Supervision in Clinical Practice
A practitioner's guide

D0221641

Since the publication of the first edition of this book, originally entitled *Supervision in the Mental Health Professions*, supervision has become of even greater significance in health, education and social care settings, with no let up in the trends towards mandatory registration, managed care and clinical governance.

In *Supervision in Clinical Practice*, Joyce Scaife, along with her guest contributors, draws on three decades of experience to illustrate ways of thinking about and doing supervision. Using practical examples, she explores often-encountered dilemmas, including:

- How can supervisors facilitate learning?
- What are the ethical bases of supervision?
- What helps to create and maintain a good working alliance?
- How can supervisors balance their management and supervision roles?
- How can supervisors work equitably in an increasingly diverse and pluralistic world?

Supervision in Clinical Practice is a comprehensive, practical and indispensable text for supervisors and supervisees who practise clinically in a range of professions, including applied psychology, counselling, psychotherapy, psychiatry, nursing, and social work.

Joyce Scaife, former Director of Clinical Practice for the Doctor of Clinical Psychology training course at the University of Sheffield, is a clinical psychologist with a career-long interest in supervision. She particularly values supervision when it encourages the full commitment of personal qualities and creative talents to clinical practice and when it helps to create a sense of fun and excitement at work.

Supervision in Clinical Practice

A practitioner's guide

Second edition

Joyce Scaife

With contributions from Francesca Inskipp, Brigid Proctor, Jon Scaife and Sue Walsh

Routledge
Taylor & Francis Group

LONDON AND NEW YORK

First edition published 2001
by Brunner-Routledge as *Supervision in the Mental Health Professions:
A Practitioner's Guide*
27 Church Road, Hove, East Sussex BN3 2FA

This edition published 2009
by Routledge
27 Church Road, Hove, East Sussex BN3 2FA

Simultaneously published in the USA and Canada
by Routledge
270 Madison Ave, New York, NY 10016

*Routledge is an imprint of the Taylor & Francis Group,
an Informa business*

Typeset in Times by
RefineCatch Limited, Bungay, Suffolk
Printed and bound in Great Britain by
MPG Books Ltd, Bodmin, Cornwall
Paperback cover design by Sandra Heath

British Library Cataloguing in Publication Data
A catalogue record for this book is available from the British Library

Library of Congress Cataloging-in-Publication Data
Scaife, Joyce, 1950–
    Supervision in clinical practice : a practitioner's guide / Joyce
Scaife; with contributions from Francesca Inskipp . . . [et al.] –
2nd ed.
        p. cm.
    Rev. ed. of: Supervision in the mental health professions / Joyce
Scaife. 2001.
    Includes bibliographical references and indexes.
    1. Mental health–Study and teaching–Supervision. 2. Mental health
personnel–Training of. 3. Supervisors. I. Scaife, Joyce, 1950–
Supervision in the mental health professions. II. Title.
    [DNLM: 1. Mental Health Services—organization &
administration. 2. Administrative Personnel. 3. Ethics, Professional.
4. Interpersonal Relations. 5. Personnel Management–methods.
WM 30 S278sa 2008]
    RA 790.8.S33 2008
    362.2068—dc22
                                                    2008007520

ISBN: 978–0–415–44999–1 (hbk)
ISBN: 978–0–415–45000–3 (pbk)

Contents

Illustrations

Figures

Tables

Contributors

Brigid Proctor and **Francesca Inskipp** met at the first BAC (then SCAC) Trainers' Conference in 1973 when they were both employed as full-time counselling trainers – Francesca at NE London Polytechnic and Brigid at SW London College. Since then they have been engaged in the development of counselling and supervision training as trainers, supervisors, external assessors, consultants and writers. Joint publications include a set of three audiotapes and two booklets entitled *The Skills of Supervising and Being Supervised*, produced in 1989. In 1993 and 1995 they produced *The Art, Craft and Tasks of Counselling Supervision*, two workbooks – *Making the Most of Supervision* and *Becoming a Supervisor*, both illustrated with audiotapes. They have both published books on counselling and counselling skills and in 2007 produced a DVD, *Creative Supervision with Francesca Inskipp and Brigid Proctor* (Newport: University of Wales School of Health and Social Sciences). Brigid is currently working on a second edition of her book *Group Supervision: A Guide to Creative Practice*, first published in 2000.

Jon Scaife teaches in the School of Education at the University of Sheffield. His main research interest is the development of radical constructivist accounts of learning and their implications for teaching and assessment.

Sue Walsh is a lead clinical tutor in clinical psychology at the University of Sheffield where she is also Director of the Diploma in Clinical Supervision. She completed her Ph.D. at the Social and Applied Psychology Unit, University of Sheffield and her clinical training at the University of Exeter. Her primary interests lie in the interface between clinical and organisational psychology.

Preface to second edition

Still the world is wondrous large, – seven seas from marge to marge, –
And it holds a vast of various kinds of man;
And the wildest dreams of Kew are the facts of Katmandhu,
And the crimes of Clapham chaste in Martaban.

Here's my wisdom for your use, as I learned it when the moose
And the reindeer roamed where Paris roars tonight:
There are nine and sixty ways of constructing tribal lays,
And-every-single-one-of-them-is-right!

> (from *In the Neolithic Age* by J.R. Kipling, n.d.)

Since authoring (and coordinating co-authors of) the first edition of *Supervision in the Mental Health Professions*, I have enjoyed being involved in the creation of a postgraduate diploma course in supervision, of continuing to supervise and be supervised, and of meeting a range of colleagues who share an interest in the process. There has been a sustained burgeoning of articles and books about supervision, and a range of ongoing research efforts aimed at making links between supervisory inputs, supervisee experiences, and client outcomes. Supervision has been described as psychology's (and other mental health professions') 'signature pedagogy'; its profession-specific primary instructional strategy (Goodyear, 2007). For this reason I see the development of knowledge and skills in supervision as the central strategy for enhancing learning in the next generation of recruits to these professions.

This revised edition incorporates new ideas related to the original chapter headings, some of which have undergone a major rewrite, while some of the more technical chapters incorporate developments that have taken place since their original conception.

In finding a route through the ideas expressed in the supervision literature, I am repeatedly struck by the importance of the underlying values and beliefs of the authors. In the introduction to a special 2005 edition of *Issues in Mental Health Nursing*, John Cutcliffe asked whether the nursing academe should be searching or striving for homogeneity or heterogeneity in clinical supervision. He suggested that there is a body of literature and an associated practice base that lacks internal consistency. Along with his co-authors, he reinforced his previous statement (Cutcliffe *et al.*, 2001: 3) that 'there is no one single correct way to carry out supervision', and argued that an educational and supportive system should take account of variations, nuances and differences in the broad church of mental health nursing.

Milne (2007a) also identified what he called a 'casual consensus' around the definition of supervision and, in contrast to Cutcliffe, suggested that there are good reasons for defining terms carefully, such as its importance for the consistent implementation of a given method. He suggested that there are many examples of the importance of definition in mental health research, with perhaps the most prominent being that of treatment fidelity. This concerns the careful definition of a therapy in order to provide consistency in training therapists in the method, and in order to make comparative outcome evaluations possible.

In my view, supervision is a complex process which does not lend itself readily to simple statements of linear causality. So, what is available to guide the practitioner is intuition based on critical and unprejudiced reflective practice that includes within its compass the imperfect research literature. Evidence-based practice is the integration of best research evidence with clinical expertise and client-related values (University of Toronto Libraries, 2000).

This book aims to offer ideas about supervision practice and theory that are derived from a multiplicity of sources in the literature and which are also based in experience with a view to encouraging you, the reader, to reflect upon and review your own espoused beliefs and ideas about supervision and to develop your skills in applying these congruently in practice. The ideas presented in this book can only gain life and meaning through application in your own supervision.

I also believe that supervision in different contexts and settings is much more similar than it is different. I have encountered a view of supervision as exclusively a technical intervention. During the process the participants enter a 'cognitron' where all that happens is rational thinking. Only when they emerge might they think that something was missing. If you think of supervision like this you may prefer to read no further. In my experience there is always a need to engage with more than rational matters, to respond (even if this is to minimise them on occasion) to feelings. In supervision of practitioners and researchers, supervisees are in all cases opening up their work and their committed behaviours, performance, practice, writing, thinking and feelings, to scrutiny by another. Judgements will be made, usually by a person with greater experience and often in the context of a formal power relationship. The supervisor is handling supervisees' education and development but also their vulnerability, needs and defensiveness. Supervisees will bring (explicitly or not) their varying degrees of distress; my intervention went wrong; one of my clients died today; I don't know how to write my report; and their joys. The main difference, in the case of supervised *practice*, is the need to maintain respectfulness towards the social order whereby the supervisee has status in relation to clients, service-users, students, people or patients.

Underlying beliefs and values

In the education literature there is a concept known as 'diagnostic teaching' in which the teacher seeks first to understand the learner's current conception of the subject matter in order to devise a learning programme that fits the needs of the individual student. It is argued that teaching which fails to take account of current knowledge and understanding may be at odds with and therefore irrelevant to the learner. As you embark on this book, why not begin by reviewing or 'diagnosing' your current beliefs and ideas about supervision? Contrasting views about supervision have already been described in this preface. You may have recognised similarities to and differences from your own ideas. What strong beliefs do you hold that you would resist being challenged by what follows? What issues in supervision interest you? What do you want to find answers to or questions about as you read the chapters that follow?

In the majority of the literature, supervision is regarded as a process which encourages learning, development, growth and maturation. This is also an aim of therapy and counselling. What are your own theories (formal or personal) about the process of change and how this is facilitated? What other beliefs inform your ideas about supervision? These are some of mine:

- The most common supervisory need that I have encountered is for people to develop greater confidence in their work.
- Learners need to feel safe enough within the supervisory relationship to acknowledge their vulnerabilities and anxieties. Rather than seeking to avoid anxiety, supervision works best when it supports learners in facing their anxieties.
- Supervisors can have greater confidence in their own work if it has been seen.
- However it might appear at times, people are generally doing their best at work.
- Supervision is an entitlement that safeguards clients and workers.
- Supervisors need to be able to exercise the authority vested in the role.
- The tasks of supervision are best accomplished when both/all parties take responsibility for the outcomes.

Use of language

I have taken the decision to use a range of terms interchangeably. Practice is variously referred to as work, professional helping, therapy, counselling and practice; the people who do it as workers, professional helpers, counsellors, therapists, practitioners; and the people they do it with as people, patients, clients and service-users. Practitioners include those who work in health, social work and education settings, and the book draws on literature from each of these contexts.

Acknowledgements

In my career I have been very fortunate to work with many colleagues who have stimulated and contributed to my ideas about supervision. These include, in particular, many supervisors, supervisees, team members and other colleagues to whom I am especially grateful for allowing me to try out my ideas and for sharing their ideas about supervision. Most recently they have included Linda Buchan, Jason Davies, Barrie Evans, Grace Hoskins, Jan Hughes, Sue McCarthy, Manya Merodoulaki, Charlotte Merriman, Derek Milne, Liza Monaghan, Mike Pomerantz, Graham Turpin, Robin Waller and Irenie Zelickman. I would also like to thank my commissioning editor Joanne Forshaw and her assistant Jane Harris for their tolerance, sound advice and practical support.

Jon Scaife and Sue Walsh jointly authored with me Chapters 2 and 3 respectively. This is because my ideas about learning and about the way that work is saturated with feeling have developed enormously through the many lively and enjoyable conversations we have had over a number of years. I first encountered Brigid Proctor and Francesca Inskipp through the very helpful sets of books and tapes on supervision that they had produced. Having listened to their work on tape, I invited them to lead a supervisor training workshop in which these two 'retired' counsellors delighted and entertained us while ensuring that we went away with a wealth of new ideas and evolving skills. Their experience of group supervision is much wider than my own and I wanted this breadth to be reflected in this book. My grateful thanks are due to Jon, Sue, Brigid and Francesca, both for their contributions and also for their inspiration.

Special thanks to Hannah and Jon P for putting up with me when I was plugged into the keyboard rather than to their needs; to Jon, for the excitement of our journey as we intertwine our way through life and its challenges, resting to ponder when we can on sunny balconies; and to Pat and Ray for a peaceful and loving place in which to write.

Acknowledgements are also due for permission to reproduce illustrations as follows: Prentice-Hall Inc., Upper Saddle River, N.J. for figure 2.1 which was originally published in *Experiential Learning: Experience as the Source of*

Learning and Development by D. Kolb in 1984; Open University Press for Figure 5.2 which was originally published on page 82 of *Supervision in the Helping Professions* by P. Hawkins and R. Shohet in 2006; Taylor and Francis Books (UK) for Figure 5.3, Overview of the Supervision Model which was published as figure 3.1 on page 36 of *Supervising the Counsellor: A Cyclical Model* by S. Page and V. Wosket in 2001; Open University Press for Figure 6.1 which was published on page 82 of *Supervision in the Helping Professions* by P. Hawkins and R. Shohet in 2006. Reproduced with the kind permission of the Open University Press Publishing Company; the American Counseling Association for Figure 12.2, which was published on page 157 of volume 28 of *Counselor Education and Supervision* © ACA 1988 in an article by F.I. Ishiyama. Reprinted with permission; Figure 5.4 from *Clinical Supervision: A Systems Approach* by Elizabeth Holloway. Copyright 1995 by Sage Publications Inc Books. Reproduced with permission of Sage Publications Inc Books in the format Textbook via Copyright Clearance Center; Barnet Enfield & Haringey Mental Health NHS Trust for table 9.1 entitled Lead Responsibilities for Managerial and Clinical/Professional Supervision published in *Integrated Supervision Policy for Mental Health Community Teams* in 2005; John Wiley and Sons Inc. for table 13.1 entitled Comparative structures of cognitive therapy sessions and supervision sessions published in *Handbook of Psychotherapy Supervision* by C.E. Watkins Junior in 1997.

   Finally, acknowledgements are due for permission to reproduce excerpts as follows: Henry Holt and Company, LLC, for the excerpt from *I Never Promised You a Rose Garden* by Joanne Greenberg, Copyright 1964, 1992 by Joanne Greenberg. Reprinted by permission of Henry Holt and Company, LLC.; also Copyright © 1964 by Joanne Greenberg. Reprinted by permission of William Morris Agency, LLC on behalf of the author. The excerpt from *Human Traces* by Sebastian Faulks, published by Hutchinson in 2005. Reprinted by permission of the Random House Group; Aitken Alexander Associates for the excerpt from *Human Traces* copyright © Sebastian Faulks, 2005; Taylor & Francis Group, LLC for the poem from Copyright (2000) *Some Stories Are Better Than Others* by M. Hoyt. Reproduced by permission of Routledge, Inc., a division of Informa plc; British Psychological Society for the excerpt from 'Homoworld' by Catherine Butler on page 15 of *Clinical Psychology Forum* in 2004; Greenwood Publishing Group for the extract from *Client-Centred Therapy* by R.F. Levant and J.M. Shlien. Copyright © 1984 by Praeger Publishers. Reproduced with permission of Greenwood Publishing Group. Inc. Westport, CT.

Chapter 1

Introduction

Gillie Bolton (2001: 15) used the metaphor of 'the hawk in your mind constantly circling over your head watching and advising on your actions – while you are practising' to elaborate the process of reflection-in-action described by Donald Schön (1987). The process of supervision, when the focus is reflection-on-action, might be regarded as one in which the hawk in your supervisor's mind circles overhead, watching, advising and, if it could, enquiring into your thinking, feelings and actions.

The hawk may suggest the presence of an aggressor waiting to pounce on its prey; and although this might fit well for the case of self-reflection, in supervision it implies a state of impending danger for the supervisee. While supervision may be construed in this way, one research finding about which there is relative consensus is the necessity, if the aims and purposes of supervision are to be achieved, for the creation of a supervisory relationship which allows the participants to reveal their vulnerabilities to each other (Beinart, 2004; Ellis and Ladany, 1997). In the context of a trusting relationship, the sharp eye of the hawk might be put to constructive use. While the nature and quality of the relationship is fundamental to the venture, in itself this does not guarantee that supervision will be useful. In this regard, supervisory relationships might be thought to parallel therapeutic ones.

I believe the word 'supervision' conjures up a variety of ideas and emotions in people. Practitioners' prior experiences can lead them both to seek and to avoid further involvement in the process. I have met people who have felt wounded by the words of a supervisor twenty years earlier and who are still smarting. There are others who feel aggrieved if the work context does not provide ongoing supervision throughout their professional career. In my own practice I have come to regard supervision as an entitlement, an activity which acts as a safeguard for client well-being and facilitates my ongoing personal and professional development. It is not an imposition by an organisation in which I am not trusted to work without being 'overseen'. This chapter reviews some of the different definitions and ways in which supervision has been viewed. It addresses questions such as 'What is supervision?', 'What is it for?', 'What are my responsibilities?' and 'What are my roles?'

Getting help with your work

However supervision is defined, it may be regarded as one way of getting help with your work. There are many others. Most ways involve talking with other people and these might include family and friends, and informal conversations with colleagues over lunch or in the kitchen. While such conversations have the potential to jeopardise confidentiality, there is evidence that they are widespread. The results of a study (Pope *et al.*, 1987) examining the ethical beliefs and behaviours of therapists found that while three-quarters of the sample believed it unethical to disclose confidential information, including unintentional disclosures, almost two-thirds reported that they had engaged in behaviours that jeopardised their clients' privacy. While only 8 per cent of the sample reported discussing clients by name, about three-quarters said they discussed clients without naming them with friends. Ninety-six per cent of participants reported disclosing client information to their significant others in a study by Boudreaux (2001).

McAuliffe and Sudbury (2005) interviewed 30 social workers in depth regarding their sources of support and consultation in cases where they had experienced ethical conflict. All respondents regarded supervision as critical in their work but less than half had discussed the matter in organisational supervision. Social workers were more likely to bring the matter to supervision when this was external to the organisation. In many cases ethical dilemmas were discussed with colleagues who were thought to have had relevant experience, and to a lesser extent with family and friends. Dudley (1988) stated that one of the most common problem areas faced by the American Association for Marital and Family Therapists is 'pillow talk' or therapists sharing clients' confidential information with their spouses or other family members. A formal and effective supervision arrangement can obviate this threat to professional integrity.

Providing the client is unidentifiable, therapists may discuss their thoughts and feelings with a range of people without breaching confidentiality. The nature of the work, in which other humans are the materials worked upon, has the power to evoke strong feelings which need an outlet. One function that can be served by supervision is that of 'restoration', providing a space for thinking, reflecting on and exploring these feelings. The space provided by supervision is not only an outlet for such feelings, but can also provide the opportunity for working out how to make use of them constructively in the work.

Many attempts have been made to define supervision and these differ both within and across professional disciplines and cultural contexts. One of the most significant differences lies between the North American conceptualisation which typically emphasises a training context and a supervisor more experienced and expert in the specialty, and the European view which emphasises the development of practitioners throughout their entire careers (Cutcliffe and Lowe, 2005). In the latter view, management is regarded as independent of clinical supervision. Cutcliffe and Lowe stated, 'When clinical supervision is conflated with managerial supervision, it ceases to be an emancipatory process and becomes analogous to Bentham's "Panoptican"; a process more concerned with surveillance' (Clouder and Sellars, 2004). These views raise many significant issues about supervision: its definition, its aims and purposes, and the potential effects of multiple roles.

Aims and purposes of supervision

A distinction between the purposes and functions of supervision was helpfully made by Carroll (1996). Following Carroll, the primary purposes of supervision are defined as ensuring the welfare of clients and enhancing the development of the supervisee in work. In order to effect these purposes the supervision needs to perform the functions of education, support, and evaluation against the norms and standards of the profession and of society. These functions are described as 'formative', 'restorative' and 'normative' respectively by Inskipp and Proctor (1993) and they are applicable irrespective of employment arrangements, both in private practice and public service settings.

Definitions of supervision

The following are examples of definitions of supervision from the North American literature:

> Supervision provides an opportunity for the student to capture the essence of the psychotherapeutic process as it is articulated and modelled by the supervisor, and to recreate it in the counselling relationship.
> (Holloway, 1992: 177)

> Supervision is that part of the overall training of mental health professionals that deals with modifying their actual in-therapy behaviours.
> (Lambert, 1980: 425)

> Supervision is 'an intensive, interpersonally focused one-to-one relationship in which one person is designated to facilitate the development of therapeutic competence in the other person.
> (Loganbill et al., 1982: 4)

> An intervention provided by a more senior member of a profession to a more junior member or members of that same profession. This relationship is evaluative, extends over time, and has the simultaneous purposes of enhancing the professional functioning of the more junior person(s), monitoring the quality of professional services offered to the client(s)

she, he, or they see(s), and serving as a gatekeeper of those who are to enter the particular profession.

(Bernard and Goodyear, 1998: 6)

Supervision is a distinct professional activity in which education and training aimed at developing science-informed practice are facilitated through a collaborative interpersonal process. It involves observation, evaluation, feedback, the facilitation of supervisee self-assessment, and the acquisition of knowledge and skills by instruction, modeling, and mutual problem solving. In addition, by building on the recognition of the strengths and talents of the supervisee, supervision encourages self-efficacy. Supervision ensures that clinical consultation is conducted in a competent manner in which ethical standards, legal prescriptions, and professional practices are used to promote and protect the welfare of the client, the profession, and society at large.

(Falender and Shafranske, 2004: 3)

These definitions have in common an emphasis on supervision as a means of facilitating the development of *practice* skills, and typically emphasise a training context in which the student is in a relationship with a more senior member of the profession. The definitions are more or less prescriptive about how the supervisor will intervene in aiding knowledge and skill development.

European definitions also emphasise practice skills while typically being less specific about the relative seniority of the participants. The definitions below emphasise that supervision is a formal arrangement that takes place regularly in the context of a relationship, involves reflection on practice and is relevant to experienced as well as neophyte practitioners.

Supervision is a working alliance between a supervisor and a worker or workers in which the worker can reflect on herself in her working situation by giving an account of her work and receiving feedback and where appropriate guidance and appraisal. The object of this alliance is to maximise the competence of the worker in providing a helping service.

(Inskipp and Proctor, 1988: 4)

[A] formal arrangement for counsellors to discuss their work regularly with someone who is experienced in counselling and supervision. The task is to work together to ensure and develop the efficacy of the counsellor/client relationship. The agenda will be the counselling work and feeling about that work, together with the supervisor's reactions, comments and confrontations. Thus supervision is a process to maintain adequate standards of counselling and a method of consultancy to widen the horizons of an experienced practitioner.

(British Association for Counselling and Psychotherapy, 1996: 1)

[C]linical supervision usually involves meeting regularly to reflect on prac-tice with the intention of learning, developing practice and providing high quality care to patients. It is distinguished from more informal forms of staff support and development by a 'contract' between supervisor and supervisee(s), setting out ground-rules on issues such as confidentiality, commitment to attend and contribute, and format of sessions.

(Department of Health, 2000: 1)

[R]egular, protected time for facilitated, in-depth reflection on clinical practice aimed to enable the supervisee to achieve, sustain and creatively develop a high quality of practice through the means of focused support and development.

(Bond and Holland, 1998, cited in Hyrkäs, 2005)

Case management supervision

In some professions, such as social work, and some multi-professional ser-vices (Richards and Suckling, 2008) the supervisee may be designated as case manager. The role of case manager has been seen either as focusing exclu-sively on the needs of the client (Gowdy *et al.*, 1993; Tower, 1994), or focusing on the case management system of service provision (Roberts-DeGennaro, 1987). In the latter instance the role of the case manager is to balance the needs of the individual client against available resources. In the former, clients' wishes and desires take precedence over all else. It has been argued that the resource gatekeeping role can generate stress for the case manager who simul-taneously acts as the agent both of the client and the system, the needs of which may be in conflict with each other (Applebaum and Austin, 1990).

The literature on case management supervision presents different views about the legitimate focus and purposes of supervision (Bowers *et al.*, 1999). Some authors argue that the task of the supervisor is 'planning of the work, delegating work, helping the case manager deal with work problems, review of the work and modification of current and future tasks' (Roberts-DeGennaro, 1987). This definition is oriented rather towards the supervisor as manager. Others argue that the role involves administrative, educational and supportive functions (Kadushin, 1985; Mordock, 1990). This orientation fits with the purposes of clinical or professional supervision.

In their interviews of twenty case management supervisors Bowers *et al.* found that a large majority of supervisors saw themselves as engaged at the level of the service system rather than at the level of particular clients or case managers. In a previous study (Bowers, 1995) case managers themselves described the difficulties they felt had been created by less client-centred supervisors. One case manager, referring to the importance of the supervisor, said, 'I think I can do it [care management] because of my boss. He knows because he's been a case worker. He says client contact is most important.

He's not one of these guys who says, "Is your paperwork done?".' Bowers *et al.* argued that in situations where mismatches in approach between the supervisor and case manager occurred, less client-centred supervisors attempted to minimise the problem through becoming quite deliberate about employing case managers who did not have extremely client-centred practice approaches.

In the context of a service providing high-volume, low-intensity treatment to clients in the UK, Richards and Suckling (2008) suggested that therapists may not be the people best equipped to provide clinical supervision when there may be a requirement to discuss the clinical progress of up to twenty clients per case manager a week. The issue of the distinction between clinical and managerial supervision is explored more fully in Chapter 9.

Clinical supervision

The term 'clinical supervision' is now widely used in the literature and in government policy documents in the UK. It is often used interchangeably with the term 'supervision', although implicit in the former term is a focus on supervision of clinical work or practical work in the field. To my knowledge, the first use of the term was by Cogan (1973), referring to a very specific approach to the supervision of student teachers. The word 'clinical' was chosen to emphasise a focus on professional practice in field settings rather than in the training institution.

A defining feature of Cogan's clinical supervision was that it rested on the conviction that performance of a skill can only be improved by direct feedback to a person on aspects of her or his practice that are of concern to that person rather than items on an evaluation form or the pet concerns of the supervisor (Reavis, 1976). The model offered a process for the analysis of performance but also emphasised the importance of the supervisory alliance, and it relied on the establishment of a collegial relationship between supervisor and supervisee in which it was the responsibility of supervisees to define the supervisory focus, their strengths and weaknesses and the goals of supervision. The approach has been used in both pre-registration and post-qualification supervision.

I have conceptualised the phases of the process as follows:

1   Establishing a collegial relationship in which a stance of openness is taken by the supervisor.
2   Planning the arrangements for data collection and observation in order to minimise the anxiety of the supervisee while being observed live.
3   Planning the supervisory conference which may be undertaken by the supervisor alone or by supervisor and supervisee together.
4   Observation of the supervisee's practice by the supervisor.
5   Undertaking the supervisory conference in which both participants together examine what has taken place in order to develop understanding.

6   Analysis of the data by both parties, focusing on critical incidents and pattern analysis and following the wishes of the supervisee.
7   Planning a programme for subsequent change and development.

The approach is principally behaviour-focused and was devised for a context of live supervision. It emphasises mutuality in the supervisor–supervisee relationship with the goal of developing self-sufficiency and freedom to act. Enquiry, analysis, examination and evaluation, especially when self-initiated and self-regulated, are espoused. The person responsible for initiating the clinical supervision model is the supervisee and the process is shaped to be congruent with the 'internal landscape' of the supervisee (Sullivan, 1980). This emphasis gives the model congruence with ideas about adult learning which are described in Chapter 2. Cogan's original specificity regarding the definition of clinical supervision has been lost and I would argue that it is helpful for authors to state at the outset how they are using the term or to define what characterises the process they are describing or researching.

Pre-registration and post-registration supervision

As stated above, in North American literature, usage of the term 'supervision' is typically restricted to the context of student–supervisor where the supervisor has managerial responsibility for the work of supervisees, and this is also the case in some European literature (Cottrell *et al.*, 2002). When used in this way (for example, Morrison, 2001), a distinction is usually drawn between 'supervision' and 'consultation', the former involving a position of authority for the supervisor which includes a mandate to direct the supervisee if necessary. The term 'supervision' has also been restricted by some authors to the situation in which the focus of the conversation is exclusively on direct work with clients (Shohet, 2003). Such an arrangement might preclude the discussion of work context or relationships with colleagues which could be dealt with through a consultative arrangement.

In the European literature, relationships that aim to accomplish the normative, formative and restorative functions of supervision come under the umbrella term 'supervision' whether these are between peers, members of the same or different disciplines, and between staff at any stage of their careers, pre- or post-registration. Distinctions have been attempted by the use of terms such as 'training supervision', 'practitioner supervision', 'peer supervision', 'peer consultation', 'consultative supervision' and 'consultation'. Some departments have introduced supervision constrained to highly specific and narrow aims such as the reduction of risk to staff and clients (Fleming *et al.*, 2007).

Coaching and mentoring are also practices which seek to encourage client development. The Coaching and Mentoring Network website (n.d.) describes the role of the coach or mentor as that of facilitating the exploration of needs, motivations, desires, skills and thought processes to assist the individual in making real, lasting change. The coach or mentor is advised to maintain unconditional positive regard for the client, which means that the coach is at all times supportive and non-judgemental of clients, their views, lifestyles and aspirations. Parsloe (1999: 8) stated that coaching is:

> a process that enables learning and development to occur and thus performance to improve. To be successful a Coach requires a knowledge and understanding of process as well as the variety of styles, skills and techniques that are appropriate to the context in which the coaching takes place.

There are clearly some similarities and differences between supervision, coaching and mentoring. Supervisors typically are not proscribed from making judgements of performance and in pre-registration supervision undertake this as a central activity in the role. Coaching and mentoring are usually associated with the world of business where supervision is more likely to be used in the context of managerial control.

For the purposes of this text, the term 'supervision' is used in its wider sense and thus includes what some authors have defined as 'consultation'.

Features that characterise supervision

The above discussion was intended to orient the reader towards the term 'supervision' while showing that the meaning given to the word will differ between individuals, professions and cultures. There will be no attempt here to offer another definitive meaning of the term 'supervision', since words mediate between the meanings located within the speaker and the listener so that, 'strictly speaking nothing we know can be said precisely' (Polanyi, 1958: 87–88). Instead, a number of features that characterise supervision are proposed:

- The purposes are to secure the welfare of clients, and to enhance the services offered to clients by workers. In so doing, the supervisory focus may be almost exclusively on the needs and experiences of the supervisee.
- Effective supervision takes place in the context of a formal relationship/s in which there is mutual respect and trust.
- Supervisory relationships should either preclude the simultaneous existence of other role-relationships between participants (friendships, managerial relationships) or, where dual relationships pertain, this should be acknowledged and the implications expressly addressed.
- Supervision is characterised by an agreement or contract (with varying degrees of formality) which specifies the purposes, aims, methods, agenda, term, frequency, location and so on of the supervision.

- Supervision does not aim to address the personal and development needs of the supervisor, but is focused on the personal and professional development of the supervisee.
- Supervision can serve formative, restorative and normative functions.

In pre-registration training, supervision is also characterised as follows:

- The effects of supervision are to socialise the new recruit into the profession, to replicate institutional canons and to propagate the norms of the profession.
- The supervisor performs a gatekeeping function which allows for the exclusion of those deemed unsuitable for membership of the profession.
- Supervision occurs in the context of a power imbalance in which the assessment of the work of those in training can have a profound impact on their subsequent lives at work.

In this book the above characteristics define how the term 'supervision' is being used, and it is intended to be inclusive. This is not to argue that supervision is the panacea for dealing with work-related issues; its aims and purposes can also be achieved through less formal relationships, and the existence of the above features does not necessarily guarantee that the aims of supervision will be achieved. More detailed characteristics of European conceptualisations of 'clinical supervision' were proposed by Cutcliffe and Lowe (2005) and are reproduced in adapted form below.

Clinical supervision:

- Is supportive.
- Takes place in the context of a facilitative relationship.
- Is centred on developing best practices for service users.
- Is challenging.
- Is brave (because practitioners are encouraged to talk about the realities of their practice).
- Is safe (because of clear, negotiated agreements by all parties with regard to the extent and limits of confidentiality).
- Provides an opportunity to ventilate emotion without comeback.
- Is not to be confused or amalgamated with managerial supervision.
- Provides the opportunity to deal with material and issues that practitioners may have been carrying for many years (the chance to talk about issues which cannot easily be talked about elsewhere and which may have been previously unexplored).
- Is not to be confused or amalgamated with personal therapy or counselling.
- Offers a chance to talk about difficult areas of work in an environment where the other person attempts to understand.

- Is regular.
- Takes place in protected time.
- Is offered equally to all practitioners.
- Involves a committed relationship from both parties.
- Is an invitation to be self-monitoring.
- Is at times hard work and at other times enjoyable.
- Is concerned with learning to be reflective and with becoming a reflective practitioner.
- Is an activity that continues throughout one's healthcare career.

The aspirations implied within this list suggest the need for high levels of commitment to the enterprise, not only from supervisors but also from the people they supervise and from managers within the organisation. Cutcliffe and Lowe (2005) argued the case for 'clinical credibility' of the supervisor because the focus of supervision will frequently be on clinical performance. This is of particular importance when performance evaluations are to be made; the supervisor benefits from having had relevant experience in the clinical practices that are to be assessed.

Responsibilities in the supervision system

A number of different parties constitute the stakeholders in the supervisory process. At the least these include the client, therapist and supervisor. In addition, the work generally takes place in a host agency which will have norms and morés of its own. In pre-registration supervision there is also a host training institution. All of the participants and agencies that constitute the supervisory system have roles and responsibilities which will influence the process of supervision to a greater or lesser extent. In this section, the responsibilities of the different stakeholders are explored and the author's views presented.

The client's responsibilities

The identity of the client is not always obvious. The client may be an institution, the referrer, the carer, the identified client or the client's family. The client is the person or system that seeks change for the purpose of relieving distress or solving problems. The client may be seeking change in another rather than in self as is often the case, for example, when a child is referred. In such instances the person presented as the problem may become the client but not necessarily at the point of referral. Problems can be solved through many different approaches and through various processes of change. For instance, a child may be referred with sleep problems, the resolution of which might include a change in the child's pattern of sleep, the parents coming to accept that they can tolerate and adapt to the child's pattern of sleep, redefinition of the problem as a marital-sexual one in which the sleep pattern focuses attention elsewhere, or relocation, as a result of which the neighbours no longer complain about disturbance in the night. The problem may also be defined as arising from a socio-cultural context in which infants are expected to sleep alone rather than in physical proximity to their parents and could be resolved by resisting contextual pressures and allowing the child into the parental bed. Supervision can aid both the process of client identification and choice of direction for the intervention.

Once the client has been identified, the definition of the problem and the decision to work towards change usually lie with the client, albeit with the help of the therapist. While the work may not begin with this degree of clarity, an appraisal of motivation or capacity for change at a more or less formal level is part of the ongoing assessment. Without the commitment of the client to change, continuing efforts are likely to be experienced as frustrating for the worker. However, ongoing assessment of motivation to change is the responsibility of practitioners and their supervisors and is an appropriate focus of supervision.

The supervisee's responsibilities

Responsibilities to clients

The responsibility of the supervisee is to strive towards creating the conditions that will facilitate change for the client. Whether or not clients respond is up to them. In addition, workers have responsibilities to act ethically and within the professional guidelines established both by their employer and by their professional body. Actively participating in supervision and remaining open to learning as part of continuing professional development help practitioners to ensure that they are fulfilling these responsibilities to clients.

Responsibilities for supervision

Supervisors sometimes assume that the burden of responsibility for what happens in and the outcomes of supervision lie principally if not exclusively with them. Supervisees also fall into the same trap and as a result may approach supervision passively, as if it is something done *to* them, not something in which they have responsibility for making sure that their needs are met. When the responsibilities of the supervisee are abdicated, a set of unreasonable expectations of the supervisor may be created. Understanding of the different responsibilities of supervisors and supervisees can be drawn from considering a parallel between the supervisee–supervisor system and the client–therapist system. Essentially, the supervisor is responsible for participating in and creating the conditions in which learning and development can take place, and in which the client's needs can best be addressed, but grasping these opportunities is the responsibility of the supervisee.

Inskipp and Proctor (1988) developed an excellent set of materials to aid supervisees in identifying and developing their skills in taking this responsibility. The following list is derived from their materials and from Carroll and Gilbert (2005: 19):

- Identifying your learning objectives.
- Preparing for supervision.
- Using supervision time effectively.
- Being aware of cultural, religious, ethnic, gender, disability and sexual orientation differences between yourself and others.
- Being aware of the influence of and responsibilities to all stakeholders in the supervisory arrangement.
- Considering how to share your current understanding of your strengths and points for development with the supervisor.
- Taking a position of openness to learning which includes communicating your thoughts and feelings in supervision.
- Noticing what you find threatening in supervision.
- Noticing how you typically show defensiveness.
- Identifying your own ideas about boundaries in supervision and working out how to let your supervisor know should he or she begin to stray beyond them.
- Being prepared for and having the skills to negotiate disagreement.
- Identifying your expectations about the focus of supervision.
- Being clear about the roles that you expect of your supervisor.
- Working out how to stay in control of feedback that might be given by the supervisor.
- Examining your views about having your work observed either directly or indirectly.
- Working out how to show your supervisor your fears and anxieties without undue apprehension in anticipation of negative evaluation.
- Letting the supervisor know what is proving helpful and unhelpful to your learning and development.
- Acknowledging errors with a view to learning from them.
- Applying your learning from supervision.
- Keeping a record of supervision sessions.

The responsibilities of the supervisor

Depending on the context of the supervision, the supervisor has various wide-ranging responsibilities for the client, the supervisee, and for ensuring that the mores and standards of their own and the supervisee's employing body and any involved professional and training institutions are maintained.

For the welfare of the client

Supervisors will need to identify with whom the responsibility for case work lies. In pre-registration training this will often be their responsibility, whereas in post-registration arrangements it is more likely to lie with the supervisee. In a survey of counsellor supervisors working in private practice, none of the respondents regarded themselves as legally responsible for their supervisees' work (King and Wheeler, 1999). It has been argued by Storm *et al.* (2001) that supervisors frequently erroneously assume that they are less responsible for their supervisees' cases than they are, which might lead them to focus on a few ongoing cases but ignore the remainder of the caseload, for example. If the supervisor is deemed responsible, they argue the case for a formal agreement specifying that supervisees will inform them regularly about any 'risky' clients, specifying procedures for the handling of emergency cases, and confirming that supervisors will be accessible to provide appropriate guidance or arrange alternative cover (Engleberg and Storm, 1990).

The location of the responsibility for case work will influence the manner in which supervision is conducted. Supervisors who have direct responsibility for their supervisees' client welfare will need to have a more 'hands-on' awareness of the work being undertaken in order to effect their responsibilities and in order to protect themselves and their supervisees from potential litigation. Even in post-registration arrangements, supervisors have responsibilities towards clients and cannot 'unknow' things that they have been told or have observed in supervision.

The dual responsibility for the client and for the supervisee can give rise to some of the most difficult dilemmas for supervisors. The needs of the two parties may conflict and supervisors in such circumstances need to steer a course that is fair to both and which they themselves can tolerate, even if this entails a sense of discomfort. Such a conflict of interest can arise, for example, as a result of the supervisee experiencing debilitating levels of anxiety in the presence of clients so as seriously to impede the formation of a relationship in which the client is able to change. The supervisor is faced with the dilemma of ensuring that needy clients are provided with adequate help, while simultaneously aiding the supervisee in dealing with her or his anxiety. Paradoxically, the supervisor may find that raising the issue with the supervisee further escalates anxiety levels. However, for some supervisees, clear statement of a problem confirms what they already implicitly knew and allows them to undertake the task of remediation with the help of the supervisor.

Generally speaking, where the client is at risk or where someone else is at risk from the client, supervisees will value the input of the supervisor in helping them to steer a safe course. If the supervisee is not taking the danger sufficiently seriously, the supervisor is responsible for pursuing the matter further with the supervisee until satisfied with the course of action agreed and taken. Dilemmas can also arise should supervisors find themselves questioning whether the supervisee should be practising at a particular time. While there is clearly a gatekeeping function in pre-registration supervision, a course of action is not so obvious in practitioner or peer arrangements. Where the difficulties are acknowledged by the supervisee, the supervisor's role may be to help the supervisee to determine how to act. In the face of a failure to acknowledge and act appropriately, the supervisor may be faced with taking the matter outside supervision, discussing *how* not *whether* to do this with the supervisee. In private practice supervisors are particularly sensitive to the tension between practitioners needing to stop working for personal reasons but needing to continue practising for financial reasons (King and Wheeler, 1999).

While the supervisor's responsibility may be clear, there is evidence that supervisors find it very difficult to take matters beyond the supervision itself. King and Wheeler (1999) found that counselling supervisors in the UK were very reluctant to invoke the British Association of Counsellors' (BAC) complaints procedure even if obliged to do so. When undertaken, the process had been experienced as distressing for both supervisor and supervisee. King and Wheeler advocated a cautious approach by supervisors in private practice to taking on a supervisee, but pointed out that paradoxically, counsellors with less experience or skills, in whom the supervisors had least confidence, might find it most difficult to obtain supervision from well-regarded colleagues.

Supervisors need to be clear that they share responsibility for the welfare of their supervisees' clients, and that this may present conflicts with their responsibilities to their supervisees. This is discussed further in Chapter 7.

To the supervisee

The supervisor cannot make the supervisee learn and develop but is responsible for participating in, and working to create and manage the supervisory process so as best to facilitate the supervisee's learning at work. Many of the skills required are versions of the skills of supervisees. In addition, supervisors have responsibility for the process of establishing a contract for supervision and for being open to development of their own knowledge and skills in supervision.

Supervisors are responsible for effecting any designated tasks that arise from the regulations of other involved parties. Where a number of different parties are involved, the supervisor may be faced with dilemmas regarding the priority of conflicting needs. For example, if an employer pays for the supervision of one of its employees, and it emerges in the supervision that the supervisee is acting ethically but against the stated aims and objectives of the employer, to whom do supervisors owe their principal allegiance – the supervisee or the employer? It is best to establish this before entering into the supervisory arrangement. When the arrangement is clear and in the open, the supervisee can make an informed decision about what he or she can safely reveal in supervision and what would compromise the supervisor. In this instance, the supervisor can in any case help the supervisee to explore the options for acting both ethically and within the aims and objectives of the employing body. Where this is not possible, the supervisor will be able to act according to the initial agreement regarding primary allegiance.

To the employer/s

Different employers may be involved in a supervisory arrangement. Super-visees may be employed by their own agency but undertake work in the supervisor's agency. In this case, it will be necessary to establish the specific contractual responsibilities of the different parties and how disciplinary and grievance procedures will be effected in the rare event of this being necessary. An additional complication arises when the supervisee works in the super-visor's agency but on a voluntary or self-funded basis. Supervisors would be wise to clarify their responsibilities to their own agency including the liability of the agency for the work of the supervisee. While the majority of super-visory relationships work to the satisfaction of all parties most of the time, the rarity with which serious difficulties arise makes it essential that the supervisor take responsibility at the outset for clarifying the procedures to be followed when the supervisee's work performance is problematic.

To the training institution

When the supervisee is a student it is the responsibility of the training institu-tion to inform the supervisor of its expectations, but subsequently it becomes the responsibility of the supervisor to act in ways congruent with the agree-ments that have been made. Should the supervisee be required to produce case material based on the work carried out under supervision, the supervisor has responsibility for ensuring that appropriate clients are available to enable the completion of such work, and that appropriate confidentiality is maintained. A process of obtaining informed consent from clients will be necessary.

Training institutions usually require that the supervisor make a formal assessment of the supervisee's work. Supervisors will need to familiarise themselves with assessment procedures and have responsibility for working out how best to carry out their role in such a way as to include both formative and summative evaluation.

To the profession

In supervision of pre-registration training, the supervisor may also have responsibility to transmit the values and standards of the profession. This can be more or less conscious and explicit, but the underlying values of the profession are likely to be manifest in the way in which the supervisor thinks and acts. In a research context, this tendency to act consistently with the 'school' in which one's learning has taken place was described by Kuhn (1962). Ekstein and Wallerstein (1972) described this socialisation into the profession as the development of professional identity arising by association with senior members of the trainee's own professional discipline.

In this section the responsibilities of stakeholders beyond the more immediate triad of client/practitioner/supervisor have been explored only peripherally but the supervision takes place in a wider context which confers responsibilities beyond the immediate triad. In agreeing to provide supervision, by implication the supervisor accepts the responsibilities associated with each of the agencies concerned and as a result must deal with the implications that arise.

Boundary issues

Personal and professional

The extent to which the supervision focuses on personal issues is determined partly by the model of intervention in which the parties are engaged. Historically, for example, while there has been disagreement in the psychoanalytic school about the extent to which the same analyst might both analyse and supervise a student (Doehrman, 1976), the feelings experienced by the supervisee have nevertheless been regarded as a legitimate and desirable focus of supervision.

When the personal qualities that supervisees bring to their work are the focus of supervision, the potential for misunderstandings, affront and hurt feelings is at its greatest and the supervisor's role as personal developer presents particular challenges. In carrying out formative and normative functions, the approaches available to the supervisor include the use of feedback and constructive challenge. It is relatively straightforward to give feedback about or to challenge technical skills or theoretical knowledge, but to raise issues that are intended to be, or are construed as personal is much more risky, with greater potential for the creation of a rupture in the relationship.

If the supervisor is going to be helpful to the supervisee in terms of personal development, the establishment and maintenance of a good working alliance is an essential prerequisite. Supervisees need to feel confident enough in the relationship to disclose issues about themselves in the work, and to manage the feelings of vulnerability that this may entail.

The emphasis on the personal is a matter for negotiation in the supervisory relationship. It is important that the supervisor does not stray beyond the territory agreed and also that the supervisor is aware of the supervisee's other sources of support should life events or other personal issues compromise the work.

Supervision and therapy

While there is a clear distinction between therapy and supervision in terms of a focus on learning for life as distinct from learning for work, there are also commonalities of purpose regarding development and change. Supervisors are likely to draw on skills common to both tasks that include active listening, collective meaning-making, information giving, supporting and challenging. Additional dimensions relevant to the supervisory task include evaluation and probably a greater degree of supervisor self-disclosure than is usual in therapeutic relationships.

Because of the commonalities in the supervisory and therapeutic roles, supervisors need to beware of straying from the tasks of supervision, particularly where they are invited into the role of therapist by the supervisee. This process is often outside the awareness of the supervisee and possibly of both parties. It is useful always for the supervisor to have in mind the question, 'How is this relevant to the work?' as an aid to maintaining the boundary between the two different roles.

Supervision and teaching

At times in supervision, it is appropriate for the supervisor to act as a teacher either by giving information, or by focusing more generally on the learning of the supervisee using enquiry, exploration, role play, modelling and so on. The common aims of developing knowledge and skills are relevant to both roles, but supervision covers a wider territory through its restorative function in which the supervisor helps supervisees to understand and manage their emotions at work. Supervision is also less likely to be constrained by an externally determined curriculum. Supervisees working with clients will generate a personal curriculum for their learning based around the specific encounters of their day-to-day work.

Dual relationships: friendships/managerial relationships

When participants in a supervisory relationship have no prior or ongoing relationship that was established for other purposes, there is a greater freedom in which to work out the new relationship. Many people participate in managerial supervision at work and it is a moot point to what extent this concurrent role relationship restricts and limits the potential achievements of the supervision. When one person has power to influence the progression and promotion of the other, there is bound to be some influence over what takes place in supervision, and in my experience the roles of supervisor and manager are often conflated. The authors of original conceptualisations of clinical supervision for nurses in Europe were adamant in highlighting that the roles of line manager and clinical supervisor should not be blurred (Cutcliffe and Lowe, 2005). Butterworth (1992: 9) was averse to the conflation of clinical supervision and managerial supervision and wished to dissociate the role of supervisor from a position of authority and power, stating: 'People at work tend to think of their supervisor as authoritarian and that the whole concept of supervision is linked conceptually to an authority figure. . . . Supervision is often negatively associated with more traditional disciplinary dealings between managers and their staff.' In a keynote presentation he stated, 'Clinical supervision is about empowerment – not control' (Smith, 1995: 1030).

This dual-role relationship is likely to pertain in pre-registration training as well as in other managerial relationships. The influence of the disparity in status may be contained by discussion during and following the contracting process, but its influence may readily be underestimated. Because this particular dual-role relationship is so widespread, Chapter 9 of this volume is devoted specifically to ways in which supervisors might manage the situation.

Given a choice, people may be tempted to select someone whom they know and like as their supervisor. Supporting evidence for this was reported by Lawton (2000) in a study of qualified counsellors working in further education colleges. She found that convenience of location and familiarity with the supervisor took precedence over all other considerations. In many cases this will present no problems and may facilitate the development of a very effective supervisory relationship. However, where the relationship extends beyond the context of work, potential problems arise. If the supervisor makes a negative evaluation of the supervisee's work, there is a risk that this could lead to a redefinition of the relationship from 'friend' to 'enemy'. When supervisors prioritise the friendship, are not prepared to compromise it, and thus withhold negative evaluation, they are failing to fulfil all aspects of the role that they have contracted to provide.

In my experience, people tend to be reluctant to acknowledge the potential difficulties that can arise when friendships and formal work relationships coincide. Attempts to manage this have led people to agree not to meet each other outside work for the duration of their relationship in supervision and this may prove satisfactory. Such an arrangement clearly acknowledges the potential for the blurring of roles and allows role conflict to be addressed as an agenda item in supervision.

Further potential for the development of a dual relationship occurs when supervisor and supervisee find themselves sexually attracted to each other. Professional codes of conduct are explicit that sexual relationships between supervisors and their supervisees violate professional standards since they exploit the person in the relationship who holds less formal power. Feelings of sexual attraction towards colleagues and clients are ubiquitous. Between 80 and 88 per cent of psychologists report having been attracted to or having had sexual feelings for at least one client (Falender and Shafranske, 2004: 168). A distinction needs to be made between experiencing such feelings and acting upon them which constitutes a boundary violation with serious nega-tive consequences. Education about the risks of such behaviour is advocated by Hamilton and Spruill (1999) who developed a very useful checklist of risk factors for trainees and supervisors. Positive answers to the items on the list are indicators of the potential for boundary violation and this measure would serve as a useful document on which to base a discussion between supervisor and supervisee about sexual feelings at work.

Choice or allocation of supervisor

The degree of control over selection of a supervisor will often be influenced by the stage of the supervisee's career development. The greater the opport-unity to choose, the more likely the supervisee will positively anticipate engaging in the supervisory process. When choice is possible there is a view that experienced practitioners benefit more from the challenge and stimula-tion of a new approach rather than gravitation towards the familiar (Page and Wosket, 1994). Particularly during training, supervisory allocations are likely to be made by the training institution. Supervisors will have reputations in the training community deriving from their previous input, and this can have extensive repercussions for what subsequently takes place.

Generally speaking supervisors perform this role through choice and are interested in carrying it out well. Supervisees who are allocated a supervisor whose reputation generates concern have a responsibility to consider how this might affect the establishment of the relationship, and would benefit from discussing this with the person responsible for the allocation. Supervisors have a responsibility to be interested in their reputations in the professional community and to seek feedback with regard to their supervisory role. In the knowledge of their reputation they can bring it into the contracting process by suggesting, 'You may have heard that . . .' which signals that reputations are appropriate material for discussion and exploration.

In a similar fashion, supervisees themselves acquire reputations which may also be handled through disclosure and discussion. Secret knowledge is likely to generate adverse effects that will interfere with the process of supervision.

It may be considered that 'bad' reputations are more problematic than 'good' ones. However, supervisees allocated to a 'good' supervisor who fails to conform to expectations may struggle to make meaning of this failure, and may conclude, probably unhelpfully, that the fault lies with them.

In a study by Teasdale et al. (2001) 56 per cent of their study sample had been able to choose their own supervisor and in this case showed a preference for supervision by colleagues (69 per cent) as opposed to managers (22 per cent). When nurses were not permitted to choose, nurse managers (65 per cent) predominated as preferred supervisors. This suggests that while workers prefer to choose colleagues as supervisors, they ultimately prefer what they get. Wherever feasible it is desirable for there to be an element of choice of partner in supervisory relationships, including a built-in review process which enables participants to reassess the suitability as both develop and change.

The organisational context of supervision

Supervision takes place in organisational contexts that define and delimit the options available to the participants in the endeavour. This topic is explored in terms of the potential emotional impact of the organisational culture in Chapter 3 and as an issue to be addressed in the contracting process in Chapter 4. Supervisory practices and attitudes are embedded in service settings which may involve more or less well-qualified staff, different types of intervention with clients, various supporting technology (discussed in Chapter 10), clinical governance demands, and service prescriptions. The latter may, for example, constrain supervisors to limit the time available for supervision, and to focus on a predetermined and preselected number of the supervisee's cases in any one supervision session (Richards and Suckling, 2008) through a process of supervision management. Such constraints offer a challenge to supervisors in their capability to perform the normative, restorative and formative functions of the task. Taking these issues to supervision (supervision of supervision) can aid perspective-taking and self-care for practitioners who work in pressured environments. Mohtashemi, cited in Bolton (2005: 15), stated, 'The workplace is a tough, manipulative environment where people are often expected to comply without challenge, to "live the company's values", to "display the right behaviours", and even to adopt the corporate language.' This observation applies no less to health and social care 'businesses' whose objectives and practices, with the best will in the world, are nevertheless subject to ever-changing economic and political demands. When supervision focuses on service systems, it is nevertheless with the ultimate aim of enhancing client welfare and outcomes.

Chapter 2

Supervision and learning

Joyce Scaife and Jon Scaife

A vessel to be filled? A flame to be kindled?

Practitioners in the helping professions are in the business of applying theories about human nature to their practice. A theory provides the conceptual basis for action. Supervision can draw on theories of psychotherapy and extensions of them. An example would be the notion of parallel process which is based on the psychodynamic concept of transference. Developmental approaches to supervision have typically been based on stage theories. While there are many models and frameworks for supervision that can guide the process, the main body of theory (i.e. proposed explanations of what takes place in supervision) on which the supervisor can draw is learning theory. Learning theories attempt to account for changes in knowledge and they are of particular value to supervisors and supervisees in addressing the crucial formative function of supervision.

This chapter aims to outline a coherent contemporary account of learning, relate this to traditional accounts, and address how supervision might contribute to learning in practice. It explores approaches to adult learning and also draws attention to the literature on learning styles.

Traditional theories of learning

Traditional theories of learning are underpinned by empiricist or innatist assumptions. The former stresses the role of the senses in the creation of knowledge. A legacy of the seventeenth-century philosopher John Locke is the widespread assumption that the mind is a container into which knowledge flows through experience. Some approaches to teaching and training, such as lecturing and instructing, are consistent with this doctrine. The widely held views that people are characterised by fixed abilities (she's naturally musical) or general intelligence (he's not very bright) illustrate an implicit commitment to innatism.

Innatist beliefs have a history dating at least as far back as the ancient Greeks. Plato had no access to genetics or any other scientific basis for his innatist position; instead he adopted reincarnation as his explanatory story.

Plato's story of Socrates' conversation with Meno is a good illustration of an innatist account of how learning can occur. Socrates asserted that everyone has innate knowledge. Meno challenged him to demonstrate this. Socrates put a series of questions to a slave, culminating in the young man correctly solving a non-trivial geometric puzzle. Socrates then challenged Meno: Did I tell the boy anything? Meno conceded that he had drawn out – educed – knowledge through well-judged questions. Socratic questioning, based on this idea, has become a technique used in cognitive behaviour therapy.

Perspectives like innatism have been held long enough to warrant being called traditions. They have been viable within intellectual discourse for centuries but, as we aim to show, some cracks have begun to appear. In our contemporary professional contexts of pluralism, diversity and contestability, traditional epistemologies are sometimes found wanting.

A contemporary account of learning

In evolutionary terms, what makes human beings special, what marks us out in the animal world, is our capability to learn 'good tricks' (Dennett, 1993: 184). What we lack compared with other creatures in speed, strength, mobility and fecundity we make up for in mental dexterity: we are great learners. Unlike other animals we also create learning 'fast tracks' for each other, in the form of cultural and material environments that highlight for those around us what we regard as important things to learn. The supervisory context is set up to capitalise on this skill.

Supervision offers a formal way of learning 'good tricks' in a professional context. 'Formal', here, is used to contrast with the informality of serendipitous learning in everyday living. It implies intention and purpose.

In this chapter, the term 'learning' is being used to refer to a process of change. This change process cannot be observed directly but the outcomes of the process can be modifications in any or all of the following, which collectively we take to comprise 'knowledge':

• Declarative knowledge; that which can be stated. This is sometimes described as 'knowing that'. It consists of theories, concepts, principles and facts that can be stated by the supervisee (Anderson, 1980).
• Understanding (such as being able to make a critical choice from a range of possible models in a given situation).
• Skills, sometimes known as procedural knowledge or 'knowing how'.
• Other behaviours, such as interpersonal interactions.
• Values.
• Attitudes, such as openness, curiosity, caution.

These inclusive definitions reflect our view that competent practitioners employ a broad spectrum of personal and professional qualities in their work. Interpersonal skills, attitudes and values are at the heart of the therapeutic enterprise and the effective practitioner needs to be able to develop and sustain an emotional bond that can weather the vicissitudes of the endeavour (Ladany *et al.*, 2005: 25). Acts of encouraging hope in the face of despair or challenging a client to further self-responsibility are moral acts as well as technical interventions (Falender and Shafranske, 2004: 31).

In contemporary accounts of learning, references to constructivism and constructionism have appeared with increasing frequency from many areas of the globe. The literature includes several varieties of constructivist thinking. Categorisations include psychological and social constructivism (Phillips, 1995), social constructionism (Gergen and Gergen, 1991), and trivial and radical constructivism (Glasersfeld, 1995). Approaches to intervention with clients increasingly are taking account of these views of learning (Mahoney, 2003). All of these accounts assert that knowledge is built up and constructed, rather than poured or written in. They all reject an 'instructionist' view of learning. Computers are designed to operate on the basis of instructions but neither human beings nor human societies appear to be the products of design and there is no evident 'program' at work.

The various strands of constructivist and constructionist thought have their own lineages and champions (Steffe and Gale, 1995). Glasersfeld (1995) argues that in order to form a joined-up picture of human learning we need to reach an understanding of how we come to be the knowers and doers that we are. In other words, we need to ask: Where did our knowledge come from? At one time this question might have been directed to the development of knowledge from birth onwards. Now there are evolutionary perspectives which address the question by considering changes over periods of hundreds of thousands of years. Over such time-scales species evolve and adaptations emerge. Adaptations are interpreted in evolutionary psychology as forms of knowledge located in the gene pool of the species (Plotkin, 1994). Some of this 'knowledge in the lineage' is inherited by newborns and has the effect of marking out roughly defined developmental and behavioural pathways. This is important in the context of supervision because it means that people, whether newborn or adult learners, are anything but the blank slates that they were held to be in some empiricist accounts of learning.

Traditional views of learning held that infants experience objects in the world and gradually build up knowledge of them. Our view is that whatever is experienced, it comes with no labels stating what it is (Edelman and Tononi, 2000: 81). The experiencer has to construct personal semantic content; this does not come prepackaged. Second, following Glasersfeld (1995), the learner has access only to her or his own experiences. Learners cannot step outside their experiential worlds. Each of us is a 'closed system' (Maturana and Varela, 1980).

Recurrent regularities in experiences come eventually to be 'objectified' into something which in due course attracts a label (Segal, 2001). Labels specific to helping professions might include 'negative automatic thoughts', 'transference', 'externalisation', 'IQ' and so on. This process may best be understood with reference to a newborn's learning because it is possible confidently to say that learning is going on in the absence of language.

Segal (2001: 122) gave an illustration from the work of Heinz von Foerster of how recurrent regularities in what an observer of the infant would call visual and tactile experiences could eventually be 'objectified' by the child into what he or she would later call a rattle. Objectification acts as an experiential short cut, a mental economy: in short, a memory. What distinguishes this constructivist account from traditional instructionism is that it holds that the world, and the objects in it that a person comes to know, are constructed objectifications from the person's experiences. The objects arise from the experiences, not vice versa. The causal origins for the person's experiences are, in this perspective, unknowable. This is because there is no way for any of us to step outside our own experiential world to check what gives rise to our experiences. Our experiences are all that we have.

If learners each construct their own world and set of objects within it does that mean that they are each free to construct anything they like? This is unlikely. Learners' constructions are constrained by human ways of experiencing. For example, people have no way of experiencing how it feels to fly like a bird. The constraints on human ways of experiencing can change over time. Monet suffered with cataracts in his later life. In his paintings, tones became muddier and darker, and forms became less distinct as his contrast sensitivity declined. His later works are typified by large brush strokes, indistinct coloration, and often an absence of light blues. The sense of atmosphere and light that he was famous for presenting in his earlier works disappeared (Department of Psychology, University of Calgary, 2005).

People are also constrained by the mental tools available for constructing knowledge from their experiences. For example, one of the authors has the mental resources to solve hard chess problems but not easy crosswords. Learners are constrained by what they have already constructed because this serves as the starting point for the learning of new knowledge. The contents of our experiences are also constrained by whatever was beyond the experiences that caused them. This last constraint manifests itself at every moment of experience. It is not possible to walk through walls; people have to fit with the constraint. A wall is an objectification of experiences; presumably there is something that gave rise to them but this cannot be sidestepped to find what is behind and beyond experience. Knowledge is neither true nor false, since there is no way of stepping outside it to check if it matches its underlying causal origins. The quality of knowledge that matters is the extent to which it fits with the learner's experiences and enables the learner to navigate pathways through life.

People have to fit with more than just walls – fitting with other people is an even more profound constraint. Social interaction and communication present conceptual challenges to a constructivist account. A traditional view of communicative language is that a speaker draws a listener's attention to something by speaking about it. In a constructivist account there is no commonly experienced 'something'. There is a something for the speaker and what he or she says may orient the listener towards something in the listener's own experiential world, but there is no sense in which the two 'somethings' can be said to be the same thing. This is because there is no way that one person can have another's experiences or step outside her or his own.

How, then, is communication possible? Glasersfeld (1995: 129) argued that communication is possible if there is a functional fit between the intentions and actions of the communicating parties. For instance, if a supervisor said, 'Which of us will write up the case notes?' the supervisee's conception of 'write' and 'case notes' or what sounds she or he hear or even that she or he has no way of knowing these things in the supervisor's world are of no matter. All that determines supervisors' judgement of the effectiveness of the communication is the fit or lack of it between what happens next and her or his intentions. It is a convenient shorthand to treat 'case notes' as an object in common to both parties but this conceals the inescapable inferential nature of communication, even more so when communication involves abstract ideas. To get by and communicate, people read each other. Everything in social interaction is inference.

In the above example, the assumption that there is something in the world, case notes, that is experienced as the same thing by the two people, is an 'objectivist' assumption. Objectivist assumptions have the benefit of providing considerable economy in communication and thinking. They work successfully most of the time – but not always. Misunderstandings, collisions of intentions and unfulfilled expectations arise when objectivism fails. When this happens a constructivist perspective can enable a route to be found through the maze.

Implications of a constructivist account of learning for supervision

The above account of learning informs supervisors about how they might approach the formative function of supervision. It suggests that supervisees' knowledge is unlikely to change in any profound way as a result of being told or instructed. Their current knowledge has been constructed to fit with their whole life history of experiences to date. In most cases this knowledge appears to be fairly stable and unlikely to change unless a misfit is experienced. Misfits are rarely sought and they tend to generate affective resistance. The task of influencing someone else's learning is more demanding than is

portrayed in an instructionist account. Anyone working in the helping professions will be aware of this from their clinical case work. From a constructivist
perspective, learning is a process of coming to a subjectively better fit with
one's experiences. In order for people to help others to learn, their challenge
is not to tell things to their colleagues but rather to help them to be open to
change, to see value in changing, and to see a possible pathway of change for
themselves. By acknowledging, for example, that supervisees' knowledge is of
their own construction and that it fits more or less well for them, even if the
supervisor cannot see how this is possible, and that appeals to 'how things are
in the world' is ineffective as a lever for change, the prospect of contributing
to learning is enhanced. It follows that it would be helpful to create a supervisory relationship in which tolerance, exploration of difference, and curiosity about the individual and subcultural learned beliefs underpinning the
approach to the work may be expressed.

These ideas about learning are consistent with those of Carl Rogers:

> I have come to feel that the only learning which significantly influ-
> ences behaviour is self-discovered, self-appropriated learning. *Such self-
> discovered learning, truth that has been personally appropriated and
> assimilated in experience, cannot be directly communicated to another*. As
> soon as an individual tries to communicate such experience directly,
> often with quite natural enthusiasm, it becomes teaching, and its results
> are inconsequential.
>
> (Rogers, 1974: 276; italics in original)

Rogers took the view that for meaningful learning to take place, the learner
must be at the centre of the process. In questioning whether another can
assist the learning he rejected the idea of direct communication of knowledge. The question then becomes whether the supervisor can do something
else that acknowledges the central position and the values of the learner and
from which learning can result. Gagné (1967) suggested that actions such as
supervision or teaching involve:

> The institution and arrangement of the external conditions of learning
> in ways which will optimally interact with internal capabilities of the
> learner, so as to bring about changes in these capabilities.
>
> (Gagné, 1967: 295)

In this view, the task of the supervisor is to work out, together with the
supervisee, what supervisory environment and interventions will best connect
with and constructively challenge the current knowledge and beliefs of the
supervisee.

The implications of these ideas about knowledge and learning for supervision are:

1   That the supervisor's actions and resources are in competition with other aspects of the learner's environment for the learner's attention.
2   That in order for learning to take place, what is to be learned must connect with the current knowledge of the learner.
3   That in addition to observation, description and experience, there are internal implicit processes that are less amenable to analysis and study that also contribute to learning.

Formulatory or diagnostic assessment

How might supervisors begin their task of designing a learning environment that will best support the learning needs of the supervisee? Formulatory or diagnostic assessment can be conducted with the aim of enhancing the supervisor's understanding of the current knowledge and learning needs of her or his supervisees.

The direct beneficiary of formulatory assessment is the person who wishes to influence the learning of those being supervised. Formulatory assessment is for the supervisor's learning. Formulatory assessment is highly compatible with constructivism. A supervisor seeking to contribute usefully to a supervisee's learning experiences is, in the absence of formulatory information, relying on habit and guesswork. Formulatory assessment enables supervisors to tune their interventions to the current knowledge and ways of learning of the supervisees. Cycles of formulatory assessment and intervention operate as guided feedback loops.

Formulatory assessment operates through an attitude of curiosity, and 'attunedness' on the part of the supervisor to the supervisee's inferred knowledge and ways of learning. In practice this requires the supervisor to explore the supervisee's current knowledge through conversation, through reference to intended learning outcomes, observation and discussion of the supervisee's practice and so on.

Other perspectives on learning

From a constructivist perspective, conceptual frameworks are not seen as right or wrong but as more or less useful. This makes it reasonable for a constructivist-inclined practitioner to consider other perspectives, such as behaviourism, as potentially useful alternative ways of describing situations and processes. Behaviourist theories focus on what can be observed rather than on mental content and seek to account for learning through the interaction of the individual with the environment. Behaviourism can guide what to do in a particular type of situation in order to optimise the likelihood of a particular outcome. This may be exactly what is needed. While it may be that attempts to set out a conceptual basis for the success of behavioural procedures would rest on an instructionist rather than a constructivist premise, in terms of practical action a constructivist should have no problem at all in adopting behavioural (or any other) methods if they are judged suitable for the purpose at hand.

Participating in supervision from a behavioural standpoint, one would expect that learning might be facilitated by the supervisee observing the work of the supervisor or other practitioners either in real time or recorded. The supervisor acts as a model for supervisees, demonstrating the 'good tricks' he or she has learned in work and exploring how these might fit for the learner. This can be of particular relevance where the procedures are relatively common across work with different clients, for example, in introducing oneself and the way of working, or in following a standard assessment procedure. Other behaviour that could be modelled includes responding to certain events in the work where safety is at a premium, such as assessment of risk where a client is threatening suicide, or explaining to the client the issue of confidentiality and its limits.

In addition to direct observation, the supervisor may provide a model by illustrating what to say, making suggestions with: 'You might have felt, thought, said, done . . .' or 'I might have felt, thought, said, done . . .'. Supervisees who are at an early stage of training often have yet to learn the different style of communication undertaken in professional practice in which typical social conventions might be breached. The sorts of questions or statements used might in other contexts be construed as 'rude' or might require the use of language normally reserved for intimate relationships. Examples include asking clients diagnosed as anorexic how much they weigh, asking suicidal clients about the plans they have made to kill themselves, in sexual therapy asking questions about erectile functioning, or in a child who is soiling asking about the consistency of the stool. Supervisees may avoid such issues in their attempts to be 'therapeutic' or to avoid feelings of embarrassment. Seeing how it might be done is likely to enhance the confidence of supervisees since they might take something from their observation which they can fit with their own practice. This process is one of construction rather than direct imitation.

While some learning can derive from observation, further development can hinge upon behaviour rehearsal or practice, perhaps with opportunities for feedback from the supervisor. This can be accomplished through enactment in supervision or by supervisees practising alone or making recordings of their attempts to bring to supervision for further discussion.

The behavioural concept of reinforcement is also applicable to the supervisory situation. Supervisees can be encouraged by positive feedback from the supervisor. Some supervisees regard *any* sort of evaluative feedback as preferable to the uncertainty of none at all. In addition, and ultimately perhaps of greater importance is the reinforcing experience of success which occurs when practitioners observe the positive outcomes achieved by their clients as a result of their interventions. In this regard, it is helpful if the supervisor is able to arrange for the supervisee to work with at least some clients for whom good progress might be predicted.

Piaget's ideas applied in supervision

Piaget (1972) proposed a theory, consistent with constructivism, of knowledge growth through a process of equilibration which arises from the interaction between individuals and their environments. Equilibration is a process of resolution of incompatibilities that can occur between what the person currently knows, and the perception and meaning made of an experience that does not fit with current knowledge.

Piaget's account of the growth of knowledge is based on the idea that knowledge is adaptive; it enables people to navigate through their lives, and it derives from activity. When the outcome of activity fits with an existing action scheme, the experience is 'assimilated' into the action scheme. Glasersfeld (1995: 62) put it concisely: assimilation is a process of 'treating new material as an instance of something known'. In Piaget's account, 'knowing an object or an event is to use it by assimilating it to an action scheme' (Piaget, in Glasersfeld, 1995: 56).

Assimilation is a useful economy measure because what matters is an adequate, not an exact, fit with current knowledge. A judgement about the adequacy of fit requires the presence of some system of value which acts as a discriminator. An example of a value system that humans appear to have evolved in common with many other animals is our own form of thermostat. We can readily make discriminations between 'too hot', 'too cold' and 'adequate'. The 'too hot' discrimination interacts rapidly with a 'withdraw' response. Unless they are able to survive adequately within a very large temperature range, animals that have such a value system are at an advantage over others that don't whenever things get hot.

What happens if the fit is inadequate? Inadequacy of fit is experienced as *surprise* (Bickhard, 1995: 246). The psychological state underlying the experience of surprise is known as 'cognitive conflict' or 'cognitive dissonance'. If the experience is not too traumatic the individual may do a second 'take' – that is, look at the situation again. This happens in a flash when we experience 'getting' a joke. A joke is funny if it contains some surprise, some misfit between what is expected and what is heard. Having experienced the misfit we then reconstrue the story and make it fit in a new way. In so doing we have assimilated the story to a different part of our current knowledge, having at first tried and experienced inadequate fit.

In an experience of cognitive conflict, if a retake does not lead to assimilation, two possibilities remain. One is that the person may disengage from the situation associated with the conflict. By disengaging, the individual escapes the experience of cognitive conflict and also disengages from action that might alleviate or resolve the conflict. This could be regarded as a state of denial; it could turn out to be beneficial or harmful for the person. The other possibility involves a persisting experience of misfit. This is known in Piagetian theory as disequilibration. In this case there is a deeper, more profound review of the new material which ultimately leads, if not to disengagement, to the construction of a new action scheme – some new knowledge – that accommodates the new material. This process is known as accommodation. Unlike assimilation, accommodation involves a radical restructuring – a construction of a new action scheme. This is a process of learning which sometimes involves the experience of confusion. It is illustrated by the response of voice recognition software to this stanza from Lewis Carroll's 'The Jabberwocky':

> Twas brillig, and the slithy toves
> Did gyre and gimble in the wabe,
> All mimsy were the borogroves,
> And the mome raths outgrabe.
>   (Carroll, 1872)

The software's version:

> Was really, and the slightly clothes
> Did go and kindle in the way,
> all Lindsay Werther borrowed Road's,
> and the rats out great.

The software tried to assimilate the new information into its existing structure. What is needed is for the software to accommodate, to change its own structures by the 'teaching' it some new vocabulary. A little like the software, supervisees receive sensory input from which they select, categorise and assimilate those elements which they perceive as relevant based on their previous learning history. The selection process appears to take place without conscious awareness; this selection and construction process is likely to differ from that of the supervisor. States of confusion can be very fertile ground for significant learning, but often result in resistance.

Vygotsky's ideas about learning

Vygotsky, like Piaget, was interested in the development of thinking and behaviour. Also in common with Piaget, he believed that in order to understand higher levels of thought it was necessary to study the processes that preceded and led up to the higher levels. The scope of Vygotsky's interest in development was wide; he referred to three distinct strands of development: phylogeny, the evolution of species through natural selection; ontogeny, the set of processes involved in the development of an individual organism (such as a human being); and 'cultural-historical' development. Much attention has been paid to Vygotsky's work in the third strand, principally because he asserted that 'higher mental functioning' emerges from participation in social processes, processes which are cultural-historical in origin. This is the basis for the label 'social' in Vygotsky's constructivist account.

The zone of proximal development (ZPD) is probably the most widely known of the ideas derived from Vygotsky's work, and with good reason, since it combines elegance, simplicity and applicability in the fields of education and psychotherapy. Vygotsky defined the ZPD as follows:

> The zone of proximal development . . . is the distance between the actual developmental level as determined by independent problem solving and the level of potential development as determined through problem solving under adult guidance or in collaboration with more capable peers.
>
> (Vygotsky, 1978: 86)

A useful application of the ZPD concept is that it shows where to target teaching or supervision in relation to its formative function. If supervision presents supervisees with experiences inside their current developmental profiles (CDP) the learner will be unchallenged and probably bored. At the other extreme, if the supervision demands thinking beyond the ZPD the learner probably won't be able to cope. Optimal formative supervision presents challenges inside the ZPD.

Piaget's and Vygotsky's theories inform supervisors about the learning environments they might attempt to create in order to support supervisees' learning needs. First, a lack of fit must be experienced by the supervisee before it can generate a response. If the gap between the understandings of the supervisor and supervisee is too great, it may not be possible for supervisees to perceive that something has occurred that is of relevance to their learning; it may be regarded as outside the ZPD. This is encapsulated in the four stages of learning readiness described by multiple authors but often credited to Howell (1982). This model describes a cycle where learners move from a comfortable state of unconscious incompetence in which they are unaware of not knowing or possessing a skill. Recognition of not knowing leads to a less comfortable state of conscious incompetence (or self-conscious incompetence). This may arise as a result of having seen another perform the skill, or when something is tried unsuccessfully. There is then a decision to be made about whether to attempt to learn the skill in the knowledge that the process of learning will be accompanied by clumsiness and failure. The next stage is that of conscious competence when the skill can be performed with intellectual effort. Finally, the stage of unconscious competence is reached when the skill is overlearned and can be performed without conscious effort.

A first step may be for the supervisor to draw the attention of supervisees to something salient for their learning. If supervisees do not perceive this as material to their learning, they might respond with incomprehension, with resistance or avoidance. As hypothesised by Piaget, a conservative initial response would be expected. When there is a significant gap in knowledge and experience between supervisors and supervisees it may be very difficult for supervisors to 'de-centre' and understand the current status of the learner with respect to the knowledge that they wish to encourage, a point made by Donaldson (1978).

For example, in teaching interviewing skills it was the intention of one of the authors and a colleague to ensure that we addressed issues of difference, and in particular ethnicity, gender, age and disability in the session. To this end, we asked the group members to think about their own personal features that might be noticed by a client on first meeting. People talked about their age, gender, ethnicity, hearing losses and the like at some length. The feedback given by the participants in this session was that issues of difference had not been addressed. On further exploration it became apparent that the learners had not regarded their own personal characteristics as relevant to learning about difference – they were focusing exclusively 'out there' on the client, seeing difference as a characteristic of the other person rather than lying between them. On reflection it would have been helpful explicitly to bridge from the students' personal characteristics to those of clients in order better to connect with the students' learning needs.

In the application of Piaget's ideas, some authors go so far as to prescribe that the teacher or supervisor instigate a series of problems designed specifically to produce a state of disequilibration in relation to the topic to be learned (Rowell, 1989). Our experience is that sufficient unsolicited examples present themselves, creating a frequent state of uncertainty often accompanied by the unpleasant emotional states of confusion and anxiety. Supervisors might anticipate normal self-preserving defensiveness as a common response.

Knowledge-in-action

In professional training, theory is usually taught within a curriculum defined by the training institution or professional body. The knowledge acquired through the completion of course work assignments or through the reading undertaken at any stage in a professional career could be described as 'declarative knowledge'. When this knowledge is applied in practice, what is learned may be referred to as 'procedural knowledge' (Anderson, 1980). This form of knowledge is regarded as tacit and automatic and is referred to by Schön (1987) as knowledge-in-action. Knowledge-in-action takes place during skilled performance. It may not be possible to put this into words. Even when key features can be described, learners cannot acquire the skilled performance without their own active involvement.

Skilful performance necessarily involves procedural knowledge. This can be seen by considering performances such as riding a bicycle, playing a sport, making music or learning to speak a second language. There is not time consciously to think of all the knowledge that is applied while effecting these skills, even if it had a conscious form. Bringing some features to awareness can even undermine performance; for example, thinking too hard about particular aspects of a golf swing. Professional helping involves procedural knowledge. Binder and Strupp (1997) argued that what is needed is a particular sort of procedural knowledge that allows for on-the-spot appraisals and reappraisals of the problem situation while simultaneously acting within it. Following Schön they referred to this as 'reflection-in-action'. They suggested that true therapeutic competence and effectiveness involve becoming proficient in the capacities for reflection-in-action and improvisation. Many examples of such improvisation are given in Mahoney (2003).

Binder and Strupp (1997) regard treatment manuals as offering a sketchy map of the therapeutic terrain on which moment-to-moment movements must be improvised. The method that they recommended for the development of these skills is through structured sequences of therapeutic problem-detection and problem-solving exercises under conditions that simulate actual clinical experiences. This fills what they saw as the gap between classroom teaching and work with clients in which the material brought by the client cannot be controlled.

They argued that video-records and segments of real or simulated therapy situations could be used both to illustrate theory, and to provide opportunities for coaching and practice of skills in interpersonal processes. Supervisors may be in an ideal position to offer such simulations and exemplars and, with technological developments, supporting materials have begun to appear (Open University, 2005).

The adult learner

The literature on adult learning acknowledges the capacity of adults to reflect on their own learning. Brookfield (1986) suggested that 'educators should assist adults to speculate creatively on possible alternative ways of organising their personal worlds' (p. 233), 'developing in adults a sense of their personal power and self-worth . . . and fostering a willingness to consider alternative ways of living' (p. 283).

Learner and educator in an adult learning context are encouraged to engage with each other as peers. This involves a conscious effort on behalf of the educator to reduce the influence of prestige, counter the right–wrong dialogue commonly found in schools, and encourage critical reflection in a context of openness towards alternative perspectives (Mezirow, 1997: 13). Mezirow regards the adult learner as capable of transformative learning which is a process of becoming changed by what is learned in a highly meaningful way. 'We transform frames of references – our own and those of others – by becoming critically reflective of their assumptions and aware of their context – the source, nature, and consequences of taken-for-granted beliefs' (Mezirow, 2000: 19). He proposed that transformative learning can result from a 'disorienting dilemma' (Mezirow, 2000: 22) which may be triggered by a major life transition. It has been suggested that teachers are able to promote transformational learning in the context of less dramatic predicaments (Torosyan, 2001).

Self-reflection may be aided by the supervisor's taking an enquiring approach to the supervisee's work. This can be accomplished by asking questions such as, 'How did that feel?', or 'What might you have done differently?' Questions can convey alternatives to the meanings made by the supervisee or to the 'normative' meanings of the culture in which the work is being carried out. For example, the supervisor might query the potential impact of an arranged marriage where the assumption is being made that couples will form partnerships through social dating.

The relevance of context

Weil (1993) argued that the tasks for the supervisor are to help supervisees to recognise factors that limit their understanding and behaviour, and to help them to develop a critical consciousness with respect to their own assumptions, behaviour and effectiveness in different situations. There is also the need to help supervisees to understand the values of the systems in which people work, and the parts they play in maintaining the status quo or in unsettling these meaning systems. These issues are explored further in Chapters 3 and 8.

Mezirow (1985) regards the most important aspect of adult learning as problem posing rather than content mastery or problem solving. He emphasised that adult learning and education do not occur in a social vacuum. This acknowledgement of a social and political context is particularly important when examining historical views held within the helping professions. Both normative values and the body of knowledge change over time. This is illustrated by the pseudo-science that was used to argue against higher education for women in the nineteenth century, for example. In 1879, Gustave Le Bon, a leading French scientist who was one of the founders of social psychology, published an article in France's most respected anthropological journal. In it he concluded:

> In the most intelligent races, as among the Parisians, there are a large number of women whose brains are closer in size to those of gorillas than to the most developed male brains. This inferiority is so obvious that no one can contest it for a moment; only its degree is worth discussion. All psychologists who have studied the intelligence of women, as well as poets and novelists, recognize today that they represent the most inferior forms of human evolution and that they are closer to children

and savages than to an adult, civilized man. They excel in fickleness, inconstancy, absence of thought and logic, and incapacity to reason. Without doubt there exist some distinguished women, very superior to the average man, but they are as exceptional as the birth of any monstrosity, as, for example, of a gorilla with two heads; consequently, we may neglect them entirely.

(Le Bon, cited in Gould, 1980: 152–159)

Looking back it is hard to comprehend the development and propagation of such ideas within the professional community without reference to the prevailing social, economic and political climate. History suggests that future generations looking back will find aspects of our current canon of knowledge just as alien and perhaps similarly distasteful.

Experiential learning theory

Learning to be a professional helper involves the construction of new knowledge and the development of skills in its application in practice. Experiential learning theory (Kolb, 1984) attempts to account for the processes by which this learning takes place. Kolb described a cycle of learning in which there are four stages, namely 'concrete experience', 'reflective observation', abstract conceptualisation' and 'active experimentation' (see Figure 2.1). The cycle repeats and may be entered by the learner at any of the four stages but the stages are followed in sequence.

For example, at the stage of concrete experience, the supervisee might discuss in supervision methods for identifying the client's schemas in cognitive behaviour therapy. He or she then tries to use these methods with a client. The results of this are brought to the following supervision in which the

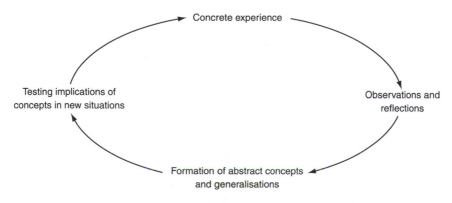

Figure 2.1 The Lewinian experiential learning cycle.

Source: Kolb, David A., Experiental Learning: Experience as a Source of Learning & Development, 1st,© 1984. Electronically reproduced by permission of Pearson Education, Inc., Upper Saddle River, New Jersey.

supervisor helps the supervisee to reflect on her or his experience through a process of enquiry. This might lead to new understandings at the level of abstract conceptualisation, arising from which the supervisee tries the method differently on the next occasion.

Weil (1995: 14) identifies the key features of experiential learning as follows:

- Learners are involved in an active exploration of experience. Experience is used to test out ideas and assumptions rather than passively to obtain practice. Practice can be very important but it is greatly enhanced by reflection.
- Learners must selectively reflect on their experience in a critical way, rather than take experience for granted and assume that the experience on its own is sufficient.
- The experience must matter to the learner. Learners must be committed to the process of exploring and learning.
- There must be scope for the learner to exercise some independence from the teacher. Teachers have an important role in devising appropriate experiences and facilitating reflection. However, the transmission of information is but a minor element and the teacher cannot experience what the learner experiences or reflect for the learner.
- Experiential learning is not the same as 'discovery' learning. Learning by doing is not simply a matter of letting learners loose and hoping that they discover things for themselves in a haphazard way through sudden bursts of inspiration. The nature of the activity may be carefully designed by the teacher and the experience may need to be carefully reviewed and analysed afterwards for learning to take place. A crucial feature of experiential learning is the structure devised by the teacher within which learning takes place.
- Openness to experience is necessary for learners to have the evidence upon which to reflect. It is therefore crucial to establish an appropriate emotional tone for learners: one which is safe and supportive, and which encourages learners to value their own experience and to trust themselves to draw conclusions from it. This openness may not exist at the outset but may be fostered through successive experiences of the experiential learning cycle.
- Experiential learning involves a cyclical sequence of learning activities. Teaching methods can be selected to provide a structure to each stage of the cycle, and to take learners through the appropriate sequence.

This kind of open-minded problem exploration is advocated by Coulshed (1990), who argued that the more staff are encouraged to rely on so-called rational decision-making tools, procedural manuals and routinised service delivery methods, the more they stop thinking for themselves. Such blinkered responses can lead to narrow and superficial discussions in supervision, trapping supervisor and supervisee into a happy conclusion that all is inspected and under control. The idea that staff should be able to think for themselves has become enshrined in a wide range of professions through the notion of 'reflective practice'. Reflective practice models abound (Boud *et al.*, 1985; Gibbs, 1988; Johns and Graham, 1996) and the requirement to demonstrate skills in reflective practice has become a demand in the standards specified by professional associations and quality assurance bodies. Reflective practice is at the heart of the supervisory enterprise and will be addressed in depth in a forthcoming text (Scaife, n.d.).

Experiential learning theory prescribes a particular role for the supervisor as a facilitator and designer of environments to support learning. It is compatible with many of the ideas described earlier in the chapter. Supervisors' knowledge of theories of learning is likely to underpin their approach to supervision when attending to the 'formative' purpose of the task. In addition, the cycle might be referred reflexively to a supervisor's learning of supervisory skills.

Selection of what to learn

So far, this chapter has addressed the process of learning but what can be said about that which is to be learned? To some extent, each profession that works to alleviate human suffering will have devised its own subcultural ideas of what is considered appropriate to learn and what is excluded. In learning the profession, individuals become encultured within that school of thought, the tenets of which do not always become obvious except when coming up against people schooled in alternative professional cultures.

An exercise designed to show how individual beliefs and convictions are implicitly brought to supervision and influence the process was designed for a training workshop as follows.

Participants were divided into three groups, each given the same task of wrapping an egg. Each group was given a different card on which were written the directions for what should be achieved in wrapping the egg. One group was invited to wrap the egg for aesthetic effect, the second for durability, and the third for economy. Upon completion, the products of each group were passed to another group whose task was to give feedback and critique the product. Initially some of the comments made about other groups' efforts were negative to the point of being scathing. Emotions ran high. After a few minutes of loud debate and laughter, one person asked another group's members why they had wrapped the egg in that particular way. This prompted a gradual realisation that the different groups had been assigned different values from which to approach the task.

Guidance as to the material to be learned is typically provided in pre-registration education through required professional learning outcomes and programme specifications. In the UK there is an overarching framework for higher education qualifications specified by the Quality Assurance Agency with subject benchmark statements for broad subject areas (Quality Assurance Agency, 2001). Each institution of higher education writes programme specifications setting out in detail the knowledge, understanding and skills the successful student should acquire. The achievements of individual students are recorded in personal progress documents. In conjunction with key government agendas such as National Service Frameworks (NSF) and the Knowledge and Skills Framework (KSF), Skills for Health is in the process of developing National Occupational Standards (NOS) and National Workforce Competences (NWC) for use within the health sector (Skills for Health, 2007).

Specifications have also been devised for the skills of supervision (American Association of Directors of Psychiatric Residency Training, 2005; British Psychological Society, 2007b: Appendix 5). The skills devised by the latter are listed in Appendix 3. It has been suggested that there will be a high focus on supervisory skills and competencies and how they are assessed in the next few years (Turpin, December 2007, personal communication). Practitioners might benefit from keeping in mind the value base from which these prescriptions derive and subjecting them to critical review over the course of a professional career in which repeated modification is to be anticipated.

Personal learning styles

The 1970s saw a surge of interest in the idea of learning styles which has continued to be popular in Britain, the USA, Southeast Asia and further afield. It is claimed that learners have their own natural learning style. Different categorisations have been proposed by a range of authors. Pask (1976) argued for two distinguishable processes involved in the learning of complex material – building a description of what may be known (a conceptual model of how topics interrelate) and building procedures that represent a more detailed sequential study. Individuals may show a dominance of one of these processes over the other. Those who show a preference for the development of an overview are described as holists who tend to adopt a global study approach. Those preferring procedure building are described as serialists who adopt a local approach to study whereby they focus on local facts and details. The holist typically focuses on several aspects of the subject at the same time.

Ford (1985) explored to what extent postgraduate students could adopt either holist or serialist strategies. Two groups of students were identified, each showing a preference for one strategy. They were then taught with two different teaching strategies designed to suit either holist or serialist learners. The majority of students showed evidence of greater learning taking place as a result of the teaching designed to suit their preferred learning style.

Pask's is not the only attempt to identify distinctive individual learning styles. Riding (1992, 1994; Riding and Rayner, 1998), for example, identified nine categories of learning style based on the dimensions of analytic-holist and verbaliser-imager. These differences were accounted for in terms of the individuality of human brain activity.

The implications of these ideas for supervision are that supervisees might find it helpful to identify whether they have preferred learning styles and, if they do, the way these styles vary with the task. In the light of this knowledge the supervisor might strive to create the conditions for learning that would best suit the preferred learning style.

Methods for the exploration of personal learning styles

A number of questionnaire methods are available for exploring personal learning styles, for example, the Study Preference Questionnaire (Ford, 1985), the Short Inventory of Approaches to Study (Entwistle, 1981), the Cognitive Styles Analysis (Riding, 1994) and The Manual of Learning Styles (Honey and Mumford, 1992).

A technique for exploring which environments and interventions have previously enhanced the supervisee's learning has been described by Judy Hildebrand (1998a). She invites supervisees to draw a professional 'geno-gram' of their previous learning. This can be pictorial, in words or images according to the preferences of the individual. The task is to map the histor-ical influences on learning that have been of relevance to the way the person conducts her or his work. This might include people and relationships, books including novels, films, 'gurus', personal crises and so on. The exercise is private with a view to the supervisor asking, 'What would it be helpful for me to learn from your having completed this exercise?' 'What does it tell me about the conditions I should try to create that will be most helpful to your learn-ing in supervision?' This is an example of formulatory assessment discussed earlier in this chapter.

A further method for exploring personal learning styles is to offer a prob-lem that acts as a metaphor for an issue in professional helping, and to ask the supervisee to attempt to solve it. The supervisee then thinks about how he or she approached the task – through a logical and steady progression, with impatience, through guesswork and the like. Information about super-visees' approaches to this problem might shed light on their approach to problem solving more generally. Examples of such tasks are described in Scaife (1995).

The notion of a fixed learning style is potentially problematic because there seems to be no convincing evidence that people approach learning tasks in ways that are independent of context. In addition, the implications of the categorisation are unclear, and labelling, especially in a dynamic context like learning, risks closing down willingness to engage with events and processes that lie outside the scope of the label. Brookfield (1995) said, 'Sometimes the last thing learners need is for their preferred learning style to be affirmed.

Agreeing to let people learn only in a way that feels comfortable and familiar can restrict seriously their chance for development.'

The learning styles literature has, however, served the positive function of drawing attention to learning as opposed to intervention; that is, to the 'end' as opposed to one of the 'means'. It encourages a spotlight on the learner as opposed to the teacher, a focus which is congruent with contemporary views of learning.

Chapter 3

Personal development and the emotional climate of work

Joyce Scaife and Sue Walsh

> He was beginning to feel an ache of anxiety because this person towards whom he felt kindly was a crazy person (even though the doctor had told him to call them mentally ill) and he could make her crazier if he said the wrong things. The doctors and all the books he had been reading told him not to be too definite, not to argue or show strong feelings, but to be cheerful and helpful. In spite of these instructions, he knew that he could move her, and this made him try, and the trying made him feel something for her, and his success at this feeling made her a human being to him.
>
> (Greenberg, 1992: 257)

This chapter focuses on the role of the supervisor in relation to the emotions of supervisees because these affect and are affected by their work. It also addresses the role of personal issues, personal histories and personal qualities in the work of supervisees, and the supervisory tasks of providing support and aiding the development of self-understanding and knowledge.

There are two themes within the chapter. The first addresses how work contexts, events, and the attitudes and behaviour of clients and colleagues can have significant consequences for the emotional state of people working to help others (i.e. the influence of work on self). The second theme focuses on the issue of personal and professional development and how the personal qualities, values and beliefs of helping professionals are of central importance in their work (the influence of self on work). The development of self-awareness is often referred to in the helping professions as 'personal and professional development'. The chapter moves from a focus on wider cultural and institutional influences to specific relationships between clients and therapists. In the final section some exercises designed for the exploration of values and beliefs are described.

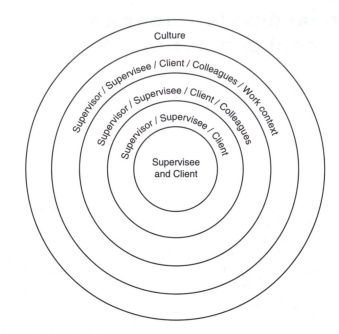

Figure 3.1 Levels of the helping system.

The emotional climate of organisations – its effects on supervisees

Professional helping often takes place in institutions which are influenced by the wider social, political and economic context. In an ideal world, people might hope to experience their institutional context as compatible and congruent with their own values and aspirations, but this cannot be assumed or guaranteed. Within the institutions in which we work there are social, political and economic forces that can be construed as dangerous, disturbing and destabilising, which may evoke feelings of vulnerability in the employees. Political changes can reverberate throughout organisations and lead to staff experiencing dislocation and alienation from the tenets upon which the employing organisation becomes based.

Morrison (1993) argued that practitioners in the helping professions expect to experience some primary stress arising from the work they undertake, but are far more distressed by the secondary stress arising from the organisation's response to them when this happens. He offered a theoretical framework to explain the damaging effects of this process on staff: the Professional Accommodation Syndrome (Morrison, 2001: 248).

The ethos and functions of the employing organisation and the motivation of individual employees can be at cross-purposes. People's motivations for becoming professional helpers can be explained at a number of levels, which include family scripts and wider cultural values. At the level of the individual, people usually express a desire to be useful in the service of others – they want to help. Employers may have other priorities – to make a profit, to cut costs, to reduce waiting lists, to increase bed occupancy and the like. One view would regard employees as 'economic cogs' whose role is to undertake the tasks of the organisation. An example would be the concept of 'scientific management' (Taylor, [1911] 1998), in which the worker is reduced to executing management thinking.

Faced with the task of attempting to help another individual, organisational priorities may be frustrating and restricting in terms of the action to be taken that would best suit the needs of client or patient care. The incompatibility of the purposes of the individual and of the organisation can produce a sense of misery, helplessness, outrage and alienation (Obholzer, 1994). Using psychoanalytic and systemic theories, Fotaki (2006) and Hoggett (2006) have critiqued the disconnection between public health priorities and the effective and benevolent care of vulnerable and sick individuals. These disconnections can have significant negative impacts upon the staff who are trying to provide a service within poorly functioning and disconnected systems (Heginbotham, 1999).

In training contexts additional constraints and potential conflicts result from the involvement of the third party; namely, the training institution. The priorities of this institution are likely to include successful completion of the course by as many students as possible. In a university, the status of staff and students may depend on seeming to know more, or, for example, publish more, than colleagues. Bernard and Goodyear (1998: 76) highlighted this particularly in relation to postgraduate students when they stated, 'the achievement orientation, competitiveness and evaluative nature of the academic climate tend to exacerbate anxiety'. Such a climate may be fostered further by a 'marketplace' political context in which funding of public services such as universities and health and social services depends on outputs and quantification.

During the 1980s and 1990s in the UK, the change of emphasis in the political climate away from caring to production and output was reflected in the language used in these contexts where 'patients' and 'clients' became 'service users' and 'customers'. University staff gave up 'teaching' in order to 'deliver the curriculum', and when library books were borrowed on loan there were no longer other 'readers' but 'customers' waiting. Treating the health and public services as a marketplace economy is almost certain to be accompanied by distress and a reluctance to make the transition in meaning for staff who entered their professions in order to 'care' or to 'teach'. This clash of values was highlighted by Llewelyn and colleagues (2007) when seeking to explain the distress experienced by course staff faced with students who appeared to be disturbingly self-oriented in the consumer-oriented, complaint and entitlement ethos of wider society.

In our opinion, the effect of the organisational context and climate on the supervisee is a legitimate focus of supervision. Supervision can serve as a restorative function for helpers afflicted by this sense of alienation and dislocation by offering a reflective space in which the influence of these conflicting ideas can be understood and moderated. Different contextual dimensions may be analysed in order for supervisees to develop a clearer understanding of their own position and the influences to which they are subject at work. Pearce and Cronen (1980) offered a hierarchical model for this purpose, while other authors (Hoffman, 1991; Scaife, 1993c) proposed a more heterarchical relationship between the elements.

Such analyses can assist people in making sense of their position in the work system and this may help to take the sting out of what may have been construed as personal. Actions taken in an organisation often lead to hurt feelings, particularly when an asset previously enjoyed is threatened with removal. The loss of an office, secretarial support or staffing cuts can evoke a response in which workers doubt their value to colleagues and the wider organisation. In supervision it is possible to identify self-destructive reaction patterns and consciously to experiment with different strategies. This does not have to involve passive acceptance, but rather constructive conceptualisation and action planning. Negative labelling, in contrast, tends to block productive avenues for improving matters.

Learning cultures

Hawkins and Shohet (2006) described a number of working contexts or cultures and the climates that they produce. These include 'hunt the personal pathology', 'strive for bureaucratic efficiency', 'watch-your-back', 'driven by crisis', 'the addictive organisation' and the 'learning developmental culture'. They argued that nearly all organisational cultures are a mix of these types but that the learning developmental culture supports reflection on experience with a view to making sense of this in a way that allows the experience to challenge one's way of seeing and thinking about the world. We would argue that such a culture effectively provides nurture for its staff and clients with contingent personal and professional development mediating the negative experiences that may be induced by aspects of the work context.

In order to create opportunities for restoration, reflection and developing meanings, a focus on the *process* of learning rather than the outcomes (information or knowledge) is desirable. For example, a colleague described how he was educated by people whose vision of education happened to be to develop understanding rather than to acquire factual knowledge. On taking up a place at university he was amazed to find that he had significantly greater understanding of the subject than many of his peers with better grades than his own who had been educated to pass examinations.

If the process of learning is valued, to not know is the impetus to try to find out rather than to pretend to know already. It implies a focus on questioning and curiosity rather than on premature closure. Premature closure may be advantageous in certain contexts – for example, emergency health services where decisions must be made quickly. But most work in health and social services is not carried out in conditions of emergency. If supervisees can see that the supervisor's interest is in facilitating learning, then the context of safety will allow them to disclose uncertainties and minimise the sense of threat that can produce a veneer of competence and resistance to learning.

Relationships with colleagues

Professional helpers are likely to spend a significant proportion of their lives at work. Shared interests offer ground for the development of intimacy with colleagues which could threaten pre-existing close personal relationships and partnerships. Supervision can help people both to manage their needs for intimacy at work and to maintain appropriate boundaries. The emotional demands of working with distressed clients may heighten this tension between the need for intimacy and the need for distance.

Close proximity with colleagues who are experienced as annoying, harassing, boring or dim-witted can evoke hostile emotions that make work an undesirable place. Work offers as much opportunity as life outside work for the experience of pleasure and displeasure in the company of others. The difference is that at work it may be impossible to avoid colleagues who distract, annoy or irritate. To add further complexity, these people may occupy positions of influence in which they cannot be avoided and as a result of whose actions careers can be made or broken.

Supervision may provide the only context in which it is possible to stand back from relationships in order to analyse and understand the interpersonal processes taking place and to construct action plans in order to alleviate the distress arising from them. It has been argued (Hawkins and Shohet, 2006: 174) that it is more effective to address issues about colleagues when all parties are present. This requires much skill. Individual supervision can help to prepare individuals for this challenging experience. The dynamics of team meetings can be so powerful as to preclude rational discussion of interpersonal issues, particularly when they have not been thought through in advance.

Some contexts may be experienced as particularly unsupportive to the development of effective interprofessional working. For example, multidisciplinary teams (MDTs) can be the source of tensions that undermine relationships with colleagues (Roberts, 1985). Professional bodies have attempted to help their members with this issue by providing guidance on responsibilities within such teams (e.g. British Psychological Society, 1998b). By definition the professional helpers who constitute the team bring with them different training, have been encultured into different professional schools of thought and as a result see the work through different lenses. Tensions are inevitable, particularly where the structure of the team elevates the views of one discipline above others. Instead of the multiple lenses providing a comprehensive overview, competition can generate factions and splits within the team and differences of opinion can become personalised.

In a study employing in-depth semi-structured interviews of 20 members of five teams caring for older residents in Metropolitan Toronto (Cott, 1998) it emerged that one of the larger teams comprised two subgroups differentiated as 'nursing' and 'multidisciplinary team'. The latter group proceeded with their work tasks with relative autonomy and independence. They met regularly with supervisory nurses in meetings which were rarely attended by direct care-giving staff. Cott found that the structure of the teams, counter to the prevailing teamwork ideology of collaboration and cooperation, reinforced status differentials. In this case, the nurses who provided direct patient care occupied lower status positions. The team structure promoted alienation in the nurses who were key to the implementation of decisions made by MDT staff who had no authority in relation to the nurses. Cott concluded that 'not only do team members not share understandings of roles, norms and values, they do not share similar meanings of team work'. Gomez *et al.* (1980) reported a study on an inpatient unit in which role confusion and insecurity among the staff had relegated patient care to second place as major interpersonal conflicts were played out among staff along ethnic and cultural lines. The situation was resolved through offering training to the staff members who provided direct patient care and emphasising the value of their contributions to the well-being of residents. Good arrangements for supervision outside managerial arrangements can provide a medium for minimising adverse effects of conflicting perspectives in multidisciplinary teams by encouraging an analysis of team structure and dynamics.

In our experience, the range of emotions aroused at work in relation to clients is at least equalled if not exceeded by those evoked by colleagues. After all, these feelings can in some ways be given freer rein since one is not setting out to help colleagues in the same way as setting out to help clients, and the expectations about behaviour from within the two roles (colleague, client) are quite different. Supervision may be the place in which a more distant perspective can mediate the effects of relationships with colleagues, providing that the material is used to promote compassionate understanding rather than mutual moaning.

Emotions generated within the supervisory relationship

The supervisory relationship itself is a subset of relationships with colleagues. It is sometimes argued that supervision implies a complementary relationship in which there is a difference in status between the participants (Wynne *et al.*,

1986). This feature is of particular relevance when supervision occurs in the context of a training relationship in which the supervisor has a formal and crucial assessment function. It has been argued that this structural feature of the supervisory relationship makes it inevitable that intense emotional reactions will develop in the relationship in one or both partners (Doehrman, 1976).

Salzberger-Wittenberg (1983: 12) and Lee and Littlejohns (2007) argued that an adult entering a new relationship with a teacher is inevitably anxious and that feelings associated with earlier relationships with authority figures are evoked. Salzberger-Wittenberg stated, 'Any new relationship tends to arouse hope and dread, and these exist side by side in our minds. The less we know about the new person the freer we are to invest him with extremes of good and bad qualities.' She argued that helpers such as teachers, counsellors and doctors are often imbued with immense power for good and evil. More realistic expectations include the hope of benefiting from the supervisor's greater knowledge and experience, that the relationship will be characterised by tolerance, and that unreasonable demands will be understood yet met with firmness.

The differential status of participants, particularly in training supervision, cannot be denied. However, its influence can be circumscribed by acknowledgement of its potential impact and discussion of how it may be contained. A good beginning, effected through a sound contracting process (discussed further in Chapter 4) can establish a foundation for the development of trust, which in turn allows for the possibility of openness and risk taking.

A good beginning is not enough to guarantee an ongoing stable and effective working alliance. In particular, making sense of any threatened ruptures in the relationship, such as when the supervisor has to give the supervisee difficult feedback, is important. Such experiences are invaluable for the supervisee, and if handled well can create a stable sense of trust and hopefulness in the relationship such that openness and assessment can go hand-in-hand. In general, a respectful attitude towards the supervisee and to other colleagues can go a long way towards the creation and maintenance of a climate of trust in supervision.

Personal and professional development (PPD)

People who decide to work in the helping professions bring with them a wide variety of expectations regarding the relevance of self both to the work and as a focus of supervision. The extent to which the exploration of self in the work is seen as relevant differs according to profession and theoretical models. At one end of the continuum is the view that the experience of personal therapy is essential to competence. In the centre is the perspective that awareness and development of self in work is crucial, and it can be achieved through a range of methods. At the other end of the continuum there is greater emphasis on skills learning with little attention to how personal issues might be relevant in the work. We take the view that it is impossible to leave the issue of personal growth out of the equation when undertaking the roles and tasks of the therapist or professional helper, and learning about oneself in work is central to an ethical stance in relation to the work. The understanding and development of self in work is referred to as personal and professional development. This differs from personal therapy, although personal therapy might result in personal and professional development.

Learning about psychological methods, approaches and techniques occurs in the context of personal qualities. While personal growth is not necessarily a primary goal of supervision, it is an instrumental goal that works in the service of making the supervisee a better practitioner (Bernard and Goodyear, 1992). It has been argued that a keen sense of self-awareness, insight, and control of one's feelings and behaviour are necessary if one is to be empathic and understanding with clients (Middleman and Rhodes, 1985). Falender and Shafranske (2004: 92) argued that personal influences accompany every technical intervention and facet of training, and that interventions 'are guided by science and yet are influenced by our humanity'. Wheeler and Richards (2007a) took the view that when the 'wounds' of the supervisee impact on the work with the client they cannot be avoided in supervision. They described types of issues that the supervisee might address under the headings of paradigmatic difficulties (linked to stable personal attributes of the therapist), situational difficulties (such as work with severe abuse or trauma), and transient difficulties (emanating from particular circumstances arising from the nature of the work). These categories were derived from research into therapist difficulties conducted by Schröder and Davis (2004).

In the nursing profession there have been attempts to research the impact of supervision on personal development, particularly in relation to the role it plays in preventing burn-out and encouraging creativity (Berg and Hallberg, 1999). On the basis of a large-scale exploratory study which included interviews with a subset of participants, White et al. (1998: 189) reported that supervisees

> welcomed the development of their confidence and self-esteem, the support they derived from peers and the sense of 'actually taking responsibility' for their own practice which resulted from supervision. Interviewees variously claimed that clinical supervision had made them more honest, relaxed, enthusiastic and less competitive. For some, clinical supervision had helped them to 'cope with the fear of being seen not to cope'.

Arvidsson and colleagues (2000) analysed interviews of ten nurses following their experience of two years of group supervision. One of their descriptive categories was 'a feeling of personal development'. They found that the participants in the study were more likely to be able to identify issues of personal development in the second year of supervision than in the first. They concluded that as a result of supervision, 'the nurses gained increased trust in their own abilities, feelings and work performance. They became more courageous, dared more and worked independently to a greater extent.'

Using Proctor's framework concerning the restorative, normative and formative purposes of supervision, Bowles and Young (1999) conducted semi-structured interviews to explore the benefits of supervision. Nurses reported that clinical supervision had, among other reported impacts, improved self-confidence, had made them more aware of their own behaviour and had increased their self-awareness. Positive influences of clinical supervision on self-awareness and self-value were similarly reported by Bégat et al. (1997).

What is personal and professional development?

Many authors have attempted to define the elusive concept of personal development and to develop profession-specific models (Sheikh et al., 2007). Definitions of PPD are reviewed in Hughes and Youngson (in press). Three key features identified by Mearns (1997: 94) are:

- A preparedness and willingness to become more and more aware of self.
- A preparedness and willingness to try to understand one's self.
- A preparedness and willingness to explore and experiment with one's self, i.e. to risk doing things differently, face fears, invite challenge, examine one's character and personality, learn to confront and so on.

It may help to use a metaphor to get across the idea of personal and professional development. If you think, for example, of professional musicians playing classical music, in order to have become accomplished in their playing they will have studied music theory, learned appropriate techniques and practised extensively with the help of an experienced teacher. It may be possible to know everything that there is to know about music theory, have flawless technique, and yet fail to please an audience. There is something more to a musical performance which derives from the personal qualities of the performer. As a rule, one of us prefers a passionately rendered performance with some inaccuracies to perfect technique with a wooden delivery that suggests the performer's heart isn't in it.

What is the factor that makes the difference? It is about performers saying something with the music; they have put into it their own personal interpretation. We talk about the 'feel' that they have for the material and by their rendition they can move the audience, the other humans who are participating in the event. Technique is foundational but if it is the focus of the performance it is more than likely to get in the way of the communication between musician and listener. As a client we hazard that you would prefer to be treated by someone who keeps you in mind. For example, consider the frustration generated when the bank clerk, the garage mechanic or the builder fail to recognise your need for an individualised response but rather send you a recorded message, lose your documentation or pass you from one member of staff to another. How much more galling if your therapist cannot remember what is important to you, turns up late for your meeting, loses your notes, does not take the action promised, looks bored or discourages you from talking about what you need to discuss.

The essence of personal and professional development is an ongoing learning process about aspects of the self in relation to others. An aim is to develop the capacity simultaneously to be affected by the client's communications, while reflecting on a range of meanings of the communication and choosing how to respond to the benefit of the client. Without a good understanding of self, the therapist is more likely to participate in habitual patterns of responding developed in the client's or his or her own life histories.

Aspects of self that constitute the domain for personal and professional development in the work context may be understood in three categories.

1 Acknowledging the personal impact of client work

At the heart of the therapeutic enterprise is compassion and caring. 'The client–therapist relationship provides a special context for vital experiments in living. . . . One clear and crystalline moment of understanding and caring can ripple across endless lives and generations' (Mahoney, 2003: 15). As soon as the worker cares, the whole spectrum of feelings including elation, anger, uselessness, sexual arousal, confusion, depression, amusement, disgust and the like may be experienced in relationships with clients. These can be very difficult to handle since feelings of warmth and empathy are espoused. Those clients that get under one's skin can be taken home in the head and ruminated upon endlessly unless there is a process for making meaning of these feelings and using them to inform the work. We would contend that maintaining distance from clients and failing to acknowledge such feelings would significantly impair the work and is not an option. Rather, if these feelings can be consciously recognised, they can be used constructively in the work (Falender and Shafranske, 2004: 84).

Mollon (1989) gave examples of how clients' behaviour towards novice therapists can generate feelings of inadequacy that interact with the more general feelings of incompetence associated with early stages of professional development. In one case example, having found previous encounters with the medical profession unhelpful to her long-standing anxiety state the client had requested the assistance of a psychologist. Initially the therapist felt hopeful and attributed the client's dissatisfaction to previous inappropriate medical interventions. Over time, the client conveyed a feeling that the psychologist should do something other than listen and talk, and her stance in sessions was passive – the psychologist feeling pressure to identify topics herself. The client questioned frequently whether the work was going to be of help to her, thereby dismissing the activity in which the therapist was currently engaged as having the potential to be of help. While the client's behaviour was not overtly hostile, it was experienced by the supervisee as a sustained attack on her state of mind and her professional identity.

Supervision enabled the novice therapist to obtain a more distant perspective on the work and to make a meaning of the interaction with the client which provided information about the client's other and earlier relationships. This allowed the focus of the work to move to the current interaction between client and therapist, and to the nature of the relationship between the client and her parents. Mollon argued that a task of supervision is to bring the supervisee's anxiety and mental pain into the discourse so that feelings of incompetence and disillusionment regarding the capacity of psychotherapy to be of help may be seen as meaningful material that informs the work. Typically such feelings engender a sense of shame and inclinations towards reticence and concealment. Shame can manifest in supervision through 'withdrawal', 'avoidance', 'attack on self' and 'attack on others' (Hahn, 2001). Since supervisees are not disposed to bring such reactions to supervision, a proactive stance by a watchful and supportive supervisor is advocated (Falender and Shafranske, 2004: 111).

It is not only novices who are affected by client distress. There is a whole research literature addressed to staff burn-out, vicarious traumatisation and compassion fatigue (Bennett *et al.*, 2005; Figley, 1995, 2002; Myers and Wee, 2005; Rothschild and Rand, 2006). Burn-out results from cumulative stress and hassles experienced at work. Compassion fatigue is a state of tension and preoccupation with the individual or cumulative trauma of clients which can be manifested in a number of ways including re-experiencing the traumatic event, avoidance of reminders of the event, and persistent arousal. It can be regarded as secondary trauma arising from contact with the experience of traumatised clients. Figley (1995) argued that professionals who listen to clients' stories of suffering may feel similar fear, pain and suffering because they care, and that those who have the greatest capacity for feeling and expressing empathy tend to be more at risk of compassion stress.

Clients with particular kinds of presentation can be almost invariably challenging. Relationships with clients who self-harm and who are at high risk of suicide, often diagnosed with the label 'borderline', can wreak havoc with the emotions of workers (Capodanno, 1998). Some treatments, such as dialectical behaviour therapy, designed for such clients, specify support for staff through weekly therapist consultation team meetings which are intended to enhance therapist motivation and skills and to provide therapy for the therapists (Linehan *et al.*, 2006; Palmer, 2002). Supervision is one of the few activities provided by an employer that can help to identify and allay such emotional disturbance in the worker.

It is not just that working with clients can generate *negative* feelings that can be problematic for someone trying to occupy a professional helping role. Goffman (1968: 79) asserted that, 'A . . . general way in which human materials differ from other kinds, and hence present unique problems, is that however distant the staff tries to stay from these materials, such materials can become objects of fellow feeling and even affection.'

A piece of reflective writing by a nurse, Lindsay Bucknell, reported by Gillie Bolton (2005), illustrates how a ward sister was able through example to help her understand how to love her patients professionally:

> The door opens and the ward sister comes in. She has trust in me that I can nurse her patient. She asks if I would like her to help me turn him. It is a question, not an order, in the way she says it she acknowledges that today Simon is my patient and she is simply offering to help me. She is cheery and competent, not cheery which might suggest avoidance of the situation, she is just present but lightly so. She says, 'wouldn't he have hated this'. She is right – he is a diffident and intensely private young man . . .
>
> Now he lies, totally dependent, his body exposed to anybody. She is right: he would have hated this. As we turn him she is very careful with the body which is on loan to us, because he can't protect it himself at present, careful to protect his dignity. We talk to him, not across him. In this care of this young man is our understanding that he is still a person with right to care and dignity, whether he knows or not.
>
> In that moment I learned the truth of empathy; I received permission to have empathy with my patients, to believe in their rights as individuals, to allow myself to love them, but as a professional, not as a friend. She didn't talk about it, she didn't analyse it, she simply modelled it and all I'd heard about not getting involved which had never made sense inside me fell away. I understood something profound about the nature of being truly involved in a professional relationship with my patients.
>
> (Bolton, 2005: 53)

Making sense of these feelings and working out how to respond as a human being while maintaining professional boundaries is an appropriate focus of supervision.

The second category of issues that constitute the domain of personal and professional development is the influence of life events.

2 The influence of events outside work on relationships at work

In every life there is an ongoing series of transitions which can include major life events such as bereavements, ill-health, the formation and breaking of relationships, births and the like, but also a broken leg, a car accident, moving house, falling in love and taking a holiday in a different culture. Each of these events can generate changes in the meanings that people make in their lives. People may experience anger, profound sadness or elation, and these feelings, mediated by thoughts and ideas, are brought to work and influence the ways in which it is undertaken.

Each person's emotional context for the work and her or his values and beliefs about the world are thus in constant transition. Exploration of this in supervision can help to identify how these experiences might help or hinder the work. For those who have experienced a recent bereavement, the sadness evoked by being in the presence of a bereaved client may lead workers to be unable adequately to attend to the client's needs as they become overwhelmed by their own. On the other hand, the experience may ultimately help the worker to understand how the client's grief may be capable of exerting such a debilitating effect on the client's ability to function.

It is not proposed that the supervisor intrude excessively into the supervisee's personal life, but instead that an appropriate focus of supervision is the effects of life events on the work rather than on the events themselves, and that it is permissible and desirable for supervisees to bring such matters to supervision. Supervision is also a forum in which the influence of people's values, beliefs and personal characteristics on their work can be explored.

3 The influence of personal life history, values, beliefs and personal characteristics on relationships at work

If we acknowledge the psychological significance of individual differences, it follows that each person will approach the work differently, even when adopting the same model and techniques. Often, one's beliefs and values are taken for granted and do not come into focus except when brought up against difference. This can occur when travelling and visiting a different culture, or by meeting individuals who hold different beliefs from one's own. Issues of difference encompassed by ethnicity, religious beliefs, socio-cultural status, gender, disability, age and sexuality are explored further in Chapter 7. Other personal characteristics are addressed here.

FIRST IMPRESSIONS

The first thing that clients are likely to notice about a worker is her or his appearance and general manner. The influence of first impressions may attenuate over time but is likely to affect the initial process of engagement not only between client and therapist but also between supervisor and supervisee. Visually apparent features such as age, gender, disability, height, weight, skin colour, dress and hairstyle are mutually assessed at some level before a word is spoken. Some features are enduring and relatively immutable while others are more amenable to change. It is worth considering what clients might make of badges, styles of dress, jewellery and the like, and this may be an appropriate focus of supervision.

Sometimes these factors have an influence from the beginning to the end of the work. A referral was made to one of us after the client had attended a public meeting led by a middle-aged male who favours formal dress and a serious manner. Although not identified at the point of referral, it later transpired that the client had specifically wanted to work with this person whose appearance had conformed to what he perceived as the features of someone who could help. He did not want to be seen by a female whose style was less formal. The work was 'stuck' from the beginning, although not identified as such until several sessions had taken place. Had the issue of the client's preferences regarding the personal characteristics of the worker been taken to supervision earlier, much of the frustration experienced by both client and therapist might have been avoided. Supervision offers a forum in which participants might speculate about the first impressions that they make, checking this against the actual first impressions of the other.

Some personal characteristics might benefit from explicitly being introduced to a client at the outset, particularly if there is reason to believe that the client may have expected someone different. 'I may seem very different from the kind of person that you expected to work with and, as you get to know me, if you feel that this is an issue that is getting in the way I would like you to tell me so that we can work out if you would prefer to continue with me or with someone else.' This would not usually constitute part of an introduction to the work of therapy or supervision but can be used to constructive effect if cues suggest that a specific personal feature is adversely affecting the engagement process or is known to 'throw' people on first meeting in a more general social context.

Another strategy might be to ask colleagues, friends and relations how they think others perceive you on first meeting. Ideally choose someone who is prepared to be open and direct and someone whose opinion you respect! These approaches to this issue are congruent with, for example, a systemic model of therapy. The influence of personal features and characteristics on the therapeutic process might be managed differently within other models, and the example of transference and counter-transference is discussed in a later section of this chapter.

USE OF PERSONALITY AND TEMPERAMENT IN THE WORK

Extensive research in temperament and personality (e.g. Thomas *et al.*, 1968) has provided evidence for individual differences that have a degree of stability from infancy to adulthood. These qualities will influence the way in which people approach and are experienced by others in their work, irrespective of the model or theory adopted. For example, some people are generally quiet and calm, others more extrovert; some people are adept in the use of humour, others are more serious. These qualities may be a focus of discussion in supervision. Supervisees might be interested to explore how they can use a personal quality that is apparent in their personal life to more effect in their work.

VALUES AND BELIEFS

Personal biases can inadvertently or explicitly result in therapists encouraging clients in particular directions without considering the full range of options and exploring what is most suitable for the client. For example, those who hold the view 'marriage is for life' may not create space for clients to consider leaving their partners as a solution to their difficulties. Those who have a desire to look after and make things right for their clients may not foster the development of problem-solving skills in the client. Practitioners who believe that it is never a good idea to suppress emotions may not acknowledge this as an adaptive response for some people some or all of the time. Bringing these values to awareness enables them to be examined, their effects on the work explored, and a conscious decision taken as to how to use them in the service of the work. This does not imply that a worker cannot hold beliefs and values, only that awareness of them encourages the possibility of understanding that they are not universal and that the client's may be different. Where such differences pertain, the most helpful route for the client may not necessarily be that which in similar circumstances would also suit the worker.

In our experience, many a member of the helping professions is assailed by a desire for perfection. When this is challenged by clients who do not progress, feelings of failure, depression and reduced motivation may result. It is the supervisor's role gently to challenge such beliefs that serve to hinder the work, and to help supervisees to notice their strengths and capabilities. People have often had to struggle to become fully fledged members of a profession by meeting demanding academic standards, engaging in extensive processes of personal exploration, or after giving up a well-established career in order to find more rewarding work. In consequence, the high esteem in which they hold the helping professions, particularly during training, can suffer a severe blow as they become more familiar with the task. The resultant feelings of disappointment in the profession and in themselves can be devastating. How difficult to strike a balance between accepting that this is all there is while being able to show that, despite the limitations of the art, it can nevertheless make a profound impact on some lives, and some impact on many more. Crises of confidence in supervisees can be particularly demanding of supervisory skill. This might be a time when a measure of self-disclosure can assist.

There are a number of enlivening and honest books which further explore the way in which the practitioner can helpfully develop awareness of the connection between self, values and client work (see Casement, 1985, 1990;

Mahoney, 2003; Yalom, 1989). Other authors have published materials containing exercises designed to facilitate personal and professional development (Cross and Papadopoulos, 2001; Wilkins, 1997; Wosket, 1999).

Processes in the exploration of personal material

In some psychotherapies (such as psychoanalysis) exploration of personal issues has been a required undertaking during training, usually through concurrent personal therapy. Other approaches to the work (such as systemic family therapy) have viewed reflection on personal values and beliefs as essential to training and ongoing practice, but see this as being accomplished through alternative mechanisms such as group work focused specifically on personal and professional development (Hildebrand, 1998b). Some approaches include multiple mechanisms within which trainees can find those best suited to their own learning needs (Walsh and Scaife, 1998).

We take the view that the exploration of personal issues when undertaken with a lens that focuses consistently on relevance to and implications for the work is an essential component of an ethical approach. It may happen that such exploration is more generally beneficial to supervisees, having spin-offs in their private lives. This is serendipitous and not the purpose of supervision. The boundary between supervision and therapy needs to be kept in mind.

Personal and professional development can be addressed by a range of different mechanisms, but is likely to arise in supervision and can be explored while continuing to adhere to appropriate boundaries. Where supervision leads to the identification of personal issues that would benefit from exploration outside of supervision, the partnership can continue the discussion by working out where and with whom the supervisee can continue the exploration.

In making a distinction between supervision and therapy, Mollon (1989) said:

> Both should provide a space for thinking, but the tasks are different and the points of focus are different. In supervision, it is the therapy that is the 'patient' and the supervisee's feelings and fantasies are examined only insofar as they might throw light on what is happening in the therapy. The crucial task is to create a supervisory setting in which uncertainty, ignorance and feelings of incompetence can be tolerated and discussed – a culture quite different from the one of 'being supposed to know'.
>
> (Mollon, 1989: 121)

Mollon regards the state of 'being supposed to know' as characterised by the profession of clinical psychology. Holt (1969) believes that this expectation develops much earlier and provides evidence that it is already present in the thinking of primary schoolchildren.

Some of the literature focusing on personal and professional development and the emotional context of work tends to emphasise the negative, or the ways in which these issues can adversely interfere with the work. Our own orientation is to regard personal qualities, life experiences and emotions generated at work as having the potential for both positive and negative effects. The task of supervision is to aid identification of both the benefits from and barriers to effective work that arise from personal factors.

Transference and counter-transference and their relevance as a focus of supervision

There is not the space here to devote to a thorough review of the impact of transference and counter-transference upon the supervisory process. However, some broad definitions and starting points are offered. If the reader is interested in exploring in more detail the enactment of these two fundamental analytic principles as they are used primarily within psychoanalytic therapy there are a number of texts which may be useful (Casement, 1985, 1990; Goldstein, 2006; Hinshelwood, 1994; Laplanche and Pontalis, 1973). Their influence in non-analytic therapy has also been examined (Schaeffer, 2006).

Transference is a process whereby the patient invests the therapist with meaning which belongs to the patient's internal world (Casement, 1985); for example, when the patient perceives the therapist as the withholding and judgemental father. Counter-transference is the way in which a worker feels as an indicator of the patient's state of mind (Hinshelwood, 1994); for example, when the therapist experiences the client as boring or seductive. Depending upon the nature of the supervisory model provided and the skill of the supervisor, such processes, which are traditionally located between the therapist and her or his client, can usefully be located between supervisor and supervisee. For example, one of the authors has the experience of discussing in psychodynamic supervision a very angry 'borderline' client. A mirroring process occurred between the therapy relationship and the supervisory relationship. In the former, the client was experienced by the therapist as constantly attacking her for not making anything better and for being useless. In the latter relationship the therapist began to feel that her supervision was poor, her supervisor ineffective, and started to arrive late for sessions as a mark of unexpressed contempt for her supervisor. It was only when this process of re-enactment between therapy and supervision was reflected upon in the supervision that the therapist felt held enough in her own anger and fear, so that she was able to provide such holding for the client.

Ruptures experienced in the client–therapist relationship can often be tracked to issues of transference. Research evidence suggests that workers are not always skilful in recognising such tensions (Lambert *et al.*, 2005). In a series of studies, clients completed questionnaire measures, including information about their experience of the therapeutic relationship, prior to each session (Harmon *et al.*, 2007). This information was given to the therapist before the client's next appointment. Client outcomes were enhanced, particularly for those who had been predicted to deteriorate. Therapists reported using the data in different ways but some discussed the results with the client, using them as a prompt to discuss the relationship, to explore process issues, and to review the client's expectations and goals.

Using concepts such as counter-transference and transference within the context of supervision requires sensitivity, a light touch and a high level of supervisory skill. Identifying such a process within the room can be challenging and thought-provoking, and it is the view of the authors that there needs to be an explicit contract between the supervisor and supervisee about the 'theory-in-use' or the therapeutic model which informs the supervisory process. Creativity and depth can emerge from the supervisory use of these therapeutic processes. However, if the making of such connections is poorly executed, disruption and disconnection between the supervisor and supervisee are likely to result.

Exploration of attitudes, beliefs and values

Attitudes, beliefs and values are learned through assimilation from groups to whom individuals belong, beginning with the family of origin and extending through schooling, peer groups, work and other social groupings. These are constantly revised to accommodate the beliefs of significant others and in response to life events and experiences. Certain events, such as becoming a parent, promote revision of values through being faced with far-reaching decisions as to what should guide approaches to the upbringing of a child. The repercussions are highly significant for the future of the child and for the future of the parental relationship in which family histories are brought together and differences brought into focus.

New perspectives on the self can arise serendipitously through interactions that take on a particular significance. Contexts aimed at teaching and learning can be particularly fruitful sources of such experiences. In the novel *Human Traces* by Sebastian Faulks, Jacques, who is of humble social origins, has little confidence in his capabilities as a medical student. He attends the final viva to defend his thesis convinced that he will fail. To his amazement, at the end of the viva the assessment committee all stand to shake his hand and offer their congratulations. Later, he reflected thus:

> His own life sometimes seemed to him to have that quality of being made up of a series of separate phases, barely understood at the time, for all that they formed part of an unwinding whole. The moment of his appearance before the examiners to defend his thesis had marked the dramatic end of one such section. He had prepared very little for the interview – dangerously little, when he came to think of it. It was as

though he could not bring himself to imagine it in advance because too much depended on it; yet he could not have foreseen what really resulted, which was not just the ending of the student years or the acquisition of a licence to practise, but the sense that he had become someone else: for a moment in the churchy upstairs room where the test took place, he had seen himself from the outside, as the examiners saw him, and he no longer felt provisional or disqualified, but filled with power and confidence. If they believed in this strange Dr Rebière, then why should he not do so too? And then, why not send the fellow out to do his life-work for him – this awe-inspiring doctor whose work of 'first-rate scholarship' had brought his superiors – no, his equals – to their feet?

(Faulks, 2005: 243)

Supervisor assessment of performance can have a remarkable impact on the confidence and self-perception of supervisees.

The experience of 'stuckness' or becoming aware of incongruity between actions with clients and institutional prescriptions can be useful clues to personal development issues. These include giving a client a cigarette when the service setting prohibits smoking on site, running over planned session time, offering reassurance and advice when having planned to take an enquiring stance, or giving out a home telephone number. These behaviours may be appropriate to certain circumstances but boundary transgressions invariably benefit from closer examination. Daniels and Feltham (2004: 182) argued: 'In every personal development endeavour there is some notion of difficulty, defence mechanism, resistance, stuckness and so on.' While we do not agree with this assertion, these feelings are often useful cues to issues of personal growth.

Hughes and Youngson (in press) argued that the first hint that an issue may need attention may be described as a 'clue'. Clues come in a whole variety of guises and may not be immediately obvious to the individual, while others are an inescapable message. They may be internal, within us, or external, a message from others. They may be an intense one-off experience or an ongoing sense that something is 'not quite right'. Examples include the following.

Internal

- A nagging worry or intrusive thought
- A repeated and unhelpful behaviour in relation to self (e.g. addictive behaviour, self-harm)
- A feeling of distress/psychological pain
- A sense of existential discomfort
- An urge to understand an aspect of the self
- Reaching for the glass of wine every evening
- Waking up in the middle of the night with an uncomfortable feeling.

External

- Feedback from clients/colleagues/manager/annual appraisal
- Struggling to maintain relationships
- Comments from friends
- A repeated and unhelpful behaviour in relation to others
- A demand from others to understand aspects of the self (e.g. from trainers on a training course).

In supervision, the identification of the factors underlying the supervisee's responses to others can help to bring greater flexibility and curiosity to the exploration of the client's difficulties. Our own underlying assumptions lead us to believe this to be of value in the work.

Mechanisms for exploring values and beliefs in supervision

Alert supervisors may notice elements of their supervisees' values and beliefs in the language they use to describe their work. What people say about their clients may be conveying at least as much about the speaker as about the subject. One option for exploring this is to record a supervision session with a view to reviewing it specifically to identify the values and beliefs of *both* supervisor and supervisee. Here is a passage from a supervision session which is described in Scaife (1995). This supervisor seems happy to take control of the pace, and aspects of the direction of the supervision. The passage which follows (where S = supervisor and T = therapist) is offered as an example of a transcript of a supervisory conversation. Readers are invited to make their own judgements about the values and beliefs implicit in the conversation.

T: Well, where shall I start to tell you about this one?

S: Well, right, if you start, who does it involve? Let's get a genogram up.

T: There's mum who's 35, Mary. She's divorced.

S: Did she have lots of children by this marriage?

T: There's only two. They've been separated for about three years. Two children, Emma, 17, and Peter who was the identified patient, 13 now. I have been seeing this family for nearly two years.

S: I'd hazard a guess what your problem is.

T: Well, yes and no. It could be that that's what's my problem. She has another partner now, Chris, who's about 45, and they've been together for a year, and she met him after he'd come out of prison for offences of sexual abuse against children. He previously had a long-standing relationship of about eight years.

S: What sort of age were the children who he abused?

T: Teens.

S: Girls? Boys?

T: Yes. One was his partner's daughter, one was her friend's daughter and one was a lad, and it was supposed to be . . .

S: She had to search hard to find a suitable partner . . . [ironic comment]

T: Right. Her ex-partner was abusive towards her.

S: Physically?

T: Physically.

S: And sexually?

T: Er, yes, I would say so, and she had been sexually abused as a child by an uncle. She had a mum and dad and an older sister.

S: Now do you know whose brother it was?

T: I think it was the father's brother. I think I need to put you in touch with what my main problem is now because I've worked with the family for a long time. And a lot of the work – when I met Mary she was very depressed, clinically depressed, and in the course of which she did take an overdose, but I did a lot of individual work and she's certainly not depressed any more. And I was about to discharge the family when she met up with this new partner and I got notification from Social Services that they were going to hold a case conference on Peter, and that was when I discovered that Mary was wanting to get married to Chris and if he moved in, Social Services were concerned about the children.

S: She knew all about that?

T: Yes. And Peter was put on the register because of that case conference.

S: Is he still registered?

T: No, he's just become deregistered.

S: OK. So you have a problem which is?

T: As a result of the case conference, I was designated, because of the relationship that I have with Mary, to work with Chris and Mary to look at the abusing behaviour and to try, I suppose, to do two things. One would be to assess the likelihood that abuse will occur.

S: For the case conference?

T: Yes, I suppose that's one thing but that's not the one that's bothered me so much as the other one which is to work with Chris to give therapy for the abusing . . .

S: These two seem like aspects of the same thing.

T: Yes, I think they are. I actually did this latter work jointly with the probation officer and I think maybe this is where an issue comes in. I've come to realise over the course of time that probation officers and clinical psychologists have different training.

S: And different agendas possibly?

T: And different genders, yes.

S: No, agendas. Right, genders too. Now just hold on. How long ago was this case conference?

T: Not quite a year, but approximately a year.

S: Right, so there's you and there's the probation officer, who I now gather is male.

T: My current problem is not about the assessment aspect because I've stated to the case conference that I think that how Mary is and how Mary and Chris's relationship is, means that it's very unlikely that these children will be abused. As a result the child has been deregistered, but I wouldn't put any money on Chris if he were in a different context.

S: The next-door-neighbour's child or whatever. He will have a next-door-neighbour wherever he lives so that's not matter for action really, is it, unless he lives in HM [colloquial for prison].

T: So the thing that's been the difficulty, is the thing about 'curing' him, and what's happened is that he's come to sessions and I and the probation officer have tried to get him to complete various tasks. A particular one was to write down his cycle of arousal so that we can find the position where one would need to intervene in that in order to introduce the normal boundaries.

S: Where *he* would need to, I mean I say that deliberately.

T: Right, and he consistently says he will do that, then it's not brought to the session.

S: Can I just ask you, are we still finding out what your problem is or have we moved beyond it? Because at the moment I'm still not quite sure what your problem is.

T: No, we've moved beyond it haven't we?

S: I feared we might, yes.

T: The problem is that I think I've decided that I can't do any more work with Chris constructively. I think I've decided I can't 'therapise' his abuse, but I'm not quite satisfied with myself for deciding that, and so what I need to do is to check it out: to either make myself content with that and say, 'OK. I can't do any more work with that', or if not, decide to pursue it further in some way. So it's making a decision about whether to drop it or carry on with an attempt to therapise Chris.

S: So the problem is, 'Have you done everything you can?'

(Scaife, 1995: 124–128)

The authors reviewed the above extract with a view to identifying the implicit values and beliefs of the participants. The purpose of the exercise is to identify underlying beliefs and values in order to challenge them and explore their impact on the way the work is being conducted. The authors identified the following, which may coincide to varying degrees with those identified by the reader:

- That family and wider context is relevant to the work.
- That the named referred person may not be the actual client as perceived by the worker and that the worker has some right to make this decision.

- That supervision focuses on solving a problem.
- That asking questions is an appropriate activity for a supervisor.
- That therapeutic work lasting for two years could be indicative of a problem.
- That supervisees have the right to define the focus of supervision.
- That the gender of workers is material to the work.
- That in therapy the therapist does a lot of work.
- That therapy is something that is 'done' to people.
- That there are such things as 'normal boundaries' that prevent people from sexually abusing others.

It is not being suggested that these are desirable or undesirable positions, only that any such dialogue might inform practitioners about the underlying views that may be influencing their work.

Another method for attempting to access underlying beliefs and values was devised for a group, but could be adapted for individual supervision. The exercise may be used with a variety of topics. Value statements are written on individual file cards. Suggestions for content are made below. The statements are provided by the supervisor, a process which protects supervisees from the disclosure of their own values at this stage. The file cards are distributed randomly between the group members. They are asked to imagine a line on the floor that corresponds to a continuum from 'agree' to 'disagree'. Group members take it in turns to read out the statements on their cards and to place each card on the continuum, explaining their decision to place it at the selected point. Other group members then debate the placement of the card, giving reasons for their different opinion. When the issue has been explored to everyone's satisfaction, another card is selected.

The advantages of the method are that people do not have to disclose their own issues and the group facilitator can provide riskier topics than might otherwise emerge. The method also highlights the diversity of views and opinions in any group. The following are examples of items that might be used in the above exercise. They fall into two categories – namely, beliefs about therapy and beliefs about wider issues in life.

- You can have anything if you work hard enough.
- You cannot understand how events have affected people unless you have been through it yourself.
- It is inappropriate to make jokes in work with clients.
- People who are victims need protecting.
- It is never a good idea to suppress one's emotions.
- One should always admit to not knowing.
- Children should only be raised by heterosexual couples.
- Professional helpers are responsible for the outcomes of therapy.
- Clients need to have confidence in the expertise of the therapist.

- Women who are in violent relationships should be helped to extricate themselves.
- It is wrong to feel sexually attracted to clients.
- Arranged marriages stand a much greater chance of success.
- It is unethical to offer therapy without having been in personal therapy oneself.
- Religion is for people who feel insecure.
- Shameful things should always be kept to oneself.
- When people grow older they are less able to do things.
- Wealth is a sign of hard work and commitment.

The impact of life experiences

From time to time adverse life events can have an impact so profound as temporarily to disable practitioners in their work with certain clients. For someone recently abandoned by a partner, working open-mindedly with clients who are in similar circumstances may not be feasible. Tasks of supervision include clarifying such conflicts and helping the supervisee to make alternative arrangements for the work to be conducted by someone else until the personal matter reaches a state of greater resolution and stability.

There are a number of ways of exploring one's own life history that may be used with clients and also by professional helpers in learning more about themselves. In addition, such exercises provide an opportunity for people to experience the perspective of clients when they are requested to carry out similar tasks.

LIFELINES

Drawing a lifeline provides an opportunity to put on paper past life events and the accompanying emotions. Large sheets of paper are called for on which the person draws a line or shape on which events can be noted. In order to get started, people often find it helpful to note dates around school changes or moves of house. Details may include events such as birthday parties or holidays and visits. In our experience there is great variance between people in the extent of the detail that can be remembered, particularly about childhood and about unhappy events from the past. Some are shocked by how little they recall and are prompted to ask friends and relatives in order to attempt to fill in the gaps. Some can recollect in detail even early life events, recalling tastes and smells and the fine detail of every day.

This task is best conducted as a private exercise, with the results of a secondary task brought to supervision. The secondary task is to identify how these experiences might be relevant to and influence the way in which the person carries out her or his work. For someone who has detailed recall of childhood episodes, the meaning of minimal recall by a client might be perceived as pathological, whereas for therapists with minimal recall of their own childhood, minimal recall by the client would not be expected to seem odd.

The completion of lifelines might bring forth issues for therapists which they recognise as continuing to have an adverse impact upon their life and their work. In order for supervision to retain a clear work-oriented focus, identification of a suitable alternative exploratory forum is an appropriate task.

DRAWING ONE'S OWN GENOGRAM

Genograms or family trees are used as a shorthand and compact way of illustrating family relationships. They may contain basic information such as gender, ages and names of family members but may be further elaborated to include identification of patterns of role relationships and can be illustrated with family 'sayings'. This can aid exploration of the underlying values transmitted by families of origin. The following are examples of ideas that have emerged from the construction of family trees in workshops for professional helpers:

- 'Whatever else, you should always provide a good table.'
- 'Never let your neighbour starve.'
- 'A table has four sides – one for each person in a family.'
- 'You can only do your best.'
- 'Hard work is its own reward.'
- 'Some things are best left unsaid.'
- 'If you say it you will make it happen.'

What also emerge are repetitive intergenerational patterns such as number of children in a family, age of having first child, gender roles, positions of power and influence, leaving or staying at home, patterns associated with birth order, and so on. From these ideas may be constructed the family script into which the person was born. These were described by Byng-Hall (1995) as a family's shared expectations of how family roles are to be performed within various contexts. He views the family plot as scripted although the cast can change. Family scripts are revealed when repeating patterns of family interaction are either observed or described. He proposed the notions of replicative and corrective scripts in which people to some degree reproduce previous family patterns or make pacts with themselves to live their lives differently. Either kind of script will be represented in the beliefs and values that professional helpers bring both to their personal and professional lives.

IDENTIFYING A PROBLEM

It is not the task of supervision to explore the personal problems of the supervisee, and the first stage of the following exercise is therefore privately conducted. The supervisee identifies a problem of her or his own. The problem can be at any level from seriously debilitating to what to buy as a present for a friend. While the latter would seemingly constitute a relatively straightforward dilemma, such a choice may be underlain by more significant dilemmas and can evoke significant personal responses.

Having identified a problem, the person then thinks about what questions she or he would like to be asked in exploration of the problem. It would be possible to choose the kinds of questions or an approach such as free association prescribed by a particular model of therapy or to think of questions at random. The task in supervision is to consider what the selected questions or approach reveal about the expectations of the supervisee about how therapy is conducted. The problem itself need not be disclosed. Through the exercise supervisees learn about their own orientation to how helping is carried out and gain ideas about the potential impact of such methods on clients.

UNDERTAKING PERSONAL THERAPY

Traditionally there has been a wide variety of views about therapy and its place in training. And this is just among mental health professionals! For some models of therapy, such as psychoanalysis, undertaking personal therapy is a core requirement. It was not seen as relevant in early behavioural approaches which emphasised sound and technically adequate application of method. Similarly, in the early conceptualisations of cognitive behaviour therapy it had no place (Laireiter and Willutzki, 2005). Today it is accepted that it may be helpful in attaining important training goals such as the development of a self-reflective working style, the promotion of self-knowledge and of greater empathy with clients.

Macran and Shapiro (1998) found that most therapists who had undergone personal therapy stressed its value, although there was limited evidence that undertaking personal therapy led to better client outcomes. A number of studies (e.g. Orlinsky et al., 2005) exploring therapists' experience of personal therapy have reported that 85 per cent or more of therapists found personal therapy of great or very great benefit with 75 per cent indicating that it had a strong positive influence on their development as therapists. These authors also reported that personal therapy was ranked third in a list of sources of positive influence on professional development, following direct experience with clients and formal case supervision. Studies attempting to link personal therapy directly with client outcomes have produced variable results but Orlinsky et al. (2005) argued that this is not surprising given the large number of variables at play.

Some practitioners make a distinction between personal therapy that is undertaken with the explicit purpose of enhancing training, and therapy undertaken in response to personal distress (Beail, 1998, personal communication). The following potential benefits have been proposed (Orlinsky *et al.*, 2005):

1   It improves the emotional and mental functioning of the clinician.
2   It enables the development of a more complete understanding of personal dynamics and thereby reduces the potential for unhelpful countertransference enactments.
3   It leads to an improved ability for the participant to distinguish between personal issues and those of the client (Grimmer and Tribe, 2001).
4   It alleviates the emotional stresses and burdens inherent in the helping professions.
5   It offers a profound socialisation experience establishing a sense of conviction regarding the transformational possibilities of such intervention, whatever the model.
6   By having experienced the role of client it increases awareness and respect for the client's struggles.
7   It provides a firsthand intensive opportunity to observe clinical methods, both interpersonal and technical.

Murphy (2005) proposed a model to account for the impact of personal therapy on the trainee through the emergence of four key processes: reflexivity, growth, authenticity and prolongation. It may be argued that to work with people's distress on a day-to-day basis without in some way experiencing one's own therapy is at best naive and at worst hypocritical. Many professionals are deeply self-neglectful and it is easy to slip into an 'I have no needs' form of working of which one should beware.

For those who choose to embark upon the course of personal therapy there are a number of publications available which are helpful in the selection of a therapist (MIND, n.d.), and, as a mental health professional, asking colleagues for the names of well-respected practitioners is also effective. It is often useful to talk to a supervisor about the process of identifying a practitioner who could meet one's needs. It is also worth considering whether to undertake one-to-one therapy or join a group.

IDENTIFYING THE NEED TO BE AWAY FROM WORK

The exploration of emotions, values, beliefs and the impact of life history and events is part of the landscape of supervision and enables the supervisor to effect a supportive and restorative function. From time to time the impact of these factors involves supervisors in helping supervisees to decide when they should and should not be continuing to work. Professional helpers are sometimes reluctant to prioritise their own needs when ill, under stress or in a personal crisis. The supervisor can play a significant role in helping supervisees both to acknowledge the magnitude of the difficulty and to give themselves permission to take time for themselves in order to restore health and well-being. On more than one occasion in such circumstances when supervisees have been asked to 'reverse roles' and give advice on well-being, they have responded by saying, 'You would be crazy to carry on working'. From this emerges a plan for self-care which in the long run is a better option for staff and ensures the welfare of clients.

The conclusion that time out of work should be taken is often the result of a very painful and protracted decision-making process. It is the experience of the authors that the view of most professionals is that it is better to struggle through, no matter what life throws at you, and no matter what emotional burdens you are bearing, than to stop. The reasons for this are complex. First, there is a sense of shame about being personally vulnerable or in need, and that such vulnerabilities are more acceptably located in the client rather than in the professional. Second, stopping work is a very public way of saying that one needs time out. Individuals may hold legitimate or irrational fears that their careers or professional standing with colleagues may be irrevocably damaged if others see them as not coping. Ironically, individuals may actually find themselves the objects of envy on the part of their colleagues because they have been able to give themselves time away from work. Third, some orientations towards therapy disconnect self-needs from the work as a legitimate focus of exploration; taking the view that damage is 'out there' and not located in the self. Thus, if personal issues become pressing and have to be acknowledged, as opposed to being defended against or projected into clients or other individuals, there is little or no permission to address personal needs. Fourth, for clinicians in private practice the tension between needing to stop working for personal reasons and the need to continue to practise for financial reasons is evident (King and Wheeler, 1999). Finally, in periods of acute distress (something that comes to us all) one of the primary fears about stopping work may be the fear of never being able to pull oneself together.

In conclusion, it is our view that self and emotions play a crucial part in work. Their appearance in supervision is inevitable and desirable. Supervisors can occupy a pivotal role in helping supervisees to explore these issues.

Chapter 4

The contracting process and the supervisory relationship

Averting pitfalls and problems

> During luncheon – which was excellent, of course, as everything at Toad Hall always was – the Toad simply let himself go. Disregarding the Rat, he proceeded to play upon the inexperienced Mole as on a harp. Naturally a voluble animal, and always mastered by his imagination, he painted the prospects of the trip and the joys of the open life and the roadside in such glowing colours that the Mole could hardly sit in his chair for excitement.
>
> (Grahame, 2005: 14)

Mole, affected by the enthusiasm of his friend, fell into the journey which ended when the canary-coloured cart lay on its side in the ditch, an irredeemable wreck. It is easy to be swept along by an exciting idea. Implicit expectations are revealed only later. It may have been wise for Mole to clarify matters in advance through, however informal, some kind of contracting process.

Contracting is usefully thought of as a process that occurs over a number of sessions, regularly or irregularly, and from time to time for the duration of the supervisory relationship. It is wise to negotiate a contract at the outset of the supervisory relationship, and to review the initial agreement regularly to see if matters are on course and whether supervisory needs have changed as learning has progressed. The process is enhanced by the supervisor showing sensitivity to the needs and preferences of the supervisee (Page and Wosket, 2001: 46). These authors contrast the approach of a counsellor attending an initial contracting session with a written list of preferences because she had previously experienced supervision as straying outside acceptable boundaries, with an inexperienced trainee plunging straight into presentation of her case material.

Contracting can involve the drawing up of a relatively formal written contract or working agreement which is a statement of intent, although the discussion in and of itself is key. A written contract is likely to be a requirement in preregistration education and some authors offer sample contracts which can be adapted to meet individual needs (American Association for

Marriage and Family Therapy, 2004; Falender and Shafranske, 2004: 233; Sutter *et al.*, 2002). Contracts may be seen as increasing the accountability of the parties to supervision, and may be used to promote ethical practice by including the requirement to adhere to professional and ethical standards (Bernard and Goodyear, 1998: 213). It has been argued, however, that in some cultures the parties to supervision would regard a written contract as an indication of mutual mistrust (Tsui, 2005: 130). This might be an issue appropriately addressed early on in the contracting process.

The contracting process benefits when supervisors adopt an approach in which they are genuinely curious about and interested in supervisees (Engel *et al.*, 1998; Nelson, 1978). Supervision is an interpersonal process, the success of which owes much to the quality of the relationship between the supervisor and supervisee. Alderfer and Lynch (1987) stated that, 'the relationship between the supervisor and supervisee has more impact on the success of the process of supervision than any other factor'. This finding has been replicated repeatedly in empirical research reviewed in meta-analyses such as that reported by Falender and Shafranske (2004: 95). The finding appears to be independent of therapeutic approach, the profession studied, or the perceived wisdom or experience of the supervisor (Beinart, 2004; Cottrell *et al.*, 2002; Horvath, 2001).

Creating a supervisory relationship in which the participants experience mutual respect, are open about their fears, difficulties, blunders, successes and challenges, learn from each other and stay within the boundaries of the supervisory task is a tall order. Establishing such a relationship at work is no less challenging than creating satisfactory and rewarding relationships at home. At work, long periods of time are spent with people who may take care of, love or hurt each other. Hillman (1983) stated that:

> Freud said that the whole business of therapy was to bring the person to love and work. It seems to me we have forgotten half of what he said. We have been talking about what goes wrong with love for eighty years. But what goes wrong with work, where has that been discussed?
>
> (Hillman, 1983, quoted in Hawkins and Miller, n.d.)

Models and frameworks that conceptualise supervision typically support the notion of a contracting process through which the participants negotiate and reach agreement about such matters as the requirements of their agency contexts, timing and frequency of contacts with each other, supervisory role relationships and the purposes and processes of supervision (Carroll, 1996; Scaife, 1993a; Page and Wosket, 1994). While organisations in which supervision is mandatory typically specify the topics to be covered in the contract, Lawton (2000), in a study of eight supervisory relationships, found that the majority of participants reported a very patchy experience. Furthermore, information obtained about the nature of the relationships which then developed suggested a strong link between the rigour of the contracting process at the outset and the quality of the working alliance which subsequently evolved. On the basis of his own experience of training in psychiatry, Rhinds advised senior house officers:

> At the initial meeting, take control – supervision is for the benefit of the trainee. The consultant has educational responsibilities towards his/her trainee, but benefits by having a trainee as part of the clinical team. . . . Plan setting realistic objectives, how to obtain them and how to measure them. Also write them down, ensuring that your supervising consultant has a copy. Remember, failing to plan is planning to fail.
>
> (Rhinds, 2003: 352)

Why establish a supervisory contract?

The supervisory contract can serve to highlight the formal contractual obligations of the parties to supervision both to each other and to the organisations which hold them accountable. In addition, the 'psychological contract' involves the implicit mutual obligations which the parties expect.

Discussing the formal aspects of a contract serves to increase the explicit accountability of the participants by requiring them to commit themselves to the agreement and by flagging up their formal obligations regarding issues such as policies and procedures, leave arrangements and indemnity insurance. The host agency may require those working with its clients to undertake various procedures to ensure that it is not inadvertently liable for any errors perpetrated by the supervisee. Discussions centred on principles of ethics and codes of conduct can promote ethical practice by reminding participants of these duties. The formal contract may also specify the standards which must be met (for example, by students in order to pass the practicum or field placement), and this serves to draw the attention of the supervisor to the appropriate focus and level of complexity of the work that will meet the student's current learning needs. Training institutions may specify how many or what type of client presentations should be seen and what submissions will be required for coursework assignments.

The contracting process supports supervisors in effecting their ethical responsibility in relation to supervisees' informed consent. Supervisees need to have a reasonable idea of what might take place in supervision and of the expectations of the supervisor regarding their work. They need to give informed consent to participate, although not all eventualities can be covered. Because in some circumstances, supervisors are legally liable for their supervisees' errors (Falvey, 2002; Knapp and VandeCreek, 2006; Sacuzzo, 2003), it may be helpful to provide supervisees with guidelines regarding the types of events, personal experiences and problems about which supervisors want to be informed. These may include disputes with clients or impasses in the therapy; allegations of unethical behaviour by clients, colleagues or others (e.g. a client's family members); threats of a complaint; mental health emergencies requiring immediate action; high-risk situations; cases in which clients evidence suicidal thoughts, gestures or attempts or a significant history of attempts; cases in which clients present with a history of, propensity for or threats of violence; contemplated departures from standards of practice or exceptions to general rules, standards, policies or practices; suspected or known clinical or ethical errors; contact with clients outside the context of treatment; and legal issues, such as possible reporting obligations related to suspected abuse of a child or vulnerable adult or ethical violations by other professionals (Thomas, 2007). Thomas addresses the issue of informed consent with useful thoroughness.

The contracting process is never more important than when addressing the covert expectations of the parties to supervision. Where different desires are implicit and unexpressed, a mismatch can lead to misunderstandings from which it can be difficult to reinstate a functional relationship. Covert expectations usually become apparent when an injunction or unspoken rule is broken.

In the contracting process supervisees can be prompted to think about their learning needs and desire for support, knowledge about supervision can be shared, and a joint framework developed within which to structure and understand the process. Importantly, the negotiation of the contract indicates that these matters are open to debate and can be revisited in the event of any difficulty or changes in needs. The discussion sets a context of candour in which different ideas and values may be acknowledged and accommodated. There is an overt plan and purpose rather than reliance on a risky, random, hit-and-miss process.

When the supervisee is a trainee or student, negotiation of a contract should also include discussion about each party's ideas regarding the evaluation of the supervisee's work. Students are likely to find it helpful to know what the supervisor regards as evidence of adequate knowledge and skill and how this compares with their own assessment of their work. Similarly, the contract might include agreement regarding trainees' actions that would be negatively evaluated by the supervisor and what would constitute evidence of failure. The purpose here is to ensure fairness by making the student aware of the supervisor's assessment criteria in advance.

While flexibility to meet the needs of the supervisee is regarded as a virtue in supervisors (Bernard, 1979), the contracting process may also be used to define what the supervisor can and cannot provide. Where there is a choice of supervisor this might mean that supervisees will seek an alternative supervisor better matched to their expectations and needs. Similarly, supervisors themselves should usually be in a position to decide not to accept a supervisee if they are of the view, after attempting to establish a contract, that they are not able to offer what is required. The contracting process thus serves to avoid establishment of a relationship in which the likely outcome is frustration or disappointment for either or both parties.

In summary, I believe the reasons for undertaking a contracting process to be:

- To clarify contractual responsibilities to external agencies and stakeholders.
- To promote ethical practice by reminding each party of the requirements of ethical conduct.
- To fulfil the requirement for the supervisee to give informed consent to the supervision.
- To give a kick start to the supervisory relationship by showing interest in the supervisee and beginning with a process of negotiation.
- To clarify the desires and expectations brought to the relationship by the different parties and to agree what is and is not possible.
- To set a context of openness and candour in which processes in supervision and the supervisory relationship are matters for discussion, negotiation and renegotiation, rather than being left to chance.
- To set a context in which different beliefs and values can be expressed and are acknowledged.
- To prompt supervisees to think about how supervision can best support and develop them at work and to share the responsibility for their learning.
- To facilitate a sharing of knowledge about the supervisory 'field'.
- To establish a pattern of paying attention both to process and content in supervision, mirroring the importance of both process and content of therapy.
- To explore the evaluative role of the supervisor and to identify the criteria that will be used in judging performance.

Setting up a supervisory contract

The opening discussion of the contract should probably take place after an initial meeting between supervisor and supervisee. First requirements are to get to know each other a little and this might best be accomplished in a fairly informal way. Information regarding professional history, how each came to choose their work, geographical origins and the like might be discussed before focusing on the contract. When the supervisee is joining a service, perhaps for a time-limited training placement, a first priority is an induction to the service which might include introductions to other staff at the base, an explanation of systems for booking rooms, keeping files and keeping a diary, car-parking arrangements, access to a confidential telephone line, arrangements for refreshments, conventions of dress, case management processes, collection of statistics and audit, authorisation to work in the host agency, required attendance at meetings, methods of accessing suitable resources such as computers and the library and what to do in an emergency. A list can usefully be constructed as a reference for general use. During this initial meeting, some appropriate self-disclosure can enhance intimacy. A study of supervisory relationships conducted by Ladany and Lehrman-Waterman (1999) focused on the impact of legitimate supervisor self-disclosure on the working alliance. Not only was it found to help build and enhance the supervisory relationship, but it also helped to repair any ruptures created as a result of conflicts and tensions. Supervisees particularly valued self-disclosure in which supervisors shared feelings of vulnerability through discussing their own struggles with therapeutic dilemmas. On a cautionary note they warn against excessive self-disclosure, particularly where the specialness of the supervisor is emphasised. Jacobs and colleagues suggested as a guideline:

> The litmus test of self-revelation in supervision is the degree to which it contributes meaningfully to the therapy of the patient and the education of the therapist. Will the self-revelation relate to or interfere with the basic goals of supervision?
>
> (Jacobs *et al.*, 1995: 159)

During this discussion of practical matters, supervisor and supervisee can feel their way with each other, paving the way for the negotiation of the supervisory contract. This is more likely to be necessary where the supervisor and supervisee have no prior knowledge of each other and particularly where the pairing has been allocated by a third party such as a university, rather than selected and requested by the supervisee.

Supervisors typically take a greater share of responsibility for beginning the contracting process than supervisees. A number of pre-supervision questionnaires are available that can be completed by each participant as a self-assessment exercise prior to discussion of the supervisory relationship. These can help in the identification of learning needs, the exploration of a person's typical responses to characteristics of other people, identification of strengths and points for development, and so on. An example of a questionnaire for supervisors may be found in Hawkins and Shohet (2006: 127) and for supervisees in Appendix 1 (this volume).

What topics might be included in a supervisory contract?

Formal contractual obligations

The need to discuss formal contractual obligations will depend upon the nature of the organisation and the employment arrangements of the parties to supervision. The latter may include arrangements for payment, sick leave and annual leave, hours of work, the requirement to adhere to the policies and procedures of the host organisation, how to keep records, informed consent to supervision, arrangements for indemnity insurance and so on. These matters may be encapsulated in an honorary contract where a supervisee employed in one organisation is hosted for training purposes by another.

Ethical imperatives

The contracting process provides a forum in which principles of ethics and formal Codes of Conduct for the relevant profession may be highlighted and personal ethical codes explored. Personal convictions form the most effective basis for moral and ethical behaviour and these have been described as a necessary basis for responsible professional practice (Husband, 1995: 99). The moral responsibility of the individual has been emphasised as the central tenet for ethical practice over and above the roles adopted in professional practice (Baumann, 1993: 19). Discussion of these personal convictions is particularly important in a postmodern world where individual histories will reflect the wide-ranging values of the pluralist societies in which we now live. Increasingly clients demand that services are responsive to their values rather than those imposed by a particular profession (Banks, 1998), and the need to meet this demand can also be raised in contracting discussions.

In any supervisory arrangement it is possible for the supervisor to face ethical dilemmas regarding the supervisee's practice. Within the contracting process, these potential dilemmas and potential responses of the supervisor can be discussed, much as the limits of confidentiality might be raised with a client. Should the supervisor later develop concerns, the prior discussion has indicated that these matters will be addressed, and the supervisee will already have a sense of the approach the supervisor is likely to take.

Ground rules

Ground rules are about the practicalities and basic conditions under which supervision will proceed. In addition to an agreement regarding the timing, frequency and location of supervision, it may be helpful to address availability in the event of an emergency between sessions, or opportunities for informal contact, particularly relevant in training placements. Ground rules include clarification of the boundary between personal and professional issues. In the event of a pre-existing personal relationship or friendship there will need to be a discussion of the implication of the dual-role relationship for the supervision. In such circumstances it may be very difficult for a supervisor to make a wholly frank negative evaluation of a supervisee or, in the event of so doing, later to re-establish the friendship.

Ground rules also include clarity regarding the responsibility for work undertaken. In pre-qualification supervision the responsibility usually lies with the supervisor which may make a difference to how willing a supervisor would be to agree to a supervisee deviating from recommended action. Post-qualification non-managerial arrangements generally identify the supervisee as the person responsible for the work carried out. The responsibility of the supervisor will be to meet the needs of the supervisee as laid out in the supervision contract.

Stakeholder requirements, standards and learning

Particularly in training placements, the education institution will place requirements on supervisors to provide suitable learning opportunities, and to help students to achieve required standards and learning outcomes. These matters may be encapsulated in documents complementary to a contract such as an Aims and Activities Plan, Evaluation Checklist (Hall-Marley 2000, published in Falender and Shafranske, 2004), professional specifications (British Psychological Society, 2002) and/or the programme specification of the education institution.

Supervisees vary in the extent to which they are clear about what they hope to learn in the course of supervision and how this learning might be expected to take place. More experienced supervisees usually have a clearer idea than beginners. Learning goals might include the development of skills in a particular model or theoretical approach, a focus on learning more about personal responses in the work, or the identification of strengths and blind spots. Supervisees may want to learn more about why they are experiencing difficulties in some of their work but not across the board.

The negotiation of how the learning will take place can begin with a discussion of what supervisees have previously found helpful to their learning. Some supervisees welcome advice and information giving, others prefer a more questioning and enquiring style while at times a sympathetic listener may be required. Some of the frameworks for supervision described in more detail in Chapter 5 can support the exploration of the role relationship that will best support learning.

Written records of supervision

It has been suggested (Bernard and Goodyear, 1998) that supervisors are far more careful about client records than about supervision records although these can be equally important, particularly when problems occur. In pre-registration training, records relating to student progression will invariably be required by the educational institution. More generally, what is recorded will depend on the agreements that have been reached with relevant employers, balancing issues of confidentiality, safe practice and time constraints. In some cases, written records are restricted to confirmation of attendance and a broad annual statement to the funding body concerning the supervisee's ongoing fitness to practise. In my experience, even this limited information is often not required. In contrast, some authors have emphasised the importance of consistency in documentation and the need to manage risk in the domain of legal liability through detailed written records (Bridge and Bascue, 1990; Falvey *et al.* (1996), cited in Bernard and Goodyear, 1998). These authors offer suitable pro-formas. Some services maintain detailed electronic records of supervision (Davies, 2007).

In the case of post-registration clinical supervision of nurses, Cutcliffe (2000) recommends that the supervisor's records need to meet the minimum requirement of audit, that keywords may be used as an *aide-mémoire*. He advocates the option of maintaining minimal records which helps to keep the supervision supervisee-led and avoids overlap with managerial supervision. It is advised that in the rare event of a supervisor prescribing a course of action, this should be recorded. In the light of such diverse views, it is wise within the contracting process to discuss this issue in detail and to ensure that the agreement reached is acceptable to all stakeholders.

Diversity

The helping professions are 'socio-political' in nature (Katz, 1985) and reflect the values and ideologies of the dominant group. Diversity extends to expectations about interpersonal relationships and individual belief systems. It would be easy to make assumptions about these, with the possibility for mismatches further into the supervisory relationship. The contracting process can address diversity as it relates to the participants in supervision, to clients and to the assumptions upon which the service is predicated. The aim is to accommodate diversity rather than to override or ignore it. The supervisor can flag up the centrality of cultural awareness to ethical practice. This topic is addressed more fully in Chapter 8.

The psychological contract

The term 'psychological contract' was first used in the early 1960s, but became more popular following the economic downturn in the early 1990s. It has been defined as 'the perceptions of the two parties, employee and employer, of what their mutual obligations are towards each other' (Guest and Conway, 2002). These obligations will often be informal and imprecise: they may be inferred from actions or from what has happened in the past, as well as from statements made by the employer, for example, during the recruitment process or in performance appraisals. Some obligations may be seen as 'promises' and others as 'expectations'. The important thing is that they are believed by the employee to be part of the relationship with the employer.

The psychological contract can be distinguished from the legal contract of employment. The latter will in many cases offer only a limited and uncertain representation of the employment relationship. The employee may have contributed little to its terms beyond accepting them. The nature and content of the legal contract may only emerge clearly if and when it comes to be tested in an employment tribunal.

The psychological contract on the other hand addresses the situation as perceived by the parties, and may be more influential than the formal contract in affecting how employees behave from day to day. It is the psychological contract which effectively tells employees what they are required to do in order to meet their side of the bargain, and what they can expect from their job. It may not – in general it will not – be strictly enforceable, though courts may be influenced by a view of the underlying relationship between employer and employee, for example, in interpreting the common law duty to show mutual trust and confidence. The psychological contract in the context of supervision represents the implicit expectations of each other that the parties bring to the relationship. In my view this term covers the most important issues to be addressed in the contracting process if the supervisory relationship is to be effective.

Role relationship/supervisory alliance

The contracting process plays a crucial role in facilitating the establishment of a supervisory alliance. The beginning of the relationship is important; at this stage anxieties can be most pronounced. Liddle (1986) argued that counsellor trainees worry about their professional adequacy, impressing their supervisors, their clients, colleagues and themselves. A common response to these anxieties is resistance, which is defined as 'any coping behaviour by a supervisee that interferes with the learning process'. In the contracting process, anxiety can be 'normalised' as commonly associated with significant learning.

The term 'supervisory alliance' derives from the notion of a working alliance between client and therapist. The alliance is regarded in both cases as making a significant contribution to outcome. The contracting process aims to explore what kind of relationship would work to meet the aims of supervision. A number of frameworks have been adapted from a therapy context to a supervision situation in order to facilitate an understanding of the working alliance in supervision. These include attachment theory (Watkins, 1995) and the notion of 'collaboration to change' (Bordin, 1979). This latter notion was extended to encompass the supervisory relationship (Bordin, 1983) and proposes three elements: the bond between the parties, the extent to which they agree on goals, and the extent to which they agree on tasks. In my view, the negotiation of the psychological contract is crucial in beginning the process of establishing the working alliance.

Heading off potential ruptures in the relationship

While it may not be desirable in establishing a contract to dwell for too long on potential problems that might develop in a supervisory relationship, it is probably better to have undertaken some exploration of how these might be handled at the outset. In the event of problems occurring, the above discussion has already indicated that these are matters for exploration and resolution through talking. A relatively brief discussion in the contracting process may be revisited when the supervisor and supervisee have developed greater familiarity with each other, ideally nipping problems in the bud before they intensify. Three of the more common problems are discussed below.

EVALUATION AND REVIEW

Review of the contract and reciprocal feedback can ensure that the supervision stays on track. Typically people encounter some anxiety in giving and/or receiving feedback and can feel very hurt, particularly if they feel problematised in the process. Supervisors who fear to hurt feelings will tend to make bland statements if asked to comment on the work of the supervisee. Supervisees who are repeatedly told that their work is 'fine' tend to feel insecure about their competence and often prefer more specific information about their strengths and how their skills could be further developed. One way for the supervisor to give feedback without hitting a sensitive spot is to suggest a number of hypothetical alternative ideas or approaches while showing honest (not affected) acceptance of the supervisee's current practice.

In order to help supervisees begin to take responsibility for letting the supervisor know how things are going, supervisors can indicate at the outset that they will be inviting an assessment of what they themselves are trying to achieve; giving the message that their learning is ongoing. A general invitation may be too nebulous to result in anything other than a neutral response from the supervisee. One way around this is to ask supervisees to complete a questionnaire or rating scale (examples are listed in Appendix 2). Such questionnaires can be adapted to make the supervision itself the clear subject of the assessment. By their design the questions can imply that both parties share responsibility for the success of the venture; what are *we* doing that is working/needs modification? Sample questions of this type are provided in Chapter 9. Questionnaires or rating scales may be used in a variety of ways and, in addition to helping supervisees to think about the evaluation of their own work, the process of inviting structured comments also provides information to the supervisee about what the supervisor values and gives the message that these matters are negotiable. Further aspects of evaluation and feedback are addressed in Chapter 14.

Another way in which the potential negative effects of the evaluative role may be ameliorated is to discuss the supervisor's potential reaction were the supervisee to reveal a perceived error. Hypothetical examples can be described by the supervisee and hypothetical responses given by the supervisor. In this way, the underlying values and beliefs about what is important in the work may be explored. Most typically, supervisors value openness, disclosure and willingness to learn in their supervisees significantly more highly than exemplary performances. Open expression of this in the contracting process may make it more possible in the longer term for supervisees to disclose the work which they themselves have doubts about or evaluate negatively.

THE DISINTERESTED OR BUSY SUPERVISOR

Particularly in training placements with senior clinicians, workload constraints may limit the amount of time that is available for supervision and the supervisor may be distracted by seemingly more important concerns. One of the most difficult tasks for supervisees is to bring this up with the supervisor as they also typically perceive other concerns to be of greater importance and may feel guilty about raising the primacy of their own needs. This may again be addressed in the contracting process before the problem arises by supervisees asking what course of action they should take in the event of feeling neglected. This could be attributed either to their apparently excessive needs in comparison with other supervisees or to the other roles and demands on the supervisor.

To raise these issues from the position of supervisee is usually experienced as more tricky than from the position of supervisor, and busy supervisors may prime supervisees about how best to approach them in circumstances where they feel that the supervisor's lack of attention to supervision is by default rather than by design. It is easier for supervisees to raise such issues if given advance permission, rather than waiting until they occur.

The following is a somewhat extreme example of a supervisee raising this problem with a supervisor having tried and failed in all other approaches to have their needs met. It occurred in the context of a workshop in supervision and is a role-played exchange set up with a supervisor who fails to respond to more usual appeals. The role play (where *S'ee* = supervisee and *S* = supervisor) is well underway at this point with no progress having been achieved in relation to the issue.

S'ee: I know that it is difficult to meet with me for more than half an hour a week with all your other work commitments at the moment. I understand that, but I do seem to need more than that to feel confident that what I am doing is OK and safe for the clients.

S: I have a lot of confidence in you and you make very good use of supervision. I think it's more to do with how you feel about your work than what you really need.

S'ee: Yes, but, look, I haven't told you this before because what happened didn't feel just right, but last week Mr X suggested that we have our session in the pub because he feels embarrassed about coming to the office. He made a very good case for it and I agreed to meet him next Wednesday. He thought it would be much more helpful to him because he'd be more relaxed and comfortable.

S: [Looks startled] I don't think that's a very good idea. What about confidentiality and how will you feel about raising issues that might have a powerful emotional impact? Don't you think it would be a bit public?

S'ee: Well, since it was his idea I thought that he would have thought about all that.

S: Might his suggesting meeting in the pub have other meanings – I was wondering how he sees his relationship with you?

S'ee: Actually, I didn't really agree to meet a client in the pub. I was just making that up. [S looks even more surprised and confused] You see, I know that that wouldn't be OK in this service although I know some of the people who work in HIV services do go to pubs to try to help clients to connect with their service. The problem is that I might be doing other things that you could help me to see were not very useful or even harmful, but I don't know that. You have a lot of experience and I'd really value being able to draw on that to help me with issues where I don't even know that there's an issue or other ways of thinking about things. That would help me to feel safe.

S: Let me think about it. We'll make a time for next week and put it on the agenda for then.

In this case it seemed that the only recourse for the supervisee was to frighten the supervisor who was responsible for the case work into giving the supervision greater priority. In the contracting process it is helpful if the supervisor is clear about how much time can be devoted to supervision with a view to keeping to the agreed arrangement. This can be particularly difficult for senior clinicians. In order to give supervision reasonable priority, a reduction in case load will almost certainly need to have been negotiated with the employer. If the issue has been fully explored at the beginning of the supervisory arrangement it is then legitimate for either party to revisit the matter should problems occur. While in the example above the problem is being experienced by the supervisee, the boundary issues of time-keeping, non-interruption of sessions and so on might just as well be problematic for the supervisor and may also be included in the contracting discussions.

DIFFERENCES OF OPINION

One of the anxieties frequently cited by supervisees is that of having to deal with different styles and approaches to the work and to supervision adopted by tutors and supervisors. An anxiety for supervisors is dealing with unsatis-factory work, about which there may well be a difference of opinion. These were two of the difficulties listed by Pomerantz and colleagues (1987) in a survey of trainees, university tutors and fieldwork supervisors who partici-pated in an educational psychology training programme.

Resolving differences of opinion in a satisfactory manner may be more difficult in supervisory dyads than in some other relationships. Doehrman (1976) proffered an explanation for this from the perspective of a psycho-dynamic framework. She contended that supervisees (in training relation-ships) typically experience intense emotional reactions towards supervisors because the development of professional identity is closely linked with per-sonal identity, and changes to professional self can therefore be experienced as threatening. She also argued that supervisors may experience powerful counter-transference reactions to supervisees which result from the position of authority and their ideas being challenged. Supervisees who challenge their supervisor's stance may find themselves in a double bind if their objec-tions are construed as resistance (Bernard and Goodyear, 1998: 79), which serves to emphasise the desirability of raising possible differences of opinion in the contracting process.

How the participants might approach a difference of opinion will depend on whether the relationship is for the purpose of training, managerial and/or peer supervision. Discussion might focus on how to elicit the most positive response from each party in the event of a disagreement, what each person's most typical defensive response might be, and the approaches to this that are generally most constructive.

Individuals have been found to adopt different personal styles in approach-ing conflict resolution. In their 'dual concerns theory', Blake and colleagues (1962) proposed that people experience a conflict between progressing their own goals while seeking to sustain their interpersonal relationships. Holt (2001) identified five styles of conflict resolution: forcing, avoiding, accom-modating, compromising and problem solving. She found differences between preferred styles according to gender, organisational role and ethnicity. You may like to try to locate your own preferred style along these dimensions in preparation for a discussion with supervisees.

In establishing a contract, it is possible to discuss these matters hypothetic-ally before actual content has contaminated the relationship. Agreeing to notice the process of a potential disagreement, externalising the process, ana-lysing the process together, and returning later to the content if necessary, offer more channels for successful resolution of differences of opinion than hoping that they will not occur in the first place.

Discussion of potential problems and how to respond to them gives the message that these matters are subject to some negotiation within the bound-aries of ethical practice. It is implicit that concerns about practice are not necessarily pathological. It is not necessary unduly to dwell on potential problems, but rather desirable to engage in a concise discussion that sets the scene for later negotiation should the need arise.

Personal characteristics

Each of the participants in a supervisory relationship brings some qualities by accident rather than by design. These include personal features such as ethnicity, cultural history, gender, age, years of experience, and the specific experiences of working with different clients, in different models and in different services. Some of these characteristics may purposefully be selected by supervisees and supervisors but inevitably some of them will arise through happenstance. During one supervisor training course, delegates were asked carefully to select someone to work with whom they perceived on the surface to be very different from themselves. The feedback suggested that this selection for difference opened up greater learning opportunities than had people selected someone who on the surface was perceived as similar.

Identifying personal characteristics and discussing the potential influence of these characteristics may form part of the contracting process. A young supervisor paired with an older supervisee might question what they are able to offer, as in the following example in which two experienced senior nurses retrained as specialist mental health nurses:

> What they felt happened was that the people who were training them had their defences up, presumably because of their lack of confidence about these two experienced people being around, and basically it was, 'The less you bother me and the further away from me you are, the happier I will be. Just keep out of the way and I'm sure you both know how to do it anyway and that'll be O.K.' What they both said they wanted more than anything early on was somebody who was prepared to be totally open with them and reveal their own feelings and thoughts and incompetencies and to just accept them as they were at that stage of training. I think that was how they found each other.
>
> (Scaife, 1995: 75)

Difference in age and experience can also affect how people feel about working with different client groups. Not infrequently, younger workers express anxiety about how they will be perceived and received by older adults or by people who are parents when they themselves are childless. It is important that an open mind is kept for explanations of what happens in therapy and supervision that take account of these factors without them dominating inappropriately.

The characteristics of each party and their ideas and fantasies about the other people in the supervisory relationship might usefully be explored in the contracting process. Sometimes such self-awareness does not emerge until bumping up against difference – for example, views about domestic violence when faced with different perspectives on the matter. Including them in the contracting process indicates that they are appropriate material for supervision. Not only is permission granted to address them, but also each party will have gained an idea of how best to go about raising them.

Supervisory style

If supervisors are aware of their supervisory style, this can be a useful topic to be addressed in the contracting process. Rowan (1989) identified a number of styles which were regarded with varying degrees of esteem by supervisees. Valued approaches included 'insight-oriented' in which probing and questioning encouraged the supervisee to reflect upon the material, and 'feelings-oriented' also effected through enquiry specifically into the supervisee's affective experiences with clients. Rowan's findings may to some degree have been determined by the humanistic model in which the work was conducted. Supervision which adopted an approach based on the development of insight and which addressed feelings would be congruent with the model of therapy and might offer a good fit with supervisee expectations.

Less highly regarded were a number of approaches characterised together as 'constrictive supervision' in which supervisees characteristically felt that they were not given sufficient autonomy in how to conduct the work. In the 'authoritative style' the supervisee's work was closely monitored and regulated. While this may be preferred by some novices, it can come to be experienced as oppressive and induce resistance on the part of the supervisee. The 'didactic-consultative' style was characterised by instruction and the giving of advice and suggestions. Rowan suggested that the danger of this style is that it can turn into a virtuoso performance by the supervisor which can disenfranchise supervisees of their own clients. Also found to be unwelcome was the 'laissez-faire style' in which supervisees were largely left to their own devices. The style was manifest as vagueness and the supervisor failed to provide guidance about what was expected. This style was considered particularly unsuitable for new recruits. Also referred to as 'confrontational supervision', Rowan identified an 'unsupportive style' in which supervisees were exposed to critical and unsympathetic responses to their doubts and insecurities. This style can serve to exacerbate rather than allay doubts and fears.

Least popular of all was 'therapeutic' supervision (Rosenblatt and Mayer, 1975) in which supervisees felt problematised themselves when the supervisor appeared to attribute their struggles in the work to personality deficiencies in themselves. It can be surprisingly easy for supervisory interventions unintentionally to have this effect. Supervisory challenges are important to the development of skills and they need to be handled carefully in order to avoid the risk of leaving supervisees feeling vulnerable and exposed. The issue is discussed further in Chapter 14.

In a study of 137 counsellor supervisors, Ladany and colleagues (2001) found a significant positive relationship between self-reported attractive, interpersonally sensitive and task-oriented supervisory styles (based on the three dimensions of the Supervisory Styles Inventory) and a positive working alliance. They argued that an attractive style enhances the development of a supervisory bond whereas a didactic and directive supervisory style may emphasise the hierarchical aspects of the supervisory relationship, thus inhibiting the development of an emotional bond.

Magnuson and colleagues (2000) reported on the results of interviews with 11 experienced counsellors about their unproductive experiences as supervisees. The results of a category analysis revealed six aspects of supervision which were labelled as 'lousy' supervisor behaviours:

- *Unbalanced*: The supervisor who gets hung up on detail, or focuses too much on one aspect of supervision at the expense of seeing the bigger, systemic picture or context.
- *Developmentally inappropriate*: These are supervisors whose approach is fixed and static and who fail to acknowledge or respond to the changing needs of supervisees.
- *Intolerant of differences*: Characterised by the supervisor who does not encourage autonomy and individuation in supervisees and, instead, tries to persuade the supervisee to become a clone or close replica of the supervisor.
- *Poor model of professional and personal attributes*: These are supervisors who fail to observe professional boundaries and are intrusive, exploitative or abusive.
- *Untrained*: Supervisors who enact the role without adequate preparation or professional maturity.
- *Professionally apathetic*: Frequently described by research participants as 'lazy' supervisors who are not committed to the profession, their supervisees and, by inference, their supervisees' clients.

In my view, it is worth bearing in mind that supervision involves two or more people and only one of them is providing the above descriptions. It would not have surprised me to have heard myself being described in any of the above categories at some time in my career as a supervisor. I have certainly been untrained, regarded as overly intrusive and hung up on detail at various times. In general I don't like to be described in these ways and my interventions and supervisory style have been well intentioned. I suspect that this is the case for most if not all supervisors.

Ensuring that features of supervisor style are a topic for open exploration in the contracting process can offset Rosenblatt and Mayer's finding that supervisees typically adopt the strategy of 'spurious compliance' when faced with an unpalatable supervisory style.

Supervisor preferences and capabilities

While much of the discussion regarding the contract is likely to comprise supervisor enquiry, the contracting process also provides an opportunity for supervisors to state their own needs and preferences. This is also a useful skill in other circumstances, for example, in dealing with the unsatisfactory performance of a supervisee. In contracting, the supervisee might identify a need or wish that the supervisor cannot or prefers not to meet. It is beneficial for supervisors to be clear that they are unable or unwilling to meet this request. Similarly, supervisors may have requirements of their own and these need to be clearly stated at the outset. For example, 'When I am supervising people in training, it is my belief that I need to see the work being carried out if I am to be properly responsible to my clients. Before I see your work I would like you to see mine and we will work out a way of doing this together that is as comfortable for us both as we can make it. What are your thoughts about this?'

This statement makes it clear that the supervisor has certain requirements. It also indicates the purpose of the requirement and invites the supervisee to join with the supervisor in deciding *how* but not *whether* to meet it. The statement provides an opportunity, when the supervisory arrangement is elective, for the supervisee to decide against making a contract with this particular supervisor. Were this information to emerge at a later stage, withdrawal could be more difficult.

Mini-contracting for specific supervision sessions

Being prepared for supervision can take a variety of forms. The process of negotiating a supervisory contract acts as one form of preparation. In addition, it is helpful if the supervisor and supervisee have thought beforehand about what they wish to be on the agenda for this particular supervision. Mini-contracting helps to stop supervision from becoming routine, predictable and/or boring! Needs of supervisees are likely to change over time and this can readily be accommodated when each session begins by addressing the supervisory focus and process for today. In each party's mind, the questions in this regard might be, 'What do you/I wish to accomplish as a result of today's supervision?' and 'How shall we go about accomplishing that?' While being prepared is generally useful, from time to time supervision may be used to explore why the supervisee is having difficulty in clarifying what he or she wishes to achieve in supervision. This can arise, for example, where high levels of stress and workload have evoked a pattern of disorganisation and rushing from pillar to post. In such a case the supervisee may need time to relax into the supervision before being able to identify and explore work issues. The following is an extract from a supervision session (where $S'ee$ = supervisee and S = supervisor) in which the supervisee's stress level prevented her from being able to think about her work until she had an opportunity to let off steam (Inskipp and Proctor, 1988).

S'ee: I feel so tired, I don't know where to start. I had a terrible weekend on top of a bad week. My boyfriend had to go to the Continent and didn't get in touch when I expected him to. I found, it turned out that he had a minor accident – he's OK now. I was so worried over the weekend and then had to go straight back to work only to find that there were two staff short. I really haven't had any time to think about supervision.

S: It sounds as if you've had a really tough time, and you're feeling like that – what would you like to do now at the moment?

S'ee: I'd just like to sit quietly for a few minutes and relax. I really feel like having a good cry. [voice becomes tearful] [deep sigh]

S: That feels better.

S'ee: That feels good. I think this is the first quiet time I've had all week. [deep sigh]

S: 'Long and deep sighs', my yoga teacher says. It reminds me of a sea where we go to camp in Ireland and you can hear it coming in and out with a big sigh.

S'ee: It reminds me of the sea at home but I bet that's a lot hotter than Ireland.

S: Yes.

S'ee: God, I could do with some sun now. I feel so cold. Just thinking about that sun makes me feel warm and alive.

Inskipp and Proctor noted that this supervisee was fortunate in that her supervisor noticed and responded to her need to let off steam and relax.

When supervisors carry direct responsibility for clients, they will need to know what is happening with every client. Early on in training, it is likely that the supervisee will want to focus on what to do rather than on a deep exploration of the interpersonal dynamics. As the supervisee gains in confidence and experience, the conversation may focus on a particular client or a particular technique, the application of particular theory or the dynamics of the therapeutic relationship. When the supervisee is prepared in advance, time is not wasted as a consequence of lack of preparation, in identifying a supervisory focus during supervision itself.

When it does not result from a failure to prepare, time taken to identify a suitable focus during supervision may have a very valuable function. For example, where a supervisee is struggling to understand the therapeutic process or is finding the work confusing or distressing. Spencer (2000) stated:

> a counsellor may be consciously hoping to bring their work with clients but may be in such a state of dilemma, confusion or defensiveness that

they are unable to communicate in a way which brings their client or their work clearly or to allow themselves openly to be met by the supervisor. The supervisor's task begins with clearing a space to think together, to overcome such barriers and achieve open communication.

(Spencer, 2000: 517)

The issue is thus one of noticing the underlying processes about preparation for supervision. Habitual over-preparation might indicate anxious avoidance; under-preparation a lack of understanding about or commitment to the supervision.

This section has explored the reasons why a contract for supervision can contribute to the establishment and maintenance of a good working alliance. Further ideas about contracting may be obtained from Borders and Leddick (1987), Bradley (1989), Carroll (1996), Carroll and Gilbert (2005), Inskipp and Proctor (1993) and Page and Wosket (2001).

The ongoing supervisory relationship

As discussed above, contracting is part of the process of establishing a supervisory alliance. Social influence theory (Egan, 1994: 58–61) suggests that the more trusting an interpersonal relationship, the greater the potential influence of one person upon the other. Trustworthiness of the supervisor was found to relate significantly to measures of supervisees' judgements of supervision, and accounted for larger proportions of variance than did expertness and attractiveness in a study by Carey and colleagues (1988). Trustworthiness of the supervisor has also been found to relate to trainee performance in counselling (Carey et al., 1988; Dodenhoff, 1981; Friedlander and Snyder, 1983; Heppner and Handley, 1982).

Building trust takes time and is facilitated by an attitude of openness and authenticity whereby supervisors show evidence of knowing about their own foibles and blind spots and a continuing interest in developing this knowledge further. Genuine respect for the views and circumstances of the other is also important, as is a flexible and curious approach to the work. The supervisor's awareness of the potential vulnerabilities of supervisees should encourage a structuring of supervision sessions so as to prevent a level of disclosure that goes beyond the needs of the work. This is facilitated by the supervisor ensuring adherence to agreed boundaries by always having in mind the relevance of what is taking place in supervision to the work.

In a qualitative study (Worthen and McNeill, 1996) which employed in-depth interviews of eight experienced therapists, effective supervisors were characterised by an empathic attitude, a non-judgemental stance towards the supervisee, the conveying of a sense of validation or affirmation, and encouragement to explore and experiment. These qualities are illustrated in the following comments from one of the participants.

And what was so great, was that my supervisor was really affirming of and validating of my ability to speak clearly. I felt very much understood by her and I felt also like she appreciated those abilities that I had taken pride in the past and which I had felt, I just hadn't felt were being recognized at all, at any level.

(Stoltenberg *et al.*, 1998: 113)

In a study by Beinart (2004), rapport and the experience of support were found to be specific qualities of the relationship that contributed to effectiveness. When sessions 'go wrong' or do not turn out as expected, for example, where clients leave the session before the planned ending, express anger or dissatisfaction with the therapy or therapist, state that they feel worse than before and so on, the therapist can feel responsible, blamed and shamed. When feeling vulnerable in this way, one reaction is to hide this from the supervisor and to present a facade of competence rather than seek to learn from the experience (Ladany *et al.*, 1996; Yourman and Farber, 1997). Ladany *et al.* (1996) found that one of the frequent reasons for nondisclosure in supervision was a poor alliance and that negative reactions to the supervisor were the most frequent type of nondisclosure. Most nondisclosures to supervisors were discussed with someone else, typically a peer. It is particularly helpful in these situations if a position of curiosity and open-mindedness is adopted by the supervisor whereby the explanation for the difficulty may be attributed to multiple sources. In the following example, it is helpful that the supervising team is familiar with the work of the therapist and is able to state that the pattern of interaction is atypical of the worker's usual approach. Multiple hypotheses are proposed to explain the events in the session and the therapist reaches her own conclusions about her options in future.

A family was referred to the family therapy service by a headteacher who was concerned that there had been significant deterioration in the behaviour of all three children since the acrimonious separation and divorce of the parents within the previous year. The referral noted that the children spent alternate days with each parent and that the mother had remarried and was expecting a baby. The initial appointment was attended by both birth parents and the three children. The therapist introduced herself, explained the method of work which involved a live supervising team and the interview proceeded as follows:

Th:	Could I be introduced to the people who are here?
Child:	[points to youngest child] He'll tell you.
Father:	[Names each person present by their first names]
Th:	Could you tell me what brought you to our service?
Father:	It's him, [points to youngest child] his behaviour at school.
Th:	Are there any other things that concern you?

Mother: No [assertively] just his behaviour at school.
Th: Are there any difficulties at home?
Father: No, [loudly] just his behaviour at school.
Th: I'm afraid that we don't deal here with problems in school. You need a different service for that.
Father: [aggressively] We've waited 12 weeks for this appointment and now you tell us that this is the wrong place.
Th: I'm very sorry. We know that that is a problem.
Father: What do we do then about the problems at school?
Th: I'm very sorry but the school thought that there were some difficulties at home as well.
Father: What sort of difficulties?
Th: They mentioned that you had separated and that the children spend some time with each of you and that might be difficult for them. But as you say the problems are at school and I can tell you how to get help there.
Father: [stands up and says to family] Come on then, we're off. [father strides out and rest of family follows]

The therapist then joined the supervising team and concern was expressed that the children might have lost an opportunity to talk about the effects on them of the separation and divorce. There was exploration of why this session might have ended so quickly and why it had not been possible to move the family on to a wider discussion as might more typically happen (*S* = supervisor, *Th* = therapist).

S: Wow, that was the shortest session I've ever seen you do. I was wondering how the family might have organised you into finishing so much more quickly than you usually do.
Th: I don't know. They really surprised me. It felt as if they really didn't want to be here. Even when they got up though, I was still expecting them to carry on.
S: What did it feel like in there? Did the father seem like he might be violent?
Th: No, I don't think it was that. I felt safe. It was just that they seemed like they didn't want to be here.
S: Was that just the father?
Th: No, the mother as well.
S: I noticed them in the car-park on my way in – just the mother and the boys and they looked a bit uncomfortable then. What happened in reception?
Th: Well, I didn't know the mother's new married name to invite her down and when I asked, they said she wasn't remarried and they didn't know what I was talking about.

S: I wondered if they didn't like the idea of the screen and team, but they'd had the leaflet explaining that it would be this way.

Th: I don't think it was that.

S: When they insisted the problem was just at school, sometimes you would have chosen to carry on exploring that and then other things might have emerged. What was it that made you choose to say it was the wrong service?

Th: I think it was the change in my job – I have to be very careful about not taking on anything that doesn't fit with what I'm supposed to do. Yes, and it's to do with being in the allocation meeting. I'm very aware that we have a long waiting list and recently there's been a change so that instead of accepting everything we have been turning a lot more away.

S: So that we work with those who can most benefit?

Th: Yes. But now I think maybe I could have chosen to talk for longer about the school problems but I didn't think it was appropriate at the time.

The team members commented that they had been very successful in fitting the new referral criteria. Further consideration was given to the possible loss of an opportunity for the boys to talk about the effects on them of the separation and residence arrangements, and how other opportunities might be provided; to the context of the school which has been designated as 'failing' and made many referrals to the service; how referrals might contain misinformation; and to what extent it was legitimate for the therapist to reveal the concerns of the referrer to the family.

Reducing fear and increasing trust

In my experience, one of the most important factors contributing to a functional working relationship is the experience of feeling safe. In a study of counselling within a psychodynamic model, some of the conditions that helped to create a positive working alliance in which supervisees felt more confident to disclose difficult issues to their supervisor were one-to-one rather than a collective arrangement, when the supervisor had been chosen rather than allocated, and when supervision took place independently of the setting in which the work was conducted rather than in-house (Webb and Wheeler, 1998). Within a specific relationship, while the conditions of warmth and empathy may help, they may not be necessary or sufficient, and sometimes generate a superficial 'feel good' relationship designed to make both supervisor and supervisee feel good because they want to be liked. This may work well when the going is easy but come unstuck in the event of problems.

Bob Johnson (1996) argued that fear is the most dominant of human emotions, controlling our thinking and actions and distorting our perceptions. He stated that the antidote to fear, often hidden fear, is trust, and his approach to creating trust in relationships is to react spontaneously, 'deploying his full personality'. A number of other factors involved in trusting relationships follow. Some of them have already been introduced earlier in this chapter, and they continue to play a part as relationships develop.

Familiarity

The greater the knowledge that we have of another person, the better our ability to predict what the other will say and do in relation to us. The longer the duration of the relationship, and the greater the consistency with which the other behaves, the greater sense of security is likely to result. This can often be seen in well-led workshops where people initially tend to show reserve, the level of disclosure increasing as confidence in the facilitator grows. This is particularly the case where care has been taken to show respect and value for contributions offered. At its extreme, the saying 'familiarity breeds contempt' might be invoked – if you are able reliably to predict at all times what the other might say, then what they say may not be worth hearing. In long-standing supervisory relationships it would be wise to review at intervals the continuing capability of supervision to stimulate learning.

What does this mean for supervision? Probably that first and foremost the participants need to get to know each other. This process can be helped along by talking together about aspects of professional history, possibly informally, and with a degree of personal disclosure. While the focus of the conversation will be on work, it will be important for each of the parties to see the person behind the professional.

Self-esteem and self-confidence

Some people rely more heavily on affirmation from their social world than do others who have developed what might be called greater ego strength. A measure of uncertainty or self-doubt is probably essential to learning. Elsie Osborne (personal communication) argued that the behaviour of noviciates to a profession tended to lie between two ends of a continuum. At one end, they cope with a lack of confidence by seeming to feel that they have to know everything and this can give an impression of arrogance. At the other, they appear to believe that they know nothing and consequently act helpless and dependent. She proposed that for the majority of students the position lies somewhere in between. For those at the extremes, Elsie's hypothesis offers supervisors a benevolent explanation from which to take the matter forward.

The Integrated Developmental Model (IDM) (Stoltenberg and Delworth, 1987; Stoltenberg *et al.*, 1998) accounts for such attitudes and offers a framework within which supervisors can understand and respond constructively to supervisees at different stages of their professional development. It is discussed in more detail in Chapter 5. The issue of defensiveness can usefully be discussed early on in the supervision relationship. Supervisors can describe their own typical responses when experiencing a sense of insecurity and enquire as to the supervisee's responses. It is also possible to ask about helpful ways to respond in the event of noticing such behaviours. At the least, this signals that such matters are appropriate topics for discussion and that defensiveness is an adaptive response to perceived threat.

Feeling accepted

Relationships are usually helped along by mutual respect. While this seems obvious, there is plenty of evidence that working contexts can legislate against such an ethos. The idea of taking a 'both-and' position can foster mutual respect, each lens offering a perspective which adds to or enriches the overall picture.

The supervisor can take this position in relation to the ideas offered by supervisees. After all, having and expressing ideas is probably more crucial to the work than the specific nature of those ideas. So the supervisor can take an attitude of 'that's a good idea and here's another one'. This is a particularly effective strategy in group supervision where a fear of looking stupid to colleagues by giving a wrong answer has been implanted as people have progressed through the education system (Holt, 1969). Supervisees benefit from having their ideas and capability to learn challenged, and this can be undertaken in ways that build upon strengths rather than expose weaknesses.

Containment

Many of the issues that are pertinent to working with clients translate to the supervisory relationship. Containment is one of these. It can be effected through many channels and strategies. Some models of therapy prescribe that clients should be seen in the same place and at the same time throughout their episode of care, and that paying attention to time-keeping and proscribing interruptions is crucial. These map directly on to supervision arrangements and give the message that the supervision is important. Knowing who to contact in an emergency is another feature of containment.

Supervisees often express the wish to have feedback about their performance and in my experience this can be a dangerous thing. Without containment, supervisees are, by their invitation, exposing themselves to evaluation of any aspect of their work or person and this can be shocking. The same goes for supervisors who offer an open-ended invitation to supervisees to give them feedback. My own preference under most circumstances is to confine requests for feedback to comments on a specific issue identified by the inviting party. For example, rather than ask, 'What did you think of that session?' try, 'What do you think the client made of my introduction to the session?' or 'Did you think I came in too early when the client was silent?'

A sense of containment can also be generated by knowing what to expect, although individuals will have different preferences based on their cultural histories. Are you more the kind of person who is happy to throw yourself into an unprogrammed open-ended event with colleagues, or do you prefer to have a written programme outlining what to expect from the day? I think that it is safer to assume the latter in the first instance, the implications being that in a new supervision relationship it is likely to be helpful for the parties to outline their ideas and expectations regarding the task in hand.

Self-disclosure and moderation of the 'expert' role

Too much self-disclosure by the supervisor can become self-serving but a little can help to normalise 'good enough', and occasional 'not good enough' performance. It probably helps for supervisors to feel that they are able to do something well, while showing awareness that their knowledge and skills would yet benefit from further development. Supervisees might appreciate the supervisor taking shared responsibility for their difficulties, being prepared to make statements such as 'I think I have not explained that concept adequately', or 'In retrospect I underestimated the complexity of this client's difficulties'.

Through such interventions the supervisor can model openness to learning and that there is no need to fear getting things wrong. There is probably no better way of illustrating this than by allowing supervisees to see the supervisor working. While daunting in the first instance, it is possible to reach a position where feelings of vulnerability and exposure are supplanted by the benefits of sharing responsibility for what transpires in a session. Live supervision is explored more fully in Chapter 11.

Taking one step at a time

When there is a significant gap in knowledge and experience between supervisors and supervisees it may be very difficult for supervisors to 'decentre' and connect with the learner's position (Donaldson, 1978). If you were helping someone to learn about diving you would probably not expect them to jump head-first off the highest board during the first lesson. The capability of supervisors to stay connected with their own earlier stages of learning, and to break down complex skills into manageable chunks will probably be helpful to supervisees, but can be easier said than done. Taking a position of curiosity towards the supervisees' current state of awareness should help, as can focusing on a particular and specific topic or skill to be learned.

For neophyte practitioners there is some mileage in encouraging them to focus away from the development of technique. This may run counter to the tendency of beginners to be preoccupied with what they did in the session and for supervision early in training to be oriented towards case management. Such a focus may be driven by the fear of getting things wrong and the need actively to be doing something that is helpful to clients. This tendency can also affect beginning supervisors. Inskipp and Proctor (1995) used the term 'under-standing' to highlight the central role relationship of super-vision, rather than the supervisor being blinded by anxiety into privileging the role relationship as super-vision (i.e. overseeing). While both may be neces-sary, it is understanding that supports the establishment and maintenance of both the supervisory and therapeutic alliances.

Difference

This is a theme which is addressed more fully in Chapter 8. It is introduced in this section on the basis that the greater the social and cultural differences between us, the less secure we may tend initially to feel with each other. This has been borne out in studies, for example, of selection for jobs where interviewers tend to choose people similar to them (Eder and Ferris, 1989; Silvester, 1996). It accounts for the development of equal opportunities policies in the workplace.

Differences between us can be immediately apparent, as in the case of ethnicity, gender and age, or may be hidden, for example, in relation to sexu-ality and some kinds of disability. Difference does not stop there. We tend to have preferences for different degrees of formality, different styles of dress and different philosophies with which we make sense of our experiences and with which we approach our world. Joyce Stalker (1996) argued that healthy, positive discussions, challenges and negotiations are more possible in a learn-ing situation when the 'secrets' of the assumptions which underlie the learn-ers' and the teacher's approaches to the learning experience are evident. She provides a framework developed as a result of finding herself working in a different culture from the one in which she was brought up. She offers this to students with a view to helping learners to understand and to analyse their own and others' experiences.

Clarity and purpose of task

Imagine finding yourself in a room with another person. Neither of you know quite why you are there or what you are supposed to be doing. How would that feel? It could be quite exciting but on the other hand quite anxiety-provoking. At least one theory of group dynamics (Adair, 1983) iden-tifies 'task needs'. Relationships tend to work better when the tasks are clear and when there is reasonable consensus about the tasks among participants.

Individual and group supervision

There is a tendency for people to feel safer in one-to-one relationships than in groups, and the dynamics of groups change with increasing membership size.

This is not to say that groups do not offer a rich tapestry for learning, but rather that the group supervisor will probably have to work harder to create a climate of safety than the supervisor in a one-to-one supervisory relationship.

On the other hand, it is more possible for individuals to 'hide' in groups than in one-to-one relationships, although not possible for the group supervisor. Since the dynamics of groups are more complex, the beginning supervisor might wish to start with an individual supervisee. While able to draw on experiences in the role of supervisee, beginning supervisors would do well to find themselves a circumscribed role with an experienced and respected supervisor, perhaps being involved on a case-by-case basis in a form of joint supervision. In this event, care needs to be given to the possible experiencing of multiple-role relationships which can muddy the waters and generate competitive and potentially destructive interactions.

Conceptual security blankets

As we become socialised into our professions, we tend to acquire particular philosophical, theoretical and practice perspectives or habits. Gitterman (1988) stated that 'our favourite theories are often so overly cherished that we inevitably begin to fit people and their situations into them. These conceptual security blankets can become worn and frayed.' He argued that our needs for safety, certainty and stability compromise our curiosity and blind us to the ordinary details and actualities of people's lives. If supervisees' needs for safety can be met within the supervisory relationship, then their willingness to take risks, learn from mistakes and engage with their creativity will be enhanced.

Ruptures in supervision

From time to time there will almost inevitably be discordant episodes in a supervisory relationship that has, up until that point, been working well. These are sometimes known as 'ruptures'. Conflict is regarded as a natural part of supervision by Ladany and colleagues (2005: 215) because of the complexity inherent in the different role relationships between the participants. Research findings have suggested three types of ruptures: transient difficulties associated with a lack of experience and skill deficits which can be remedied by further learning, paradigmatic difficulties related to a supervisory style involving limited interpersonal sensitivity and greater task orientation, and situational difficulties related to specific circumstances. The latter were the most frequently reported, were such that most supervisors would find them difficult, and were typically reported by supervisors with greater experience and higher skill levels in a study by Monaghan (2007).

One strategy is to ignore ruptures in the hope that they will go away; often they don't. Another is to try and make sense of them either together with the other party at the time of the occurrence, or later in reflection alone or with a colleague, subsequently bringing the new understanding back to the supervisory relationship. Episodes from supervision can be the focus of supervision (supervision of supervision).

The concept of 'immediacy' can be helpful, an approach in which attention is drawn to the process as it is taking place in the session. Once the problem has a formulation an action strategy may be devised. Apologies may be in order, or agreement to differ. It may become appropriate to revisit the initial contract and to make changes or to remind each other of the preferences expressed at that time.

As a brief guide to making and sustaining trust in supervisory relationships, the following dos and don'ts for supervisors are offered for consideration:

- Don't ask the supervisee to do anything that you are not prepared to do first.
- Show your own work to the supervisee openly either live, on recordings or by modelling.
- Retain the main focus on the client and draw everything back to this in the end.
- Always take a respectful approach to clients and colleagues so that supervisees know you will not 'bad mouth' them behind their backs.
- Don't break confidences.
- Don't say one thing and act in a different way.
- Discuss how supervisees can 'manage' you should they find their security threatened (i.e. the manner in which they might raise issues with you so as not to provoke a defensive reaction).
- Make sure that challenges are specific and related to the work.
- Comment on areas where you yourself are unsure, don't know or feel you have made an error, and talk about what can be done next.
- Where relevant, talk about your own training experiences and how you may differ now from then.
- Don't show off your knowledge in the service of your own ego.
- Be prepared to take responsibility and give instructions where client safety is at issue.
- Let supervisees know that they will not be allowed to act outside the boundaries that keep the system safe.
- Share some personal information in a way that you might not with clients – to allow yourself as a human being to show through your professional bearing.
- Show interest in the supervisee as a person as well as a professional.
- Notice the supervisee's knowledge and skills.

Endings

I am grateful to Derek Milne (personal communication, 2008) for pointing out to me the lack of much discussion in the supervision literature about the ending or closure of supervisory relationships. This contrasts with the issue of endings in therapy and since the evidence suggests that in both cases the working alliance is key, I was led to puzzle over this apparent omission. Two obvious contrasts between therapeutic and supervisory relationships are that the latter involves the supervisor in an assessment role and that unlike therapeutic relationships, which typically mean that at closure the relationship is terminated, supervisors and supervisees may well continue in a professional relationship. Termination of supervision may create the opportunity to socialise more freely. Issues of loss are likely to be less to the fore.

Chambers and Cutcliffe (2001), who have addressed this issue, argued that there is a well-established literature indicating that a healthy ending is often associated with a negotiated ending (Lendrum and Syme, 1992; Tschudin, 1997; Worden, 1988). Gradual endings rather than abrupt terminations allow each partner to carry out desired ending tasks or rituals, and, particularly in training placements, there is usually an opportunity for a winding down as the supervisee no longer takes on new case work. The completion of end-of-placement paperwork can often facilitate a review of the strengths of the participants and help to draw a line under any of the more challenging aspects of the relationship. Where possible a celebration of accomplishments and successes is likely to make for a satisfactory conclusion, and to serve as a platform for further learning and development for both parties.

Chapter 5

Frameworks for supervision

To paraphrase Lev Vygotsky (1962: 115): 'If someone is taught to operate within a system without coming to understand that it is one among other possible ones then he has not *mastered* the system but is *bound* by it.'

There are available many models or frameworks within which to conceptualise the purposes and processes of supervision. These are useful in enabling participants to organise their ideas about what is happening either while it is happening or in later reflection. They are also useful in the study of supervision. It is often beneficial for supervisor and supervisee to share their understandings of supervision frameworks with each other. If a common framework is adopted, this may be used to explore events, thoughts and feelings evoked through the process. As in therapy, ideas may be drawn principally from a single structure or from many.

This chapter draws the attention of readers to a number of such frameworks. The selection reflects the interests of the author and is by no means comprehensive. The decision to facilitate reflection with the aid of a structure is probably of greater importance than the specific choice of model.

In this chapter, Inskipp and Proctor's (1993) model addresses the question, 'Why are we doing this?'; Hawkins and Shohet (2006) address the question, 'What are my experiences in supervision telling me about the work?', and Page and Wosket (1994, 2001) focus on the process of each supervisory session as it cycles towards the identified supervisory goals. Scaife and Scaife's (1996) framework explores supervision focus, supervisory role, and the medium on which the data studied in supervision is captured. Elizabeth Holloway's (1995) model seeks comprehensively to address the supervisory system, while Frawley O'Dea and Sarnat (2001) emphasise the relational aspects of supervision. Developmental models aid the supervisory partnership in thinking about how the needs of individual supervisees might differ according to the experience levels of the partners in the enterprise. While these are the central aspects of the models described, each of the authors addresses much wider issues. The selected frameworks are summarised here; interested readers may wish to consult the original sources for further information.

A model addressing the functions of supervision (Inskipp and Proctor, 1993)

A number of propositions have been made regarding the functions of supervision, the emphasis varying according to the role relationship of the participants. Particularly in training contexts, the learning and development of the supervisee has a place centre stage. Keeping Inskipp and Proctor's (1993) model in mind helps the supervisor to stay on track with the functions of the supervision as agreed within the initial contracting process. The model was developed in the context of counsellor supervision conducted independently of an employing or training institution. The contract was a private arrangement which included negotiation of a fee.

Inskipp and Proctor proposed three main functions of supervision: 'formative', 'normative' and 'restorative'. Supervision in any one session might include all of these aims either explicitly or implicitly.

Formative

When the supervision aims to be formative, it is the supervisee's learning and development that is the focus. No particular approach to the learning is implied and the supervisor might employ a range of methods designed to further the supervisee's knowledge or skills.

Normative

The normative function of supervision derives from the supervisor's managerial and ethical responsibilities. While the extent to which this is relevant will vary between settings, the supervisor will always have some responsibility to ensure client welfare. In a training setting, the managerial role is likely to be extensive and may include responsibility for the supervisee's case work and the task of ensuring that the supervisee complies with the rules and norms of the organisations in which the work is carried out. Where the contract for supervision is made within an employing organisation, it is necessary to negotiate the constraints that this might impose. For example, if the employer requires that the therapist work with a certain minimum number of clients at any one time and supervision elucidates that this is having an adverse impact on the work, is the responsibility of the supervisor either to help workers to comply with the organisational requirement, or to help them to challenge the requirements? In essence, the supervisor is contracting both with the funding body and with the supervisee and needs to be clear about her or his contractual duties to each of these parties.

When supervision is arranged independently of an employer and the individual makes a personal financial arrangement, the normative function of supervision may be less to the fore. However, the supervisor will still have moral and ethical responsibilities towards the supervisee's clients. Should the supervisor conclude that the therapist cannot meet client needs due to ill-health or substance misuse, for example, or if the supervisor learns about abuse of a client, should action follow? Whatever form this takes, the supervisor should seek to act sensitively and with regard to the welfare of all parties. Where other parties, such as a professional body, need to be informed, the first consideration may be to support the supervisee to make the report. If this is not possible, the professional body should be informed with the knowledge, and ideally with the consent, but if necessary without the agreement of the supervisee. It is easier to take such action if the possibility has been discussed in the contracting process. Holding in mind a framework which includes the normative function enables supervisors to monitor and review what they are doing and why when faced with such dilemmas.

Restorative

The restorative function acknowledges the emotional effects of work on the individual, and in particular of work with people in distress. The social, political and economic forces that can have a significant impact on employees are explored in more detail in Chapter 3. Links have been suggested between the emotional experiences of employees and the organisational process and structure (Czander, 1993). The potential sources of emotional arousal at work are multiple, arising not only from the organisational process and structure, but also from relationships with colleagues, relationships with clients, and relationships and life events outside work. Any of these can be a relevant and appropriate focus of supervision, the aim being to explore the level and sources of arousal and their impact specifically upon the work.

Mollon (1989) called the negative emotional impacts of direct work with clients 'narcissistic insults'. Typically these are experienced as shameful because they include proscribed feelings such as hostility or sexual arousal towards people whom the practitioner is supposing to help. Feelings of shame are not infrequently concealed. When the restorative function of supervision is acknowledged, revelation of these feelings is legitimate. The supervisor's role is to provide support, facilitate understanding and enable the supervisee to learn by using these feelings to inform the work. The feelings can be treated as information that is useful in understanding the client's issues. Failure to reveal these feelings can lead clients and therapists into liaisons that may prove a danger to both.

Inskipp and Proctor used the analogy of miners obtaining agreement from the employer to wash off the dust of their labours in the employer's time to elaborate this function of supervision. Supervisees in training may find it difficult to believe that supervision can be used for this purpose without adversely affecting the supervisor's assessment. The research evidence suggests that hiding things from the supervisor is a very widespread practice

(Ladany *et al.*, 1996; Webb and Wheeler, 1998; Yourman, 2003). Supervisors typically take the view that they would prefer to know about the messes made by supervisees and are more concerned positively to evaluate openness in supervision and progress through learning from mistakes.

Because the focus of the restorative function can be so wide-ranging it is essential that respect is paid to relevant boundaries. When difficulties are being experienced with a colleague shared in common between supervisor and supervisee, or when personal issues in the wider life of the supervisee need attention, exploration in other settings may be preferable. One of the tasks of the supervisor in carrying out this function is to monitor the level of intrusiveness into personal issues and how necessary this is for the task in hand.

Sessions that have a substantial restorative function may be experienced as less structured than others. They sometimes begin with the supervisee not knowing what issues to address and the supervisor listening attentively while the supervisee presents a confused picture that may include a vague awareness of not feeling 'right'. The supervisor listens for openings as to what may be happening for the supervisee and may use her or his counselling skills in order to try and connect. If a trusting relationship has been established, the supervisee will be able to give voice to frustrations, upsets and disappointments which may in itself be sufficient in order to move on. Without the restorative function the difficulties of the day are likely to be taken home and explored or enacted with family and friends (McElfresh and McElfresh, 1998).

Models addressing the process and content of supervision

The General Supervision Framework (Scaife, 1993b; Scaife and Scaife, 1996)

The General Supervision Framework comprises the three dimensions of supervisor role, supervision focus and the medium that provides data for supervision. The model owes much to the work of Bernard (1979, 1981) and Levine and Tilker (1974). While the dimensions are categorised under discrete headings, it is not intended that these be regarded rigidly or as the only categories possible. It offers a structure within which supervision may be conceptualised both in practice and for research purposes. In the General Supervision Framework (GSF) the spotlight is on the supervisor. Alternative focuses on the supervisee and/or on the relationship between the participants are also feasible. For a view from the perspective of the supervisee, see Carroll and Gilbert (2005). Each of the dimensions of the model is elaborated below.

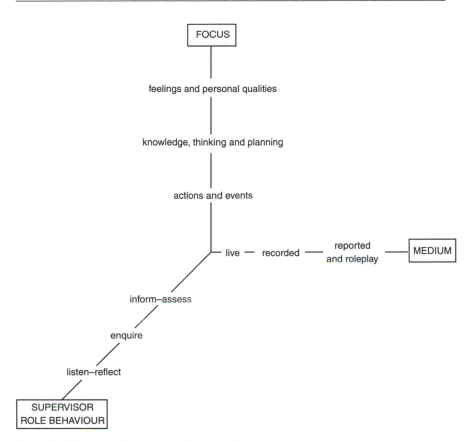

Figure 5.1 The general supervision framework.

Supervisor role behaviour

In the GSF, supervisor role behaviour is categorised under the three discrete headings of Inform–Assess, Enquire and Listen–Reflect. Inform–Assess role behaviour tends to emphasise complementarity in the supervisory relationship in which there is the informer and the informed. The role behaviours of Enquire and Listen–Reflect tend to give the supervision a more reciprocal feel. Bernard argues, in relation to preregistration counsellor training, that the approach used by the supervisor or the role adopted should represent a deliberate choice based on the needs of individuals at different stages of learning. It is also important to recognise that supervisee role behaviour can evoke particular responses from the supervisor and that this can be very difficult to resist, even when recognised and deemed to be unsupportive to learning. A commonly encountered example is where the supervisee invites Inform–Assess role behaviour by asking the supervisor for her or his views and opinions. While entirely appropriate at times, this can signal a lack of confidence which can be perpetuated if the supervisor is repeatedly drawn into an information-giving response. The three categories of supervisor role behaviour are described further below.

INFORM–ASSESS

This category involves making observations and judgements of supervisee performance, offering critical comments and 'telling' things to the supervisee. Supervisors take responsibility for their own expertise and there is an implicit assumption that supervisors have some knowledge and insights not available to the supervisee. It is when acting in this category that supervisors carry out the tasks of gatekeeping admission to a profession and discharging their ethical responsibilities to clients. The balancing of responsibility to clients with responsibility to supervisees was ranked second in a list of issues which are difficult to deal with in supervision by educational psychologists (Pomerantz *et al.*, 1987). This accords with Doehrman's (1976) finding that supervisors generally have a preference for a more collegial role than this category of role behaviour exemplifies. It is usually helpful for the supervisee and supervisor to negotiate under which circumstances such role behaviours will be appropriate. Supervisees might also use Inform–Assess behaviours to provide information to the supervisor about what is proving most helpful to their learning. Negotiation and agreement about how and when to adopt Assess–Inform role behaviours can avoid the dilemmas posed by wholesale adoption of a partnership or collegial relationship in which supervisors may feel constrained about evaluating the work of the supervisee or suggesting agenda items for supervision.

Inexperienced supervisees or those new to a particular specialism may be the most likely to prefer the Inform–Assess approach. At this stage supervisors might suggest relevant reading material, describe some of their own case work and experiences, point out key issues and dilemmas that might arise in the work, or conduct mini-seminars exploring such issues. This is not to say that the role behaviour is no longer relevant in the case of greater experience as in peer supervisory relationships. Supervisees may continue to find it helpful to hear about the supervisor's approach and to obtain feedback on their work. However, it is likely that the balance will change with the development and experience of the supervisee.

Because Inform–Assess role behaviour tends to carry with it a tacit assumption that supervisors are experienced, expert practitioners whose role is to instruct novices, it is wise for supervisors to ask themselves whether this role is pedagogically efficacious; does it aid learning? Telling things to the supervisee carries the risk of inhibiting the development of the supervisee's own critical faculties.

ENQUIRE

When the supervisor adopts Enquire role behaviour, the supervisee is likely to experience reciprocity in the supervisory relationship, which is often preferred by supervisors (Pomerantz *et al.*, 1987). In this role supervisors ask questions. The spirit of the role is of enquiry from a position of curiosity and exploration rather than of interrogation. Asking a question to which the supervisor has a preconceived notion of the 'right' answer would exemplify veiled Inform–Assess role behaviour and in such circumstances it is usually better to 'come clean' rather than to expect the supervisee to read the supervisor's mind.

The Enquirer role equates with that described in partnership supervision (Rudduck and Sigsworth, 1985) and is also a significant feature of the Interpersonal Process Recall (IPR) model of Kagan (1984) and Kagan and Kagan (1991), a more detailed description of which appears in Chapter 10 (this volume). Skilful questioning is a central feature of several approaches to learning and development. For example, Socratic questioning was named for the renowned Greek philosopher and teacher. This approach involves the posing of thoughtful questions to aid learning and draw out knowledge. There is debate as to whether the questioner will already have in mind what is to be learned. The questions typically follow a sequence which involves selection of a question or issue of interest, clarification of the issue, critical examination of the assumptions and evidence related to the central statement, exploration of the origin of the statement, critical examination of the implications and consequences of the statement and investigation of conflicting views or alternative viewpoints (Paul and Elder, 2002).

Circular and reflexive questions are characteristic of systemic approaches. Their aim is to facilitate change by prompting people to make new connections and to develop novel ideas and understandings. Each of these enquiring approaches can produce similar open-ended questions, the difference between them lying in the aims of the questioner and the structure within which the questions are devised. Knowledge attained through a questioning process stands a very good chance of being owned by the learner.

LISTEN–REFLECT

The supervisor using this category of role behaviour is often placing a premium on the supervisee's personal needs in the professional context. The role involves attentive listening and reflection of what has been said in such a way as to provide illumination of the issues raised. The process of reflection may introduce a development and overview of the supervisee's own ideas. While the focus of this role is often on the feelings, needs and issues of the supervisee, it can also help supervisees to clarify their thoughts about the professional task in which they are engaged. For example, a supervisee may, generally speaking, exhibit well-developed skills in a particular kind of work, but may be struggling to apply the skills effectively in a particular setting or with a particular client. The supervisor in Listen–Reflect mode may help the supervisee to derive her or his own explanations of the difficulties in this case. This role behaviour exemplifies Stones' (1984) and Bernard's (1981) counsellor role in which the supervisor is sensitive and attentive to the mood and personal needs of the supervisee.

In practice these three categories of role behaviour rarely obtain in pure form. In each session these and other role behaviours might be expressed, the aim of the supervisor being to move between roles according to need. The pattern of role behaviours results from the dance between participants in terms of what is unconsciously evoked and what is deliberately chosen. The extract below (where S = supervisor and $S'ee$ = supervisee) illustrates how a supervisor might respond differently within each of the categories to a particular stimulus introduced by the supervisee:

S'ee: When she started to talk about how she couldn't go out anywhere because she couldn't be bothered to get ready, I wanted to challenge her about how she managed to attend the sessions with me, but she looked so fragile I was worried that she would just think that I didn't understand. I wanted her to know that I could empathise with that, particularly given her history, and that I felt upset as well. Then I started to think that what I could offer was pretty useless and superficial given the depths of her distress. As soon as I thought that, I didn't know what to say to her.

Supervisor using Inform–Assess role behaviour:

S: I think that perhaps what you were experiencing was a dilemma about whether to try deepening the empathy, which you might do by saying something like, 'You feel so depressed that nothing seems worthwhile anymore?' or making a distinction on a difference by drawing her attention to the exception to what she was describing – the evidence that maybe she can do more than she thinks she can because she is able to attend her sessions with you.

Supervisor using Enquire role behaviour:

S: If you were to have followed your inclination to point out that she had managed to attend the session with you, can you think now about how you might have said that without risking her thinking that you didn't understand?

S: When you focused on your empathy with her feelings of sadness, was that the point at which you started to feel that you had nothing to offer?

Supervisor using Listen–Reflect role behaviour:

S: So it sounds as if you're saying that there was a dilemma for you about making a choice of direction and that when that happened, you kind of got stuck and lost your confidence.

These role behaviours may be selected by the supervisor to suit the specific occasion or to suit the supervisee, may reflect a preferred *modus operandi*, or may result from the supervisor being invited into a particular response by the supervisee's role behaviour. This can be more or less explicit. Supervisees who expect to begin a session by describing their previous meeting with the client often invite the supervisor into Listen–Reflect role behaviour for the first few minutes of the supervision. Alternatively, as part of the agenda setting for supervision the supervisee might explicitly invite Enquire role behaviour, saying, 'I have a number of conflicting ideas about the work with this client and I would like you to help me to think through which to use at this point in the work.'

Supervision focus

Supervision focus is the topic or topics to be explored in supervision. The focus is the material under discussion, which may be addressed in a range of ways and for varying purposes. Both parties may contribute to decisions regarding the choice of supervisory focus. In some models of supervision (e.g. Goldhammer *et al.*, 1980; Sullivan, 1980) the focus is primarily oriented towards skill development. Arguably, the term 'coaching' is more appropriate to a specific skill development orientation (Megginson and Clutterbuck, 2005: 4). In models of supervision that emphasise partnership, it has been found that supervisees often prefer a focus on feelings generated in the relationship between the professional worker and the client. In the work of Rudduck and Sigsworth (1985) with student teachers, supervisees tended to select a focus on personal and ethical issues such as the impact of the student teacher's youthful appearance, or ensuring fair and equitable treatment of all children.

Bernard (1979) proposed that supervisors are likely to have preferred focus areas, often based on their own special interests. There is also likely to be a relationship between preferred focus and preferred model of therapy. A behavioural approach is likely to emphasise observable behaviour; a cognitive approach, thinking processes; and a psychodynamic approach, the feelings and unconscious dynamics occurring in the relationships of client/therapist and therapist/supervisor.

Bernard categorised supervisory focus under three discrete headings. Adopting a similar structure, Scaife and Scaife labelled these categories 'Actions, Events and Responses', 'Knowledge, Thinking and Planning' and 'Feelings and Personal Qualities'.

ACTIONS, EVENTS AND RESPONSES

This focus category is behaviour and skills oriented. It includes what was said and done during sessions by the client and/or supervisee. The supervisor might ask questions or make observations about events that took place during the work. It could include supervisees asking questions about events and responses that they have observed in the supervisor's work. Descriptions or demonstrations of technique would exemplify this focus. It may also involve noticing a pattern or process in the session; for example, the client responding by giving information about behaviour whenever invited to discuss feelings.

KNOWLEDGE, THINKING AND PLANNING

Knowledge, thinking and planning can either be raised directly as a focus, or inferred from the content of the supervisory conference. This focus would be exemplified in supervision by the reading of case-relevant literature followed by a discussion of how these theoretical ideas could be used in the work with a particular client. Supervisees in training often value this approach to supervision in helping them to link what is being taught in the academic context with their experiences of being with clients. It is within this category that understanding and conceptualisation of the client's difficulties and the process of formulation are located.

FEELINGS AND PERSONAL QUALITIES

This focus includes the expression of individual style, the use of personal qualities in the work and the supervisee's feelings. It may include reflection upon a person's values, expectations and prejudices; the impact of life events; and feelings generated at work. An example would be a focus on the effects of a powerful felt imperative to produce symptom change (referred to by Hawkins and Shohet (2006: 91) as 'aim attachment counter-transference') which can be fuelled by professional demands to produce results, or how a recent or past bereavement in the lives of workers may be affecting their approach. Within this framework, the value direction (negative, neutral or positive) of specific personal qualities and the experience or lack of experience of specific life events is not assumed. The focus is on self in the professional role and when these issues are explored it is important to keep in mind the relevance of the exploration for the work. Where issues go beyond work, the role of the supervisor is to ensure that these are addressed in other more appropriate relationships, for example, with a mentor or in personal therapy.

This focus is also on the ways in which the work affects the mood and feelings of the supervisee and how these in turn affect the work. Ashforth and Humphrey (1995: 98) go so far as to argue that the 'experience of work is saturated with feeling'. Mood at work can have multiple determinants and the initial contract for supervision may be used to decide the extent to which issues that go beyond direct case work can be explored. Different models of therapy use different language to describe the dynamics of the client–therapist relationship. The notions of transference and counter-transference (Hawkins and Shohet, 2006: 90) are helpful here, as is the idea that feelings will inevitably be evoked by the work, and the task of the therapist is not to deny their existence, but rather to make meaning of them in order most usefully to employ them in the service of the client.

Adoption of this focus does not convey an implicit need for 'support', but rather is a legitimate focus of development in what was referred to by Goffman (1968) as 'people-work'. Supervisees might thus choose agenda items for supervision such as 'How can I use my liking for this client positively in the work?'; 'How can I understand my reluctance to take on the ideas proposed by my social work colleague?'; 'How can I deal with my anxiety about the session getting out of control if I allow people to shout?'; 'Why do I find myself feeling angry with Mr Smith?' Questions may be addressed to the supervisor by the supervisee, for example, 'What strategies do you adopt to help you to cope with the distress that this work generates?'

In workshops described by Bernard (1981) and Scaife and Scaife (1996) supervisors and trainees respectively were found to differ significantly according to preferred focus, although this may vary according to the nature of the work being undertaken. There is also likely to be a relationship between focus and model of therapy and focus and stage of development of the supervisee, the choice of focus changing according to the stage of professional development. Shared knowledge of the framework can facilitate negotiation of focus to optimise use of supervision.

As with the supervisor role, the above categorisation of focus is adopted for convenience and simplicity when studying the supervisory process. During the course of a supervision session, participants typically would move between focuses according to planned or unplanned agendas.

Supervisory medium

The third dimension of the General Supervision Framework categorises the media that provide the data for supervision. As with Role and Focus, the selected medium of supervision is likely to relate to the theoretical model in which the supervised work is being conducted, and to reflect the preferences and experience of the parties involved. The medium of supervision is referred to by Levine and Tilker (1974) as 'stages' and by Pomerantz et al. (1987) as 'modes'. The possible options for the medium of supervision include non-participatory observation, role play, simulated therapy sessions (West, 1984), sitting in with the supervisor, bug-in-the-ear/eye, audio- and video-recordings, verbal reporting, telephone and email communications, and video-conferencing (Wood et al., 2005). Survey findings suggest that retrospective reporting (mode III supervision, Pomerantz *et al.*, 1987) has been the most commonly adopted medium for supervision of preregistration training in the professions of educational and clinical psychology in the UK.

Scott and Spellman (1992) reported that despite British Psychological Society guidelines on training, it was not then uncommon to encounter trainees who, towards the end of their training, had never seen their supervisors working with clients, or to find that trainees had never been observed working themselves. Pomerantz *et al.* (1987) reported that 32 out of 57 trainees claimed that observation of their supervisors' work had taken place in fewer than 10 per cent of supervision sessions, and 41 claimed that their own work had been observed in fewer than 10 per cent of sessions. This contrasts with teaching practice supervision in which the most commonly adopted medium is live classroom observation of the student by the supervisor. It has been argued that the use of reporting back as the medium of supervision implies the ability to practise with relative independence, and is therefore more appropriately employed towards the end of training. Arguments against the use of live methods tend to emphasise a fear of undermining the status of the supervisee in the eyes of the client, the potential negative side effects of raised anxiety levels, or intrusiveness into the relationship between clients and trainees.

LIVE SUPERVISION AND OBSERVATION

There are many possible ways of conducting live supervision in which either the supervisee or supervisor takes the lead in relation to the work being carried out. These methods are explored in greater depth in Chapter 11. In contexts where the technology is available, a one-way viewing screen may be used. Communication between supervisor and supervisee may take place during scheduled breaks, via a 'bug-in-the-ear' device through which the supervisor can speak directly to the supervisee as the work is carried out, by a 'bug-in-the-eye' whereby information is provided to the worker via a computer screen shielded from the client, by telephone, or by use of a 'reflecting team'. A reflecting team involves the supervisory team speaking to each other about their ideas in front of the client and therapist, who choose how or whether to use these ideas in the remainder of the session (Andersen, 1987). Variants are common in family therapy approaches when a supervising team tends to be employed as a matter of course.

Reluctance on the part of supervisees to adopt live supervisory methods may arise from the discomfort of being the subject of another's observations. There may be associated expectations that the focus of supervision will be Actions and Events selected by the supervisor and that the role behaviour adopted by the supervisor will be Inform–Assess. Such expectations may be overcome through prior discussions between the supervisor and supervisee and by working out a method for live supervision with which both parties feel comfortable.

RECORDED SESSIONS

Video- and audio-recordings provide opportunities for 'action replay'. Some data will be lost compared with live supervision (for example, the 'feel' of the session) but these media offer the advantage of multiple review. They may also be perceived as less intrusive than live methods while providing an opportunity for indirect observation. Issues raised by the use of these media include confidentiality of the recorded material, and 'ownership' of the recording during the process of supervision. Technical considerations also apply. Written consent is an ethical requirement when recordings of sessions are made, and efforts to protect the material (for example, using a numerical referencing system) are advisable. These issues are explored in more depth in Chapter 10.

Some methods of supervision, for example, Interpersonal Process Recall (Kagan and Kagan, 1991) and micro-counselling (Ivey, 1974) are based primarily on the use of recordings. Playback may include whole or selected sections of the material, the former being a relatively time-consuming option. Selections may be made by supervisor, supervisee or both participants in the supervisory process. Developments of the use of these media include the option to involve the children, families or professionals with whom the work has been carried out in the review process (Kagan et al., 1963; Open University, 2005; Pelling and Renard, 1999). Recordings can be particularly valuable when the supervision discussion focuses on subtle or rapidly changing processes in a session.

For the supervisee, the use of recordings can offer a different kind of 'realism' compared with verbal accounts of practice. The opportunity to review one's practice on a recording may evoke lines of thought not so readily stimulated by other media.

REPORTING

Reporting is a popular and versatile medium through which supervision is conducted (Pomerantz et al., 1987). In much of the writing about supervision practice, the worker 'presents' material to the supervisor or supervision group and this is usually an account of what they have been doing, thinking and/or feeling. Work may be discussed in advance at the planning stage, and/or retrospectively in debriefing a session already conducted. While this medium may be perceived as less threatening than live or recorded supervision, information may be lost or forgotten, or not raised because it is considered to be too sensitive. The supervisor's awareness is constrained by the narrative offered by the supervisee (Pelling and Renard, 1999). It has been argued that supervisees in a training context find it easier to focus on the problems of the client rather than on their own experiences, interventions and responses when this medium is used (Levine and Tilker, 1974).

Reliance on reporting carries an implied respect for the judgements of the supervisee. One approach that the supervisor might usefully take is to encourage supervisees to examine and question their judgements, perhaps so as to locate them in a theoretical framework or in a practice model.

ENACTMENT

Role play, role reversal, simulated interviews and behaviour rehearsal may be used during supervision in order to pose a variety of hypothetical problems, to demonstrate and practise skills and techniques, and to explore difficulties arising in the work. This medium also includes an option for interviewing the 'internalised other' in which supervisees are asked questions in the first person as the 'other' with whom the work is being conducted (Burnham, 2000; Epston, 1993) (see Chapter 12, this volume, for a fuller description). Enactment can be a powerful aid to learning and offers the opportunity for reflection and exploration of relationships and for practice in a situation which is relatively safe for both worker and client (Yardley-Matwiejczuk, 1997). It can provide the experiences, and the opportunity to reflect on those experiences, that help to change attitudes or behaviour. It can enable supervisees to put themselves in hypothetical situations they have never previously experienced with the possibility of learning better to understand other people's motivations (Bell, 2001).

It has been argued that when using enactment, the supervisor should initially take the role of therapist in order to demonstrate protocol and procedures, and in order to provide the supervisee with the experience of being 'on the other side of the desk' (Levine and Tilker, 1974). Whether or not this is an appropriate starting point will depend on the nature of the supervisory relationship. Experienced therapists in supervision are less likely to require the supervisor to do this. Agreement can be reached as to whether the supervisee takes the role of client, the role of therapist trying out a range of different approaches, or of another 'player' in the client's problem system. Groups have also been regarded as useful settings in which supervisees can request another group member to adopt the role of a client whom they are finding problematic. It has been proposed that such simulations are helpful vehicles for identifying counter-transference issues (Altfeld, 1999).

TELEPHONE AND EMAIL COMMUNICATIONS AND
VIDEO-CONFERENCING

Increasingly, with developments in technology, opportunities have been taken to exploit media that allow supervision at a distance. This is at a premium in rural areas of sparse population where supervision may not be easy to come by. It has been questioned (Robson and Robson, 1998) whether email, for example, is adequate for building the kinds of relationships that support effective supervision. Fewer cues are available for the participants to make sense of the communication between them. In contrast, some emailers have reported that the lack of such cues has enabled the development of deeper relationships without the distractions of face-to-face communication (Goss, 2000).

Supervision by video-link has become a possibility (Gammon *et al.*, 1998). All participants in their study of video-conferencing supervision would recommend it as an acceptable supplement in psychotherapy supervision provided that this method is built on an already established relationship.

These media have been used to enable immediate access to supervision following a difficult session, have widened access to supervision, and can minimise the potential for prejudicial assumptions based on physical appearance. Supervision using the telephone was a topic at a round table discussion during the 2005 spring meeting of the psychoanalysis division of the American Psychological Association (Manosevitz, 2006), the conclusion of which was that it must be seriously considered as a useful adjunctive method in training programmes.

Positive effects might be anticipated from gaining experience with a range of supervisory media. While different professions historically have tended to adopt their own preferred media as the norm for supervision, these assumptions may be questioned, and constitute an appropriate issue for discussion in the negotiation of the supervisory relationship.

The General Supervision Framework may helpfully be used during the contracting process as a structure to aid the identification of supervisor and supervisee preferences regarding the three dimensions of focus, role relationship and medium. While the majority of practitioners tend to prefer flexibility of focus and role relationship, individuals often lean towards a preferred specific medium. Should a relatively fixed pattern of role relationship and focus tend to develop, the framework may be used in a review process with the aim of encouraging greater experimentation along each dimension.

A process model of supervision (Hawkins and Shohet, 1989, 2006)

Hawkins and Shohet's model is embedded within a philosophy emphasising the importance for clinicians of a support system at work which holds them when they are facing the negative feelings of clients and are feeling inadequate in relation to the tasks they have set themselves. To this end they emphasise the importance of supervising networks which involve the individual, team, department and wider organisation, and they advocate the need for supervision at all levels. They take the view that 'helping organisations' by their nature import distress, disturbance, fragmentation and need, and that in consequence the importance of containment cannot be overestimated.

Where this containment is not provided, workers who are stressed incline to take this out on colleagues with the potential for arguments and team splits, irritability and high rates of sickness absence. They argue that the culture of the organisation can have a significant impact on the likelihood of such developments occurring, and in particular advocate a 'learning culture' in which staff development and supervision are valued.

Hawkins and Shohet's model of supervision is addressed specifically to supervisory focus concerning the processes taking place in the relationships of the participants in therapy and supervision. It includes within its compass the quartet of the client, the supervisor, the supervisee and the work context. It uses the notions of transference and parallel process to aid the understanding of these interactional patterns, and the authors suggest that the supervisor needs to pay attention to seven interlocking focuses. They refer to this as 'seven-eyed supervision'.

Mode 1 Focus on session content

In this mode, the focus of the supervision is on the client – what was said, how the client came to seek help, how the client looked, her or his gestures, use of language and metaphor. This focus encourages the therapist to attend to the

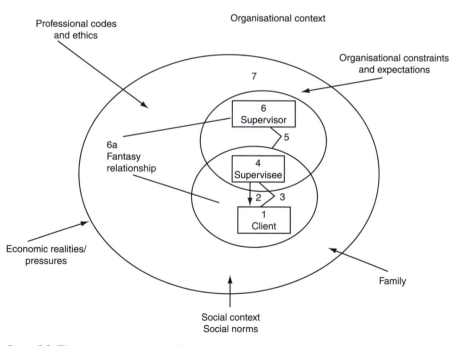

Figure 5.2 The seven-eyed model of supervision.

Source: Hawkins and Shohet (2006: 82). Supervision in the Helping Professions. Reproduced with the kind permission of the Open University Press Publishing Company.

unique human qualities of each client and to stay open to the different options for making meaning of what the client brings to the session. This may be particularly helpful for supervisees early on in training when anxiety may lead them to feel uncomfortable with uncertainty. To minimise this discomfort they may move too hastily to reach a formulation or explanation for the presenting problems, thus 'objectifying' (Shainberg, 1983) the client and neglecting the unique characteristics of each individual. Content has face validity as appropriate material for supervision, and may be experienced as safer than more self-focused material.

When focusing on content, the supervision may be used to make links with other content either from previous sessions or from different points in a single session, with a view to identifying patterns or gaining a deeper understanding. Content may usefully include events outside of the sessions themselves, such as the pattern of keeping, rearranging or failing appointments; between-session contacts initiated by the client; or what happened in the waiting room. The spotlight is on the client and relationships external to the therapy itself.

Mode 2 Focus on the therapist's strategies and interventions

This focus includes both the actions and the thoughts of the supervisee, including the choices made in the session and the consideration of other alternatives. It can be pitched at the level of technique and can help supervisees to become more aware of their own actions and thoughts in sessions. Hawkins and Shohet caution against the supervisor making too many suggestions for intervention in case this acts as a brake on the supervisee's own creativity. The ideal balance between making and eliciting suggestions is likely to differ according to the level of qualification and experience of the supervisee and is a matter for negotiation. It is often much easier to think of alternatives during supervision without the pressing presence of the client.

Mode 3 Focus on the process and relationship between client and therapist

Here the focus is on the transaction between therapist and client. This includes the patterns that develop; for instance, of the therapist making a suggestion and the client stating that this has already been tried, of the client becoming tearful and the therapist becoming silent, of the therapist asking about feelings and the client responding with information and facts, and so on.

The supervisor helps the supervisee to 'stand outside' the relationship with the client, taking an observer perspective on the interplay between the two. Hawkins and Shohet suggest a number of approaches that the supervisor might take in order to help the supervisee to find this view. These include creating an image or metaphor to represent the relationship, imagining how the relationship would develop were the client and therapist to be cast away on a desert island, and telling the story of the history of the relationship with the client, beginning with the referral.

Supervision with this focus also explores the client's transference – the patterns brought by the client to this relationship that have been learned in earlier interactions with others. This might include how clients seem to invite the therapist to punish them, to take care of them, to flirt with them, to reject them or to fight with them. Supervision can be particularly helpful in encouraging supervisees to use their feelings as information that tells them about the client and how best to proceed.

Mode 4 Focus on the internal experience of the therapist

Mode 4 addresses the internal experience of the therapist which is seen as resulting from the reciprocal influences of the client and therapist on each other. In this mode the supervisor attends to the therapist's counter-transference – the therapist's reactions to the client that are taking place predominantly out of conscious awareness. Hawkins and Shohet identify five different types of counter-transference:

- Feelings stirred up in the therapist which have their origin in the therapist's previous relationships.
- Feelings that arise from the therapist playing out the reciprocal role to the client's transference.
- The therapist's feelings, thoughts and actions that are used to counter the transference of the client.
- Projected material of the client that the therapist has taken in.
- 'Aim attachment' counter-transference whereby therapists desire that clients change for the benefit of the therapist rather than for themselves; a perspective fuelled by the service's demands for results.

Counter-transference is regarded as a response to the client that is primarily out of conscious awareness. The task of the supervisor is to help bring this material into awareness in order that it may be used constructively rather than impede the work. The supervisor attends to the gestures, images and metaphors shown by supervisees and tries to elucidate the supervisees' values and beliefs as evidenced by their choice of vocabulary, such as the adjectives they use in referring to their client. The following extract (where *Robin* is the supervisor and *John* is the supervisee) is used in illustration by Hawkins and Shohet.

Robin: Why are you allowing this staff member to drift and not confronting him?

John:	Well I do not want to be a punitive boss.

John: Well I do not want to be a punitive boss.
Robin: What would that be like?
John: As you asked that, I got the image of a little boy outside a head-master's office.
Robin: So there is a link for you between confronting and being a punitive head teacher. If you were this staff member's head teacher, how would you want to punish him and what would you be punishing him for?

(Hawkins and Shohet, 2006: 92)

The supervision would then go on to explore whether the therapist could challenge the staff member but in ways that would be less affected by punitive associations.

At times, the feelings evoked in the therapist towards the client can be almost overwhelming. A clue to some counter-transference reactions is to experience feelings towards the specific client that differ from one's typical feelings towards clients. Without supervision, these feelings can lead the therapist in dangerous directions. Bringing them to awareness offers the opportunity to use them in the service of the work.

Mode 5 Focusing on the here-and-now process between supervisor and supervisee

In modes 5 and 6 the supervisor moves away from focusing on the client and the therapist to focusing on herself or himself. In mode 5 the focus is on what is happening between the therapist and supervisor, on supervisors noticing their own reactions to the supervisee, reflecting on them and developing understanding to inform the supervision. The mechanism by which the difficulties in the therapy relationship present themselves in a similar fashion in the supervisory relationship is known as the parallel process (Searles, 1965). In a fairly straightforward example, the supervision can feel flat and hopeless when the therapy is with a profoundly depressed client.

The notion of parallel process was extended by the research of Doehrman (1976) who studied 12 cases in depth. She concluded that paralleling occurred in every client/therapist/supervisor relationship she studied and that it could occur in either direction. In other words, aspects of the relationship between the supervisor and supervisee could also be replayed in the client–therapist relationship. More recent research by a number of authors has supported the notion of parallel process (McNeill and Worthen, 1989; Miller, 2004; Morrisey and Tribe, 2001; Raichelson *et al.*, 1997; Williams, 1997) although some authors remain sceptical (Miller and Twomey, 1999; Mothersole, 1999).

Mode 6 Focusing on the internal experience of the supervisor

This focus is on the 'disruptions' that are experienced out of the blue by the supervisor during supervision. This might be experiencing a sense of boredom when a particular client is being discussed, seeing spontaneous images at a particular moment in a discussion, or suddenly feeling anxious or upset. This occurs in the context of the supervisor's knowledge of what he or she typically experiences in the presence of a particular supervisee.

Supervisors might use the concept of 'immediacy' (Egan, 1994, 2002) to employ these experiences usefully in the work. Using this technique, supervisors state what they are experiencing and wonder what this might mean, as in the following example:

> I am getting very sleepy as you 'go on' about this client. Often when that happens to me it seems to indicate that some feeling is being shut off either to do with the therapy or right here in the supervision. Perhaps you can check what you might be holding back from saying?
>
> (Hawkins and Shohet, 2006: 96)

Within this mode the focus might also be on the fantasy relationship between the supervisor and client. Some clients appear to direct much attention to the unknown supervisor and supervisors may incline to visions of their supervisees' clients. The speculations of the supervisor about the client are viewed as providing potentially useful material, particularly where these are at odds with the reported experience of the supervisee.

Mode 7 Focusing on the wider contexts in which the work takes place

Therapeutic work is embedded in a range of contexts and systems which influence the supervisory process. These include the contexts of clients and the question of why they have presented at this time and place; the worker's profession and employment arrangements; the role relationship of supervisor and supervisee; and the supervisor's own personal characteristics, orientation and style. Issues such as the meaning of therapy and supervision to the participants, often implicit, are appropriately addressed within mode 7. Hawkins and Shohet liken this to moving the focus of supervision from figure to ground.

They take the view that good supervision of in-depth work with clients should involve all seven focuses at some point in the work. They also suggest that the selection of focus should be linked to the learning needs of the supervisee. In my view, the complexity and challenge of using the seven modes increases from mode 1 to mode 7. A focus on the client seems much safer than on the relationship between the therapist and supervisor. In learning how to use modes 3 to 7 supervisors might benefit from role rehearsal or exploration in their own supervision. Hawkins and Shohet's model serves usefully to highlight the range of choices and complexities of the client/ therapist/supervisor triad of relationships.

This model encourages the supervisor to keep in mind what is happening in the relationships between supervisor, therapist and client. It requires the skill of participant observation in which supervisors are attentive to their own emotional responses and spontaneous thoughts during supervision, reflecting on these with regard to their meaning for the therapy. Hawkins and Shohet give examples of how to raise these matters with the supervisee.

A contemporary psychodynamic approach (Frawley-O'Dea and Sarnat, 2001)

Frawley-O'Dea and Sarnat present a contemporary psychodynamic perspective on supervision which emphasises the importance of relationships and the embeddedness of supervision within a work context. They cite Greenberg (1996: 201) who asserted that it is the lived experience of the therapeutic relationship that accounts for the effect. They advocate congruence in the processes of supervision and therapy, proposing that the supervisory medium needs to convey the supervisory message.

The relational model of supervision presented by Frawley-O'Dea and Sarnat has its roots in the development of a relational school of psycho-analytic theory, based on attachment theory. The human infant is viewed as genetically programmed to form social relationships with care-givers with a propensity for this experience to influence the development of further relationships throughout life.

> It is a central premise of relational theory that analyst and patient inter-penetrate each other's subjectivities from the beginning and, over the course of treatment, create and re-create one another and themselves in ever more accessible and delineated forms.
>
> (Frawley-O'Dea and Sarnat, 2001: 54)

These authors analyse models of supervision along three dimensions: the nature of the supervisor's authority, the supervisory focus, and the supervisor's primary mode of participation.

The nature of the supervisor's authority

Traditional models of psychoanalysis emphasised the power and authority of the supervisor who acted as the ultimate authority on the supervisee's clients. Freud's training model portrayed the senior analyst as the trans-mitter of knowledge to the supervisee. The training paradigm was primarily didactic which was reflected in the Berlin School's subsequent separation of supervision from personal analysis. Frawley-O'Dea and Sarnat reject this tradition in favour of an emphasis on mutuality, on shared and authorised power, rather than imposed authority. They present a case for the construction rather than the discovery of knowledge.

In the relational model of supervision the supervisor's authority derives from the process that unfolds in the supervisory relationship and relies on the ongoing authorisation of the supervisee rather than on the supervisor's qualifications and experience. The supervisor cannot be regarded as an authority on the supervisee, the client or the specific work being supervised. Within this conceptualisation of supervision, the supervisor is more likely to divulge personal information than would a therapist to a patient. Boundaries are held with a degree of flexibility in that supervisor and supervisee may socialise at professional functions and become friends, especially after the termination of the supervisory relationship.

Frawley-O'Dea and Sarnat do not deny the asymmetry of the supervisory relationship and the role of the supervisor as gatekeeper. They argue that supervisors must uphold the core beliefs, values and standards of the profession while acknowledging that these are in perpetual flux. The supervisor is responsible for:

- Defining and managing boundaries.
- Sustaining the focus on the task.
- Sustaining an analytic attitude.
- Assessing supervisee needs and adjusting the approach to supervision to meet them.
- Maintaining their own values and beliefs while accepting that it may not be possible to resolve some disagreements.
- Acknowledging their own power as evaluators/gatekeepers.

Relevant focus of supervision

In traditional models of psychoanalysis, the supervisory relationship is typically excluded as a possible focus of attention. From the viewpoint of Frawley-O'Dea and Sarnat, consideration may legitimately be given to the patient's dynamics; the supervisee's counter-transference, anxieties and self-esteem; supervisees' conscious and unconscious expressions of their experiences of the patient, self and supervisor; and the supervisory relationship itself. The latter might include transference and counter-transference within the supervisory relationship, relational enactments in the supervisory relationship that arise from the influence of the supervisee's personal analysis, parallels from the supervised treatment, and enactments arising from the supervisor's or supervisee's relationships within the organisation. The authors include in this the reputations that the participants bring to the relationship at the outset, arguing that neither party brings a blank slate but rather sets of expectations based on prior knowledge.

The relational model accepts as inevitable and welcomes regressive experiences in both supervisee and supervisor. For example, a supervisor may experience a desire to laugh and identify this as evoked anxiety about the material being presented. If the supervisor is prepared to make this link explicit to the supervisee, this models the appropriateness of such material as a focus of discussion. The material can then be analysed and contained rather than split off and hidden.

Primary mode of participation

In the relational model, supervision is considered to be an analytic endeavour in itself (Rock, 1997). Mutuality and an ongoing process of negotiation are emphasised. Disagreement is seen as permissible and useful since it expands the range of potential meanings and narratives, so long as it does not lead to supervisory impasse. This is prevented through mutual discussion of each party's experience of the other, in addition to a focus on information emanating from the patient. What are generally regarded as 'undesirable' reactions, such as feelings of guilt and embarrassment, are used as information about what is taking place. Traditionally, these intense affective responses were regarded as signalling a process of regression to which supervisors were not expected to fall prey.

A mode of participation which involves mutuality and negotiation demystifies the idealised and omnipotent supervisor. Mutuality is defeated if the supervisor presents self-disclosures as the 'truth' rather than as material for further discussion. Frawley-O'Dea and Sarnat also argue against the rigid delimitation of teaching (supervision) and personal growth (therapy), stating that this is neither attainable nor desirable, particularly where there is a central emphasis on transference and counter-transference. They take the view that it is not possible to make a clear distinction between professional development and personal growth; thus 'treating is indentured to teaching'. The supervisee may be empowered to limit the extent to which the supervision focuses on personal material, although those with less experience may need the supervisor to monitor the extent to which interventions are being experienced as overly intrusive.

Frawley-O'Dea gives an example of how the supervisor's behaviour, thoughts and feelings might become a supervisory focus. She describes having offered a student a highly sensitive microphone that she herself had used as a postdoctoral student. Over the course of the subsequent week she recognised that the gesture might have represented the shedding of her own student status; handing on the baton. It may also have served as a reminder of the hierarchical nature of the supervisory relationship. She brought this insight to supervision, presenting it as a possible enactment of self-celebration on the part of the supervisor. The discussion around the loaning of the microphone was regarded as having opened up the possibility of this type of material being a permissible focus of supervision, signalling for the future that issues in the supervisory relationship were not outside the box.

This model of supervision places the relationship at the centre, challenging some of the central tenets of traditional approaches to supervision of psychoanalysis. No longer is the supervisor the arbiter of truth, the analyst a neutral interpreter of the client's material beyond falling prey to regressive processes. The relational model is based on a constructivist paradigm which acknowledges the impact of each party in the client/therapist/supervisor triad on the others.

Cyclical model of supervision (Page and Wosket, 1994, 2001)

Page and Wosket's model is addressed primarily to the structure of supervision sessions. It identifies a number of stages through which each supervision session proceeds. It outlines options for what to do in supervision and may be used to help the supervision stay on track, ensuring that there is movement towards the agreed goals. The supervision process is presented as a cycle of five stages proceeding from contract to focus, space, bridge and review.

Contract

The contracting stage has commonalities with the process described in Chapter 4, and is influenced by the view of Page and Wosket (1994) and of Horton (1993) that there is little place in supervision for the student–teacher aspects of training where the supervisee is viewed as a 'recipient' of the acquired wisdom and knowledge of the more experienced supervisor. The task of the supervisor is to help supervisees to enhance and fully utilise their own knowledge, skills and attributes, bringing them to bear on work with particular clients. The factors that the authors list as topics to be addressed in the first step of the contracting stage are duration; timing; frequency; fees; codes of ethics and practice; and dealing with cancellation. Step two comprises boundaries between supervision, training and therapy; confidentiality; and role boundaries. Step three deals with accountability, step four with expectations, and step five with the nature of the supervisory relationship. A 'mini' version of contracting may take place at the start of each supervision session. The authors take the view argued by Hewson (1999) that effective contracts serve to minimise hidden agendas and create mutuality that guards against the abuse of power in supervision.

In the contracting stage, Page and Wosket explore the issue of duration of the supervisory arrangement and suggest that after qualification counsellors often choose to stay with the same supervisor for several years when a change might have proven more stimulating or challenging to their work. They also report some supervisees having stayed with an incompatible supervisor because they lacked the assertiveness to terminate the relationship. They

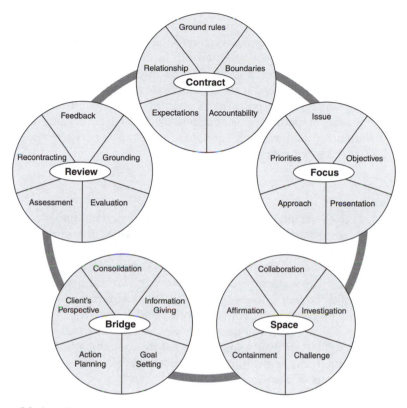

Figure 5.3 A cyclical model of supervision.

Source: Page, S. and Wosket, V. (2001: 36). Supervising the counsellor. (2nd edition) Figure 3.1 overview of the supervision model, Taylor and Francis Books (UK).

suggest that two years allows sufficient time to develop a trusting relationship without becoming stale, and that a longer duration might suit experienced practitioners who have learned better to self-challenge.

Page and Wosket consider the issue of the timing of supervision sessions, wisely counselling that it is the responsibility of both supervisor and supervisee to ensure that they are mentally as fully present as possible for the supervision work. This guards against the phenomenon of 'presenteeism' (Proctor and Ditton, 1989: 3) where physical attendance masks a lack of full engagement with the task in progress. Supervision sessions scheduled at the end of the day or crammed into lunch hours are unlikely to allow for unhurried, well-prepared and creative interchanges.

Discussions based on expectations, the beliefs and desires of the participants are viewed as crucial to the development and maintenance of an enabling and supportive relationship. It is recommended that the supervisor spend time eliciting the supervisee's anticipations, preferences, learning styles and learning history as an aid to planning the supervisory experience (Webb, 1983).

In the contracting stage homage is paid to the research findings concerning the primacy of the supervisory relationship in the success of the enterprise. The forging of the relationship is not seen as an end in itself but rather as a foundation on which successful supervision may be built. Page and Woskett advocate that supervisors express their hopes for a relationship characterised by trust, respect, empathy and genuineness at the outset, arguing that this conveys humanity and warmth, and reassures the supervisee about the intentions of the supervisor.

Focus

The next stage of the model, the focus, refers to the material under consideration in a supervision session, and is the point at which the work of supervision begins. The purpose of the focusing stage is the identification of issues, prioritising where necessary, and clarification of the objectives for the session. Sometimes these can be identified through straightforward questioning such as, 'What would you like to focus on today?'; 'What would you like to happen as a result of us having this conversation?', and 'How would you like to approach this – shall I ask you questions, would you like to take the role of one of the characters or would you like to tell me something first?' Page and Wosket liken the focus to the 'figure' standing out from the 'ground' of the supervisee's therapeutic work.

It is argued that wherever possible the supervisee should take a major role in identifying the issue/s for supervision and generally begin a session by bringing an issue. Advance preparation is usually helpful, while it may be agreed that the supervisee will come to some sessions relatively unprepared. In this case supervision typically begins with identification of the supervisory focus as in the following extract from Page and Wosket (2001), in which a supervisee has chosen to experiment with a different approach to supervision, having experienced the power of free association in getting to the heart of issues.

Counsellor: We agreed at the last session that I would not prepare this time. That feels a bit scary. So all I've done is just look briefly through my file and it feels quite strange. In a way I'm sitting here, not terribly sure what to do, because I'm used to being very well prepared. I feel quite anxious now . . .

Supervisor: . . . and a bit, sort of, adrift from it?

Counsellor: Yes, because we agreed that I would do that and that we would work psychodynamically, and yet I've never done that before and so I'm thinking 'What am I supposed to be doing?' So I may need some help.

Supervisor: OK, perhaps I can give us a hand in getting started.
Counsellor: Please.
Supervisor: You said all that you did was look through your file. Did anything come up when you did that – about any of the people you're working with? Or now, when you think about going through your file, does anything come to mind?
Counsellor: I think what comes to mind is – how many people I'm seeing and the messiness of it. That's how it feels now, quite messy. And I think that's reflected in – you said 'adrift' before – and I think I feel a bit adrift in my counselling. Not in the actual process, but how I'm handling the overall counselling – the beginnings and endings – the whole series of counselling sessions.

(Page and Wosket, 2001: 75)

The authors suggest that the supervisee did have a clear issue which the supervisor helped to bring into focus early on in the session. While typically priority is given within this model to the issues identified by supervisees, it is regarded as legitimate for supervisors to introduce foci, and at times as incumbent upon them, particularly where issues of client welfare become pressing.

The effects of stress and variable levels of motivation towards the work are regarded as a legitimate focus for supervision. Doubts and uncertainties about effectiveness and the capability to create the conditions in which people can solve their problems are common. In developmental models of supervision such uncertainties are seen as a normal and passing phase of development. It has been argued that these doubts and anxieties can go to the core of the professional self (Eckler-Hart, 1987). If the quality of the supervisory relationship allows, and the supervisee's doubts are accepted by the supervisor, the risk of the work being undermined by them is lessened. If not, the practitioner may attempt to overcompensate for feelings of 'fraudulence' by trying too hard. Noticing that we are trying too hard with a client is often a good trigger for taking the work to supervision.

Page and Wosket argue that necessarily, supervision often tends to focus on stuckness and difficulties being experienced by the supervisee. They counsel that an exclusive focus on stuckness would preclude acknowledgement and celebration of successes. They suggest that it is pertinent from time to time to ask questions such as, 'And what are you doing well with this person?' The effect can be confidence generating, enabling the supervisee to 'return to the fray'. Such interventions can also model for supervisees ways of challenging the strengths and resources of their clients.

The second step in the focus stage is that of objective setting. Dependent on the degree and type of previous experience of the supervisee he or she is more or less likely to have objectives in mind at the beginning of the supervision session. The measure of clarity about objectives can also be influenced by the supervisee's emotional state generally or in relation to a particular client. As an example, objectives might encompass a number of different goals such as updating the supervisor on work in progress following on from a previous session, presentation and review of a new client, and exploration of an issue related to work context. The objectives step includes agenda setting and identification of potential end-points for pieces of work.

Supervisors may also have objectives for the session which are similar to or different from those of the supervisee and these will need to be negotiated. Managing the time to meet the supervisee's objectives will be one of these, as might be a wish to challenge supervisees to stretch their skills in a particular domain.

The next step in the focusing stage is the supervisee's presentation of the issue. Most typically, presentations are verbal, although they can include recordings or pictorial representations. Page and Wosket advise that supervisees prepare their presentation by already having asked themselves questions such as, 'What is my particular difficulty or problem in working with this client?'; 'If I could risk telling my supervisor what really concerns me in my work, what would that be?'; 'What do I need to tell or off-load to my supervisor so that I can work more freely with this client?' This can prevent supervisees from introducing important issues 'just remembered' towards the end of a session when insufficient time remains.

Space

Emphasised in this stage of the model is the fundamental requirement for successful supervision: the establishment and maintenance of an effective relationship. Page and Wosket emphasise the powerful nature of affect, the complexity of the supervisory dynamics and their potential for both creative and destructive effects. Taking place in this phase is a process of collaborative exploration in which the supervisor may provide containment, affirmation of the supervisee's views and actions, or may challenge the approach to the work. This exploratory space is regarded as the heart of the supervision process in which new ideas and understandings can develop. In the context of a collaborative relationship the supervisor can both participate in the discussion taking place and simultaneously notice her or his own reactions to the supervisee and to the material being presented. These reactions can then also be explored in what Page and Wosket deem the 'reflective alliance'. At this point in the supervision the aim is the generation of ideas rather than answers. The process of finding answers or ways forward in the work is addressed in the next stage of the model – the bridge.

The bridge

The purpose of the next stage, the bridge, is to link the thinking undertaken in the space stage to proposed action. This can involve giving information, consolidating some of the ideas that emerged in the 'space', deriving action plans and goals, and working out how the client might respond to the proposals. Awareness of this stage helps to keep the supervision goal oriented and grounds the ideas considered in action. The supervisor might facilitate theory–practice links by providing a reference to a journal article or book, by describing and discussing some aspect of theory with the supervisee, by sharing experiences, or by introducing a new idea or technique. It may involve self-disclosure, and a sharing of struggles in common. On the other hand the task may be to help supervisees to summarise their own emergent ideas and to explore the implications for action.

In my view, the process of sifting through ideas that emerged in the supervisory space sometimes occurs alongside the exploration itself. Some ideas seem more immediately attractive although it is useful to have a process for the retention of others that may later prove their worth. Page and Wosket suggest that some identifiable form of bridging process is desirable so that clients do not experience a discontinuity in the work following a change of emphasis brought about through supervision. They state that it is not always necessary for each of the following five steps of the bridging process to be undertaken.

The bridge stage involves a process of consolidation which can be stimulated by questions such as 'What would you like to have in mind from this discussion when you next see your client?' or 'I wonder what you want to do with what we have been discussing?' If the exploration has been particularly emotional, this step needs to be taken in time to allow the dissipation of feelings before the end of the supervision session. The process of consolidation is described as one in which insights, hypotheses and new understandings are gathered up. The process might stop at this point with the new material noted and the supervisee left with the task of deciding how to apply what has been explored. It is suggested that with beginning practitioners the supervisor take a more active role in sifting through the material and deciding with the supervisee which ideas to develop further at this point.

The bridge phase also involves goal setting: therapeutic goals for work with the client, learning goals for supervisees, and goals specifically for the supervision process itself. Therapy is conducted to different time-scales according to a number of factors such as the therapeutic model, the constraints of the service, and the preferences and needs of clients and therapists. Page and Wosket point out that time-scales can be influenced by the economic climate and that practitioners in recent years have often been required to work in a time-limited fashion. Under such conditions it may be more important for practitioners to leave supervision with a clear idea of attainable therapeutic goals and strategies for moving towards them.

The fourth step of the bridge phase is action planning. Page and Wosket advise that although the supervision may serve to develop a plan related to therapeutic goals, rigid application of the plan may be of disservice to the client, and may lead to the work being carried out in an inflexible and mechanistic way. The best-laid plans still need to be responsive to the client's needs. It is probably useful to review the extent to which the work deviates from action plans. It would be reasonable to expect that at least some plans might follow the anticipated route.

The final step of the bridge stage is that of the client's perspective in which the potential effect upon the client of the planned strategy is explored. This empathic process has been termed 'trial identification' (Casement, 1985: 35). Page and Wosket suggest that the supervisee face an empty chair in which the imaginary client might be sitting. The counsellor or therapist then runs through the proposed action, afterwards changing chairs and trying to imagine the impact from the client's perspective. Strategies can then be reviewed in the light of any new awareness that this brings.

Review

The final stage within the model is that of review. Mutual feedback (step one) is encouraged in order to keep in mind how the supervision is proceeding in relation to what was agreed in the supervisory contract, and how the supervision relates to the intended beneficiary – ultimately the client. Page and Wosket, following Gilbert and Sills (1999: 181), caution that 'most people have emerged from such a shame-based educational process that any feedback which is in any way critical seems to "devastate" the person'. It is incumbent on supervisors to develop their thinking and skills in this domain, not least because they may have experienced little in the way of a good model during their own education.

The second step of the review stage is grounding. It is described as a process of disengagement from the exploratory and planning work undertaken in the previous two stages and involves winding down before looking back over the session that is coming to a close. Attention is shifted from the supervision work itself to the appraisal of the supervision. The parties to supervision might ask themselves whether a suitable stopping point has been reached; habitual occurrences or a change of pattern in the supervisory process might be noted. Comment might be made on the outcome of the supervision. Following this is the step of evaluation with a focus on mutual evaluation of the cooperative enterprise, rather than assessment of the supervisee which occurs in the following step.

The fourth step of the review stage is that of assessment. There is no dodging the supervisor's role as assessor, most clearly when the supervisee is in training. There is a professional mandate for the supervisor to take this role and fudging the subject can undermine the supervision process. Bernard and Goodyear (1992: 105) pointed out that 'formative evaluation does not feel like evaluation because it stresses process and progress, not outcome'. The purpose of formative assessment is to foster the development of the supervisee. It can be undertaken in collaborative ways through dialogue, judicious questioning and the encouragement of self-assessment.

The final step in the review stage is that of recontracting, when supervisor and supervisee revisit their original contact and make amendments and renewals. Since supervision is a dynamic process it has to take account of changes in the development of the parties to it and of their changing needs. Recontracting can take place at scheduled intervals or as and when either party requires. It need not be unduly formal but ensures that the parties to supervision are continually making readjustments to the agreement in response to events.

Page and Wosket's framework offers a system of five stages, each of which is divided into five steps. As with all models and frameworks, it is not intended that supervision inevitably proceed in an orderly and structured way, each stage following seamlessly from the one before. The structure is something to be kept in mind to help the process remain useful and to effect its identified aims and purposes.

A systems approach (SAS) (Holloway, 1995)

Holloway argued that seven dimensions of supervision have arisen from the empirical, conceptual and practice knowledge bases of supervision. The supervisory relationship is seen as the central core and is represented dia-grammatically in this way with the six other dimensions of the model radiating out as wings. Four of these are contextual factors: those of the institution, the supervisor, the supervisee and the client, with the fifth and sixth dimensions being the functions and the tasks of supervision.

Identifying tasks and functions in practice

Holloway asserted that teaching the body of professional knowledge is a task of supervision. This body of knowledge includes counselling skills, case con-ceptualisation, professional role, emotional awareness and self-evaluation. She suggested that the supervisor make choices in response to the supervisee's presentation, for example, by focusing on a teaching or intervention strategy rather than on the supervisee's emotional response. The supervisee's emo-tional response may be acknowledged, or on a different occasion become a focus of supervision. It is argued that through supervision, learners need to develop case conceptualisations that link with theory, while remaining con-gruent with the supervisee's beliefs about human development and change. Within the supervisory relationship the supervisee learns professional behav-iours in context and develops awareness of interpersonal style. Both inter- and

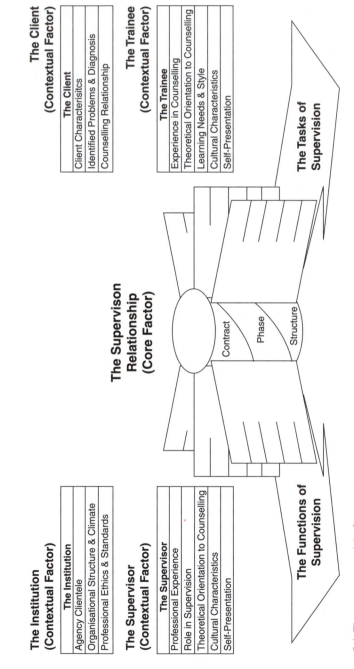

The Institution
(Contextual Factor)

The Institution

Agency Clientele

Organisational Structure & Climate

Professional Ethics & Standards

The Supervisor
(Contextual Factor)

The Supervisor

Professional Experience

Role in Supervision

Theoretical Orientation to Counselling

Cultural Characteristics

Self-Presentation

The Client
(Contextual Factor)

The Client

Client Characterisitcs

Identified Problems & Diagnosis

Counselling Relationship

The Trainee
(Contextual Factor)

The Trainee

Experience in Counselling

Theoretical Orientation to Counselling

Learning Needs & Style

Cultural Characteristics

Self-Presentation

The Supervison Relationship (Core Factor)

Contract

Phase

Structure

The Tasks of Supervision

The Functions of Supervision

Figure 5.4 The systems model of supervision.

Source: Holloway (1995: 58–59)

intrapersonal awareness are considered to be crucial skills in conducting the counselling task. The supervisor may draw the supervisee's attention to an emotional reaction to a client or a response to something stated in supervision which could be indicative of parallel process. The supervisor constantly models the skill of self-evaluation and can prompt supervisees to take a self-reflective stance rather than offering the supervisor's judgement of performance.

Holloway named the five primary functions of supervision as monitoring and evaluating, instructing and advising, modelling, consulting and supporting, and sharing. In training supervision the supervisor conducts both formative and summative assessment. In the SAS model this function is restricted to assessment of the supervisee's behaviour as it relates to professional role. When exercising this function, the communication is often one-way from the supervisor to the supervisee, and the hierarchical nature of the relationship is emphasised.

In the SAS model the tasks and functions of supervision are portrayed in a 5×5 matrix. Hypothetically the supervision may link any of the teaching objectives with any of the functions or supervision strategies. In practice, some links are regarded as more feasible than others. For example, a supervisor is more likely to adopt a supportive stance when the focus of the supervision is on emotional awareness.

The supervisory relationship

The supervisory relationship in the SAS model is regarded as the container of the supervision process. Based on the work of Miller (1976), Mueller and Kell (1972) and Rabinowitz *et al.* (1986), Holloway argued that supervisory relationships progress through the stages of beginning, maturity and termination. She draws on the social-psychological literature indicating that as a relationship evolves, the participants rely less on general cultural and social information and more on personal knowledge of the other. In this process uncertainty reduces and people are able to make increasingly accurate predictions about the other person's reactions to their messages. This is likely to reduce the potential for conflict while there is a concomitant rise in the experience of vulnerability brought about by increased self-disclosure.

At the outset the supervisee is likely to value a relationship in which the balance is loaded towards support rather than challenge in the context of uncertainty about reasonable role expectations. Once the relationship has moved towards greater maturity, the specific learning needs of the supervisee and the idiosyncrasies of the parties to the relationship are more likely to be accommodated. Holloway discusses the power dynamic, which traditionally has been viewed as a vehicle of control and dominance. It is argued that power may be regarded as determined by both participants in the relationship and is a feature of the relationship rather than residing with one or other individual. This view is supported by Llewelyn and colleagues (2007), who regard the trainer–trainee relationship as nested within a complex weave of interrelationships in a training community and, while the power may appear to reside with the staff, the picture is more complex.

Contextual factors of supervision

The SAS model incorporates contextual factors associated with the supervisor, supervisee, the client and the institution in which the work takes place. Factors such as amount of experience, theoretical orientation, values and beliefs, individual differences along lines of ethnicity, gender, age and so on are regarded as influencing the transactions taking place in the supervisory matrix. For each of Holloway's dimensions, the interplay of factors is demonstrated through a series of transcripts of supervision sessions annotated by the supervisor, supervisee and the author herself.

Organisational norms and politics are regarded as impacting on the supervisory relationship and can be particularly complex when there is involvement of both a training agency and a service setting. Environmental stress can be carried forward from the institutional context to the supervisory relationship. In one of the transcript examples, it emerges through supervision that a trainee is concerned that the setting will not provide her with clients who will meet her learning needs. The trainee says, 'The real problem is how am I going to talk to her about something. Maybe I should just have her terminate now if there isn't anything to deal with. You know that is one of the problems of having these volunteers – they don't have "real" issues. I don't know how I'm going to learn to do this unless I have a real client' (Holloway, 1995: 102). The supervisor suggests that while the client does not seem overtly to be presenting 'a problem', she is describing developmental issues to do with separating from her family of origin which might well benefit from counselling. The trainee acknowledges that she has been overly focused on needing a really big problem in order to learn counselling skills.

This model is particularly helpful in providing a perspective which encompasses the wider system. In my experience, the longer a worker spends in a particular setting, the easier it becomes to lose awareness of the impact of institutional imperatives and practices. Outsiders can shine a refreshing new light on habitual practices providing that they have sufficient confidence in the supervisory relationship to bring their puzzlement and doubt. And it is the supervisory relationship that lies at the core of the SAS model.

Developmental models of supervision (Stoltenberg and Delworth, 1987; Stoltenberg et al., 1998)

The notion of trainee dependency is addressed in a number of developmental approaches to supervision reported from the USA and described by

Stoltenberg and Delworth (1987) and Stoltenberg *et al.* (1998). Not infrequently, early on in training, supervisees feel insecure in their role and anxious about their ability to fulfil it. Further on in training there tends to be fluctuation between dependence and autonomy, with a subsequent gradual increase in professional self-confidence and only conditional dependence on the supervisor. The process of supervision may become more collegial with sharing and exemplification augmented by challenges to personal and professional development. Developmental models lead supervisors to expect different presentations from supervisees who are at different stages of professional development. It is proposed that supervisors adapt their approach according to these different presentations. Stoltenberg and colleagues take a 'stage' approach to the description of these differences. These stages are viewed as overarching yet specific to different domains of clinical practice. Thus a supervisee might be assessed as functioning at an early developmental level in one domain while operating at a more advanced level in other domains. The context or environment provided by supervisors is regarded as playing a crucial role in the rate and ultimate level of supervisee development.

Stoltenberg and colleagues identified four stages of supervisee development within three overriding structures across specific domains. The three overriding structures are defined as 'self and other awareness', 'motivation' and 'autonomy'. 'Self and other awareness' comprises both affective and cognitive components that reflect the level of the supervisee's self-preoccupation, self-awareness and awareness of the client's world. 'Motivation' describes the supervisee's interest, investment and effort expended in clinical training and practice. 'Autonomy' is a manifestation of changes in the degree and appropriateness of independence demonstrated by supervisees over time.

In stage 1, the dependency stage, the supervisee is likely to experience feelings of anxiety and insecurity while being highly motivated in the work. Awareness is likely to be self-focused and performance anxiety tends to prevail. Supervisees at this stage are often most concerned with surviving the session with the client. Due to the need to reflect constantly on the rules, skills, theories and other didactic material being learned, it is viewed within the model as difficult for trainees to carefully listen to and process information provided by the client in the session.

The supervisor can help by providing safety and containment. Supervisees may benefit from having a structure for their interviews on which they can depend and to which they can revert when they feel stuck or uncertain. Availability of brief supervision outside of a scheduled meeting is helpful and an emergency telephone number can be reassuring. Loganbill *et al.* (1982) proposed that facilitative interventions that communicate support and encourage development by the supervisor are possibly the most helpful for level one therapists. They include praise, reinforcement of skills and careful and attentive listening. The supervisee is likely to find it helpful to see the supervisor struggling from time to time, in order to compensate for the apparent smoothness in therapy that can sometimes be conveyed by text-books. Positive feedback on specific supervisee contributions may be appreci-ated, and where the supervisor has responsibility for selecting the supervisee's case load, screening of clients may be beneficial in order to provide a graded approach to the level of difficulty of the work. At this stage, if the model for the work is too far removed from the skill level of supervisees, it may be difficult for them to extract the salient characteristics in order to build them into their own work.

Dependency and insecurity can be manifest in a variety of ways along a continuum from supervisees seeming to have to know everything, to seeming to know nothing. The former state can lead to avoidance in supervision and the latter can present as helplessness which may evoke more contributions to supervision from the supervisor than from the supervisee in a way that does not help learning. This interaction taking place between the two parties can be drawn to the attention of the supervisee, with both working alongside each other to looking at ways to modify the process and to relieve anxiety.

Stage 2 is characterised by dependency–autonomy conflicts in which the supervisee fluctuates between overconfidence and feeling overwhelmed. Supervisees may experience fluctuating motivation in the work, feel out of place, and wonder, if they are in training, how they decide to choose a career in professional helping. The focus in the work is likely to have moved from supervisees themselves to the client. At this stage supervisees are unlikely to be able both to participate in the session and to take an observer perspective on the process. They tend to exhibit a principal focus on the client's perspective, and level two therapists are regarded as capable of ex-hibiting a naive lack of insight regarding their counter-transference reactions to the client. Data obtained from other sources (when incompatible with the client's view) may be disregarded by supervisees at this level of development. Supervisors' attempts to increase supervisees' awareness of such reactions may be met by confusion or disbelief.

The supervisor might help by drawing attention to the fluctuating state, defining it as a normal developmental stage and not, as the supervisee may think, confined solely to herself or himself. Metaphors can be useful, as may drawing attention to examples of over- and underconfidence. Supervisors can provide a secure base to which the supervisee may return when feeling overwhelmed. This requires clear views and agreements regarding boundary issues as supervisees may find themselves drawn across boundaries by the needs and demands of clients. Supervisors can provide an assertive yet warm role model through their actions in supervision.

Stage 3 is that of conditional dependency. At this stage, supervisees are developing increased self-confidence, greater insight and more consistency in their sessions with clients. They are able to focus more on process and to use this to inform the work with the client even if only retrospectively. At this stage the supervision may benefit from being undertaken within an enquiring framework with a view to facilitating the development of ongoing self-supervision. There may be more opportunity to focus on the thinking and feeling that is informing the work and less on technique and survival strategies.

Stage 4 (or 3i) is referred to as that of 'master professional'. Here the therapist has personal autonomy, insightful awareness and is able to confront personal and professional issues. The work is process-in-context centred. The supervisory relationship becomes increasingly collegial and the responsibility for the structure and process of supervision is largely taken by the supervisee or shared with the supervisor. The supervisee is likely to be supervising others at this stage, and might bring issues arising there to the supervision. Stoltenberg and colleagues posit that few, if any, therapists reach this level of development across all domains of clinical practice and that the task of development is never complete.

Developmental models may also be applied to the practice of supervision and it may be helpful for supervisors to review what they see as their own stage of development in relation to this role. Stoltenberg and colleagues argue that the effectiveness of supervisory relationships can be influenced by the relative levels of development of the participants. For example, they argue that level 1 supervisors tend to be either highly anxious or somewhat naive, focused on doing the 'right' thing and highly motivated to be successful in the role. They may find giving feedback difficult and have a preference for a relatively high degree of structure in supervisory sessions. Level 2 supervisees, in a state of conflict and confusion, are seen as an inappropriate match with level 1 supervisors and it is suggested that this particular pairing should be avoided at all costs. Similarly, therapists who are moving into level 3 functioning can lose their recently acquired consistent motivation if they are confronted with an insecure, highly structured level 1 supervisor.

Developmental models have face validity in that most people tend to think of themselves as improving with experience. Worthington (1987, 2006) reviewed studies based on developmental models and concluded that there is some empirical support for conceptualising supervision in this way, that the behaviour of supervisors and the nature of the supervisory relationship change as supervisees become more experienced, but that supervisors do not necessarily become more competent with experience. He argued for a deficiency with current developmental stage theories of supervision in that they are primarily *stage* theories rather than theories of how *transitions* take place between stages. They specify, albeit broadly, what the counsellor and the supervisor experience and do during each stage but not how the supervisor promotes movement from one stage to another. Other examples of developmental models include those of Littrell *et al.* (1979) and Skovholt and Ronnestad (1992).

There is evidence to suggest that beginning clinicians tend initially to focus on self which reflects their concerns about surviving the session, and on actions and events which are relatively 'safe' territory. It becomes possible to focus on the client as the initial anxiety level decreases, eventually moving to a focus on therapeutic process in which it is possible both to participate and simultaneously to reflect on the session. Winter and Holloway (1991) examined the supervision focus for 56 counsellor trainees with different amounts of experience when a recording was the supervisory medium. The results indicated that counsellor experience level correlated directly with the supervisee's focus on personal growth and inversely with a focus on client conceptualisation.

Other frameworks

This chapter has been by no means comprehensive in its coverage of models and frameworks of supervision. It has provided a flavour of the burgeoning literature on this topic. For those who are interested to explore a wider range of such structures, works by Gilbert and Evans (2000, 2007), Ladany *et al.* (2005) and Watkins (1997) are recommended.

Chapter 6

Group supervision

Brigid Proctor and Francesca Inskipp

> [G]roup supervision can offer a rich tapestry for learning and develop-
> ment with a range of possible formats and leadership roles.
>
> (Scaife, 2001: 4)

Many supervisors run brilliant groups with unselfconscious skill. They have
learned this ability from other group leaders or have developed it naturally in
life; perhaps many more run groups which they or their participants find
unsatisfactory, uneasy or effortful. For this chapter, we are condensing what
we have done in our previous writing and training – we offer maps and some
guidance on how any reasonably skilled supervisor can set about consciously
developing the abilities that are needed for good group supervision. By good
supervision we mean supervision which is satisfying to the participants and to
supervisors and therefore enables the most effective work with clients – the
heart of the matter.

Our aim is to promote group supervision as an aid to seeing practice in a
diversity of ways – offering a tower with many windows. We value mutual
cooperation in learning and development and wish to encourage readers to
use the lively and creative opportunities provided by working with a group.
Group supervision can be a restorative opportunity in a pressured, often
lonely, working life – for supervisor and supervisees. In order to make this
feasible we want to indicate the range of different kinds of supervision groups
which can be offered and to help the supervisor who has only worked with
individuals to be confident with a group. This entails furthering the abilities
of supervisors and group members as reflective practitioners. Both need to
become confident in learning publicly through 'mistakes', as well as through
success; and in learning by imitation and social influence. Supervisors particularly have to learn what is 'good enough' group work and relinquish any
fantasies of becoming the 'perfect' group supervisor – groups are too complex
for that to be possible.

Differences from individual supervision

For the supervisee

Good group supervision demands complex roles and tasks for both supervisee and supervisor. Depending on the type of group, the supervisee may have as many as four identified professional roles in the group – supervisee, practitioner, group member and co-supervisor. Each role entails specific tasks which between them require the development of a surprisingly wide range of skills.

Supervisors have not traditionally spelt out these roles when starting a group. Often the supervisor has not realised just what he or she may be expecting from participants. People who are 'good supervisees' may have been inducted elsewhere into 'how to do it well'. However, like the good supervisor, they may have acquired their abilities along the way and now unself-consciously use them as part of their professional repertoire. We have come to believe, through experience, that some conscious understanding of the roles and tasks can help participants – even those who already do it well. For supervisors it is only respectful to have clarified for themselves what it is they are expecting of group members as they start the group. They can then choose to make that clear, or, on reflection, modify or change their expectations.

So what are the tasks of group supervision which follow from the four roles identified?

- *As supervisees* to learn the skills of preparing the work they wish to take for supervision in the group and then to present their work publicly, both economically and in a way that engages their colleagues.
- *As practitioners* to identify their own personal and professional development needs and to discern and communicate how the group could be a helpful learning resource.
- *As group members* to develop good 'group manners' – being aware of time and air space and becoming conscious of thoughts, feelings and communications which help or hinder the group's work.
- *As co-supervisors* to develop the skills of supervision – giving close attention to others' presentations and mutually supporting and challenging each other in the work through clear feedback and thoughtful responses.

It needs to be remembered that joining a group often engenders more anxiety than beginning one-to-one supervision.

Christensen and Kline (2001) in a qualitative study of qualified counsellors who were attending group supervision as part of an advanced training course found that participation anxiety was the predominant theme and context that framed all of the participants' experiences in their supervision group. Participants experienced fears about appearing incompetent and about offering feedback that could harm or potentially destroy their relationships with other supervisees and the supervisor. Anxiety was for some anticipatory, starting before the group gathered together, and often served to limit the contributions made. Over time, supervisees tended to change their views about their perceptions of participation anxiety. As trust developed within the group, supervisees seemed to master the interactive learning process inherent in group supervision and they began to believe that participation anxiety signalled a valuable learning opportunity.

In the next section we have categorised four types of groups. These inform which skills a supervisor may need to ask participants to develop in a specific type of group. Books on supervision have usually concentrated first on the supervisor. Because the findings of the research above are so typical of what we have come to expect of supervisees beginning a group we prefer to start from the perspective of the supervisee. If all group participants knew how to work well in a group the job of the supervisor would not be so complex. As it is, supervisors will probably need to do some training of the participants. Depending again on the type of group this may have to be one of their major roles.

For the supervisor

From the perspective of the supervisor there are also several additional roles which anyone who intends to supervise in or with a group (as opposed to an individual) has to be prepared to assume. The undertaking requires considerable management skill and encompasses at least the roles of manager of time and task, group leader, group facilitator, inductor, trainer, and group supervisor.

In the *role of supervisors* they will still have:

- normative responsibilities – managing the interface with the agency and training organisation and monitoring standards of practice;
- formative responsibilities – of inducting new practitioners or developing the reflective practice of the more experienced;
- restorative responsibilities – of supporting and encouraging hard-pressed workers.

These responsibilities will have to be exercised for several supervisees instead of for one.

In the role of *group managers* they will be responsible for:

- organisational and practical arrangements – place, time, payment and so on;
- setting the working agreements (by negotiation or otherwise);
- ensuring sufficient adherence to the agreements or modifying them;
- monitoring that there is fair allocation of time and attention;
- introducing group reviews or appraisals.

In the role of *inductors and trainers* they will be responsible for:

- enabling participants to have the information, skills, support and challenge (Egan, 1976) they require in order to meet stated expectations of the supervisors and of other stakeholders;
- enabling supervisees to present and engage well with group supervision.

Depending on their expectations of group members, and the type of group agreement, they may be responsible for:

- modelling good 'group manners' as above;
- modelling and teaching group awareness and skills;
- modelling and teaching supervision and feedback skill.

In the role of *group facilitator*s again dependent on the group agreement, they may be responsible for:

- creating a culture conducive for this particular group to interact in a way that builds and maintains a good group alliance and when necessary repairs it;
- modelling the core qualities of respect, empathy, straightforwardness and, we would add, intentionality;
- enabling members to get to know each other well enough to create trust in the group;
- ensuring members know each other's contexts well enough to work appropriately;
- freeing up the rich resources of the group in undertaking individual pieces of supervision work;
- taking the lead in addressing and valuing diversity in the group;
- addressing conflict, competitiveness or other interactions, which, if ignored, hinder the task.

In the role of *group leaders* they have the responsibility:

- to prioritise the task or process on which it is most important to focus from moment to moment in the group.

This conscious and unconscious making of choices among a welter of responsibilities is at the heart of the job. It is useful to have ready some maps of group process, supervision tasks, and individual development needs in groups, to name a few. Such maps or frameworks (see pp. 152–157 and Figure 6.1) need to find their place within an overall framework of professional ethics and personal and professional values.

The skills for making priorities and for undertaking these multifarious roles are worth considering and we will return to them later. However, since the skills will depend on the type of group being run we first want to offer a framework for categorising possibilities for different supervision groups.

Typology

We have identified four different types of supervision group. The frameworks they offer appear to have been useful to supervisors in helping to clarify with supervisees the respective roles and responsibilities that will be expected. We summarise the four types in Table 6.1. Type 1 could be called *Authoritative* supervision – the supervisor, treating the group members as a more or less

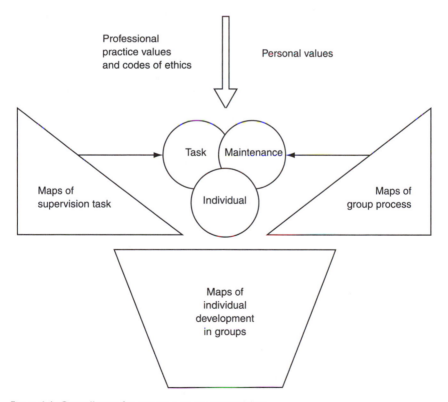

Figure 6.1 Overall map for running group supervision.

Table 6.1 Typology of groups

Type 1	**Authoritative group supervision or supervision *in* a group** *Supervisor supervises individuals; members as more or less involved audience.*

Advantages
- Releases supervisor to focus on the supervision
- Minimises group energy and therefore destructive interaction
- Allows freedom from responsibility for overworked practitioners
- Can be an excellent master class
- Safer for participants who distrust groups
- Easier to allocate time

Disadvantages
- Participants may be passive and resent not being involved
- Expertise stays with the supervisor and participants can feel de-skilled
- Richness of the group not utilised fully
- Can be stultifying for those who learn through interaction
- Supervisor does not develop group skills or flexibility of leadership

Type 2	**Participative group supervision or supervision *with* a group** *Supervisor supervises; members are taught and encouraged to participate actively.*

Advantages
- Develops the richness of the group
- Acts as a forum for the development of supervisory and group interaction skills
- Fosters active participation and commitment to a shared task
- Can raise self-esteem by mutual recognition of expertise
- Offers opportunities for the supervisor to develop active group skills, leadership and creative teaching
- Can be exciting and stimulating, therefore restorative and good for learning

Disadvantages
- Can change the focus from client/work issues to group process
- Harder to manage fair sharing of time
- Can become too busy and interfere with reflective space
- Hard work initially and more risks involved for the supervisor
- Requires skill in choosing priorities and gearing the group interaction to the task
- Can feel unsafe for supervisor or participants thereby restricting honesty of sharing
- Can be daunting for supervisors who hesitate to direct

Type 3	**Cooperative group supervision or supervision *by* the group** *Supervisor facilitates the group in sharing responsibility for the tasks of group supervision.*

Advantages
- Offers a collegial experience for established practitioners
- Encourages supervision and group skill development
- Reminds participants of shared professional accountability
- Encourages creative use of self for supervisor and participants
- Can offer a variety of models of theory, style and practice

- Freer interaction allows for serendipity – parallel process, group surprises

Disadvantages
- Supervisor can lapse into a *laissez-faire* approach and participants feel unsafe
- Riskier – more room for destructive interaction and group process
- Requires higher level skills from supervisor and participants
- Experienced practitioners may have poor group skills and 'manners'
- Can be harder to keep the focus on client/supervision work

Type 4   **Peer group supervision**
Peers take shared responsibility for supervision; members negotiate structure, leadership, roles and responsibilities.

Advantages and disadvantages
- Largely as above, plus
- Saves money
- Good peer groups often offer optimal safety and trust
- Needs clear contracting or can develop into a social group rather than a work group
- Needs mutual self-discipline for regular attendance

participative audience, supervises each member one-to-one. It can also be designated as supervision *in* a group. Type 2 we name *Participative* supervision because the supervisor negotiates with members to help them become skilled and active participants in the work of supervision – hence supervision *with* a group. Type 3, or *Cooperative* supervision, is set up in such a way that the supervisor is the facilitator and wicket-keeper for the group members sharing fully in each other's supervision – hence supervision *by* a group. Type 4 is *Peer Group* supervision – members share the full responsibility of supervisor for each other, and negotiate how leadership will be shared.

These types are not discrete but may be seen as part of a continuum in which the supervisor progressively shares, with the group, the responsibilities of supervising. The framework assumes that participants will vary in their degree of ability and sophistication for working in a group. It also allows for the fact that supervisors will have varying degrees of experience, or indeed inclination, for working in a group. Those factors, together with the particular context and its working culture, will be the major determinants of which type of group the supervisor may propose.

All these types may be well or badly run and help or hinder client work. Let us suppose that consideration is being given to setting up or taking on a group. How supervisors choose which type of group to run will depend on the above factors and also what they believe about learning, self-managed or otherwise, about expertise and about certainty and creative (or anarchic) chaos. Are they prepared to risk converting a group from the safety of receiving expertise to being collectively supervised by colleagues; to challenge the group members and themselves as they join together in supervision?

Other factors which will impinge will be the composition of the group. There may be a group of eager trainees who give the supervisor permission and confidence to teach them basic skills of supervision and cooperative group work. On the other hand, the group may comprise experienced mixed professionals who could possibly benefit from such teaching but who would not appreciate it! Perhaps the supervisor's greatest ally in either case is taking time to declare her or his intention for the group and to give the members a chance to consider and negotiate. At this stage the supervisor may be announcing which kind of group this is *going to be* or may genuinely be *exploring* what working agreement would be most suitable for these participants, their clients, the context and herself or himself. What needs to be made clear is what is negotiable and what parameters are non-negotiable.

Russian dolls: agreements and alliances

This image seems to be a useful metaphor for the interdependence of the various agreements which supervisors and supervisees need to make openly if they are to engage in a fruitful working alliance. Figure 6.2 illustrates the metaphor.

The professional contract

To some extent non-negotiable parameters will be determined, as in individual supervision, by the wider professional contract. This will determine:

- what accountability is expected of the supervisors and of the participants, whether experienced practitioners or trainees;

Figure 6.2 Russian dolls: agreements and alliances.

- the Codes or Frameworks of Ethics and Practice to which all will be working;
- the conventions of confidentiality in the particular setting;
- the overall ratio of supervision to client hours;
- supervisor and supervisee rights, responsibilities and lines of communication with all the employing organisations, agencies and training providers who may be connected with differing group members.

The supervisor's first task of management is finding a way to make that professional contract clear to participants. It may be useful to let them have it in writing before the start of the group. However, whether or not this has been done, they will need time to digest and discuss the implications of that contract in practice. This process of discussing and digesting is one way in which the group members get to know each other and begin to get a feel of working in this particular group. Using the analogy of Russian dolls we call this the Large Doll because it encloses and determines the shape of any subsequent working agreement.

In Figure 6.2 we indicate what the other useful agreements are. If the agreements are well made there will be more cooperative ownership and the supervisor will not have to take so much ongoing responsibility for determining priorities and time management. Discussing and negotiating can be an exercise through which the group, led by the supervisor, overtly sets initial norms for working together and begins the forming process (Tuckman, 1965). The DVD *Creative Supervision with Brigid Proctor and Francesca Inskipp* (Inskipp and Proctor, 2007) illustrates and discusses some of the issues involved in setting up a participative group.

The group working agreement

The second doll represents the specific agreements that need to be clarified or negotiated if the group is to be enabled to forge a working alliance. We suggest that there are four major strands to this:

- The *type* of group it is going to be and consequently the specific roles and responsibilities of supervisor and supervisee.
- The *working arrangements* for the group, which include time allocation, method of presenting, pattern of sessions (e.g. time for checking in, processing), reviews, and changes of personnel.
- The *ground rules* for interacting with each other. For example, if the group is to be a type 2 or 3 group, the ground rules might include respecting task, time and each other's opinions; clarifying what is meant before disagreeing; working to have empathic understanding of practitioner and client before advising or suggesting, and so on. Group members will each have experience as to what they find a help or hindrance when they are

working in a group and they need to be encouraged to identify and share that if they are to be working participatively.

- The *individual responsibility* of participants to identify their learning needs and what help they need. For instance, one group member may want to develop the ability to be tougher and less malleable with residents in a care home while another might identify the need to learn to be more patient and empathic.

The specific working agreement will depend on the type of group. The degree to which the features are laid down by the supervisor or negotiated with the group will depend on the type of group, and on the particular style and values of the supervisor and supervisees. What it is worth thinking about throughout the process of building an agreement and forging an alliance is:

> Even ... supervision groups need often to be a good home for their members – not an ideal or idealised home but one where there can be comfort and honesty, some love and some loyalty and the exchanging from time to time of home truths.
>
> (Houston, 1997: 2)

It is always an issue how and when to formulate these agreements. Some factors need to be agreed at the outset; others can be interim arrangements with the promise of review when people have experience of working together. It is a rule of thumb that participants seldom remember, let alone understand, 'agreements' made in the first session. They will always need to be revisited when participants are more able to give informed consent or feedback. A second rule of thumb is that some participants will become impatient if they are prevented from getting on and doing some supervision, while others will not want to work until they know where they stand. Therefore the process of making a working agreement allows supervisor and supervisees to become aware of the kind of culture which needs to emerge for this collection of individuals to become a working group. Induction of new members will require revisiting and perhaps renegotiation of the original agreement.

Session agenda

The third doll represents agenda setting – the specific agreement at the beginning of each session. The regular pattern of the session will probably have been determined by the group working agreement. However, specific agenda items such as leftovers, reviews, requests, work on particular issues (for example, group diversity or ethical dilemmas) need to be programmed in and time allocated for them. In addition to giving the group a sense of intention, agenda building helps individuals become self-managing in using and giving time. The process of checking the agenda also allows group preoccupations to become apparent.

The fourth doll is the shadow doll – which is contained by the others but which is the area where supervisors are on their own. Before considering that, we will conclude the series of contracts.

The mini-contract for a particular piece of supervision

The fifth doll brings us to the heart of the matter – what supervision is all about. It is the agreement with an individual practitioner as to what he or she wants from a piece of supervision work and perhaps how he or she would like to do it. Taking time to make a hard contract ('I want to know what to say to this client') or a soft contract ('I just want to introduce my new client and hear your responses') (Sills, 2006) serves several purposes. It focuses the supervisee and encourages taking responsibility for identifying the issues that need, or could benefit from, reflective space in supervision. It brings the group to attention around that reflective space. It allows supervisors to make informed choices about how to conduct themselves and the group in the best interests of practitioner and client.

The shadow doll representing the uncontracted space

In the illustration, the fourth doll appears as a shadow. Managing group responses remains the responsibility of the supervisor, no matter how that role is played. In a group there is a wealth of possibilities – exponentially greater than in individual supervision. The group will hopefully be well held within the various agreements we have already discussed. For instance, if an Authoritative group has been created (supervising *in* the group), the choices will have been deliberately limited. If a Participative agreement has been made, the supervisor will have undertaken to orchestrate the group responses for the most part. As a Cooperative group supervisor, the group will be more active in offering and suggesting how to carry out the work. Nevertheless, the choice – of how best to use the rich resources available at any one time – remains with the supervisor, regardless of advice or guidance from supervisee and participants. That is the supervisor's responsibility due to the overall contract with practitioner, agency and, implicitly, clients. Later in the chapter we will look at some of the possibilities and considerations involved in this.

Peer groups

In peer group supervision, the responsibility for using the group in a specific piece of work can be designated by members to one of their number, for a session or for a single presentation. At other times it can be agreed that the presenting supervisee remains responsible for how the supervision is done. In a well-working peer group, pieces of work will often 'happen' rather than being overtly 'led' – the group has become a shared improvisation group. (A warning here: this way of working needs to be honestly reviewed at regular intervals – such groups can become oppressive to less assertive members.)

Skills for supervisors

Active leadership

Leadership of a supervision group requires proactive skills and a leadership style that can manage, lead and teach without being authoritarian or bossy. Counsellors and psychotherapists can find such overt taking charge difficult. They are more used to following or subtly managing their work with clients. However, some have previously taught, or taken responsibility for a group, in more authoritarian settings and they can easily slip into being bossy. Whatever the type of group chosen, the task of the group is to enable or ensure that participants do better work with their clients. This means maintaining reflective space for practitioners and engaging them to varying extents in their own and each other's learning.

Clarity

The ability to lead requires being intentional, clear – and when necessary forthright – about defining the task and how to do (or not do) it. Confidence grows with experience, but thought and preparation beforehand, both privately and with the help of supervision or consultancy, can allow supervisors to clarify their own understanding of the tasks involved and their own expectations of the group participants.

Preparation

Such preparation is particularly necessary before the initiation (or taking over) of a new group. As we have seen, clarifying contracts and agreements in such a way that a working alliance is forged means taking leadership both:

- for *what* is to be negotiated and how, and
- for *the culture* in which the discussions and negotiations take place.

Preparation will also be essential at later stages when it may follow from pondering expected or surprising group events. What does the group need to learn next in order for participants to continue developing as practitioners, supervisees and group members? What sense can be made of some event? What needs to happen if the group is to learn from difficult or moving experiences? What personal/professional learning do *supervisors* need and how will that show in the next group?

Skilled use of frameworks

If supervisors become skilled at such pondering, they will have some cognitive maps or frameworks in their minds – about group development, group process, individual behaviour and development in groups, dysfunctional group behaviour, and how individual supervision work can be helped or hindered by happenings within and outside the group. The ability to have ready access to such frameworks, and to be thoughtful and creative in using and amending them through experience, is a core skill for group leaders. We suggest some hardy perennial frameworks, but they are only as useful as the skill in making them one's own, as the actual territory replaces the map or guidebook.

Purpose and preference stating

Clarity of purpose or intention has, of course, to be signalled as well as reflected upon. This calls for 'confident enough' communication. While developing confidence, words have to be chosen carefully for accuracy and impact. This entails communicating whether a statement of *intent* is just that – 'this is what I want and intend to enable or ensure'; or whether it is a statement of *preference* – 'I would prefer that . . . what do *you* want?' This distinction (Gilmore *et al.*, 1980) has been considered to be *the* most useful information in relieving the frustrations of even experienced managers. It is necessary, for instance, when parameters and boundaries are laid down in the professional contract. It is also useful if supervisors feel that a group needs 'taking in hand' at some stage of its development or when the reflective working space of an individual member is being disrupted.

Receptivity and following

For active leadership to be taken in a way that is cooperative rather than bossy or authoritarian, it has to be balanced by receptivity. This entails actively seeking feedback and opinions from the group, and listening to them with interest, curiosity and openness – to hearing, following and even changing style or task in response! In the early stages of contract stating or negotiation this means recognising that an 'agreement' means just that. A purpose statement is non-negotiable, but a preference statement means a genuine search to find common ground for shared ground rules or procedures, and this entails listening and hearing.

Throughout the group, receptivity shows as plenty of airspace given to participants, by listening and reflecting back or summarising to check that the supervisor has understood what is being said. In so doing, good 'group manners' and supervisor skills will be modelled to group members. At later stages of a group, it means eliciting feedback as to what is working and what is not helpful. It may entail deciding to 'go along' with what is happening even when the outcome is not clear. The supervisor may want to encourage initiative being taken by a group member, or the group as a whole being enthusiastically engaged. This active following is different from being 'pulled', whether reluctantly or suspiciously. When supervisors have sufficient trust in the goodwill and ability of the group and their own sense of overall purpose, it can lead to creative and unexpected outcomes.

Imbalance

Most supervisors have a preference (and therefore probably an ability) for either active leadership or receptivity. The latter may err towards presiding over a laissez-faire group that grows either unduly competitive for leadership, or apathetic. The former may run a tight type 1 group, which is unlikely to evolve into a Participative or Cooperative group. The trick is to work to develop the ability for both kinds of behaviour. It is a behaviour, not an identity issue – not 'I'm just not like that' but 'How could I *do* that?'

Luckily (and for this framework we owe a debt to Susan Gilmore again (Gilmore *et al.*, 1980), in addition to active leadership and receptivity, there is a third category of useful behaviour for group leaders – assertion.

Assertion

In this context, assertion means simply stating, and standing by, rights and responsibilities – one's own or other people's. So if group supervisors have risked 'going along' and then become worried about, for example, time, equity or loss of direction, they do not have to wrest themselves from receptivity to active leadership – galvanising themselves and confusing the group. They can move into assertiveness and remind the group of the time, or of responsibility for the client and each other. They can query purpose or intention or just assert their presence if the group, in adolescent fervour, is busy 'disappearing' them. Like a blocked stream, the energy and initiative remains with 'the flow', but new directions have to be found.

Choosing the right fights

Assertive behaviour can reduce the likelihood of passive or active aggression from group members which active leadership can stimulate. However, like receptivity, it should not be used as a way of avoiding conflicts of interest that are interfering with good enough supervision. If a group is to grow and develop, it will almost certainly have to address differences of opinion, values, styles and ways of working, and find ways to develop through the process.

Deciding which are 'the right fights' is helped by referring to maps for under-standing group development and processes (Houston, 1997).

Underlying abilities

Choosing priorities

The larger the behavioural tool-kit at the supervisors' disposal, the more choices with which they are faced. The skills of active leadership, receptivity and assertion may be developed at a behavioural level. However, how and when a supervisor changes gear from one to the other appropriately depends on some complex underlying abilities. Chief among these is the ability to prioritise.

By the time practitioners become supervisors they will have developed the ability to prioritise in several contexts – managerial, therapeutic and so on. For group supervision, some of that ability has to be dismantled, furnished with fresh maps and skills and reintegrated into the ability to prioritise in group supervision. Within a group there are myriad happenings each second. This speed of process allows little time to reflect. It may be necessary to be able to make decisions and act quickly without reacting impulsively. Supervisors need to adopt or develop frameworks of values, process and practice which assist them to be clear in their own intentions for the group, and which help them weigh and choose one value against another in an instant. Maps or frameworks are interesting in themselves to some of us, but to aid in the development of prioritising ability they need to be of help when the supervisor is wondering 'What do I do now?', 'What do I respond to?', 'How do I respond?'

In addition, group supervisors need to increase their skills in rapidly scan-ning their physical sensations, emotions, thoughts and images. Sensory feed-back will give them information to prioritise and act – or not act. Consciously developing physical metaphors and images can be revealing – 'in tune', 'out of hand', 'needing a touch on the reins', 'it feels like the prelude to a thunder-storm'. Often such 'physical pick-up' is more immediately 'in touch' than cognitive processing and allows the supervisor to develop spontaneity. This, in turn, can give permission to group members to risk more honest and spontaneous interaction.

Using recording, reflecting and consultation

This development of spontaneity, and even risk taking, is balanced by the time spent in reflecting about the group. Developing appropriate ways of recording group work is useful (Sharpe, 1995). Using regular consultation is both a skill and a necessary discipline:

- for identifying what worked well and what did not;
- as an aid to reflecting;
- for exploring learning;
- for furthering skill development.

The role of facilitator: working with group process

What helps to produce a good working group? To pull together some of our earlier assertions, we suggest that it requires members:

- to feel safe enough with each other and with the supervisor to trust the group with honest disclosure of their work;
- to have clarity about the task and how this will be worked on;
- to know each other well enough as individuals;
- to accept and respect difference;
- to share sufficient values, beliefs and assumptions about human beings, professional helping and groups;
- to have 'good group manners'.

And the supervisor:

- to feel comfortable to exercise authority when necessary;
- to have some 'maps' which help the supervisor to understand and act on group process;
- to arrange opportunities for feedback on how the group members are working together.

When a group comes together and interacts, the behaviour of everybody is modified by the 'forces' present – the group dynamic. The energy present can help or hinder the learning process.

There is a wide range of group dynamic theories and we give below some frameworks that we have found can help the supervisor make choices in building and maintaining a working group.

Group needs (Adair, 1983)

This framework suggests that when a group meets together there are three sorts of interlocking needs that have to be kept in balance (see Figure 6.1):

1   *Task needs* – usually the most apparent on the surface. The supervision task and methods by which it will be pursued, has, hopefully, been originally clarified by contracting, so that both supervisor and group members are clear. However, as the group develops this may well need further clarification and negotiation, so time will need to be allocated for this.

2 *Maintenance needs* – the need to develop and maintain good working relationships and a positive climate to work on the task. Again, by originally contracting for 'good group manners', for time to explore the 'process' of the group, and for reviews to evaluate and give feedback on how the group is working – or not working – together, some of the maintenance needs will be made explicit. However, as the group comes together and develops, the supervisor will have the main responsibility for meeting the changing needs of maintenance and possibly repair. As the group progresses, depending on the type of group, members may learn to share this responsibility.

3 *Individual needs* – members bring a range of needs such as to be recognised, to belong, to contribute, to exercise power and influence, as well as their individual supervision and learning needs. These two latter needs may have been made explicit in contracting, but the other needs may only emerge in different degrees in different members as the group develops. Recognising these individual needs as they emerge can help the supervisor in making choices on how to facilitate the group, and on how to work with individual members for their development.

The task of facilitating the group is greatly helped if the supervisor is aware of, and can recognise, the necessity to balance these three areas – task, maintenance and individual needs.

Developing needs (Schutz, 1967, 1989)

A second framework further explores the concept of individual needs. Within it are identified three basic needs that develop in sequence as the group comes together. As any of us becomes part of a new group, each of us will have progressively to re-create our own identity within that particular group:

- *Inclusion needs* – each member will have queries about belonging to this group, and be wondering 'Who am I here?', 'Who are the others here?', 'Am I accepted?', 'Do I want to belong?' This implies that it is important for the supervisor to encourage ways for members to get to know each other as people, to create a commitment to a group that has something to offer them, and to model acceptance of each individual.

As they get to know each other they will develop:

- *Power and influence needs* – individuals have different needs for power and influence, and they need to test out with each other and with the supervisor where they stand. These preoccupations merit recognition, and, if valued, can be harnessed in the service of good work. Sometimes power struggles can hinder the task and require space and patience – and skilful interventions – to work them through. Being prepared for them – between members and as challenges to the supervisor – can help towards making the right choices of how and when to address the issues. For instance, if a member is taking up too much air space is he or she lacking validation or a sense of belonging, or should he or she be challenged because her or his undisciplined power or inclusion needs are oppressing other members?

When a good enough accommodation has been reached (and power issues will recur as the group changes and develops) the next needs to arise are:

- *Affect needs* – the need to accept liking and disliking, tolerate or enjoy differences, and decide how to work together. If the supervisor can provide a good model of communicating empathy, respect and authenticity (straightforwardness) to individuals in the group, and can help members explore issues of conflict with each other, this will encourage the development of a facilitative climate. At best, individuals come to believe that in this group they can feel safe to 'be themselves' and deal with the consequences.

The idea that these needs arise in sequence can alert supervisors to prepare for the changing needs of individuals in the group and can help them make sense of what is happening at different times. The next framework also encompasses changes as the group develops, but concerns the group as a dynamic unit or system.

Group movement (Tuckman, 1965)

This framework describes the group, as a system in its own right, progressing through four (or five) stages:

- *Forming* – a stage of anxiety and dependence on the supervisor. What is allowed and not allowed in this group? How supportive or critical will it be? What are the norms? This stage can be helped by clarifying the task, and methods to execute it, and by helping members to communicate with, and get to know each other. It can be useful to set up simple, short inclusion exercises at the beginning of a group. For example, ask each member to describe briefly something they are wearing which says something about them. Another option is to ask them to respond to sentence stems such as, 'If I were a piece of furniture I would be . . .', or 'I am the sort of person who . . .'. Negotiating the first agreements in the group, clarifying roles and type of group all help to make this a positive stage.
- *Storming* – a stage of possible resistance to the supervisor and to the task, and of conflict between members. Issues of power, influence and

competition are being brought out and hopefully resolved. It requires restraint from the supervisor not to get involved with justifying, defending or attacking but to use basic skills to demonstrate acceptance of the difficulties and emotions involved in this stage and a willingness to work on them. As we have seen, it may require assertiveness – holding fast to some agreements and negotiating others. Some groups take a long time to reach this stage, some reach it early, some work through it easily. Attending to task and maintenance needs may 'soften' the storming. Recognising it as a normal and *necessary* stage if the group is to develop honesty, and safety to disagree, can perhaps help the supervisor ride it with more equanimity.

In looking at individuals' needs for inclusion on their own terms and for power and influence, we saw that the Schutz framework could help determine what action a supervisor might take with a vociferous group member. However, Tuckman's framework offers another possibility – perhaps an individual, in addition to seeking to fulfil her or his own identity needs, might be acting as a theme setter for the group-as-system. An argumentative member, who gradually challenges the supervisor more and more and is allowed 'to get away with it' by the group, may be signalling that the group is ready to storm its way into a fuller and more realistic sense of itself, both between members and in relation to the supervisor. Now may be the time to fight the right fights, clear the decks of unspoken disagreements and reach a new accommodation – the supervisor needs to help the group express any identity with that leader, rather than treat her or him as a trying individual.

- *Norming* – the group begins to find ways to work together on the task of supervision and to enjoy feelings of mutual support, of making progress together and of accepting difference in individuals. At this stage, the supervisor may have renegotiated, or re-emphasised, roles and responsibilities during the storming phase, and the working agreement becomes more truly 'agreed'.

- *Performing* – the group members can work together, and can resolve conflicts and trust each other to give feedback and support in the task of supervision. Individuals have sufficiently developed trust and 'freedom to be' – their identity needs (as above) have been sufficiently taken care of. The energy can be very exciting at this stage and it is ideal to reach it as soon as possible. However, it is not necessarily a linear process – some groups work backwards and forwards through the stages as the learning becomes more intense, emotions become high in the group, or people leave or join.

Some descriptions of this framework include a fifth stage:

- *Mourning* – the recognition that the group is ending and is going through the process of dissolution. The closer the group, and the more satisfying the work has been, the harder to finish, and supervisees may be very reluctant to acknowledge an ending. This process can offer useful learning about the difficulties of finishing a relationship with a client. It may be very important to give mourning time if a supervision group on a training course is moving to a new supervisor or groups are being reset. A supervisor taking over an existing group may find herself or himself involved in a mixed stage of forming and mourning – and storming, if the group is unwilling to change supervisors.

The three frameworks above give a positive view and useful pointers on how to develop a well-working group. There is a fourth framework which can be helpful in diagnosing what is holding up the working alliance if the group seems really stuck and unable to work on the agreed supervision tasks.

Bion's model of unconscious processes (Bion, [1961] 1974)

This parallels Tuckman's framework of a group system's necessary developmental processes. It sets out three group processes which are dysfunctional. If they develop fully in a group it takes drastic measures to bring the group into a good functioning mode. Bion calls these processes basic assumptions (BAs):

- *BA dependence* – the group is unconsciously dominated by the belief that only a strong leader, a god, can protect the group from the insecurity and emotional stress of coming together. All communication goes to the leader; only her or his word is valid. This process can hinder groups moving from type 1 to type 2 and may need to be brought into awareness.
- *BA pairing* – the group 'allows' the interaction to be taken over by two people and somehow believes they will produce redemption or survival of the group, or solve all the supervision issues brought.
- *BA fight/flight* – unexpressed emotions, especially negative ones, may cause the energy of the group to be used to fight or run away. Aggression or withdrawal becomes the norm for the group.

Drawing on Bion's ideas the researchers below identified four categories of group climate and their conclusions are summarised as follows:

A study by Ogren *et al.* (2001) identified four categories of group climate as follows:

1   Insecure and task oriented (the angry group)
2   Insecure and relationship oriented (the disappointed group)

3   Secure and task oriented (the sensible group)
4   Secure and relationship oriented (the solidarity group)

Using qualitative methodology the views and experiences of students and supervisors were explored, not only in the identification of characteristics of the different group climates but also in investigating the factors that contributed to the development of these different climates and the supervisory interventions designed to modify them. In insecure groups members tended to find themselves occupying roles that they did not recognise which had developed in response to the group climate. Group supervisors experienced the group dynamic to be influenced by individuals who were manifesting a lack of trust or insecurity, and by conflicts of loyalty where the constituent membership was regarded as far too heterogeneous.

We note that the group supervisors in the study tended to ascribe the climate in the insecure groups to group member characteristics. We hypothesise that, although some groups are unduly influenced by personality characteristics, for the most part it is the setting up of the group and the identification of roles and tasks that most strongly affect the working climate of the group. When a group engages in dysfunctional unconscious processes it is often because the task is not clear or is too difficult, or there are underlying agendas that are not voiced. The best coping strategies are probably to bring the process into consciousness and help the group bring out and discuss unrecognised difficulties. It will almost always be necessary to revisit the professional contract and working agreement in order to ascertain if there is sufficient 'shared desire' (Randall and Southgate, 1980) for the group to do good work.

We have found the frameworks of Schutz and Tuckman to be useful in practice. What among the welter of choices is the priority at this time? Perhaps to get on with the task of supervision regardless of distractions, or to encourage the group members to express their thoughts and feelings, or to have a showdown, or to introduce an exercise to mark an ending, or to reaffirm purpose and shared interests. These, and many more options, are available for enabling group members to work well together and a quick scan of the frameworks may help the supervisor to notice what comes to the foreground, demanding attention. We have found Bion's framework some cold comfort when a group is manifestly dysfunctional, and nothing seems to help it work well enough. Sometimes there is not sufficient 'shared desire', or willingness to trust – or indeed trustworthiness – for a working alliance to develop. 'I think I just have to accept that this is a Bion group.' In a functional group, many options present themselves when thinking about how to use group resources to undertake supervision work.

Doing group supervision

Authoritative groups and parallel process

In the supervision of an *Authoritative* group, supervision *in* the group, the method of individual supervision will be translated into a public context. It will take forethought to decide how to use the audience to supplement the work so that group members feel engaged and valuable while the supervisor is holding the full supervisory authority.

One method of working is to ask members to say, in turn, how they find themselves reacting to the material. This allows reactions to be understood as *parallel process* – a mirror of the thoughts and emotions which are present in the therapeutic alliance but may not have been explicitly recognised by the practitioner. Practitioners who work predominantly psychodynamically mainly use the group in this way. If supervisors draw their own conclusions from these responses – openly or covertly – the group would still fall into the category of *in* the group. If members are then invited to discuss their conclusions as a result, the group is better described as *Participative*. The family therapy practice of circular questioning which is frequently used in supervision is an example of this. Using this technique the supervisor asks successive questions of one supervisee and the remaining members act as a reflective team, adding their observations at the end of the one-to-one session. The supervisor of a participative group will be taking greater responsibility for managing group members' reactions to their experiences and therefore have more responsibility for monitoring the *group process* engendered by the *parallel process* exercise or by circular questioning.

For type 2, 3 and 4 groups, there are many more ways of using the group creatively. Our personal experience is that informing the supervision issue by means of identifying parallel process is not helpful until the group has established a trusting working alliance and has relatively sophisticated individual and group awareness. However, there may well be times before that when a parallel process seems to be operating spontaneously. In that case, our practice is to decide if drawing attention to it is:

- helpful to the understanding of the supervisee concerned (it can often be more confusing than enlightening), or
- necessary to break through a dysfunctional process in which the group is unconsciously caught (e.g. enacting the process of 'there must be *something* you can do'), which can be as frustrating and time-consuming in the group as it is to therapist and client!

Free-flow or structure

One distinction which may help in deciding 'what to do' with a specific piece of work in supervision is that of free-flow or structure. The two are not totally distinct – even the most free discussion will require some structure; for example, time management.

Free-flow

There is an option to choose to invite or allow the group to respond in a (more or less) random fashion to a colleague's issue. In a type 2 group, supervisors may need to make it clear that, at some stages, they may choose to be quite bossy conductors of the discussion. This is necessary in order to preserve the supervisee's reflective space, and also to take on a tutoring role with regard to responses which are unclear or inappropriate. Moreover, the supervisor may, for instance, want the supervisee to hear all the responses without speaking and then choose to respond to one which seems most relevant to her or him. If time is pressing, it may be desirable to round off the session and finish the work with the supervisee individually. In order to disperse authoritative tasks it may be desirable to ask for volunteers to monitor or manage time. Inskipp and Proctor (1993, 1995) suggest guidelines for good practice in managing free-flow.

Structure

An alternative is to offer an experiential exercise, or structure, for exploring the supervisee's issue. (Experiential exercises may also be used for individual and group awareness raising and skill training, but there is not space to consider this more fully here.) By focusing attention very specifically, an exercise can bring thoughts, sensations, emotions, images, internal dialogues (and more) to the surface which may be censored or out of access in ordinary discussion.

Any medium which may be used in client work can be equally helpful in supervision; and any which may be used in individual supervision can be even more fruitful if used in a group. That includes:

- All sorts of awareness exercises and questionnaires – 'Who does this client remind you of?', 'If she were an animal what would she be?'
- The use of drawing, painting, clay, contents of handbags or pockets to depict or convey the client, the therapeutic relationship or an organisation. This depiction can either be used to help the group discover 'the felt sense' of the subject; or to map out and look at a family system; a work system; the internal system of a client or of the therapeutic relationship.
- Group sculpting, music or mime/dance used with similar intent.

- Psychodrama and socio-drama including role playing – client, counsellor, other interested parties – the supervisee choosing who takes which part, or the group members volunteering.
- Circular questioning.

Many of these can be used by supervisees working in pairs or threes, about one of their clients, followed by space for feedback and reflection in the group. At other times, one supervisee can bring client material to work on in one of these ways, to which some or all group members are invited to answer one or two questions in turn, for example, or to take roles, enact a drama, or comment on a map or picture.

Resources for specific creative exercises

Guidelines for good practice in using experiential exercises may be found in Inskipp and Proctor (2001a, 2001b) and Proctor (2000), where you will also find full descriptions of a number of exercises.

Chapter 12 of this book discusses creative supervision and suggests many ideas which could be used in groups as well as with individuals.

The DVD *Creative Supervision with Brigid Proctor and Francesca Inskipp* (Inskipp and Proctor, 2007) also illustrates the use of such exercises.

Wilbur *et al.* (1994) describe a specific six-step circular questioning exercise.

Kees and Leech (2002) describe rounds and exercises for establishing, clarifying and deepening the focus of supervision.

Fitch and Marshall (2002) describe the use of cognitive interventions with students undergoing training as counsellors.

These exercises may result in profound insights for supervisee and group members and at the same time create strong group self-esteem. Equally, if they are not set up properly, with clear enough intention and instructions, they can result in apathy, confusion, anger or shame. Members can feel very exposed in a group, so it is particularly important to foster a culture of respect and empathy, and especially to determine a time frame and keep to it. We would suggest that the full resources of the group – the rich imagination and sensory perceptions of each individual and of the group system – surface most satisfyingly within a well-set-up and well-held structure.

Formats

In the previous section it was suggested that groups need not always work *as* a whole group. Much good and time-effective work can be done by breaking into co-supervising pairs or threes for part of a session. This heightens responsibility and offers opportunities for the development of supervisor skills.

In addition, groups may regularly operate as a group for only part of their supervision time. A peer group, for instance, may decide to meet as regular, or changing, pairs for half of each session, and as a group for the rest. They may meet as a peer group one fortnight and a led group the next.

Practitioners may arrange (or be given) a mix of individual and group supervision – possibly ideal but often not realistic. This takes care of the need for some individual 'safe space' in a life of responsibility for others, and also for affiliation needs.

Group size

We believe that there has been no research on the optimum size for a supervision group (Bernard and Goodyear, 1998: 111). Those described in the literature are reported to vary between 3 and 12 individuals. The size must be in ratio with time and function. The responsibility of the group supervisor needs to be clear, as well as there being sufficient opportunity for individual supervisees to benefit in the group. For instance, if the supervisor is the *only* clinical supervisor of each group member, then either time or number must allow for this responsibility being sufficiently exercised.

As Webb (2000) suggested, a greater number of supervision participants will probably inhibit the supervisee's ability to be open. Size may often be determined by practicalities. The larger the group, the more difficult to establish an ethos in which people do not feel too vulnerable to talk about their work openly; the smaller the group the more difficult to sustain attendance in light of sickness absence or annual leave. It is probably an issue worth serious consideration during the planning and contracting stages of group supervision.

Homogeneity and diversity

Both homogeneity and diversity are desirable and potentially useful forces in a supervision group. The one helps to ensure that there is sufficient 'shared desire' (see above) to work together. The other ensures potential for 'thinking outside the box'. Few group supervisors (or supervisees) probably have the luxury of choosing individuals, though a supervisor may have power to limit intake to a specific number or category/ies. However similar or diverse group members may be, the issue of sufficient shared expectations about task and process is one of the most important strands of negotiating an initial working agreement and developing a safe and challenging enough working group.

Relevant research

Bernard and Goodyear (1998) argued that an important factor in establishing a supervision group is the degree of homogeneity or heterogeneity with respect to level of supervisee skill, theoretical orientation, profession, and characteristics of the working context. They argued the case for relative homogeneity for novice practitioners since they are likely to have greater empathy for each other and to develop trust more readily. Heterogeneous groups are probably more challenging to lead since different trainings and levels of experience might be expected to generate different hopes and expectations for individual group members. However, too much homogeneity can stifle spontaneity and limit opportunities for learning (Getzel and Salmon, 1995).

Mixed profession and mixed orientation groups

Any of the suggestions about working agreements and choice of type of group will be particularly important where a supervisor is being asked to run an interdisciplinary group. In such groups, sufficient shared values and understanding about good practice in therapy, care and supervision; ethical codes; and group manners cannot be relied on.

It will be important to engage the group in an exercise of comparing and contrasting expectations of the supervisor and of each other. Even this may be difficult if the supervisor is not received with trust. If, in addition to a lack of goodwill on the part of group members, the supervisor feels underconfident and expects resistance or competition, it can be hard to lead with intention and determination.

In preparing for the group, it is worth remembering that members will know more about their particular setting than does the supervisor. However, the supervisor will have thought and become clearer about the purpose, roles and responsibilities in group supervision than most, if not all, of the other group members. Further, the supervisor is entrusted with the responsibility of doing the best he or she can to enable and ensure good enough service to clients, whatever that takes – and it may take surviving some quite rough or subtle testing. Discovering how to find some common concerns, interests or, indeed, passions which can unite the group in doing good work will be the first leadership challenge. Discovering how to respect and value each member and develop some empathic understanding of those who feel threatened will be the starting challenge for the supervisor both as a person and as a practitioner.

In conclusion

This chapter has been written with the assumption that if supervisors set up a group with forethought and care, taking into account:

- their own developmental stage as a group leader and supervisor,
- the context of the group – the culture and expectations of stakeholders and members,
- the developmental stage of the supervisees,
- their own values and understanding about learning, practice and living,

then there is a good chance of running a 'good enough' (Winnicott, 1965) group. We consider a supervision group 'good enough' if it encourages and enables competent reflective practitioners who will enhance the lives of their clients.

Chapter 7

Ethical dilemmas and issues in supervision

Dr. Jones's last appointment of the day is with his supervisee Ms. Smith. When they finished, Jones noted that his family was out of town, he was going to take himself to dinner, and asked Smith if she would like to join him. She agreed, they had a pleasant dinner discussing professional issues, Jones paid the bill for both of them, and they went their separate ways.

Is asking a supervisee to dinner an ethical transgression? A shared dinner typically would not be considered problematic and generally is construed as potentially beneficial, but such a conclusion requires two assumptions. First, Jones's invitation was transparent. That is, he wanted a dinner companion and nothing more. Second, Smith correctly understood Jones's intentions. That is, she inferred nothing more from his invitation and did not take it to mean something other than what he intended. When these two assumptions are met, we can reasonably assume that the dinner would be enjoyable and perhaps beneficial to Smith as well. Unfortunately, the exact same scenario could lead to significant difficulties either because Jones had unacknowledged personal motives or because Smith found the invitation inappropriate or coercive.

The above passage is taken from a paper by Gottlieb *et al.* (2007) who contended that it is seldom problematic, for example, for a supervisor to have lunch with a supervisee, discuss current events, or travel to a professional meeting together. However, they referred to the concept of the 'slippery slope', sliding down which begins when a strictly helpful, professional relationship gradually moves towards a more personal one. Supervisors may not notice that they have begun this journey until it is too late. The above example illustrates the complexity of judging where the boundary lies. Because Dr Jones had no intent other than to have a dinner companion and nothing else was inferred by Ms Smith, there were no grounds to suggest that an ethical or professional boundary had been transgressed, although both parties were putting themselves at professional risk. If Dr Jones had had no intent other than to have a dinner companion but a sexual transgression nevertheless did take place, an ethical violation would have occurred but it might not have been reported. Had the ethical violation been observed by a third party, or had Ms Smith later come to view the sexual act as coercive, the behaviour might have been reported and there would be grounds for judging that an ethical violation had occurred.

In the case where no sexual transgression took place but Dr Jones' intention had been to seduce Ms Smith, if the supervisor's behaviour had been judged by Ms Smith and/or an observer (e.g. Dr Jones' partner) to be innocent then there would be no basis to assert that an ethical boundary violation had occurred. If Ms Smith or an observer had perceived seductive intent in Dr Jones' behaviour (whatever his actual intent) then there would be a basis for proposing that an ethical violation had occurred. Judgement of the issue would need to be referred to a body mandated to make a decision. The example illustrates that in order to determine whether practice is ethical it is necessary to consider actions in terms of both intentions and consequences.

Boundary violations

Boundary violations committed by health and social care professionals have long been reported in the literature (Fournier, 2000; Gabbard and Lester, 2003; Gonsoriek, 1995; Kumar, 2000; Smith et al., 1997). Discrimination and abuse against patients has been associated with a power imbalance in which professionals occupy the higher status position. There has been a perceived lack of suitable training that would encourage workers to uphold appropriate boundaries. It has been suggested, for example, that nurses were not aware of what constituted inappropriate behaviour in the workplace, did not know what to do if they had suspicions about a colleague's practice, or how to set limits if a patient flirted with them or made sexual advances (Smith et al., 1997). Training programmes focused on assisting medical students in setting and maintaining social and sexual boundaries within their training and in future medical practice have been described (White, 2004). Today there are organisations committed to supporting people who have suffered in the course of treatment by boundary-violating professionals (WITNESS, n.d.).

Gutheil and Gabbard (1993) made a distinction between boundary violations and boundary crossings, the latter occurring when a professional departs from what may be regarded as common practice. Boundary crossings in supervisory relationships do not become violations unless they do, or seek to do, the following: exploit the supervisee, disrupt the supervisory relationship, or lead towards harm that could reasonably have been foreseen by the supervisor (Younggren and Gottlieb, 2004). Boundary crossings are regarded as common occurrences. This perspective on boundary violations suggests two separate boundaries: a boundary of common professional practice, crossing which puts the parties at risk but which may not involve a violation of the wider ethical boundary. At times these two boundaries may be indistinguishable. In my view, a supervisor considering professional bound-ary crossing is well advised to share this and her or his reasoning about it with a colleague. It can be helpful to imagine the colleague in the room at the time when consideration is being given to crossing the line. In the absence of a colleague, making a formal public record including a record of the intent also serves to reduce risk. Supervisors might also seek specific training on the appropriate maintenance of boundaries with their supervisees, one model for which, in the matter of sexual feelings, has been proposed by Koenig and Spano (2004). Figure 7.1 lays out a decision tree for judgements regarding boundary violations.

At the heart of this chapter is the belief that workers in the helping profes-sions wish to take a principled and ethical stance in relation to their work, not only in their direct work with clients but in all of the professional roles and tasks they undertake. Practitioners' own individual understanding of what is 'right' or 'fitting' is likely to exert a significant influence on their practice, and such understanding is a sound starting point for taking an ethical path through the maze of work. As Baldwin and Barker (1991: 195) stated:

> Workers are accountable to their clients, their colleagues, employers and to society. Each worker has a responsibility to determine where his or her ultimate responsibility rests. Within these constraints, many workers will decide that they are, ultimately, responsible to themselves, and will operate according to a personal ethical code.

Work in the helping professions can be guided by professional codes of ethics and conduct, legal precedents, government policies and agency procedures, although these cannot replace the difficult work of ethical thinking and judgement (James and Foster, 2006). Traditionally, codes of ethics have been regarded as being in line with the cultural values of the society in which they have been conceived, and therefore unlikely to present significant conflicts between personal and professional values (Pettifor et al., 2002). In a multi-cultural and pluralistic world, this assumption is less viable. Given the plethora of imperatives to act according to a range of prescriptions from different sources, practitioners are increasingly likely to be faced with conflicting advice in reaching decisions regarding sound courses of professional action.

The supervisor who takes a conscious ethical approach to supervision can effectively model the process of ethical decision making to the supervisee. Stoltenberg and colleagues (1998) drew attention to the need for supervisors to be well aware of the necessity to behave as a role model for supervisees what-ever their level of professional development. Supervisors have vicarious eth-ical responsibilities in relation to the work being carried out by the supervisee. Whatever the legal position, the supervisor's responsibility to clients cannot be ducked. This is typically reflected in the law and, 'in supervision, responsibility is multiplied, it is never divided' (Saccuzzo, 2003).

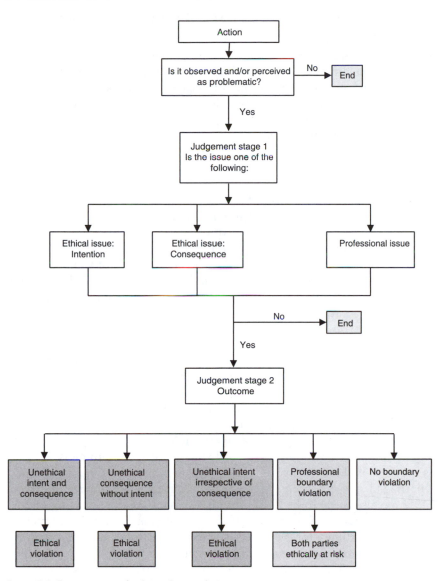

Figure 7.1 Decision tree for boundary violations.

This chapter focuses primarily on the ethical issues pertaining specifically to supervision rather than on those that arise in direct clinical work. The reader is referred elsewhere (Beauchamp and Childress, 2001; Bond, 2000; Jones *et al.*, 2000; Palmer Barnes, 2001; Pope and Vasquez, 2007) for discussions of the latter.

The role of the supervisor in the development of an ethical approach

The literature on learning ethics in psychology suggests that critical thinking and reflection are key to ethical decision making (Pettifor *et al.*, 2002). Research conducted by these authors indicated that workshop participants generally preferred small group discussion to more traditional didactic teaching when learning about 7 different ethics topics. Small group discussion provided an opportunity for participants to think and reflect together. Supervisors are in a good position to help supervisees reflect on their personal stance on ethical issues. By drawing on their own knowledge of how to conduct their work in an ethically sound manner they are able to foster such developing awareness in the supervisee. In preregistration training this may involve drawing the supervisee's attention to relevant codes of practice, legal statutes and government policies as well as exploring examples of ethical dilemmas. However, 'no ethics code or course can replace the consistent presence and modeling of a supervisor who actively helps the supervisee to integrate the principles of ethical, clinical practice, with the supervisee's pre-existing moral framework' (Clark and Croney, 2006: 52). The supervisor's role is particularly crucial because taught ethics courses often emphasise the study of doing wrong, with little attention given to best practices (Handelsman *et al.*, 2005). They argued that certificates, memberships and offices in professional associations are meaningless outward signs of competence without a firm personal grounding in and appreciation for the ethics and value traditions of the professional culture.

Supervisors may take opportunities for this modelling process in relation to firsthand issues affecting the supervisee, particularly in prequalification training where they occupy a managerial role. The supervisor is likely to require compliance with a number of local practices concerning issues such as security of the building, administrative responsibilities, hours of work, reporting of sickness absence, diary keeping, timeliness of reports and so on. There are also likely to be local procedures regarding the reporting of concerns such as issues of child protection or client vulnerability. These matters offer the opportunity for the supervisor to demonstrate authenticity, equity, transparency, responsiveness to critique, and the desirability of consulting with colleagues in areas beyond individual expertise. This beats unthinking adherence to potentially tokenistic policies or procedures that fail to do justice to their underlying purpose. Demonstration of the *process* of ethical decision making and acting is at the heart of the supervisor's role. It behoves the supervisor to explain the thinking behind local practices and to demonstrate preparedness to challenge these where they fail adequately to reflect ethical imperatives. In discussion, supervisors can explain to what extent agency policies and procedures align with their personal values and beliefs (authenticity), and how they relate to principles of ethics, legal precedents and codes of conduct. Procedures need to meet the test of fairness. By explaining the thinking behind a procedure the supervisor demonstrates transparency, thereby giving others a voice in contributing to its further development and modification through responsiveness to critique. By encouraging consultation with colleagues the supervisor demonstrates the right not to know and the desirability of sharing decision making around complex issues in order to ensure the safety of clients and staff. Such an approach is likely to communicate to supervisees a secure and non-defensive position which can be confidence generating in others.

Handelsman *et al.* (2005) advocated the use of an ethics autobiography or genogram, in which trainees outlined how they came to their present position of what it means to be an ethical professional. They argued that this can help supervisees to understand the need to learn more about how to act ethically in a professional as opposed to a personal situation.

Supervision can always be important as a space for exploration of ethical issues because even very experienced practitioners can find themselves drawn into unsound positions. For example, when a supervisee experiences a client as seductive, this can be discussed and recorded. The supervisor may take responsibility for following this up in a later session. Knowing that someone else knows helps to introduce a boundary whereby the supervisee can be kept on track by the involvement of someone more distant from the material that the client brings and the feelings that the client evokes.

Disclosure of ethical dilemmas faced by supervisees

When faced with ethical dilemmas, supervisees have a choice regarding whether to handle the dilemma alone or to bring the matter to supervision. The probability of disclosure is likely to be related to the quality of the supervisory relationship. Where supervisees fear an adverse opinion or response from the supervisor, non-disclosure and unsafe practice is more likely.

In a survey by Kent and McAuley (1995) of second- and third-year trainee clinical psychologists, only 14 out of 85 respondents indicated that they had not faced ethical dilemmas during training. The majority had discussed the matter with their supervisor, but in only 65 per cent of these cases had the trainee and supervisor agreed on a course of action. In 12 cases a conflict of view was not resolved and incompatible understandings prevailed. In five cases the trainee followed the supervisor's advice, but with significant misgivings, and in a further 12 cases the issue was not fully disclosed as the trainee reported having little faith in the way in which the supervisor would treat the information, or feared placement failure.

The following quotations illustrated the difficulties:

> I was told that I was very 'sensitive' which I took to be a criticism and this soured our relationship for a while and I felt my legitimate stance had not

been understood. She pathologized me, suggesting that I was making a huge fuss about nothing and my 'strong views' about violence towards children were getting in the way.

I didn't trust that my supervisor would treat the information confidentially.

(Kent and McAuley, 1995: 29)

Principles of ethics

Background

Currently applied principles of ethics have their roots in debates about moral philosophy that took place in the eighteenth and early nineteenth centuries. (See Warburton, 1995 for an introduction.) For example, Kant (Urmson and Rée, 1989) developed the notion of 'absolute duties' and the categorical imperative, 'Act only on that maxim which you can at the same time will to become a universal law'. Kantian ethics were based on the notion of duty, emphasising the motivations of actions and not their consequences. He believed that the consequences of actions were outside our control and could therefore not be crucial to morality. A problem with Kant's theory is its failure to address conflicts of duty. Lying, for example, is always immoral for Kant, even if a predicted consequence of telling someone the truth would be to put them in danger.

A second school of thought is that exemplified in consequentialist theories. These judge the rightness or wrongness of actions on their predicted consequences. Best known among these theories is J.S. Mill's Utilitarianism in which 'good' is whatever brings about the greatest total happiness. Various problems have been associated with this idea, including the difficulty in calculating universal happiness and the apparent justification for adding a 'happiness' drug to the water supply! It also raises other issues such as whether the trade-off of a little unhappiness in a lot of people is justified by a lot of happiness in a few.

A third school is that of virtue theory or neo-Aristotelianism. The emphasis here is on virtuous individual traits that cannot readily be encapsulated in moral rules or principles. Virtue ethics emphasises the character of the people who perform actions and make decisions. It has been argued that the virtuous judgements of healthcare professionals result in better decisions than the following of rules, codes or procedures (Williams, 1982: 50). A danger with this school of thought is that of circularity, in which individuals might define virtues in order to suit their preferences without reference to the more general good.

All of these traditional approaches have more recently been critiqued as failing to reflect the reasoning and methods of women. In particular, perspectives which focus on sympathy and concern for others have tended to be neglected. What has been proposed is an 'ethics of care' that promotes traits such as sympathy, compassion, fidelity, discernment, love and trustworthiness in intimate personal relationships (Noddings, 1984).

General principles of ethical decision making

Despite differences between schools of philosophy in the use of language and the starting points for generating ethical principles, there appears to be enough common ground to derive some general principles of ethical decision making.

Principles of ethics traditionally adopted in the profession of medicine were developed during the 1920s and 1930s out of an attempt to incorporate consideration of both the morality of an action and its anticipated consequences (Ross, 1930). In defining and applying ethical principles it was implicit that the judges were members of the professional community. An attempt was made to define and apply them on behalf of the client, although clients themselves might have defined and applied them differently. The principles were created by the professional community to guide professional action.

In light of a subsequent growing focus on consumer rights and user participation a case has been made for the full participation of individual clients and service users in the decisions made about them. An example would be parents' and children's direct participation in case conferences (Bell and Sinclair, 1993; Cloke and Davies, 1995). There is a demand for services to be provided in terms of clients' own values. Although codes of conduct generally do acknowledge that clients have their own values, views and beliefs, and that these should be taken into account, they may not go so far as user movements would wish. Banks (1998) argued that there is still mileage in retaining and developing codes of ethics, not as an imposed set of rules developed by professional associations, but as part of a dynamic and evolving ethical tradition and as a stimulus for debate and reflection on changing and contradictory values.

The principles of ethics adopted in the medical profession have been translated to the work of professional helpers. Page and Wosket (1994) proposed the use of the five principles of autonomy, beneficence, fidelity, justice and non-maleficence. Gert (2004) argued for seven principles, somewhat overlapping with those named by Page and Wosket: respect for persons, autonomy, beneficence, veracity, confidentiality, fidelity and justice.

Such principles offer frameworks which may be used to consider the ethical dilemmas that arise in supervision, either for supervisors themselves in executing the role, or in relation to the work of the supervisee. When faced with difficult decisions, supervision offers an opportunity to consider the principles in the context of the specific clinical issue, and to debate a best course of action. This process gives a degree of assurance that, whatever the actual outcomes, decisions have been taken from an ethical standpoint. Documenting the thought processes that underpin a decision embodies transparency and helps to ensure equity over time (What did we do last time and why?). It maintains an ethic of openness to critical evaluation by the wider community of practitioners and a sense of authenticity in practice, as opposed to operating in a rule-governed way in which practice has become detached from its ethical moorings. A further consideration is that such an approach can also protect the professional in the event of subsequent litigation in the light of outcomes.

Autonomy (the principle that individuals have rights to freedom of action and choice)

This is of importance in the helping professions, particularly since ways of working tend to emphasise self-actualisation and personal growth of the client as an aim of the work. Similarly, developmental models of supervision emphasise the increasing right to autonomy of supervisees as they become more experienced practitioners.

Beneficence (the principle that the actions taken should do good, using knowledge to promote human welfare)

The application of this principle needs to take account of who judges what is for the good and for whom it is judged to be good. In determining what is judged to be for the good in supervision, the participants will need to bear in mind the welfare of the supervisee, the client and involved others. The application of this principle can be particularly challenging when the work involves dependants such as children since the welfare of one family member may conflict with that of another.

Fidelity (being faithful to promises made)

Attention to this principle helps supervisors think carefully about what they can reasonably promise to supervisees during the contracting process with care taken not to go beyond what is possible. Confidentiality is an issue over which promises made must acknowledge the limits of the agreement. Clients need to be informed that supervisees will be discussing their therapy with the supervisor. In obtaining informed consent from clients, both with regard to the therapy and to disclosure in supervision, it is important to devise explanations that are not disengaging.

Justice (ensuring that people are treated fairly)

Justice is fair, equitable, and appropriate treatment in light of what is due or owed to persons (Beauchamp and Childress, 2001). Supervisors may draw on this principle to consider how to weigh the distribution of their time to different supervisees. This may be particularly challenging in the case of a practitioner who is struggling with her or his learning. The 'fair-opportunity rule' requires that this supervisee be provided with sufficient assistance to overcome any disadvantaging conditions resulting from her or his biological make-up or social context. This may mean offering a great deal more time and input than to another supervisee who is flourishing. Where time is limited, to whom is the first obligation?

Justice also encapsulates the notion of equitable treatment of people irrespective of ethnicity, gender, age, class, culture, sexual orientation, disability, religious affiliation and other individual differences. As in the above example, equitable treatment will often involve unequal treatment. To treat people in the same way would be to ignore the relative privilege or disadvantage conferred by individual and group characteristics.

Non-maleficence (striving to prevent harm)

In supervision, the needs of the supervisee and of clients may conflict. In training placements that result in student failure, the principle of non-maleficence is being applied with respect to potential future clients. It could, however, be argued that supervisees are themselves being harmed by the supervisor's refusal to sanction them in joining their chosen profession.

In the application of this principle, the question of the prevention of harm to whom arises. As in the above example, the needs of one person or group are being privileged over another. In some case examples, such as child protection, the law dictates the prevention of harm to some people over others.

In cases where the supervisee sees only one person in the system as the beneficiary, supervisors might help to create a wider perspective on the application of this principle. They may, for example, encourage supervisees to try not to cause harm to the mother and father, as well as to the child who has been the subject of abuse in a family.

Examples of conflicting ethical principles

Taken individually, the principles might suggest different courses of action, in which case the specific circumstances will determine precedence. If we adopted the principle that the worker should take whatever action he or she believes to be in the best interests of the client, this would be an exemplar based on the principle of beneficence. However, if only this principle were taken into consideration, the practitioner could take action in which the client's wishes were completely disregarded. In order to allow both considerations to influence the actions taken, the principle of autonomy (promoting the maximum degree of choice for all) would also need to be applied. It is inevitable at times that the principles will suggest conflicting courses of action. This is not as a result of inadequate thinking but rather arises due to the breadth of scope of the principles. Ethical dilemmas are inevitable and offer a rich opportunity for reflective practice.

Below are a number of vignettes that illustrate how the ethical principles might conflict with each other in regard to the decisions and courses of action a supervisor might take. They are offered as examples in which readers might ask themselves, 'How would I go forward from here?' One way of processing the inherent dilemmas is to identify the applicable principles of ethics, work out what follows from each principle, and then identify a course of action which might give greater weight to one principle but also takes account of the others. Rae and Fournier (1999: 67–83) included the additional steps of implementing and evaluating the decision in the process of ethical decision making. Sharing and documenting the process introduces additional valuable safeguards for both supervisors and supervisees.

- *You become increasingly concerned that your supervisee has mental health difficulties. This is reflected in an agitated state and spilling of personal material into the session, the supervisee showing an inability to contain the material any longer. On account of a disclosure of previous self-harm, you are concerned that if allowed to leave the premises, he or she will be unsafe. What principles of ethics are relevant and how might they inform your decision making and the course of action you take?*

One of the principles at issue here is fidelity. You have contracted to take the role of supervisor, not that of therapist. Were the supervisee a client of yours, you would be unlikely to find a course of action difficult to determine. The principle of beneficence would be likely to take precedence over that of autonomy in such an instance. Actions that followed from the principle of beneficence would lie within the agreed contract with a client, and there would be no conflict with the principle of fidelity. In the case of a supervisee, taking action to ensure the supervisee's safety would be likely to violate the contract agreed regarding the supervisory role relationship. The application of the principle of fidelity would influence whether you allowed the supervisee to talk to you about personal matters more fitting to therapy than supervision. Non-maleficence to clients, were the supervisee to be practising at this time, would also be a consideration. While in this example fidelity might usually be designated a less influential role than beneficence and non-maleficence, actions taken would also aim to protect, as far as possible, the original contract for supervision.

- *You become aware that increasingly you are sexually attracted to your supervisee. You take advice on this, resulting in a recommendation that you terminate the training relationship between yourself and the supervisee.*

You are reluctant to take this course of action as you would have to explain the unscheduled termination to the training institution.

An anonymous survey of 464 female psychologists (Glaser and Thorpe, 1986) elicited data on experiences during postgraduate training of sexual intimacy with and sexual advances from psychology educators. The replies indicated that sexual contact was quite prevalent overall (17 per cent), was greater (22 per cent) among recent doctoral recipients, and still higher among students divorcing or separating during postgraduate training (34 per cent). Sexual advances were reported by 31 per cent of respondents overall. Retrospectively these were almost invariably perceived as coercive. Since educators and students might experience sexual attraction without acting on these feelings, sexual issues are likely to be more prevalent than these figures indicate.

The coercion experienced as a result of sexual advances from educators violates the principal of autonomy. The experience of sexual attraction may interfere with the supervisor's capability to adhere to the supervision contract and there is a risk of the attraction resulting in a sexual advance. Where the attraction is mutual, the pull towards a dual relationship is likely to interfere with the tasks and responsibilities of supervision.

* *You are asked to provide supervision for someone who has failed a previous practice placement. This was as a result of serious concerns regarding the supervisee's failure to engage with clients in the work. The rules of the training course are such that the student must be offered a chance to repeat the failed placement or practicum.*

The dilemma here is about balancing justice for the student with non-maleficence and beneficence for current and future potential clients. Application of the principle of justice would promote the idea of the student having a second chance. In order to ensure the welfare of clients, the supervisor might introduce additional safeguards such as live supervision or observation. The dangers are that increased vigilance on the part of the supervisor might further elevate the already high levels of anxiety of the supervisee. This dilemma itself would be fair material to raise in supervision.

There are many examples where the primacy of the welfare of clients raises questions regarding the balance of ethical principles. It has been argued that, as a matter of course, supervisors should have independent meetings with the supervisee's clients. Kerby Neill and colleagues (2006: 8) gave an example in which the supervisor intervened directly with a state agency in order to secure the welfare of a child client of a supervisee. In this case the supervisee was invited to observe the supervisor's interventions which were regarded as beyond any beginner. Clark and Croney (2006: 57) stated, 'We have found that regular chart audits and independent contacts with clients to ascertain their satisfaction with ongoing treatment are very helpful, especially for

monitoring supervisees' work in homes, schools and in neighbourhoods.'
I imagine that many practitioners would find this approach quite heavy-
handed and if deemed necessary, routine contacts with clients intended to
secure their welfare are less likely to be experienced as threats to supervisee
autonomy than those set up in specific cases of concern.

- *Your supervisee is voracious for support and help to learn. Despite many
  hours of input from you the supervisee does not seem to progress. At what
  point do you decide to deny assistance in the face of her or his enthusiasm
  but apparent inability to learn?*

Again, the needs of clients and of the supervisee are potentially in conflict.
The principles of justice and beneficence applied to the supervisee might lead
you to carry on trying, although it could also be argued that the supervisee
would benefit from a change of career. When you have done all that you can
without progress then the needs of clients are likely to take precedence. In this
example there are the needs of three parties to consider, since the well-being
of the supervisor might be threatened by the excessive demands and needs of
the supervisee. There is also the issue of supervisors' fidelity to their terms and
conditions of employment, since their other work is at risk of suffering.

A further example illustrates a conflict of interest in the requirements of
the host training institution and of the supervisor.

- *The decision that employees in your position should take part in the training
  programme may have been made at an institutional level. You have not been
  consulted but are expected to participate, as supervision is a key result area
  in your job description. The supervisee explains the requirements of the
  training programme which conflict with your views about the work. For
  example, the supervisee states that he or she has to complete an assignment
  based on the use of a theoretical model to which you do not subscribe.*

Here you are expected to show fidelity with regard to promises made on your
behalf and without your consent. You cannot afford to lose your job and
your employer insists that you participate. You wish to hold faith with your
own beliefs about the work in order best to serve clients under the principles
of non-maleficence and beneficence. Ways forward might include the involvement of a colleague who works in the model prescribed by the training institution. Alternatively, a debate with your employer might refer to the principles
of ethics and the bind in which you have been placed.

- *You have become aware of a blind spot of your own – you do not feel
  comfortable with having your work observed live or recorded and therefore
  avoid it yourself in your own clinical practice. The supervisee has a preference to use reporting as the medium of supervision. You agree to this,*

enabling both of you to avoid observation of your work. The supervisor and supervisee thus find themselves colluding (possibly tacitly) in their difficulty.

The principle of autonomy might dictate that the supervisee be responsible for the choice of supervisory medium. In post-registration supervision this may be non-problematic. In preregistration training there is a question as to whether it is appropriate to qualify without having had work observed. Where observation during training is the norm, the lack of such experience threatens the integrity and breadth of the training, and it could be argued that clients are receiving an inequitable service. In addition, if supervisors fail to take action on this developmental need of their own, the principles of justice, beneficence and non-maleficence might be violated, since their work is subject to fewer safeguards than that of other practitioners.

Codes of conduct, legal requirements, government and agency policy

Decision making also needs to take account of codes of conduct, legal requirements, government and agency policies which have been devised in the context of principles of ethics but with diverse purposes in a constantly changing political and economic climate. It has been argued (Banks, 1998) that codes of ethics generated by professional organisations seem to serve at least four functions: guidance to practitioners about how to act; protection of users from malpractice or abuse; contribution to the 'professional status' of an occupation; and the establishment and maintenance of professional identity. She argued that agencies and government have largely taken over the first two functions by prescribing requirements for conduct and procedures to be followed.

Without reference to principles of ethics, codes of conduct and agency- or government-prescribed procedures can become a set of rules implemented mechanically and thoughtlessly as a professional requirement that avoids the difficult work of ethical thinking and judgement. Supervisees do need to ensure that they familiarise themselves with the codes of conduct relevant to their specific profession. Supervisors can help by drawing their attention to relevant documentation including examples where practitioners have been subject to litigation or professional reprimand. However, there can be significant gaps between the practice aspired to in official prescriptions and actual practice in the field. Codes of conduct are sensitive to the cultural and political context of the time. For example, in Britain the advent of the internal market in the National Health Service, increased litigation and the development of managed care networks, where information collected at one level of care is transferred to another, have influenced professional guidance on confidentiality and note keeping. The change towards more rigorous, detailed and transferable notes has not been at the behest of clients and there is no evidence to suggest that it enhances client welfare. A survey of practitioners in the field (Scaife and Pomerantz, 1999) concluded that there was a gap between the pragmatics of actual practice and the guidance issued by the British Psychological Society (1995, 1998a) to its members on confidentiality and note keeping. In some cases the security of notes was compromised by the absence of lockable cabinets, and files were not infrequently written up after a considerable time period had elapsed from the session being recorded. Respondents were also reluctant to record certain types of data that might compromise the position of the client – for example, the information that the client was illegally resident in the UK. The study concluded that despite guidance from professional organisations and the Department of Health, many issues with regard to note keeping were unresolved, ambiguous and subject to individual and local decision making.

Codes of conduct may also contain prescriptions regarding the recording of supervision sessions. For example, the Professional Practice Guidelines of the British Psychological Society (2007a) state that supervisors should:

> Maintain copies of all supervisory contracts and any updates, record the date and duration of each session, maintain an agreed supervision log-book and enter notes on the content of each session including decisions reached and agreed actions, and record in writing all regular reviews of supervision. Where a risk or ethical issue requiring a course of action arises, it is likely that the supervisor would expect the supervisee to record appropriate details in any client records.
>
> (British Psychological Society, 2007a: 17)

Given such guidance, it is wise for practitioners to establish with their employers and their supervisees where the supervision records fit with the client's own clinical record. The issue is complex because notes may be used by or against the practitioner, to ensure supervisor and supervisee accountability, for the purposes of licensure or professional registration, and in litigation. There is an ongoing interaction between issues of confidentiality, accountability and technological developments which means that the issue is never finally settled. To whom do supervision notes belong? Where might counter-transference issues be recorded? When should supervision notes be destroyed? How can electronic records of supervision conducted online be kept secure? At the heart of the issue is a focus on the purpose of a record and the principles captured in the Data Protection Act (1998). It states that personal data may only be used for the purpose for which it was originally collected. In addition, it must be adequate, relevant and not excessive, as well as being accurate, kept up to date and securely stored. A system for destroying records after they have served their purpose should be in place. Data must not be kept for longer than the purpose for which it was made. The client's explicit consent is required for the recording of sensitive data: this includes ethnicity, beliefs, sexual life, physical and mental health. The client must also be told what will be done with this data. Issues that need to be considered in relation to supervision notes are discussed extensively by Despenser (2004), Falvey (2004) and Hurley and Hadden (2005).

Because of inconsistencies across organisations and practitioners, and in consequence of the changing political and economic climate in which policies and procedures are devised, practice benefits from thinking and reflection based within knowledge of principles of ethics and awareness of one's personal value base. Ethical practice includes an orientation designed to influence the development of codes of conduct and policy frameworks in directions informed by consideration of client wishes, welfare and practicality.

Legal precedents have a place in ethical decision making and are often established following conflicts which it has not been possible to resolve without recourse to legal action. All professionals make mistakes. What is important is that people do their best in the knowledge of principles of ethics, codes of conduct and legal precedents. Wherever there is doubt about a course of action, the approach to the ethical dilemma benefits from careful thought and full documentation of the thinking process. It is always advisable when in doubt to consult with another and to document the conversation that took place. When consequences can be grave this process best ensures the peace of mind and safety of all concerned.

Examples of ethical and legal issues arising in supervision

The following section introduces some specific ethical and legal issues arising in supervision. It is important to keep sight of the underlying drive for ethical practice: the supervisor's responsibility for the well-being of the supervisees' current and future clients. In doing so practitioners might helpfully consider how to conduct themselves professionally at all times and to stay within the confines of the law.

Confidentiality

Practitioners in the helping professions owe a duty of confidentiality to clients. This applies to information communicated verbally and to that held in files such as recordings, test results, charts and notes. Communications made to the supervisor, whether directly by the client or by the supervisee, impose the duty of confidentiality on the supervisor (Disney and Stephens, 1994). The extent to which this duty may be overridden by the courts differs according to the laws of the country in which the participants reside, but it is wise to maintain strict confidentiality unless compelled by law to do otherwise.

In the context of clinical supervision it is essential to inform the client that confidential communications will be shared with the supervisor, and the client's consent to this should be obtained by the supervisee. It is the supervisor's responsibility to discuss with the supervisee the ethical duty of confidentiality owed to the client. The client also needs to know the limits of confidentiality where supervision is undertaken in groups. Disney and Stephens recommend that supervisors refer to seven elements defined by Bernard and O'Laughlin (1990) as essential to the assurance of confidentiality:

- Ethical standards and canons regarding confidentiality must be identified and discussed with supervisees.
- Confidentiality of client materials must be maintained.
- Security of client materials must be maintained.
- Prohibition of non-professional discussion must be ensured.
- Prohibition of disclosure of client identity must be ensured.
- Clients must be informed of service policies regarding confidentiality and ethics.
- Exceptions to confidentiality and privileged communications must be identified and discussed with supervisees and clients.

Issues of confidentiality are even more complex where the work involves clients and their carers. It is more difficult to ensure confidentiality for children, adolescents, people with learning disabilities and anyone assessed as unable to plead. In the case of children, Behnke and Kinscherff (2002) proposed the development of agreements offering levels of confidentiality which might provide greater opportunity for adolescents to disclose private thoughts and potentially dangerous or harmful behaviours to professionals.

The earlier discussion of issues relating to supervision notes illustrated the complexity of the notion of confidentiality. In all of the settings in which I have been employed, team members, secretarial and administrative staff have had high levels of access to client files. The greater the number of staff with access, the wider the use of technology, the more difficult becomes the challenge of genuine confidentiality.

Vicarious responsibility

The nature of supervision means that supervisors hear things that they cannot un-know. To know is to become to some degree responsible, although the extent of this will vary dependent upon the defined relationship. Whatever the professional responsibility, there is a personal responsibility deriving from the acquisition of such information.

In some cases this vicarious liability has been established through legal precedent. In particular there is a dramatic example established in US law through the Tarasoff case (*Tarasoff* v. *Regents of the University of California*,

1974). The university psychologist warned campus police that one of his clients had threatened to kill his girlfriend. The client was questioned by police, was later released and subsequently killed his girlfriend. The university psychologist had been advised by his supervisor not to warn the victim directly as this might be regarded as a breach of confidence (Meyer *et al.*, 1988). The family of the victim took legal action on the basis that university staff had been negligent because the potential victim was not warned personally. Although the case was settled out of court, it is widely regarded as having been found in favour of the victim's family. As a result several states in the USA have made the 'duty to warn' a legal standard for all mental health professionals.

The position in Britain is somewhat different and psychologists in such a case would not be expected to warn the potential victim directly. They would, however, be expected to inform the police in the case of the possibility of serious crime (Wadsborough Solicitors, 1999).

In instances such as the Tarasoff case, the supervisor may be held in part negligent for the actions of the supervisee. A supervisor and supervisee are both responsible if negligence occurs, but to differing degrees and for different reasons. The supervisor has an additional responsibility to apply experience and skill to predict and minimise the possibility of negligence (Ryan, 1991).

Responsibility to clients

A major consideration in supervision is to help safeguard the welfare of the client. Supervisors must address issues which call into question client welfare. Supervisors need sufficient knowledge regarding the performance of the supervisee to be in a position to make judgements about competence to practise, particularly when acting in the role of gatekeeper to the profession. Inadequacies cannot be addressed unless they are clearly and specifically identified to or by the supervisee, and the supervisor needs to develop skills in constructive challenge and evaluation. Issues that might evoke the need for challenge and ways of approaching this are discussed further in Chapter 14.

In preregistration training the supervisor's responsibility can include failing supervisees who are unable to meet the required standards of the profession. Typically, those supervisees who would benefit from being counselled out of the profession are showing relational difficulties both with clients and in supervision (Ladany *et al.*, 2005: 206). Of all the tasks of the supervisor this is one of the least palatable and, because it is rare, opportunities for gaining experience in how to handle failure are very limited. Many forms of remediation may be attempted before reaching this decision, balancing the welfare of clients with assistance for the supervisee.

Due process

'Due process' is a legal term referring to the rights and liberties of people in which any procedures to which a person is subject must be fair, considerate and equitable (Disney and Stephens, 1994). An example in relation to clients would be taking action to admit someone to a mental health facility under a legal section. This must be carried out with due process. Supervisees in training also have due process rights in that the supervisor's evaluation must be fair and equitable and the supervisee must have the opportunity to appeal.

It is important that the supervisor identifies serious concerns as early as possible in order that the supervisee can be informed of their nature and have an opportunity to address them. Use of the word 'failure' helps to make the level of concern clear to the supervisee. Since supervision is about learning and development it is important that once an issue has been identified the supervisee should have a reasonable opportunity to make progress. It is also important that the supervisee understands what is needed in order to do this. The issue of failure is explored further in Chapter 14.

Knowing about other colleagues

While supervision may principally focus upon work carried out with clients, as supervisees become more experienced they may wish to discuss issues regarding their relationships with colleagues. Particularly in professions that have only a small membership, the supervisor may become party to information about the practice of a known colleague. This can pose a striking dilemma. With no formal responsibility for this colleague's work, steering a course of action may be particularly difficult. Even when the colleague is unknown to the supervisor, gross professional misconduct cannot be allowed to continue. It is not the role of the supervisor to investigate the matter or to make judgements about the case. It may be that the supervisor can best help the supervisee by identifying to whom in the colleague's organisation the information should be disclosed, and by backing them up in the process.

Supervisor competence

Training and accreditation as a supervisor is not yet a mandatory requirement across the helping professions. While professional associations typically specify the requirements for competence to practise within the profession, the specifications of standards of competence for supervisors have been developed relatively recently (American Association of Directors of Psychiatric Residency Training, 2005; British Psychological Society, 2007b: Appendix 5; Phillips and Green, n.d.). The issue was explored by Newman (1981: 692), who raised the following questions:

- Has the supervisor had training in the theory and practice of supervision or in the supervised practice of psychotherapy supervision?
- Do supervisors conscientiously practise the skills they are helping their trainees to learn?
- Has the supervisor had training or experience in the assessment or treatment of the types of clinical problems and clients seen by the trainee?
- If the supervisor is not adequately qualified, has supervision by a qualified clinician been arranged or has the trainee's client been referred elsewhere?

In the absence of mandatory requirements it behoves supervisors to attend to issues regarding their own competence to practise in this role by seeking education, training and experience. The role is a responsible one both in relation to clients and supervisees, and an ethical approach incorporates the need to attend to personal and professional development in the role.

No matter how competent, there will inevitably be occasions when practitioners find themselves in situations in which they are wondering, 'How on earth did I get into this position?' A good test of any action is to ask oneself, 'If one of my colleagues were to be sitting on my shoulder watching what I am doing, would I feel comfortable, or could I at least justify my actions?' If the answer is 'No', beware. Having said this, I would argue that it is possible to act too conservatively and that at times it is desirable to be 'near the edge' without going over the edge. On such occasions it is wise to discuss and document the action taken and the reasoning behind it.

Some professional bodies, in recognition that there will be times despite best intentions that clients are put at risk by the acts of professionals, recommend that practitioners ensure they are covered by third party liability insurance. This is regarded as an ethical issue since clients who have been damaged have recourse to compensation. In many cases, cover will be provided by an employer. In the National Health Service in the UK, for example, staff are automatically indemnified, and claims dealt with by the NHS litigation authority. When the employer does not provide cover, it may be available through a trade union or through a private insurer. An example of the kind of case that might involve a supervisee is where a practitioner in training has been attacked and injured by a client referred by the supervisor.

Happily, the majority of practitioners work for their entire careers without having to defend themselves against claims of responsibility for the cause of serious harm. More typical are some of the ethical dilemmas outlined earlier. Bernard and Goodyear (1998) pointed out that ethical practice is a way of professional existence, not the command of a body of knowledge, and that the only reasonable approach for supervisors is to put ethics in the foreground of practice. Supervisors are then in a position to model what they aspire to teach.

Dual-role relationships and boundary violations

The potential for dual-role relationships (i.e. the supervisor having an additional role with the supervisee) is not uncommon in arrangements for supervision. These may include a line management arrangement, a pre-existing friendship, or the development of intimacy (sexual or otherwise) during the course of the supervisory relationship which might compromise the role as supervisor.

Dual relationships can be difficult to manage since the expectations and obligations of the different roles are sometimes divergent. An example from my own experience was of participating in a supervisory group in which one of the group members was the spouse of the supervisor. How was the supervisor to ensure that he did not favour his partner, or be perceived as favouring her? In this case the dilemma resulted in an apparently critical stance towards her work compared with that of the rest of the group. As a supervisee this was difficult to raise, since the supervisor had already made the decision to accept his partner as a group member.

I take the view that while in some cases dual relationships are built into the nature of the supervisory task, dual relationships of any kind between supervisor and supervisee are potentially problematic. For example, supervisors may be teachers, evaluators and also facilitators of self-awareness. Kurpius *et al.* (1991) pointed out that the American Association for Counseling and Development Ethical Standards (1988: 8, H12) state, 'When the educational program offers a growth experience with an emphasis on self-disclosure or other relatively intimate or personal involvement, the member must have no administrative, supervisory or evaluating authority regarding the participant.' At the same time, the standards require that counselling trainers 'must establish a program directed toward developing students' skills, knowledge and self-understanding' (p. 8, H3). These two standards potentially stand in conflict.

Harrar *et al.* (1990) implied that all intimate relationships between a supervisor and supervisee constitute violations of professional ethics. When intimacy develops during the course of the relationship the participants are likely to be so focused on each other as to be insulated against the outside world. It seems highly dubious that supervisors could carry out their task uninfluenced by the personal events taking place. Sometimes people who have had a social relationship with each other and then find themselves in a professional relationship agree to suspend their socialising while the professional relationship continues. This may serve as an adequate solution, although there is potential for the changed roles to threaten a successful return to friendship upon termination of supervision and people may prefer not to take the risk.

Line management supervision is not uncommon in many agencies. In such arrangements, the requirements of the employing organisation may play a relatively large role in defining the relationship and the possibilities within it.

For example, Morrison (1993: 1), in his book on supervision in social care, introduced the topic by stating, 'The task of the supervisor, at any level in the organisation, at its simplest is to get the organisation's job done through the staff s/he manages.' He argued that accountability is a central function of supervision and that supervision is a medium through which staff learn how the agency understands and exercises accountability and control. He pointed out that authority and control are often associated with punishment and punitiveness. If perceived in this way, staff are less likely to share doubts or possible mistakes as a result of which the organisation will have less control over outcomes. In a second edition, Morrison (2001: 3) drew attention to the experience of staff being stretched to the limits by unprecedented levels of demand, rising public expectations, efficiency savings, relentless change and a crisis in staff recruitment and retention. In this climate he argued that good supervision is central not only in terms of its normative function but also for its formative and restorative capabilities.

When the supervisory relationship includes line management responsibilities, it is helpful for the participants to be clear about the restrictions this may place on the material that the supervisee chooses to bring to supervision. Case management may occupy centre stage while supervision may still serve the full range of functions. The tasks of ensuring that employees meet the requirements of the employer and of appraising the work of the supervisee inevitably play a part in supervision. The complexities of the dual role of manager and supervisor are explored in greater detail in Chapter 9.

It is important for supervisors to be aware not only of the ethical issues underlying clinical practice but also to have considered those additional issues arising from the role of supervisor. If an ethical perspective is adopted as a matter of habit this not only provides a sound model for the supervisee but also serves to safeguard the well-being of clients, supervisees and supervisors themselves. Corey *et al.* (1993) proposed the following cognitive process as a map to follow when an ethical dilemma arises:

- Identify the problem or dilemma.
- Identify the potential issues involved.
- Review relevant ethical guidelines.
- Discuss and consult with colleagues.
- Consider possible and probable courses of action.
- Enumerate the possible consequences of various decisions.
- Decide what appears to be the best course of action.

It is recommended that each of the above steps be documented so that in the sorry event of negative outcomes the process of reaching a decision may be shown to have been ethically sound.

Chapter 8

Supervision and diversity

Diversity

Differences among people along the dimensions of ethnicity, culture, gender, faith, sexuality, age and disability have provided a context for discrimination in favour of the dominant group throughout our cultural history. Ethical practice under the principle of justice requires that an equitable approach be made to different groups whether these involve clients and/or supervisees. The dominant group is often in the majority but this is not necessarily the norm as, for example, in the case of South Africa under apartheid.

In the twenty-first century issues of diversity are appropriately and necessarily receiving greater amounts of attention. Supervisors whose initial training took place in former times, and I count myself among them, may find themselves ill-equipped to deal with the challenges presented by issues of diversity unless they set about educating themselves in relation both to their own practice and to their supervision.

Nowadays, preregistration training courses typically include a theoretical component addressed to cultural competence, cultural sensitivity, transcultural healthcare, cultural responsiveness, cultural capability and the like. But there is evidence to suggest that training courses may have limited effectiveness in bringing about learning in this domain (Bennett, 2007; Dogra *et al.*, 2007; Pilkington and Cantor, 1996) and that cultural diversity training brings about little, if any, significant change in the quality of service provision (Anderson *et al.*, 2003; Beach *et al.*, 2004). While in the UK the majority of employers have a diversity policy and 60 per cent offer diversity training, research into the effectiveness of such training is in its infancy, and evaluation of the outcomes of the training is either absent or limited to participant ratings immediately following the training sessions (Pendry *et al.*, 2007). This gives the supervisor a pivotal position in facilitating the development of ethical practice and equitable treatment. Supervision provides an opportunity to ground consideration of cultural issues in practice, not only in the direct work of supervisor and supervisee, but also as it concerns the supervisory relationship itself. Open and frank discussion of cultural issues can lead to reduced anxiety and enhance personal and professional development provided that the supervisory alliance remains strong (Ladany *et al.*, 2005: 60).

Learning about diversity is a lifelong journey. Personal experience suggests that awareness of a need to learn more about difference can begin with an internal sense of discomfort evoked by apparently small but significant differences between self and others, such as the newspaper I choose to read and the kind of food I have in my lunchbox. More embarrassing can be an acute sense of having got things 'wrong'. Later come questions about what I need to do when my supervisee and I have different ethnicities, genders, faiths, ages and so on. Often, being confronted with difference along a single dimension prompts thinking and learning: 'How will I work with a supervisee who is twice my age?'; 'What do I need to think about when my black trainee joins my all-white team?'

There is considerable debate and lack of agreement about the meaning of key terms, for example, *transcultural* or *multicultural* supervision and therapy, depending on perspective (Bradby, 2003; Dogra and Karim, 2005; Fine *et al.*, 2005; Mulholland *et al.*, 2001; Papadopoulos, 2006). An inclusive view (broad range) embraces differences between people along the dimensions of ethnicity, culture, socio-economic status, gender, sexual orientation, religious and spiritual beliefs, age, disability and any other group characteristic. In an exclusive view the terms are limited to 'race' and ethnicity (Burkard *et al.*, 2006; Stone, 1997). In this section I take a broad-range view such as that explicit in the definition of cultural identity adopted by the Association of American Medical Colleges (AAMC, 1999):

> Cultural identity may be affected by such factors as race, ethnicity, age, language, country of origin, acculturation, sexual orientation, gender, socioeconomic status, religious/spiritual beliefs, physical abilities, occupation, among others. These factors may impact on behaviours such as communication styles, diet preferences, health beliefs, family roles, lifestyle, rituals and decision-making processes.

Developing cultural competence

The term 'cultural competence' has been used to describe a state to which supervisors might aspire through attempts to develop their awareness of culture and its impact on themselves, their clients and their supervisees. Various authors have proposed models of cultural competence (Atkinson *et al.*, 1989; Constantine and Ladany, 2001; Helms, 1990; Lopez, 1997; Ponterotto and Pedersen, 1993). Smith (1981: 141–185) referred to a 'myth of sameness' in which workers assume that the skills of the helper are generic and applicable to all individuals irrespective of their backgrounds and personal qualities. Such an approach ignores the absence of a level playing field for minority groups and leads to the application of methods devised by one group to others in which the method used is of questionable and dubious value. One example of this was the misuse of intelligence tests to assess people from cultures other than that in which the test was devised (Poortinga, 1995).

It has been suggested that culturally competent supervision may be seen as a template for all good supervision (Rapp, 2000). 'Cultural competence, multi-cultural competence, and cultural sensitivity all concern therapists' ability to treat people of diverse cultural backgrounds in ways that respect, value, and integrate their sociocultural context' (Lopez, 1997: 570).

Page and Wosket (2001) argued that supervisors who are committed to working in a supervisee-responsive manner need the willingness and competence to acknowledge and adapt to varying degrees of difference between themselves and their supervisees, and that this can raise some complex issues. They suggest reflection upon some illustrative questions. The following points are adapted from their list:

- To what degree can a heterosexual supervisor, raised in a context in which aspects of homosexual behaviour were illegal, really get to grips with what a gay counsellor experiences in working with gay clients? It is worth noting that at other times in a Western cultural context, a different perspective was taken on sexuality:

    > Seeing gays as a group is now taken for granted, but before the 18th century the idea would never have occurred to ask the question whether homosexuality is a function of heredity or of upbringing. It was simply not seen as being a fundamental part of the person, but instead as an action, something s/he did.
    >
    > (Ehrencrona, 2002)

- How far can a white supervisor and white supervisee realistically hope to consider and understand, with any degree of accuracy, the experience of racism that a black client, living in a white-dominated society, may or will have had throughout life?
- To what extent can a self-determined female counsellor prevent herself from overlaying her own values and expectations on a female client whose identity and self-concept may be firmly grounded in family roles and responsibilities?
- To what degree can the counsellor who works in private practice with self-referred fee-paying clients hope to understand the context of her supervisee's work with non-voluntary clients in a secure setting?
- How far can a salaried supervisor in a financially secure job understand the dynamic that is enacted between her supervisees and their clients when they work for a voluntary agency with clients who are often homeless and without an income?

This is not to take the view that it is possible only to work with clients and supervisees who have had similar life experiences and backgrounds to oneself but rather to emphasise the degree of continuous effort and imagination that is required in order to address issues of difference.

Reflections on issues of diversity might lead supervisors, for example, carefully to select clients for a black, female or homosexual worker so as to protect them from experiencing rampantly racist, sexist or homophobic clients. The danger here is that of the supervisor taking responsibility in such a way that might reinforce the experience of a negative power differential. It also assumes that individuals from a minority group share similar experiences whereas the use of blanket terms can mask striking variations. Of children classified as 'Asian', 17.7 per cent of Pakistani heritage, 4.2 per cent of Bangladeshi heritage and 26.4 per cent of Indian heritage gained five or more O level passes in 1985 in the Inner London Education Authority (Nuttall *et al.*, 1989). Lumping Asians or any other minority group together can make for misleading conclusions about needs and appropriate responses. On the other hand it can be helpful to have some knowledge of cultural traditions, so long as assumptions are not made about specific individuals. For example, in a study of Hong Kong Chinese, supervisees tended to use supervision to ensure that the supervisor was responsible for decision making, and they often became frustrated when no clear instructions were given. The authors argued that the Chinese attitude towards hierarchical relationships and the practice of subordination to authority were obvious in the supervisor–supervisee relationship (Tsui *et al.*, 2005). Brown *et al.* (2006) argued that the majority culture in the USA is 'low context'; i.e. communication tends to be informal and direct, relying less on non-verbal communication than 'high context' cultures in which communication is more relational and contemplative. Miscommunication is easy when supervisor and supervisee are used to contrasting forms of talking.

Supervisors have an ethical responsibility to include consideration of minorities in their work because the helping professions are 'socio-political' in nature (Katz, 1985) and tend to reflect the values and ideologies of the dominant group. All acts within the role may be seen as to a greater or lesser degree political, and work with people who belong to disadvantaged groups tends to reveal this political nature more clearly. For example, consider the question of whether to allocate a black supervisee to a black or white supervisor. Allocation of the black supervisee to the black supervisor may represent an acknowledgement of the possibility of common experiences based on membership of a minority group. However, it may also be tokenistic and based on a false assumption that both parties belong to a common cultural group. Even the act to decide to consult with the supervisee about her or his preferences prior to making the allocation singles the person out if this is not the usual procedure.

The notion that we are disadvantaged in some contexts and privileged in others according to different aspects of our identities has been termed 'multiplexity' (Ayvazian, 1995). By providing opportunities within a group setting for learners to experience firsthand the emotional experience of the dynamics of power both from majority and minority positions, it is proposed that they are aided in developing their cultural knowledge. Connecting to personal experiences of unjust treatment, feeling unheard or silenced is likely to have the effect of increasing the ability to attune to, listen for and hear other stories in a more open way (Akamatsu, 1998). Divac and Heaphy described a workshop exercise entitled 'Monica's Fifty Questions' (McGoldrick, 2004 cited in Divac and Heaphy, 2005) in which trainees are asked to 'stand up if . . .' they answer affirmatively to the 50 questions posed; for example:

- Would you stand up if you remember the day Martin Luther King died?
- Would you stand up if you earn more than your partner?
- Would you stand up if you were ever turned down by a school?
- Would you stand up if you changed class/social status through marriage?

These questions are designed to draw attention to personal experiences of belonging to a minority group. They are also by nature culture bound. For example, younger people in the UK are more likely to recall the death of Stephen Lawrence than that of Martin Luther King, and older people to have changed class through education rather than through marriage.

Supervision that takes account of issues of diversity has been termed affirmative supervision (Halpert *et al.*, 2007: 341–358). Affirmative supervision is intended to augment the supervisor's existing theoretical model and involves taking a respectful and equitable stance in relation to the broad spectrum of individual and cultural diversities. No matter how liberal we believe our thinking to be, vestiges of influences from our earlier lives are likely to persist and it is incumbent on supervisors to continue addressing how these earlier influences emerge in our work. Even alert awareness does not guarantee against false assumptions. Manaster and Lyons (1994: 47) caution, 'It is as big a mistake to counsel someone according to a group classification as it is to counsel someone without regard to their group identity.'

Gender-specific issues in supervision

While it may be conjectured that gender plays a part in supervisory relationships, there is limited evidence from empirical studies for gender differences in supervision. A study by Sells *et al.* (1997) reported that female supervisors had a greater relational focus than did male supervisors, spending more time in supervision focused on the trainee, whereas male supervisors spent more time focused on the trainee's client. However, the impact of supervision (rated either by supervisor or supervisee) was not related to gender nor was there a relationship between gender and the supervisor's evaluation of the supervisee's work.

The arena in which gender has been found to play a part, not only in the context of supervision but more widely in an educational setting, is in regard to the confidence levels that supervisees show in their capabilities. When there is no difference between males and females in measures of knowledge or performance rated by supervisors or by formal assessment measures, women consistently tend to underestimate their accomplishments whereas men tend to overestimate them (Scaife, 2002; Warburton *et al.*, 1989: 152). Awareness of this difference might influence supervisors to approach their male and female supervisees' accounts of their work somewhat differently. One other finding is that men have been found to execute 75 per cent of all conversational interruptions (Kollock *et al.*, 1985) and if this is indicative of a sex difference in conversational style then it is likely to be relevant at least in group supervision.

'Power' and gender in supervision

Bernard and Goodyear (1998) defined social or interpersonal power as the ability to influence the behaviour of another person. They regard it as a variable to be acknowledged in supervisory relationships and report research that investigated whether the process of influencing differs according to gender. One finding of a study carried out by Nelson and Holloway (1990: 479) was reported thus:

> It appears that individuals in the expert role, regardless of gender, may assume more power in interaction with their female subordinates than with their male subordinates, either by withholding support for the female subordinates' attempts at exerting power or by simply exerting stronger influence with female subordinates. In the supervisory relationship the female trainee may respond to this stance on the part of her supervisor by declining opportunities to assert herself as an expert.

My own experience of influencing suggests the operation of a two-way process in which it is not always clear where the power lies. Undoubtedly the supervisor has more formal power than the supervisee when holding the key to qualification as a professional. However, in the context of supervision, it could be argued that the supervisor is influenced to exert more power by the behaviour of the female trainee who does not assert herself (Granello *et al.*, 1997). This may be because she has been socialised to believe that it would not be appropriate gender-role behaviour for a female. The research cited earlier on the relative 'overconfidence' of males and 'underconfidence' of females in their capabilities may explain why female supervisees are more likely to value the ideas of the supervisor over their own than might male supervisees. I am in any case reluctant to generalise or ignore the interplay of gender with other cultural factors.

As a visible difference, gender will be immediately apparent in the client/ therapist/supervisor triad. Some research suggests that the greatest satisfaction levels reported by supervisees occur in same-gender pairings (McCarthy *et al.*, 1994; Thyer *et al.*, 1988). However, the latter study drew attention to the fact that gender accounted for only 5 per cent of the variance and arguments for matching supervisor–supervisee pairs according to gender may thus be regarded as of lesser importance than other factors. Alternatively, supervisors might make the most of this visible difference by opening up a dialogue on the topic, exploring the usefulness of diversity in carrying out the work. It has been argued that supervisors can empower the affiliative behaviours associated with female gender roles through assuming a collegial posture, guiding from a knowledgeable yet tentative stance, listening actively to a supervisee's concerns and conveying openness to learning from the supervisee (Ladany *et al.*, 2005: 159). A supervisor may also notice the use of qualifiers in language suggesting deference or reduced engagement in a conversation during supervision.

Sexuality and supervision

The following is an extract from a text, 'Homoworld', devised with the aim of teaching lesbian and gay awareness:

> You wake up to the sound of your radio alarm dedicating songs to same sex couples. . . . You briefly flick on breakfast TV to catch the end of Richard and Jimmy discussing the latest face make up available for drag queens. . . .
>
> Arriving at work, one of the admin staff is showing pictures of her holiday she just took with her girlfriend in Lesbos. As you join the group to look at the photos you get asked 'Where did you take your last holiday?' Do you admit it was Corfu, a destination well known for its heterosexual holidays, and do you say who you went with?
>
> You start your working day and see your first client. During the session the client discusses her excitement at having found a sperm donor through one of the many agencies set up to match potential parents with similar outlooks on parenting. Can you relate to this and share her joy? She makes the comment: 'You know what it's like, it takes so much thought, time and testing to find the right match. Finally I found someone who wants to be there to talk through decisions but agrees to let me have the final word.' How do you feel admitting to yourself that you do not, fundamentally, know what it is like, that for you it would just be a case of stopping using birth control.
>
> The thought rekindles the awkwardness you felt finding one of the only two clinics in London set up to provide birth control. The stigma you might have felt walking towards it through the hospital grounds,

surely everyone must know that is where the heteros go? The condescending looks of the receptionist as she asks you loudly whether you have used the service before and whether you would prefer your GP not to be informed. You might find these thoughts and memories interrupting your session. Do you take this to supervision? Does your supervisor even know that you are straight? Do you know what your supervisor's personal feelings are about it? Do you fear your supervisor might be secretly pathologising you? These thoughts make you remember that you will be changing placements in a few months. You briefly hope that the next team will be more accepting.

At the end of the day people are going for a drink at the nearest gay bar on the corner. Some are bringing partners. Do you invite yours knowing that there will be staff there you are not out to? Staff whose response to your heterosexuality you cannot be sure of. Or do you go for a few hours and then leave to travel into central London and the straight ghetto of Old Brompton Street? But maybe you just want a quiet drink as you are tired and you know Old Brompton Street will be full of pumping Celine Dion and boozed pint drinkers. With no real alternative you decide to head home. Just as you have made the decision your partner texts you to say he will meet you at the tube as he is leaving for home now too. As you smile a member of staff you do not know well catches your eye and says, 'That from your girlfriend? What's her name?' Do you come out, lie or say you are much too busy to be in a relationship? You wonder what their response would be if you do come out?

- Full acceptance;
- A total lack of interest and changing the subject due to embarrassment;
- Or else they imagine they now have a licence to ask you a list of overly personal questions because 'some of their best friends are straight' and they've even been in a straight bar so they really don't have a problem with it, for example:

> 'So how long have you known you were straight?'
> 'What a waste, I would never have guessed you were straight.'
> 'Do your parents know?'
> 'Is the sex better?'
> 'What do you actually do in bed anyway?'

Finally you reach your home tube station and as promised your boyfriend is there to meet you. You feel a flood of relief at seeing him, realising how tired you are. But do you greet him with a kiss with all these people still around? As you walk home you both have to walk down a quiet street. You start to hold hands, glad of the contact. However, unexpectedly a group of youths round the next corner and you let go.

Did they see the contact? Are they going to say anything, heckle you? Worse still, is this a potentially violent situation? You both stare at the floor as you walk past.

Safe behind closed doors at last, you decide to order a pizza. Your partner is in the kitchen when the doorbell rings and does not realise you have already opened it. He shouts, 'I'll get that darling' and you notice the pizza delivery boy trying to hide a laugh as your boyfriend bounds into the hall behind you.

(Butler, 2004: 15)

Sexuality is a salient feature in which individuals' preferences are diverse, but unlike more visible differences such as ethnicity and gender, it can be revealed, partially revealed (for example, we both know this about me, but the rule is that it doesn't get mentioned) or can be kept effectively and totally hidden (Hitchings, 1999). The topic of sexuality has traditionally been a relatively secret and intensely personal issue. It is very rare that people wish to bring sexuality to supervision because exploration of this issue can be hugely revealing. The supervisor needs a mandate to discuss issues of sexuality which must come back to the welfare of the client. McCann and colleagues (2000) suggested that supervisors must endeavour to find a bridge between the private, secret sexual self of the supervisee and the more public arena where sexuality may be regarded as an important ingredient in the therapeutic and supervisory relationship. They suggested a number of exercises designed to encourage supervisees to consider questions regarding the development of their own sexuality and the conversations they might have had with others about this. They also suggested that practitioners should develop a capability to use a sexual vocabulary and to understand clients' use of language in referring to sexual practices. For example, oblique references such as 'get physical' may otherwise be misunderstood in the context of a conversation about conflict between partners.

Hitchings (1999) described a number of scenarios involving the different sexualities of members of the supervisory triad. The scenarios included complex situations where sexuality, religious affiliation and ethnicity interacted. For example, one supervisee's personal religious beliefs held that homosexuals were acceptable within the Church if they remained celibate. Through counselling, the client wished to resolve the issue of his sexual identity. The supervisor asked if the supervisee had previously encountered clients who were working out their sexuality. The supervisee concurred and described two examples in which the resolution of the client's issues of sexuality had fitted with her religious beliefs. She stated, 'Well those are my religious beliefs – yes, but I wouldn't impose them on clients I work with – I really feel that I can put them aside.' Hitchings questioned the extent to which workers can bracket their personal beliefs and argued that there is a risk of the client being damaged by a negative evaluation of homosexuality.

In a second example, a young man with previous homosexual experience had failed to consummate an arranged marriage. The counsellor faced the dilemma of whether to agree to the client's desired contract to change his sexual orientation while doubting the wisdom and ethics of such a course of action. Hitchings encourages supervisors to challenge implicit homophobia without creating shame in the relationship. He argues the case for gay affirmative supervision in which individual prejudice and institutional homophobia may become the focus of the work.

Ethnicity, 'race' and supervision

Supervisors' experience of working with supervisees from ethnic backgrounds different from their own is likely to relate to the ethnic mix of the geographical locations in which they have worked. Even as recently as 2001, Duan and Roehlke found that 93 per cent of supervisors in their study had no experience of supervising trainees who were ethnically different from themselves (Duan and Roehlke, 2001).

When participants in supervision differ according to ethnicity or other personal characteristics this can present a challenge, while at the same time offering significant learning opportunities. Proctor (2000) cited a case study example in which Carmel, the leader, encouraged her supervision group to take more risks, soon after which they became more lively and competitive and Carmel decided to discipline herself not to intervene excessively:

> Farah told Stephen that she resented him describing his client as 'an Asian girl'. Kate made some move to 'excuse' Stephen and Farah told her she should know better. Stephen asked to be told what was the right terminology and Farah told him he should discover that for himself and not rely on her to educate him. Carmel felt this remark was a sideways message to her, but decided to shelve a response. She thought that she would have been diverting Farah's challenge and protecting Stephen at a point where he was sufficiently 'in' the group and had the potential to find creative ways to meet the challenge.
>
> At the check-in during the following session, Mary said that she had left feeling uncomfortable the previous week. She wondered why Carmel had not helped Farah and Stephen out. Carmel said that since the review she had been acting on the feedback that she should be less protective. She thought both Farah and Stephen were experienced enough to be able to take care of themselves and discover something useful about their values and understanding. Kate retorted she thought that a bit of a cop out. She expected Carmel, as an Afro-Caribbean supervisor, to have some easy understanding of racist situations and have the courage to address them in the group. Carmel said 'Ouch'. Farah angrily interjected, but Carmel said, 'No, hang on a minute, Farah. Thanks for the support,

but I need to give this some thought. Are you saying, Kate, that you want me to adjudicate on what is politically correct?' Kate said she supposed not always, but she thought that people would need to know what Carmel thought under the circumstances. Carmel replied that Kate could ask her if she wanted to know, but no one had done that at the time.

There was an uncomfortable silence, until Mary asked Carmel whether she thought it was racist of Stephen to say 'Asian girl'. Carmel said she thought that 'young woman' was a more respectful description of a 17-year-old. As to Asian, she thought Farah's challenge would be useful to Stephen in becoming more educated about the variety of cultural and ethnic backgrounds from which their clients came. She could identify with Farah's irritation at having to act as the 'political arbitrator'.

(Proctor, 2000: 101)

Carmel suggested that they should all, including herself as the leader, make a point of sharing the role of political arbitrator, and of educating themselves about what could be experienced as offensive. While this example shows that diversity in group members can present challenges to the skills of the participants, it has been argued that too much homogeneity can stifle spontaneity and limit opportunities for learning (Getzel and Salmon, 1995).

Supervision and disability

Blotzner and Ruth (1995: 11) argued that when working with individuals with functional limitations, therapists and supervisors may need to take more responsibility than is traditional for practical contextual factors, including outside-the-office issues in their thinking and work. Often there is the need for contact with care-givers, for concern with the practical issues of where and how the therapy or supervision will take place, and with advocacy efforts which can be 'impassioned and protracted'. They argued that the latter can have very positive effects psychologically in terms of the client developing the capability to secure resources, and not only in regard to the practical improvements in quality of life that they confer.

This theme was taken up by Feasey (2002: 71). He reported being somewhat taken aback when a deaf client came to his room and reorganised the seating arrangement in order to lip-read better. The issue of physical contact became salient when he was working with a wheelchair user. He argued that the training of psychotherapists can 'sometimes produce a rigidity of response towards clients that impacts negatively on persons suffering a disability'. The use of the word 'suffering' here could be challenged as reflecting the therapist's assumption about the experience of the client in relation to his disability.

Olkin (1999) suggested rearranging an office in advance in the knowledge that a wheelchair user will be with you there. As a wheelchair user herself she provides helpful insights such as never pushing someone's wheelchair unless asked or if it is in danger since it is essentially an extension of the person's body. She also suggests asking whether someone would prefer to remain in their wheelchair or transfer to one of the other chairs in the office. People with disabilities who have to adapt to unsuited environments often experience pain and fatigue, the effects of which can be both physical, cognitive and affective. Olkin argues that students in particular may make what seem unreasonable demands in relation to a training programme (for example requesting a very local practice placement) without disclosing their disability. She argues that students fear making an issue of the disability since it might make them appear less competent, less able to become an accomplished practitioner, and may jeopardise their standing in the training course.

The issue of whether to raise the presence of a visible disability with a supervisee has been discussed by Page and Wosket (2001). They cited the example of a supervisee who described herself as 'an assertive amputee' as follows:

> Were you to bring up the subject of my disability during supervision without my prompting, I would at the very least be surprised. On a deeper level I think several things would happen. Initially I would feel offended but go with you on it out of politeness, all the while turning things over in my head which had little or nothing to do with my client. I would 'humour' you. Afterwards, my reflections would once again have little to do with my clients and during the weeks between supervision sessions I would gradually become angry and we would have to deal with this. The vital missing ingredients would be my clients. I *will* talk about my disability with you when it gets in the way, either on a practical level or when it is an issue within my client work. As you know, both these situations are rare. Otherwise, I simply accept that you see me as a whole person and don't treat me any differently to any of your other supervisees. Were this not the case I would feel that my clients were being overlooked in favour of my disability, and that I was being discriminated against.
>
> (Page and Wosket, 2001: 208)

Page and Wosket suggested that the supervisor adopt a flexible stance rather than fixed views about when and whether to raise the issue of a supervisee's or supervisor's functional limitation or other cultural differences between the client, supervisee and supervisor. They quoted Eleftheriadou (1997: 80): 'aim to achieve a delicate balance; to include the cultural background of the client, but not to make it the prime issue unless the client has already indicated that it is an area of importance in the therapy.' Adapted to the context of supervision the skilful supervisor may seek to achieve the recommended delicate balance in relation to supervisees and to themselves. Another possibility is to discuss in the initial contract for supervision whether (and if so, how) disability would be an appropriate topic to be addressed in the subsequent supervision.

One of the tasks of the supervisor may be regarded as raising the awareness of supervisees to issues of disability. Marks (1999) cautions against the use of exercises designed as simulations which have the intent of giving the learner insight into the experience of a functional disability:

> This might be done by getting shop assistants to use wheelchairs, attach weights to their arms or wear blindfolds in training sessions in order to increase their appreciation of barriers to shopping. However, such training often fails to capture some of the most difficult aspects of their impairment, such as the effect of cumulative frustration, pain, fatigue or social isolation. On the other hand, simulation can also over-estimate some aspects of difficulties. People using a wheelchair for the first time will not have built up their upper body strength or gained the proficiency achieved by a seasoned wheelchair user. Rather than listening to what disabled people are saying, simulation may pander to voyeuristic excitement and give non-disabled people the opportunity to colonise the experience of disability. Simulation may lead to, at best, a very distorted and reductive kind of 'empathy', a cavalier fantasy that an experience has been understood, or an increase in pity for the disabled person.
>
> (Marks, 1999: 134)

She counsels that such training is most usefully undertaken when led by people with impairments themselves who then occupy a position of expertise rather than being the objects of curiosity and concern. Supervisors who have a functional limitation themselves are probably in the best position of all to encourage awareness of disability issues. Where a supervisee has an impairment, the supervisor may usefully enquire about her or his views of disability, respecting the experience that the supervisee brings to this issue while not expecting the supervisee to take responsibility for its consideration in the work.

Olkin (1999: 325) offered advice to supervisors of workers with a disability. She argued that some of the worst stories from students with disabilities concerned their experiences in supervision since supervisors may use their responsibilities for clients as a licence to express prejudicial views to supervisees. Students with disabilities might be told that they have inadequate communications skills; that clients may experience a desire to take care of them that will interfere with the therapeutic alliance; that they need to prove that they are able to handle the disability before being allocated clients. These barriers are not put in the way of able-bodied supervisees. She stated, 'Protestations that disability is not a problem for clients inevitably lead the supervisor to pronounce that the supervisee is "denying the disability" and that once a cycle of accusation and defence begins it is very difficult to break out of it into a more constructive pattern of communication.' In her view, clients often like working with a therapist with a disability, sharing the experience of being an outsider, and of pain and struggle. She suggests that where supervisors are concerned that the disability is at issue in the work, they listen to tapes and focus on specific incidents, as might be the case in relation to the development needs of any other supervisee.

Less attention has been given in the literature to other issues of diversity such as religious affiliation. Aten and Hernandez (2004) stated that to their knowledge only two authors had addressed the issue of religion in clinical supervision. One of these, Frame (2001), described the use of spiritual genograms to raise supervisee awareness of the origins of their own spiritual attitudes. Aten and Hernandez argued for the promotion by supervisors of case conceptualisations that include religious issues and themes, and suggested that this is an area where more research is needed.

Approaches to developing awareness of issues of diversity in supervision

Pendry and colleagues (2007) have drawn attention to a range of strategies and techniques that aim to develop positive group relations and adherence to anti-discrimination laws. They categorised these under the headings 'Informative/Enlightenment', 'Dissonance or Guilt-inducing Approaches', 'Social Identity Approaches' and 'Use of Cognitive Tasks to Create Awareness of Bias'. They argued that prejudice is not only based on inaccurate information but that it has a strong affective component which serves to maintain or strengthen entrenched stereotypical beliefs in the face of contrary evidence. Confronting historically advantaged groups with their bias can incite anger, contempt or feelings of persecution (Mollica, 2003).

In an example of an exercise under the heading of 'Dissonance or Guilt-inducing Approaches' participants line up on one side of a room and take a pace forward if they agree with statements concerning privilege taken from McIntosh (1998). White participants typically take the most steps forward and this leads to strong negative feelings and thoughts expressed by those left behind. Those who have taken many steps typically express guilt about their privilege. Pendry *et al.* argued that those white participants who strongly identified with white culture tended to become more negative to the out-group through this exercise, and people from minority ethnic groups tended to have their lack of privilege further highlighted. They made a case for selecting exercises according to the specific constituency of the group being taught.

The approach which uses cognitive tasks is based on the notion that prejudiced reactions are often automatic and unintentional. Tests or exercises are used to draw out these biases. One such is the 'Father–Son Exercise'. Participants in diversity training were given the following problem to solve:

A father and his son were involved in a car accident in which the father was killed and the son was seriously injured. The father was pronounced dead at the scene of the accident and his body taken to a local morgue.

The son was taken by ambulance to a nearby hospital and was immediately wheeled into an emergency operating room. A surgeon was called. Upon arrival, and seeing the patient, the attending surgeon exclaimed, 'Oh my God, it's my son!' Can you explain this?

(Pendry *et al.*, 2007: 41)

Participants typically attempt to find convoluted solutions to this problem such as one father being a stepfather, or a Catholic priest, rather than the most plausible solution that the surgeon is the boy's mother. Pendry *et al.* have found this to be a very useful approach since it is simple to administer and understand while it refrains from humiliating or upsetting participants. It has the power to stun those individuals who do not consider themselves susceptible to the power of stereotypes.

Ongoing thinking and reflection in relation to issues of diversity throughout professional careers probably represents the most helpful way for supervisors and their supervisees to develop their knowledge and skills in this domain. A consistent finding is that when cultural variables are discussed in supervision, particularly when they are raised by supervisors, greater satisfaction results (Burkard *et al.*, 2006; Constantine, 1997; Cook, 1994; Gatmon *et al.*, 2001; Toporek *et al.*, 2004). Supervision might usefully focus on the following:

- Noticing feelings of discomfort or embarrassment in relation to the experience of difference and giving full attention to them.
- Reflecting on diversity stereotyping in the local and wider culture and in the histories of supervisor, supervisee and client.
- Finding out how the service monitors referrals by gender, ethnicity, disability, age and so on, how this relates to the constitution of the local population, and what actions are being taken by the service in regard to equity and equal opportunities generally, and minority groups specifically.
- Encouraging the supervisee to find out about services that are organised around specific groups (e.g. men's groups, voluntary services).
- Finding out about the employment of staff from minority groups within the service.
- Considering patterns of referral to the supervisee's service and service responses based on difference. For example, in most services there are gender differences in patterns of referral and in professional response patterns to males and females. In child services, boys under the age of 10 are referred significantly more frequently than girls to child and adolescent mental health services in the UK. Women have received two-thirds of all prescriptions for psychotropic drugs (Ussher and Nicolson, 1992). Gender stereotyping plays a role in how clients might define their difficulties and what they are prepared to speak about. There may, for example,

be more shame perceived in a man admitting to being hit by his female partner than in admitting to hitting her.

- Considering how one's own and the supervisee's responses to clients, colleagues and each other are influenced by individual differences and how alternative perspectives might be obtained (e.g. in same-gender supervisory partnerships).
- Considering how the client's views of the characteristics of the practitioner might affect the work.
- Including a focus on the dynamics of power and responsibility as it connects with minority issues and the presenting problem.
- Bearing in mind that invisible differences such as the sexuality of clients, supervisors and supervisees cannot be assumed.
- Considering the interplay of cultural issues such as the differential experiences of a black unemployed male with learning disabilities compared with a white female professional.
- Finding out about local organisations that represent the views of minority groups in order to determine their views about how best to provide a service.
- Listening to the radio or reading material with a mindset that considers what it is like from the perspective of a person from a minority group (e.g. imagining the perspective of someone with Down's syndrome on the reporting of tests carried out on foetuses to determine whether the parents will be offered a termination of pregnancy due to an identified impairment).
- Exploring the supervisor's, supervisee's and client's perceptions of their ethnic and cultural identities, values and beliefs, how these have developed and changed, and how they affect and are affected by the work.
- Exploring the values associated with the role of 'helper' and 'helped' for supervisor, supervisee and in different cultural groups.
- Examining the basis of psychological theory and how it might be associated with the cultural and personal histories of its inventors.
- Developing skills in finding out, rather than making assumptions, about clients' values and beliefs.
- Considering the effects on clients of core socio-political issues such as poverty, discrimination, racism, deprivation and exclusion.
- Considering the need for and availability of interpreters including for people with hearing impairments and those who use sign language.
- Considering the relevance of political issues such as migrant or refugee status and its implications for confidentiality.
- Encouraging development of awareness of population standardisation samples for any measures used in assessing clients and considering the relevance to minority groups of a measure standardised on the majority group.

- Reading and discussing fiction or short personal essays related to minority issues.
- Watching and discussing films in order to develop empathic awareness of similarities and differences across cultures. A suitable selection may be found in Bhugra and De Silva (2007).

In conclusion, here is a passage from 'The Malay Archipelago' by Alfred Russell Wallace (1869, republished 2007) who earned his living as a bird skin collector. He travelled extensively across Malaysia and Indonesia from 1854 to 1862 and it was while he was in the Aru Islands off the coast of New Guinea that independently of Darwin he realised the 'origin of species'. He stayed with the Aru Islanders for some months and this extract shows how the Islanders could not believe his story of his intentions with regard to the bird skins that they brought him. They created their own explanations, congruent with their own cultural values and beliefs, from which they could not be shaken:

'Ung-lung!' said he, 'who ever heard of such a name? – ang lang – angerlung – that can't be the name of your country; you are playing with us' . . . To this luminous argument and remonstrance I could oppose nothing but assertion, and the whole party remained firmly convinced that I was for some reason or other deceiving them. They then attacked me on another point – what all the animals and birds and insects and shells were preserved so carefully for. They had often asked me this before, and I had tried to explain to them that they would be stuffed, and made to look as if alive, and people in my country would go to look at them. But this was not satisfying; in my country there must be many better things to look at, and they could not believe I would take so much trouble with their birds and beasts just for people to look at. They did not want to look at them; and we, who made calico and glass and knives, and all sorts of wonderful things, could not want things from Aru to look at. They had evidently been thinking about it, and had at length got what seemed a very satisfactory theory; for the same old man said to me, in a low, mysterious voice, 'What becomes of them when you go to sea?' 'Why, they are all packed up in boxes,' said I. 'What did you think became of them?' 'They all come to life again, don't they? said he; and though I tried to joke it off, and said if they did we should have plenty to eat at sea, he stuck to his opinion, and kept repeating, with an air of deep conviction, 'Yes, they all come to life again, that's what they do – they all come to life again.'

(Wallace, [1869] 2007: 95)

Chapter 9

The interface of supervision and management roles

I've got the blues
The managed care blues
I just got the news
They're turning the screws
I gotta see more
They've taken off the door
They've pulled out my chair
Gotta be quick, still gotta care
I've got the blues, the managed care blues
(Hoyt, 2000: 105)

Multiple roles in different professions and organisations

The introduction to this book addressed the issue of defining the term 'supervision'. It is widely used and conceived. Even within the confines of the mental health professions, a range of approaches is adopted. For example, some of the research aimed at establishing the active ingredients of particular approaches to therapy has encouraged supervisors to prioritise therapist compliance with standardised procedures.

Supervision in the context of case management, for example, which involves an element of resource gatekeeping, can generate stress for the case manager who simultaneously acts as the agent both of the client and the system, the needs of which may be in conflict with each other (Applebaum and Austin, 1990). In the UK-based Improving Access to Psychological Therapies (IAPT) project (Department of Health, 2007), cognitive behaviour therapy interventions are provided by case managers on a high-volume, low-intensity basis. One of the demonstration sites is based in Doncaster. The aim is to address the woeful lack of resources for the common presentation in primary care settings of anxiety and depression. Only 24 per cent of people in the UK with common mental health problems receive any treatment for their difficulties, mostly in the form of medication (20 per cent), with only

9 per cent receiving another form of therapy or counselling in addition to or instead of medication (Office of National Statistics, 2000).

In the IAPT service supervisors and case workers input information to a computer system which flags up the cases that will be discussed in the weekly hour-long supervision session according to four criteria: high risk (from the risk assessment completed at each contact); if measures of anxiety and depression are severe; if four weeks have passed since the client was previously discussed; and any additional issues. Richards and Suckling (2008) referred to this as 'automated supervision'. Work with as many as 20 clients may be reviewed in a single supervision session. The supervision is essentially technical. The primary focus is on the needs of the service and the patients within it. The quality of service provision comes first, and case manager development issues second. The challenge is to provide the restorative component of supervision (Davies, 2007, personal communication).

Whatever the context, supervisors cannot escape the tasks associated with each of the formative, normative and restorative purposes of supervision, although they may be given different emphases in different settings.

The management of administrative tasks in preregistration training

When practitioners in training are placed with a practice supervisor, both clinical and non-clinical aspects of their performance become implicitly, if not explicitly, delegated to the clinical supervisor. All clinical work involves the necessary completion of some administrative tasks and these are often perceived as of less value or importance than the clinical work itself. Often, these relatively routine tasks only become of significance when there are problems; the paperwork that is missing when a client decides to take formal action against an institution, for example. It is my view that training people to complete routine administrative tasks in an efficient, accurate and timely way is an important aspect of the supervisor's managerial role. Once these good habits are established and have become a matter of routine, they no longer weigh heavily and will most likely continue to be effected with minimal fuss for the rest of a practitioner's career.

A lack of managerial skill on the part of a supervisor has been regarded as cancelling out the value of the supervisor's excellent clinical skills (Kadushin, 1992). Supervisees reported erratic communication, rushed supervision, and unclear or unused procedures as presenting difficulties in supervision. The provision of a stable administrative structure can contribute to a sound training experience. Supervisees need to be 'held'; their anxieties contained. A major contributor to this is the provision of clear administrative procedures and practices. Bernard and Goodyear (1998: 205) argued that:

No part of supervision is more immediately affected by the environment than the part that attempts to organise the experience. The organisation context will form the experience even before supervision begins . . . every organisation is maintained by a certain set of structural guidelines within which the supervision must occur.

They went on to say,

One of the greatest misconceptions of those not in managerial positions is that administration is made up of filling out forms and making on-the-spot decisions. Random power and paper work come to be identified with the managerial function of any organisation. On the contrary, the essential ingredients of managerial competence and the source of all sustained influence are planning and foresight. Beyond these is the discipline to implement the (supervision) plan in a methodical fashion, which, admittedly, often includes the creation of some paper work.

Specific managerial tasks in preregistration supervision

Induction

There are many things that students need to know even before they arrive at a practice placement, such as the name, contact address, telephone number of the supervisor, and when and where they are expected to present themselves on the first day. For supervisors who regularly provide placements it may be as well to create an induction file, available to the supervisee at the beginning or even before the start of the placement. Previous supervisees would be a good source of advice about what such a file might helpfully contain.

Case load management

When comparing notes, students on the same course often find that their case load size and mix vary. The ill-prepared supervisor may wait until the arrival of the supervisee to identify suitable cases, only to find a dearth of referrals leading to a delay in the supervisee beginning work. This can be further anxiety inducing for an already fearful student. At the other end of the spectrum supervisees may be overwhelmed by the bank of cases saved for their arrival in an overburdened service.

Orientation to the agency or service and its staff

Rather than supervisees learning about the culture of the organisation by acting out with its implicit rules and structures, it is advisable for the supervisor to provide some orientation to the service while at the same time not unduly prejudicing the student's view. A failure to fit with the tacit procedures and practices that are in place for having reports typed, or about who makes beverages for whom, can cause unnecessary ruptures in relationships which are particularly distressing for a new member of staff. Bernard and Goodyear (1998) argued against this task being carried out in an informal manner as this is likely to give the supervisee incomplete information and/or allow them to become triangulated in organisational power struggles. Such situations can be avoided if these issues are discussed in supervision, and part of each session could be reserved for these matters.

Time management

In relation to supervision, the issue of time management is about organising workload priorities to ensure that there is sufficient protected time for supervision. It is usually helpful to have a formal agreement with an employer about this, since it might mean arranging to reduce time spent on other tasks. While most supervisors can protect time in relation to formal supervision sessions, supervisees in training may also appreciate opportunities for informal contact and for being involved in the work of the supervisor in a variety of ways. This may include attendance at meetings and case conferences, and taking up opportunities to relate to other staff employed in the service.

Events that require specific action

Supervisees in training contexts need to be prepared for the eventualities that require specific action. These may be issues of risk associated with harm of self or others, child protection, the need for hospital admission or the involvement of other services or professions. Supervisees need to know in advance who to contact and how to proceed in such instances. Typically, the supervisor is not directly accessible when the supervisee is faced with these relative 'emergencies' for which there needs to be a back-up plan. Similarly, supervisors need to arrange cover when they are absent for any length of time.

To seasoned supervisors these managerial aspects of supervision may be well-established routines which require minimal attention. For those who are newer to the role, it may be beneficial to 'shadow' an experienced colleague in the first instance, gradually taking increased responsibility or 'sharing' a student in order to learn at firsthand the good habits that underpin successful practice placements.

The dual role of supervisor and manager

There is little consensus between, or even within, professions as to whether a line manager can simultaneously serve the functions of an effective clinical supervisor. The profession of counselling in the UK explicitly precludes supervision of clinical work by a line manager and it is expected that the employer or individuals themselves will fund an arrangement with a supervisor who is typically external to the employing organisation (British Association for Counselling and Psychotherapy, n.d.). In the USA approximately half of practising counsellors are receiving supervision of their clinical work from their administrative supervisors (Tromski-Klingshirn, 2006) despite the Association for Counselor Education and Supervision advising against such an arrangement. Advocates of clinical supervision for nurses in Europe have been clear that the roles of the clinical supervisor and manager are incompatible (Butterworth, 1992; Catcliffe and Lowe, 2005). The United Kingdom Central Council for Nursing, Midwifery and Health Visiting position statement on clinical supervision for nursing and health visiting (UKCC, 1996) stated that, 'clinical supervision is not a managerial control system. It is not, therefore, the exercise of overt managerial responsibility or managerial supervision, a system of formal individual performance review or hierarchical in nature.'

The balance of the administrative, educative and supportive functions of supervision in the profession of social work has been much debated (Tsui, 2005: xv) without resolution. A case has been made for educational and administrative functions to be separated because it is difficult for front-line social workers to discuss their errors in practice with someone who is monitoring their job performance. The potential conflict between growth-promoting and accountability-maintaining functions can thus lead to mistakes in practice being hidden from the supervisor (Tsui, 2005: 60). The counterargument is that the separation of the functions leaves a gap in which external support may not help with stress arising from the dynamics of the organisation, and that in such instances the most valuable emotional support comes from immediate managers because it includes the recognition of accomplishments made by the worker.

In the UK, the National Health Service National Treatment Agency for Substance Misuse (2004) defined 'managerial supervision' as involving issues related to employees' job description or their workplace, including prioritising workloads, monitoring work and work performance, sharing information relevant to work, clarifying task boundaries and identifying training and development needs. 'Personal (or pastoral) supervision' was defined as being addressed to personal issues raised through work, including discussing how outside factors are affecting work and enabling people to deal with stress. A third kind of supervision called 'clinical supervision' (or practice/specialist supervision dependent upon the culture of the work setting and the name preferred within the worker's profession) was defined as 'a formal process of professional support and learning which enables individual practitioners to develop knowledge and competence, assume responsibility for their own practice and enhance consumer protection and safety of care in complex clinical situations' (Department of Health, 1993). These distinctions appear to represent normative, restorative and formative functions respectively. The policy does not specify who is responsible for providing each of these types of supervision other than to state that clinical supervision 'can be on a one-to-one or group basis and either be provided by the employee's manager or by professional peers'. Morrison (2001) described a 'health model' of supervision which also distinguished between management, clinical/professional and personal supervision. Management supervision is defined as non-negotiable, focused on accountability for time, resources, administrative duties and communication with the agency. The prime roles of the supervisor are to delegate and monitor, and accountability is to the employing agency. Clinical supervision is focused on practice and achieving the best outcome for the service user while personal supervision addresses the personal needs of the worker arising from the work.

An integrated supervision policy for mental health community teams has been developed by Haringey Council: Barnet, Enfield and Haringey Mental Health NHS Trust (2005). They usefully try to set out the lead responsibilities for managerial and clinical/professional supervision in their Community Mental Health Teams (see Table 9.1). This seems to be a useful approach in that it covers those responsibilities which are common to both managerial and clinical/professional supervision and those which are specific to each role. Supervisors who are carrying out both roles with their supervisees may benefit from keeping in mind the aims and purposes of the supervision at any one time. They are moving between a focus on how the worker is using and

Table 9.1 Lead responsibilities for managerial and clinical/professional supervision

Responsibility	Managerial supervision	Clinical/professional supervision
Workload management	*	
Setting and monitoring objectives	*	*
Clinical/professional supervision		*
Assessing continuing professional development and training needs	*	*
Study leave – multidisciplinary	*	
Study leave – professional	*	*
Annual leave	*	
Work performance – general (timekeeping, etc.)	*	* Focus is on the impact on therapeutic relationship
Work performance – professional	*	*
Performance appraisal/knowledge and skill framework	*	*

developing their knowledge, skills, feelings and values to meet the needs of clients (the worker's needs are to the fore), and a focus on how the worker is fitting with the goals of the organisation (the needs of the service are to the fore). The difficulty for supervisors who are managers is that they may find themselves undertaking a form of surveillance or 'snoopervision' (Yegdich, 1999) due to the necessary focus on maintaining services and ensuring that staff follow increasingly bureaucratised policies and protocols. Supervisee perceptions of the supervisor who is in this position can readily militate against developing the kind of relationship in which honest and open exchanges can take place.

The tasks of managerial and clinical/professional supervision may be more or less compatible with each other. In this chapter the term 'managerial supervision' is used to refer to supervision that addresses work performance as it meets the goals of the organisation, and 'clinical supervision' where the supervisee's needs in doing good work are to the fore. Role overlap can be very confusing.

Where both roles are vested in one individual it is useful to negotiate at length in a process of contracting with the supervisee about how these functions are to be effected. When the functions are to be assumed by more than one individual, the contracting process then has an equally important role in enabling the parties to reach agreement about which matters should be discussed in which kind of supervision. The involvement of a clinical supervisor and a managerial supervisor creates the opportunity for 'splitting'; one providing 'good' supervision, the other 'bad' (Pedder, 1986). It is wise for supervisors to consider this together with their supervisees both at the outset and as the relationships develop.

The remainder of this chapter addresses those situations in which the supervisor is simultaneously identified as the supervisee's line manager or is trying to manage the service as well as supervise the practitioners providing the service. While this may be the case in post-registration supervision arrangements, the supervision of students undertaking preregistration training naturally casts the supervisor in a managerial role since the student's progression to further training and professional qualification lies within the scope of the role. In addition, since the responsibility for the welfare of clients on the case load is retained by the supervisor, the necessity for an assessment role and judgements of student performance are prerequisite.

In trusting relationships where good working alliances have been established, and when supervisees' performance is not in question, the conflation of the two roles may be advantageous. The manager is likely to have obtained greater insight into the supervisee's work than otherwise, and will be able to make better informed decisions regarding appraisals and progress within the organisation. The risks in this type of arrangement derive from the potential of a poor alliance to generate conflicts of interest and a situation in which supervisees feel unable to disclose aspects of their work in supervision that might count against them in terms of performance review and promotion.

Personal and professional issues in performance

Tsui (2005: 69) argued that staff performance is the actualisation of both the personal qualities of workers and of professional values, knowledge and skills which have been developed during professional training. Workers bring their own faiths, conscience and life goals to their work and hold themselves personally accountable according to these personal ideals which Tsui argues should not be underestimated: 'Supervisors should learn the life goals of their staff and align them with the organizational goals. If supervisors wish to motivate their staff to achieve a high level of job performance, they must provide them with the opportunity to actualize their own ideals in the job.' Such a mindset would be valuable to a supervisor attempting to carry out the dual tasks of managerial and clinical supervision.

While the majority of supervisory relationships prove positive and satisfying to the involved parties, research findings suggest that this is not invariably the case. Supervisors have been perceived in a number of negative ways: as dismissive of supervisee thoughts and feelings (Gray *et al.*, 2001), inflexible in their approach or uninterested in the development of the relationship (Nelson and Friedlander, 2001), as giving little regard to trainees' strengths, seeking to limit their independence (Wulf and Nelson, 2000), or as too busy and remote (Nelson and Friedlander, 2001). The data in these instances were collected from supervisees. Supervisor constructions of the difficulties would undoubtedly differ. It has been suggested that these findings may be accounted for by the differences between supervisees in what they seek from or expect of supervision and in the lack of prior experience they may have in identifying their needs (Barrett and Barber, 2005).

Contracting the dual relationship

Faced with the necessity to undertake both management and clinical supervision, a number of specific approaches can help to prevent or alleviate the development of problems in the relationship. The first opportunity occurs at the stage of contracting, since at this point there is the prospect of fully exploring the implications of the dual role, ways of managing the roles and what to do in the event of problems developing. A matter of particular significance is that of performance evaluation. Supervisees benefit from a clear statement regarding the aspects of their performance that the supervisor will be seeking to evaluate, and which of these aspects of performance will be the most salient. In conducting these discussions supervisors benefit from being skilled in making statements of intent and of preference (Gilmore *et al.*, 1980). Such conversations are likely to be more challenging than the contracting undertaken by supervisors who are occupying a single-role relationship. To give a flavour of the negotiation process, a transcript of a specific contracting meeting is presented below.

Transcript of a simulation of contracting between a supervisor who is also a line manager, and a supervisee

In this simulation the line manager wishes to negotiate with the supervisee the process of performance review. Normally this would take place after the relationship had been established and the more general issues of the dual roles discussed in the contracting process. The conversation is included here because it gives a flavour of the process of negotiation that would need to take place in the wider contracting process and it shows how two people with different ideas about and experiences of a process might struggle to reach a mutually agreeable arrangement, particularly where the role encompasses one person making a judgement about another person's performance.

The manager/supervisor needs to listen and respond to the concerns and anxieties of the supervisee. In this case the supervisee is open about and prepared to discuss her anxieties with the supervisor. Otherwise, supervisors themselves may need to take responsibility for introducing the idea of assessment being an anxiety-generating process. The appraisal process in this case has been defined within the organisation to be based on live observation of a session. The supervisor offers the supervisee the reciprocal opportunity to observe her work in order to demonstrate openness to observation and evaluation, but in this context it may have appeared that this offer was designed to 'show off' the superior skills of the manager. The conversation (where S = the supervisor/manager and K = the supervisee) does not begin on a good footing since the supervisee has not had prior notice about the identity of the person who will be carrying out the performance review.

S: Katherine, we're meeting today because we're going round the annual cycle of performance review and so I'm the person who'll be doing your review.

K: Right OK. [raises eyebrows]

S: And I don't know whether you knew that until I just said now but . . .

K: No, I didn't.

S: OK. And I have a position about the review that the professional development aspect is really important so I wanted to have a chance to talk to you before we do anything in terms of performance review to work out what might be the most useful way of approaching it.

K: Right, 'cos I've always thought of it as being, you know, that this was something that just had to happen and also that you tended to come in with your agenda about, obviously, my performance. I mean you'll have been talking to people and you'll perhaps already have got an opinion

and well obviously I want to do well in this. You know, I want to show
you what I'm made of because I do want to be able to progress.

S: Right, OK. I think there's an issue for me here about how we deal with-
you want to show me what you're made of because it affects your progression in terms of pay and in terms of promotion and things like that
which is a kind of managerial role but at the same time I'm interested in
what your learning and development needs might be and how as an
institution we might meet them and how I as a head of department might
help that.

K: But might that not look bad on me? I mean I'm meant to be an experienced clinician so I mean I have real anxieties about, you know, you
picking up on any of my weaknesses. You know, I need to do this well.

S: I understand that entirely and that's why I think it's helpful to talk about
it now to try and work out; 'cos you need to know what sorts of things I
would think were positives, if you like, and you've mentioned weaknesses
and what sort of things were, what I would probably call points for
development, areas in which you could develop. And what I wouldn't
want to do was to come in and for you to feel you had to do a song-and-
dance routine to impress me and then lose out for any opportunities
there might be for development. Now it might be that it's impossible to
put those two things together. I don't know.

K: I mean, talking to colleagues who've already been through the system so
far this year, I mean they had very much planned to be able to give their
best performance, for want of a better word, and I understand that they
were, as part of the observation, they were given a grade as to whether
the session was satisfactory or good or excellent or unsatisfactory. I
mean, would you be planning on doing something like that as well?

S: I hadn't got a plan as yet because I think I'd like to match what we do to
individuals' needs rather than have something very specific. I mean it
might be that we have to fill something in that we have as a standard for
the organisation, but as I say I'm more interested really in the developmental aspects, so from my point of view I think it would be a strength to
be able to say this is an area in which I need to develop my knowledge
and skills and to think about how you would get some assistance
with doing that, whether it was with another colleague or it might be
going on a course or whatever, but I think it feels important to me that
we don't ignore the areas that you would need to or would like to develop
further in.

K: What would be the knock-on effect of that though? I mean, how would
that affect my standing in the organisation? How would that affect my
performance management? I mean, if you found me wanting, yes I can
start to see what you're meaning. Obviously I need to improve and I need
to become a better clinician but how does that tie in with the actual
performance management? You know, I don't want to be in the situation

where I feel that I've let myself down or that I haven't been rewarded for having worked very hard for a year.

S: OK. Well, what I'm beginning to wonder is whether we could . . . it sounds as if the expectation is that I would come in and observe one of your sessions and I'd have a checklist and I'd kind of fill some things in on the basis of that and other information.

K: Yes.

S: OK. I'm wondering whether it would be possible to come to more than one session and we could do things differently because they have different purposes. You see I'm interested in your own evaluation of your performance as a starting point.

K: Nobody's ever asked me about that before.

S: OK.

K: So that's a big one. I mean, how would you want me to evaluate myself?

S: How would *you* want to evaluate yourself?

K: Well, I mean it's one thing if you're evaluating yourself quietly to yourself, 'cos I mean I do review my sessions and I do think about them and I like to think that then goes back into my planning and that I do do things differently. But it's one thing to think that quietly to yourself and another thing . . .

S: To be thinking it publicly.

K: To be thinking it publicly and to you.

S: To your head of department, yes I understand that. It might be that we could agree that you have some ways that you quietly evaluate yourself and you choose from among those some strengths that you would hope that I would notice and some points for development that you would be prepared to share with me that we could then talk about what would be helpful to you in terms of progressing those, and I would see that as a strength, the capacity to reflect on one's performance and identify strengths and some points for development would be something that I would give a positive evaluation to, if that makes sense. Whereas I think if someone's, if you like, hiding their difficulties, I wouldn't be very positive about that. I would want them to feel able to show both their capabilities and their areas that they wanted to develop.

K: I mean, that makes sense and I'm starting to feel a little more comfortable with it but what if we disagree? What if something that I think is a strength you think is a weakness or we come across something that you think's a really big deal? How would that affect everything? How would we move on from there because you know I don't want you thinking badly of me.

S: Of course not, no, I don't want to think badly of you either. So, you think we might disagree about something?

K: Yes.

S: I think you're right. There is a potential for that isn't there, that we disagree about something? And I think if we do disagree about something I wouldn't just want to leave it at that. I think we'd have to carry on talking about it. It might be, say there was something that you felt it was appropriate to do it in one way and I felt it was appropriate to do it in another, it might be that I could invite you into one of my sessions so you could see what sort of thing I was talking about and see what you thought of it when I was doing it. I don't know how that feels?

K: Yeah, possible. [doubtfully]

S: I mean there might be some things we could happily disagree about. You think this and I think that and we both agree to differ about it. But I guess what you need to know is whether we disagree and that affects your evaluation and your progression.

K: Yes, exactly.

S: So, would it help if I was clear about that then?

K: Yes.

S: About what the things are that I'd be looking for.

K: Yes.

S: And maybe that we have a discussion. You identify the things you want me to look for and I identify anything else that I would like to look for and then we agree about how that will look between the two priorities that we have.

K: Yeah, that sounds fairly fair. Yeah, I think if we were absolutely clear about what you were looking for then yeah, fair enough.

S: So clarity would help wouldn't it?

K: Yes.

S: Are there any things that you think that I could do that would make the evaluative role less dominant?

K: But that's what we're here for isn't it? I mean, this is such a big deal within the organisation isn't it? You know, everybody talks about it, and everybody gets worried about it and everybody plans for their performance management, so I mean it's very difficult because everybody does it differently, and you're here being quite supportive about it and I'm not used to that at all. I'm much more used to somebody just coming in and doing the session and then going away again. So I mean, what were you thinking about?

S: I don't know, I just think it would be really helpful if the evaluative role wasn't so dominant because it would allow me to perhaps be more useful, you know, in my role. I suppose I'm thinking, what about your opportunities to evaluate me in my role as performance manager? It feels that you're saying that you've had different experiences of the way this is carried out so I'm taking something from that about how I'm doing as a performance manager so I guess we're all under scrutiny but it feels more you've got somebody coming into your session and sitting there with a checklist.

K: Tick, cross, yeah.

S: I think it would be helpful if we looked at what those items were that we've agreed upon that would be the focus of the observation and just make sure that we both understand what they mean. And I don't know whether . . . I guess I'm not too keen on checklists in some ways but I'm wondering how we would think about where the scale was, you know. I don't know whether this is an area where we say you were very good at this on this particular occasion but you'd like to develop it further in another kind of lesson or in a different class or something like that. And maybe we could say that part of what's evaluated is your identification of areas that you would like to develop your skills in.

K: So that's starting to turn into a positive. Me saying, or me reflecting or me thinking about my performance if I'm honest about it and if I start to say well actually I'm not too sure about or I would like some extra help with, that that would be a positive. That I'd come out well from that.

S: That we say, yes, you've been very skilful at identifying the things that you needed to learn and develop, yes.

K: Right, yes I could go with that.

S: That would perhaps be one thing we could do to join these two purposes together, performance review and your learning and development.

K: When I've had this done before the observer has tended to say, just as they were running out of the door, 'Katherine, right that's fine. You know, you've got a 4, you've got a 5 or whatever.' And then perhaps I've had a little bit of written comment afterwards but that's been about it. If we're thinking about doing this whole, you know, me identifying weak areas, how will we work that then? How will we be able to do that?

S: Well, as you were talking it made me think it might be helpful that we met before the session so that I understand what you're trying to do in the session. So I've got a context for thinking about it so that we could then go through and agree together what it was you were trying to accomplish and how we would decide whether those things were being accomplished and then we could meet after the session and set aside a reasonable amount of time to go through again and see what you thought about what was being achieved and maybe this could be where I . . . It's a balance between my asking you questions and telling you things. So I think it would be helpful to find out what you thought about the session first.

K: OK that sounds rather scary but yes.

S: Or if that's scary then maybe you'd rather I said something at the outset about what I thought about it but perhaps I could say something quite brief and general so that you knew I wasn't thinking, 'Oh my goodness what a dreadful session,' and then you started talking about all the things that went well.

K: Yes, that would be very helpful. That would be good.

S: Anything else you think would be helpful?

K: Who is going to know about this? I mean how is it all going to be passed on because presumably you're going to need to share it with the senior managers and things like that as well. You know, if we've had quite a confidential chat about things that I've been worried about, you know, and I can see that that would be a really useful thing to do, how do I know that you're not going to be going to senior managers and saying, 'Well actually Katherine thinks she's got a real problem with. . . .'

S: OK, well I'm quite happy to agree to this generally being confidential. We'll have to produce a document that goes through the system that we can produce together. I won't produce a document behind your back. We'll do it together even if we disagree about some things. We can encapsulate that in the document. If I thought something needed to be passed on to somebody else outside then I wouldn't go and do that without talking to you about it first.

K: So I would know.

S: So you would know and we could talk about what I was going to say and what the implications of that might be. So there's a formal part that we have to do and then there's room within the process for some confidentiality around points for development and we'll note that you've identified some and that's a positive feature.

K: Yes, yes, that sounds all right. Yes.

S: Anything else you think we need to establish before we . . .

K: I think those were the main things that I was worried about, you know, the whole sort of judgement and this is a new way of doing it for me but I think you've explained things clearly and I'm starting to get a bit of an idea about what it might be like, so yeah.

This conversation is a starting point from which the two parties can begin to develop mutual understanding. It is apparent that this is likely to be a time-consuming approach. As the relationship progresses, if the manager is true to the values expressed and agreements reached, the supervisee will gradually be able to develop trust in the relationship which should allow greater openness in the future. Where there are ruptures in the relationship, a return to the negotiation process is usually helpful. Contracting is not a one-off process that takes place in a new relationship, but an ongoing process which is respectful of the views and feelings of both parties. The supervisor/manager may need to model this willingness respectfully to negotiate on repeated occasions, dependent upon the prior experience of the supervisee with this approach.

Separate meetings to effect separate functions

Another approach which can help to constrain the supervision to specific aims and purposes is to agree to meet on separate occasions in order to fulfil the different demands of management supervision and clinical supervision. The different agendas for each type of meeting can be agreed and when an issue arises in one meeting that is most appropriately discussed in the other, it can be noted and put to one side until that meeting takes place. A straightforward example might be the identification of a training need in clinical supervision. The training need might best be met by attendance on a course. A request for funds to support the supervisee in further training would then be taken to managerial supervision.

Less straightforward is the situation where a supervisee is presenting in clinical supervision with an issue that relates to the wider organisation, such as being stressed by the demands of a high case load. The expression of stress, identification of sources of stress, formulation and possible strategies by which the worker might manage the stress would be appropriately addressed in clinical supervision. The issue of the size of case load can then be referred to the next managerial supervision meeting. The manager may feel constrained by the demands of the organisation to maintain the size of the worker's case load but is in a position of greater knowledge with which to address the issue at more senior levels of management within the organisation. In addition, the worker's case load may be reviewed and agreement reached regarding different priorities in the work.

Involving a third party

During clinical supervision the supervisee may identify a developmental need, further exploration of which might compromise the supervisor's capability to be fair to the worker in the role of manager. For example, the stressed supervisee may have been trying to manage the case load by taking time off 'sick'. This could be legitimate or not, and either way is likely to be compromising the service to the client. The supervisor may suspect that this is the case, and it is crucial to address rather than avoid the matter but in a manner that is fair and just. If the supervisee is expressly questioned about sickness absence in clinical supervision and is found to have been falsifying sickness absence claims, the supervisor in the role of manager will need to take this forward in the organisation and it may compromise the worker's status.

An alternative in this case is to identify that the worker has a developmental need, and, where exploration of the issue would invoke a managerial response with negative consequences for the supervisee, make an arrangement for the worker to discuss the issue more freely with someone outside the immediate service or the organisation. This is helpful where, for example, the supervisee is showing signs of a mental health difficulty. The fact that the supervisee is struggling may be identified in clinical supervision, but full exploration can be referred to an external and confidential service such as occupational health. The practitioner might be advised to reduce the number of contracted hours worked, even, in the case of a student, where the pre-qualification period of study would need to be extended. This proposal could legitimately be brought to managerial supervision.

In order to motivate staff to achieve a high level of job performance, it is helpful for supervisors to take account of what supervisees need from their work; what working conditions best accomplish an alignment of individual aims and those of the organisation. Where trusting relationships have been developed in supervision, the supervisor as manager is likely to have obtained an overarching and detailed view of the effects of workplace demands on staff. This puts them in a better position to challenge senior management about workplace policies and procedures that are negatively impacting on workers.

The supervisor with these dual roles can attempt to steer a fine course in order fairly to realise both sets of responsibilities. Supervisors in one role cannot 'un-know' what they have learned in the other. It is helpful for the supervisor constantly to keep in mind and self-monitor the aims and functions of each supervision session, effecting clearly stated boundaries where there is a tendency to stray from managerial to clinical supervision and vice versa.

There are other occasions on which it is useful for the supervisee to have access to additional relationships that serve some functions of supervision. These may be more or less formalised. Trainees or students often belong to a cohort and are able to compare their experiences with each other. Qualified practitioners often do this informally. There are dangers that such conversations can become characterised by mutual moaning or competition between students. But they may also serve a positive function in that they may assist a supervisee who is finding an issue too apparently shameful to bring to supervision, to gain confidence to raise it once they have discovered that it is a shared experience (Davies and Coleman, 1999; Hawkins and Shohet, 1989: 137).

Mutual assessment

Typically, workers forget that their managers' performance will also be under review within the organisation. In preregistration contexts the salience of the review for the student is likely to be of greater significance in terms of outcome than for their supervisors who have already been awarded membership of the profession. Making assessment mutual and bidirectional can create an ethos in which the parties to supervision can be encouraged to be open about their learning needs and vulnerabilities. One way of arranging this is for supervisors to invite supervisees to observe their work and to reflect together upon the observed session, possibly using a structure within which to constrain the discussion. The supervisor is able to model self-reflection and review, and openness to further learning as a legitimate and desirable orientation to the work.

There is also much potential in the mutual evaluation of the supervision. Supervisees often think of it as the supervisor's responsibility to ensure that the supervision is effective in meeting its purposes. The use of assessment tools may facilitate the development of an attitude of shared responsibility for the process, in terms of both clinical and managerial supervision. There are many questionnaires addressing the evaluation of supervisor skills (Borders and Leddick, 1987; Efstation *et al.*, 1990; Hawkins and Shohet, 2006; Lehrman-Waterman and Ladany, 2001; Shanfield *et al.*, 1989; Winstanley, 2000; Yager *et al.*, 1989) and statements of learning objectives or standards for students. But shared responsibility may better be implied where the questions link outcomes to the contributions of both parties, at least in the first instance. The sorts of questions that might be considered in reviews of supervision are:

- How varied and appropriate are the learning opportunities that we are creating? What other approaches might be of value?
- What have we done that has been helpful in developing an effective working relationship?
- What have we done that has been distancing or has jarred with either of us?
- How are we finding the balance of support and challenge?
- How safe do we feel with each other? What vulnerabilities have we been able to reveal? What could each of us do to make the relationship more robust?
- How are we balancing the different purposes of supervision?
- How respectful have we been to the boundaries between the different roles?
- How effectively are we including issues of diversity in our supervision?
- How accountable are we being to the organisation/profession?
- How successfully are we negotiating our differences?

These are just a few suggestions. It is possible to take questions from measures designed for either supervisees or supervisors and to turn them into questions which convey shared responsibility for the relationship and for supervisory outcomes.

In conclusion

Supervisors would be wise in the first instance to investigate the policies of their professional body and employer regarding the position they might take regarding the dual role of providing both managerial and clinical supervision to staff. While the dual role may be challenging, supervisors may take heart from the fact that there is some evidence to suggest that the majority of supervisees in this circumstance do not regard it as problematic (Tromski-Klinshirn and Davis, 2007).

This chapter has offered some thoughts on approaches that might aid the supervisor in creating and maintaining effective working relationships when cast in both roles. Information sharing can also serve to increase a sense of collegiality and reduce the potential disadvantages of hierarchical relationships. You may wish to study this chapter together with your supervisees.

Chapter 10

Use of recordings and other technologies in supervision

Historically, the most common way of conducting supervision of clinical practice was for the supervisee and supervisor to meet together to discuss the work in prospect or to review work carried out. Although the technologies for making recordings are widely available, verbal recounting continues to be a popular supervision format, despite supervisors rating its effectiveness low (McCarthy *et al.*, 1994; Wetchler *et al.*, 1989).

Clinical work is a practical as well as theoretical endeavour, and the discussion of work without direct or indirect observation is atypical of methods adopted in the training of practical skills in other disciplines (e.g. bricklaying, sports, art, surgery, teaching), in which both supervisor and supervisee would expect their work to be viewed by the other and frequently to work alongside each other.

To adopt methods which allow supervisor and supervisee to see or hear each other's work presents a number of challenges and dilemmas but ultimately offers better safeguards to clients and enhanced development opportunities for clinicians. The use of live supervision or recorded material helps to overcome the tendency towards nondisclosure reported by Yourman and Farber (1997) in which 30 to 40 per cent of supervisees said that they withheld information (e.g. perceived clinical errors) at moderate to high levels of frequency. In this chapter the use of recordings and other technologies is discussed.

Audio- or video-recordings

Audio-recordings enable the verbal content of a session to be reviewed and in addition, pauses, tonal qualities and other emotional expression can be explored. The technology of the audio-recording machine is easier to introduce into a session, is more portable, cheaper and requires less preparation than video-recording. Video-recordings have the advantage of providing additional material in the visual domain and are particularly useful to people working with families when it can be difficult to notice the contributions of all the participants in a session. Their use enables the nuances of glances and non-verbal patterns and processes to be included in reviews of the work.

One of the dangers of introducing recording into sessions and supervision can be the fascination and complication of the technology itself. Without an operative, the camera cannot follow the movements of the client, but with an operative the film-making in and of itself can dominate. Keeping a focus on the purpose of the recording should help to avert this danger. Munson (2002) argued that the use of video-recording tends to generate excessive perform- ance anxiety. In order to make use of the advantage afforded by being able to be an observer to one's own work, Munson suggested that supervisory sessions may best be structured around a specific task and that supervisors should ensure that they safeguard the professional integrity of the supervisee whose work is being reviewed. In his experience, once students are exposed to learning and evaluation using electronic records they invariably find it stimu- lating and helpful, particularly when they are able to review recordings made earlier and recognise the progress they have made. A perspective that includes mutual evaluation and review can be promoted by recording and reviewing supervision sessions.

Types of technology

A further complexity as technology has developed is the multiplicity of dif- ferent media available with which to make recordings, each offering advan- tages and disadvantages dependent upon the intended use. It is crucial to make decisions about the intended use before reaching conclusions about the recording medium. Digital audio-recorders such as MP3 players are relatively unobtrusive but thought needs to be given to the means of replaying record- ings in supervision sessions. Some have internal speakers but realistically these can only be used to check that the recording has been successful. The headphone socket can double as a line-out and this can be connected by the line-in socket on the sound card to a computer or to a portable stereo. Conventional cassette recorders, Dictaphones or mini-disks may also be used for audio-recording.

Conventional analogue videotape on VHS-C may be used in PAL or NTSC format, depending on the local convention. These may be replayed using a VCR, television or monitor. There are currently four available record- ing media for digital video-recording: digital videotape, direct to DVD, mem- ory card or hard disk. If the recording is to be reviewed other than on the recording machine itself a DVD can be replayed on a DVD player or com- puter. Most digital video-recorders can be connected directly to a computer or television but if there is a need to navigate through the recording, a com- puter and appropriate software such as Windows media player or Cyberlink power DVD are necessary. For other than straight replay it is helpful to download the recording on to a computer using a fire wire or USB lead. This allows editing and copying on to a more transportable medium. For editing purposes, relevant software is necessary. This can range from shareware to expensive professional software and is constantly in a process of development. The editing process can take a great deal of time and trouble without the availability of a modern computer with plenty of hard disk space.

One of the serious difficulties now presented by the use of recordings is the lack of security of electronically stored information. Once material is downloaded on to a hard disk it is very difficult to erase, raising the question of whether it is possible to reassure clients about confidentiality. Some NHS Trusts refuse to sanction the use of digital recordings while these issues are unresolved (Sutcliffe, 2007, personal communication).

Sometimes people resist making recordings on the grounds that the only technology available is out-of-date. But for the purposes of learning, only adequate quality is necessary and it has been argued that black-and-white video-recordings are particularly useful since they generate fewer extraneous distractions (Berger, 1978).

General issues in the use of recordings

Before considering the use of recordings in supervision it is appropriate to reflect upon the issue of the use of recordings in clinical practice. A number of factors can present hurdles to the use of recordings in either or both contexts.

1   *The effects on empathy.* The conversations that take place between client and therapist can be very intimate and contain sensitive material which may not have been previously disclosed. The presence of a third ear or eye may be perceived as inhibiting, leading to an awkwardness and reticence on the part of either or both parties. Empathy requires that the full attention of the clinician be focused on the client, and the presence of a recording machine may distract from this. However, if the worker is comfortable with recording it is more likely that the client will also soon forget the presence of the machine, particularly if it requires no attention during the session. Urdang (1999) argued that the active involvement of the client in the decision to record offsets the potential intrusiveness into the therapeutic relationship. It can be disruptive if the machine clicks to off at the end of one side of a tape at a particularly poignant moment in the session. Similarly, the whirr of cameras moved by operatives behind a screen can also disrupt and is to be avoided in setting up recording technology.

Sometimes the presence of the machine can be palpable. For example, the client might whisper asides which are not meant for the supervisor's ears, or alternatively treat the machine as a third party to whom things must be made clear. Clients may save a particular comment or communication for the moment when the machine is turned off and this may present challenges to the therapist in bringing the session to an appropriate close. Such responses can be disconcerting for the worker at the time but also provide information about the client that can be taken to supervision and fed back into clinical practice.

2   *Self-consciousness.* On listening to or seeing themselves on recordings for the first time, people are usually critical of how they look or sound and it can take many interviews for people to become used to hearing or seeing themselves. It is possible to be distracted from content and process by perceived blemishes in presentation. Particular things said or seen can become unduly amplified in significance and may be perceived as an undermining or shameful experience. In order to avert this it is wise for practitioners who are new to recording to have experimented with viewing themselves on media in other contexts until listening to and seeing themselves on a recording becomes relatively comfortable and familiar.

3   *Confidentiality and consent.* When working in a public service context, confidentiality can be offered to clients only within the constraints of the organisation and the law. The use of recordings can present an additional challenge to the security of information owing to the client, particularly when permission is sought for their use in supervision or teaching and if there is any intention to download material on to a computer. Permission for recording needs to be sought in writing at the outset, informed consent obtained, while the recording process needs to be introduced in ways which do not act as a deterrent.

Aveline (1997) argued that being recorded may feel abusive, in particular to clients whose sense of personal mastery and proper boundaries have been subject to coercion and abuse by powerful figures in the person's earlier life. Such clients may be unable to protest and may accede to recording against their will. He advises that careful consideration be given to the meaning of the recording for the client.

It is possible to capitalise on the increasing sense of trust in their therapist that clients typically develop over time by revisiting the issue of consent to recording at the end of every session. Occasionally clients have inaccurate ideas about the use of recordings which may be disclosed as their confidence grows. For example, Hughes and Massey (2000) reported one client to have imagined that recordings of the sessions were being played to every member of the psychology department. The reminder about confidentiality and consent at the end of each session gave the client an opportunity to raise concerns about this that may otherwise have remained hidden from the therapist.

In work for public agencies written consent is essential, as is clarification about the relationship of the recordings to the overall case record. Recordings may best be regarded as transitory records to be destroyed at the end of an episode of care, or earlier. This may need to be agreed formally with the employer. The issue of confidentiality has become increasingly complex as recording media have developed. Recordings may be downloaded on to a computer hard drive in order to aid smooth playback. Agreement is necessary for the record to be erased once it has served its immediate purpose.

4   *Security*. While all records need to be kept securely in order to protect the confidentiality due to clients, recordings present additional challenges to this process. One method for enhancing security of recordings is to use a code letter or number on the recording itself with client identifiers documented in a different place. One disk or tape may be allocated to a client and recorded over at the following session provided that they are rewritable. Recordings may also be used in the work by clients taking them for their own personal review, and the client may be responsible for the ownership and disposal of recorded material while work is underway and when completed. In this case, the clinician would be advised to ensure through a written agreement that the recordings were for the client's personal review only, and not for more public consumption. The reassurance needed by the clinician in this example highlights the degree of mutual trust necessary to ensure appropriate confidentiality.

5   *Technical skills*. A frequently encountered problem in the use of recordings is the poor quality of the footage, particularly the sound quality. The person who carried out the work may be able to decipher the recording, but beyond this the use is limited without the provision of a transcript – the making of which is a time-consuming activity. There are a number of practical solutions to this difficulty, including plate microphones, lapel microphones and specially designed sound systems.

6   *The anxiety of the clinician*. Even when familiar with hearing or seeing oneself on a recording, performance anxieties can remain and there may be fears of negative evaluation, which can be particularly pertinent given the nature of the work. There is plenty of potential for feeling exposed. Beginning counsellors and psychiatrists in training have reported that the experience of recording sessions has had an inhibiting effect upon their interviewing performance (Friedmann *et al.*, 1978; Niland *et al.*, 1971). Videotapes were experienced as more intrusive than audiotapes. More recently, between 61 per cent and 72 per cent of nursing students reported their experience of being video-recorded as positive and helpful in enhancing their learning of effective interpersonal skills in clinical supervision (Minardi and Ritter, 1999).

Aveline (1997) argued that playing a recording is nearly always stressful for a worker since therapy is an intensely personal activity which confronts therapists with their strengths and limitations both as a person and as a professional. This can lead to a pattern of collusive avoidance whereby supervisees spare themselves exposure and the potential attack of a super-critical ego, and supervisors collude by becoming protective of the supervisee. While it may be explicable, one might ask whether this 'cloak of privacy' is justifiable.

Given the potential difficulties with the recording of sessions, careful consideration of practicalities and discussion of anxieties between supervisor and supervisee are best undertaken before introducing them in the work. The complexity of the process is probably best not underestimated, and it is preferable to prepare carefully rather than introduce recording hastily and be deterred by the difficulties encountered.

Advantages of recording

In spite of the above qualifiers, recording can be highly beneficial in supervision and in clinical practice and may offer particular advantages over other media.

1   *Provides the opportunity for detailed review and multiple perspectives*. The potential for use in review by the client or the therapist may facilitate the consolidation of different or new meanings or help to pick out developments made by the client or therapist over time. When recordings are reviewed by the client, therapist and supervisor, these multiple perspectives can generate an increased range of options for intervention and change.

2   *Removing doubts about competence*. For supervisees in prequalification training, reaching the end of training rarely serves to eliminate doubts about competence. Rather than encouraging confidence in the role, the process of training can serve seriously to undermine it (Scaife, 1995). Fear of being found out and of charlatanism are widespread even some years into practice. Mahoney (1986: 169) expresses it thus:

> I eventually came to recognise that I was naively (and unconsciously) assuming that there was actually an 'underground' handbook of how to be helpful that was secretly circulated among professional counsellors after their graduate rites of passage . . . I slowly began to appreciate that my expert clinical mentors were themselves operating according to abstract and tacit 'rules' rather than concrete and explicit guidelines.

Those in training who reach the end of the course without ever having been observed are particularly likely to be vulnerable to such feelings. Having one's practice thoroughly scrutinised and evaluated as competent is likely to be much more affirming in the long run.

3   *Providing an opportunity to participate and then observe*. During interpersonal interactions, a great deal of reaction and response takes place at such a pace that only a fraction may be given attention. Subsequent review

enables people to slow down the process, give detailed consideration to their own recalled perceptions and to reconsider the meanings in the light of the review. Taking the position of observer may shed new light and lead to different ways of understanding the interactions. The use of recordings offers such opportunities for both client and practitioner. It may be particularly helpful for practitioners in training who are enabled to look back on their earlier work in order to review evidence of progress.

4   *Enhanced empathy*. Contrary to the idea that the introduction of recording may result in reduced empathy, it provides an opportunity for the practitioner to give full attention to the client without the need to make notes as an *aide-mémoire*. The record enables the participants to have confidence that the material will not be lost or forgotten.

5   *Increased accountability*. The use of recordings can act as a safeguard for clients. Doubts about how to proceed can be explored with colleagues in the light of firsthand data. Clinicians working in the knowledge that their practice is open to direct scrutiny are less likely to find themselves drawn into situations against their better judgement that might otherwise be evoked by the potentially profound psychological difficulties that may have been brought into the work with the client. The openness of practice that is an automatic adjunct of the use of recordings thus acts as a safeguard for both client and practitioner.

6   *Myths and mystery*. For people learning the skills of the helping professions who do not have an opportunity to observe or be observed, the process of therapy can appear to be shrouded in mystery and uncertainty. The process of reviewing recordings enables debate, clarification and questioning, thus grounding the work in an applied knowledge base rather than its being seen as a magical and mysterious skill.

7   *Increases options for research and evaluation*. The use of recordings is probably more widespread where the process and outcome of therapy are being researched. Recorded data allows for the possibility of detailed micro-analysis which expands the evidence base of professional practice.

8   *As an adjunct to therapy*. In some approaches to therapy, recordings can serve a useful role in the work with the client. For example, recordings can be given to clients to facilitate homework tasks in cognitive therapy. While more controversial, feelings towards recordings as objects of projection can be explored in psychodynamic approaches.

Introducing recording to the client

The idea of making a recording of sessions is one among a number of issues that are best introduced early in the first meeting with the client, although these topics may be revisited later. There is a balance to be struck between encouraging the client to understand the usefulness of such a method, while not offering such a laborious explanation as to appear coercive and disengaging. Obtaining genuine informed consent is as tricky with this issue as with others such as the explanation of the limits of confidentiality. Beginners in the use of recordings may find it helpful to write out and rehearse an introduction until they feel at ease. It may also be helpful to have obtained the reactions of colleagues to a role-played introduction. Clients are likely to range from those who wish to consider such a request and its implications carefully, to those whose story cannot wait to be told. When the worker feels comfortable with recording and relaxed about the introduction, the client may be helped to feel the same. The introduction may be repeated at a later stage if there is uncertainty about whether the client has understood the full implications of consenting to a recording, and written consent gives a clearer indication of agreement.

An example of a script for introducing recording to clients might read thus:

> In my work I have found it helpful to record the sessions as a matter of course. This allows me to give you my full attention without worrying that I may forget something, and it helps me and my supervisor to make sure that you are getting the best possible service. If you are agreeable to recording, I will ensure that the recordings are kept confidential to you, me and my supervisor. If you wish, you may prefer to take the disk or tape home yourself at the end of the session and if you are not happy for it to be kept then you can erase it yourself. Later in our meeting today, when you have had more time to think about it, I will ask if you will sign a consent form. This is entirely your choice and I will be happy to work with you either way. Would you like to ask any questions now before we begin?

In introducing recording it is easy to focus on the usefulness to the clinician, but the client may feel more positive if the introduction includes an explanation of how the recording will be useful to the client. It enables the worker to give full attention to the client during the session, and allows for review and reflection between sessions in order to produce more ideas that could be helpful to the client. Where the recordings are to be used in supervision this can also be presented to the client as a safeguard to the work, drawing on the ideas of the supervisor in addition to the therapist. Recordings may also be offered to the client for self-review. Clinician and client may both review copies of the same recording. The following is an extract from a recording of a client reflecting on her review of a tape made in an earlier session (C = client, Th = therapist):

C: I've listened to these tapes.
Th: Right.
C: And this helped me as well. I listened to it over the weekend and made

some notes and things. It was quite . . . quite a surprise to me hearing it all.

Th: What bit was surprising?

C: Well, firstly, hearing myself on the tape I was surprised. My first thoughts were that if I didn't know this was me then I would think that this was an intelligent, friendly, lively person on there, and that's not the impression that I had I was giving.

Th: Right – what impression did you think you were giving?

C: I thought I was dithering, stuttering and mumbling [laughs]. I'd think, 'Oh she sounds quite nice', and thinking that I sounded nice was quite a boost for me.

Th: Yeah.

C: You know, if I can like it if it's someone else then I can like it if it's me.

Obtaining consent

In the early days of recording, clients were found generally to exhibit little resistance to the method as they moved beyond the first few sessions (Barnes and Pilowsky, 1969; Haggard *et al.*, 1965). Today, the climate has changed and people may be generally less trustful of professionals. The informed consent of the client to recording is essential, both in regard to paying due respect to the client's wishes and in order to protect the professional. As a first step it is often helpful to have enclosed written information with an appointment letter. The tone of this information might be to raise awareness of the possibility of recording and needs to avoid any sense of coercion. The usefulness of written information may be limited by the client's disability, stage of development or familiarity with the language. At least it increases the chance that the client's expectations about the session will include the possibility of a recording being made.

If the introduction to the session proceeds in such a way that recording is presented as a normal feature of the work this can help the client to feel confident in its value. The consent form can be introduced, the session proceed, and the form be reintroduced at the end of the session when the client knows what has transpired. At this stage clients may be encouraged to give fuller consideration to how they feel about the recording and it needs to be made clear that withholding consent will in no way adversely affect the subsequent service provided. If consent is withheld, clients may be given the recording to erase for themselves in order to have confidence that the record is expunged. If the recording has been made on hard disk this could be erased in the presence of the client.

Where the session involves more than one client, consent should be obtained from all, and this will include children to the extent that they are developmentally capable of understanding the decision. Special care is needed with clients whose consent may be ambiguous. This is particularly the case for clients with learning disabilities whose compliance may be almost automatic, and for those with more profound mental health difficulties.

Written consent

Written consent offers the best safeguards for clients and practitioners, since both will then have a clear record of what has been agreed and of the undertakings of the worker regarding confidentiality. Separate paragraphs should identify the purposes for which recordings may be used, and the approach that will be taken to its storage and destruction. Clients should be able to withdraw consent at a later stage and would be advised to put this in writing. Consent forms need to be adapted to suit the clients' capacity to understand and according to their needs. It may be helpful to use less specialist language such as referring to the supervisor as 'boss'. The consent form helpfully may contain a clause noting a date by which the recording will be destroyed. There are many sample consent forms available on the Internet that can be adapted to suit specific circumstances. They often helpfully require clients to sign at both the outset of the consultation and again at the end when they will be better informed about the content of the recording.

Recordings in supervision: issues

Once recordings have been made with the consent of the client, agreement needs to be reached between supervisor and supervisee as to how these may be used in supervision. The supervisee's work is potentially much more exposed than in reported work, with feelings of vulnerability and defensiveness likely unless a context of trust and safety has been established in the supervisory relationship. Neufeldt *et al.* (1996) identified the willingness to experience vulnerability as an essential quality necessary to the reflective process involved in the use of recordings in supervision. It may be helpful for the supervisor also to be recording her or his clinical practice, thus providing a model of willingness to experience vulnerability for the supervisee.

Bauman (1972) suggested that supervisees may claim that they are less effective when they are recorded, and that any 'mistakes' are dismissed as atypical behaviours that do not need to be examined. Dodge (1982) suggested that defensive strategies include intellectualisation, rationalisation and discussion of tangential issues. Liddle (1986) suggested that when supervisees object to recording sessions because clients would find this too threatening or disruptive, what is at issue is the resistance of the supervisee. This view should be balanced against that of Aveline (1997) that some clients may experience being recorded as aversive or abusive. It may be helpful for the supervisor and supervisee to identify in advance how resistance to recording might be shown and, in the event, how the supervisor might best approach this. Stoltenberg *et al.* (1998) described a beginning trainee whose reasons for being unable to bring a recording to supervision included forgetting to turn on the machine, poor-quality recording and the client's reluctance to give permission. They argued that to confront, interpret and process the dynamics around the supervisee's reluctance would only have served to exacerbate the already high levels of anxiety. Instead they suggested that the supervisor provide a clear, cogent rationale regarding recording in relation to client welfare, and issue a simple directive to have a recording ready for the following week.

Introducing recording to the supervisee

Supervisees themselves may introduce recording as a preferred medium of supervision to the supervisor. They may have used recordings in supervision previously and found them helpful to learning. In such a case, the supervisor might explore how the recordings have previously been used and discuss whether it is feasible or helpful to replicate this process or whether to try something new.

More typically, it is likely to be the supervisor who introduces the idea of recording to the supervisee. It is worth taking some time over discussion of the advantages and disadvantages of recording and to explore any pre-conceptions and anxieties expressed by the supervisee. Alternative review methods may be explored and the supervisor may initially offer a review of a recording of her or his own work in order to show how the process works.

When to introduce recording

It is often helpful to discuss with reluctant supervisees when, rather than if, they wish to experience recorded or live observation of their work. Practitioners are unlikely to be able successfully to avoid experiencing this at some stage, and the further on they are in their career the more they may feel the pressure to appear 'expert'. In preregistration supervision, trainee practitioners are usually persuaded that the earlier in their training that they practice with the use of recordings, the lower the expectation of an exemplary performance. It is similarly useful to introduce recording to clients in the first session rather than once the work is underway. Recording is then a natural adjunct to therapy or supervision rather than something special – such specialness being more likely to induce feelings of vulnerability. Initially, supervisees may prefer to review their own recordings as a private exercise, with their use in supervision programmed for a few weeks later when the supervisee has had time to adjust to the presence of the technology. To start with it is probably helpful if the focus of supervision is clearly on the client and understanding of the issues brought by the client rather than on the performance of the supervisee. Both focuses can facilitate learning.

Recordings may be used either in individual or group supervision, the latter involving additional considerations regarding the type of group that is operating and the ways in which group members might respond to the presentation of recordings by individual members. These matters would be discussed during the contracting process in which group 'rules' are established. The reader is referred to Chapter 6 for a fuller discussion of issues associated with the establishment and running of groups. The following sections explore the use of recordings in individual supervision. The considerations are also applicable to the use of recordings in groups.

Whole recording, part recording

The use of recordings of complete sessions in supervision offers some perspectives on the work that cannot otherwise be obtained. The supervisor and supervisee can gauge the whole session, including how it begins and ends. An overall impression as to the flow and changes of direction, repeating patterns and themes, openings and closing down can be obtained and discussed in the supervision. Supervisees can be sure that the entirety of their work has been indirectly observed and might thus be more reassured as to their clinical competence.

On the other hand, listening to and discussing an entire session in supervision could be infinitely time-consuming. It is possible to spend an hour of supervision discussing a five-minute extract, and it is unlikely that supervisors will be able to review whole sessions as a matter of course. During the period of a contract of supervision or over the duration of a training placement, the supervisor and supervisee might discuss one or two recordings in their entirety while there may also be sessions focusing on extracts. Sometimes supervisors may listen to an entire session outside supervision and then give written or verbal comments, perhaps focusing on issues that have been identified as points for development in advance.

Extracts may be selected in several ways. Supervisees might review recordings in preparation for supervision, selecting particular extracts to illustrate their development and skills in the role, or selecting points at which they felt confused or dissatisfied with the process, seeking ideas and clarification in discussion with the supervisor. Random extracts might be reviewed, in which case seemingly insignificant moments in the work may be found to have alternative meanings. Such snapshots might also offer an overview of the process of the session.

Choice of focus

It is probably helpful if supervisor and supervisee agree in advance of reviewing a recording what the intent of the review is; what the review will focus on – for example, what the supervisee did, thought or felt; what the client did, thought or felt; how the supervisee was using theory or techniques to address the needs of the client; or the non-specifics of the client–therapist relationship and how the client might be experiencing the session. Multiple possibilities exist. Narrowing the focus can be experienced as less exposing since only certain aspects of the work are subject to scrutiny.

Neufeldt (1999) described a particular method for reviewing extracts of recordings, the intention of which is to encourage supervisees to develop skills in reflecting on therapeutic process during the clinical session. For this purpose, the recording is reviewed without delay once the session ends in order to make the experience more immediate. The supervisee is asked to select the point in the recording at which the most puzzling interaction took place. After *each* intervention the worker is asked to describe her or his experiences *during that time*. This should include thoughts, feelings and intentions. The aim is to encourage supervisees simultaneously to attend to their own experiences and the actions of the clients while they are conducting the therapy.

Trans-theoretical focus or tracking adherence to a specific model of therapy

Particularly in those training and research contexts where the aim is to teach clinicians to work within the specifics of a particular model with a view to examining the efficacy of the approach, recordings are often used to train and monitor adherence to the model. This might involve the use of a rating scale such as the Cognitive Therapy Rating Scale (Young and Beck, 1980) or Cognitive Therapy Scale Revised (Blackburn *et al.*, 2001). Specific items from this scale include 'use of guided discovery', 'case conceptualisation', 'focus on key cognitions', 'application of cognitive techniques' and 'use of homework'. Keeping the focus on specific skills is less risky than addressing broader issues as the latter allows greater scope for personal affront and defensiveness. There are available many descriptions of the knowledge and skills required for the demonstration of competent practice in a range of disciplines and theoretical approaches. It is useful for supervisors to be familiar with relevant descriptors, particularly in training contexts (see, e.g. Binder, 2004; BABCP, 2005; Roth and Pilling, 2007; Skills for Health, 2007),

Control of focus and feedback

The approach to the use of recordings in supervision needs to be negotiated between supervisor and supervisee. Control of the focus and feedback may be the task of either party or shared between them. In order to construct a climate of openness and safety, the review of recordings early on in the relationship might be assisted by the control of the review process, the focus of the supervision and any feedback remaining exclusively within the control of the supervisee. Such an approach also pays homage to the idea that learning builds upon what the supervisee already knows. Suggestions from the supervisor might be too distant from this to be of use to the supervisee.

In cases where control of the review of recordings does lie with the supervisee, preparation for supervision could entail advance selection of a focus for the session – for example, on identifying examples of transference, responding to silences, making meaning of the client's non-verbal cues, and so on. Early on, a focus exclusively on the client might reduce supervisees' anxieties about their performance. Supervisees could also list issues on which they would appreciate feedback – 'Do you think that I would have been better to follow the client here or to introduce my own idea?' Such a process is likely to minimise surprises or shocks, although it might entail the supervisor withholding a plethora of ideas and comments. These could be noted for introduction at a later stage of supervisee development. However, supervisors managing to hold on to their own ideas in order better to help supervisees to explore their own is one of the more difficult skills of supervision.

The experiential method of on-the-job teaching

Mahrer and Boulet (1997) described a method of teaching experiential psychotherapy which they argued is applicable to teaching and supervision in other therapeutic approaches. The method is used with groups of three to six trainees who take turns to be the presenter. Extracts from a recording of work with a client is presented to the group members who are advised to focus on the recording rather than on each other. Group members are advised to choose extracts that they think demonstrate something of which they are proud; where there has been an impressive change in the client; an extract that demonstrates progress with a particular skill; where something happened that was puzzling, strange or inexplicable to the trainee; where a problem occurred or something went wrong; a repeating pattern of something going wrong for the trainee; or an extract that illustrated a compelling conceptual issue. Participants are required to be dedicated to the goals of experiential training which begins by trying to discover what is termed the trainee's own natural approach; their deep-seated framework or theory of change. The orientation of group members is described as one of puzzlement and excitement with a climate that ranges from quiet and careful listening to raucous interchanges.

Interpersonal Process Recall

One well-researched method for reviewing recordings that allows the supervisee to remain in control of the review process is that of Interpersonal Process Recall (IPR), which has been developed over a period of approximately 35 years by Kagan and his associates (Bernard, 1989; Elliott, 1986; Kagan et al., 1963; Kagan-Klein and Kagan, 1997). IPR was developed originally as a method by which people could review the interpersonal processes taking place between themselves and others. It arose when Kagan noticed that in the review of interpersonal interchanges that had taken place earlier, people were able to gain insights into the communication and to identify highly detailed reactions that were not available to them during the initial interchange. This enabled them to learn more about their own reactions and also about the effects they might be having on others.

He developed a method in which people are helped to identify their detailed reactions through the questioning of an enquirer. The role of the enquirer is precisely defined and a key feature is that enquirers do not attempt to make explicit meaning of the interchange themselves, but concentrate entirely on helping the reviewer or 'recaller' to explicate her or his own understandings. When used in supervision it can be helpful for the enquirer not to view the recording so as to avoid being distracted by her or his own hypotheses. The method aims to reduce the supervisee's fear of instruction and critical attack from the supervisor by putting the process explicitly in the control of the supervisee, and by encouraging the supervisor to avoid explanation, interpretation and advice (Clarke, 1997).

One of the key features of the IPR approach involves the maintenance of a separation of time frame from the original interchange. The enquirer helps the recaller to stay focused on the there and then of the recording and not on the here and now. This is viewed as important in that it protects recallers from experiencing feelings of vulnerability or threat during the recall. They are recalling what they *did* experience – 'I may not look it but I was frightened to death' – and not what is currently being experienced. The recaller is in complete control of the playing of the recording. The recaller starts the playback and may stop the recording at any point when interested to explore an aspect of the interchange. Exploration continues until the recaller wishes to move on, at which point the recording is played until the next halt brought about by the recaller. The capability that everyone has of holding vast amounts of knowledge about interpersonal processes 'on standby' is at the heart of the IPR method of enquiry. Recallers are regarded in IPR as the ultimate experts on their innermost thoughts and feelings. The enquirer is not trying to make sense of the session being recalled. The role is to help the *recaller* to make sense of the interaction.

The enquirer's responsibility is to ask a series of open-ended questions that respond sensitively to the recaller with a view to creating freedom and openness of exploration. These questions are not leading or Socratic in style. Some types of questions are listed below.

Self-exploration
What thoughts were going through your mind at the time?
Any cautions on your part?
How were you feeling then?
If that sensation had a voice, what would it say?

Own behaviour
Anything you were not saying?
What keeps you from saying that?
Was there anything that got in the way of what you wanted to say or do?
What did you like about what was happening?

Perception of other
What did you think the other person was feeling?
What did you want the other person to think or feel?
How do you think the other person experienced you?
Is there anything about the client's age, sex, appearance that you were reacting to?

Hopes and intentions
What did you want to happen next?
What effect did you want that to have on the other person?
Where did you want to end up?

Previous patterns
Have you found yourself feeling like this before?
Did you find yourself thinking about other people in your life?
What pictures or memories went through your mind?

The value of IPR in supervision and training is based on the assumption that clinicians always have a wealth of information that they fail to acknowledge or use productively, and that sessions devoted to uncovering these clinically important impressions and making them explicit in language help supervisees to become aware of messages that they denied, ignored or had previously not perceived. The process is viewed as helping people to improve their understanding of interpersonal processes. This might include the identification and acknowledgement of their previously unverbalised fears and vulnerabilities in human interaction. It is Kagan's (1984) view that these include: 'The other person will hurt me', 'I will hurt the other person', 'The other person will engulf me', and 'I will engulf the other person'. IPR involves a content-free enquiry that can be used to build confidence.

Another important feature of the method is that a sense of personal responsibility for one's own behaviour is fostered in the supervisee. The motivation to change may then be intrinsic rather than in the nature of 'jumping through hoops'. Given the chance, people are often more critical of themselves than would others be, and criticising oneself carries less risk of provoking defensive reactions.

Kagan and his associates went on from their original studies of recall with individuals to explore the idea of mutual recall in which the enquirer meets with client and clinician who both participate in the recall. Practitioner and client each share their thoughts and feelings about a past session, paying particular attention to how they experienced each other. This is viewed as helping clients and workers to become better able to talk about their experiences of each other in the present. Mutual recall is regarded as requiring self-awareness, sensitivity to the other person and courage, but is highly effective in producing learning. Students who had been trained in IPR appeared to show accelerated learning months after the process had been completed (Boltuch, 1975). Research suggests that client evaluation of counsellors trained in IPR is more favourable than their evaluations of traditionally supervised counsellors (Kagan and Krathwohl, 1967). IPR is a relatively non-threatening way of using recordings in supervision that has been adapted successfully to a range of different contexts. It is probably a good starting method for those who wish to use recordings to enhance their professional development. The skills of the enquirer should not be underestimated, particularly as the role requires the focus to be entirely on the thoughts and feelings of the recaller and not on those of the supervisor.

Other methods of using recordings in supervision

The development of recording technology has made possible a range of options for the use of recordings in supervision. Bernard and Goodyear (1998) referred to the use of dual-channel supervision (Smith, 1984). By use of a dual-channel cassette-recorder, the supervisor was able to record her or his thoughts and ideas while simultaneously recording the therapy session. This was conducted during sessions observed live by the supervisor. After the session the supervisee could listen either to the session and supervisor comments simultaneously, or, by turning a dial, listen in turn to one or the other. The advantages proposed for this method are that the supervisee must review the tape in order to receive feedback and that this then enables scheduled supervision sessions to focus on more global issues. A proposed alternative when this technology is not available is to copy the original tape, inserting supervisory comments on to the second recording. Digital recorders would prevent loss of quality.

Positive outcomes of using recordings in supervision

Many former trainees have reported that the use of video-recordings in their supervision was the single most important part of their training (Lee and Everett, 2004: 75). These authors suggested that positive outcomes result from the following principles:

1   Once the training system has agreed to the use of video-recordings, supervision will fare best when supervisors set aside time to establish the context of their use in the individual sessions.
2   In reviewing the recordings themselves, supervisors and therapists should

discuss how they will be used in the context of supervision. It has been reported by therapists that review of recordings is often less anxiety producing when it is informed by specific questions, most often raised by the therapists themselves.

3 The review method should reflect the developmental levels of the therapists. Lee and Everett found that it was best to select only those parts of a recording that were relevant to therapists' learning issues.

4 In viewing the recordings with trainees, supervisors would do well to use their own authority sparingly so as to minimise the experience of anxiety, self-denigration and doubt. It also makes sense to ask for examples that the therapists feel good about.

5 Supervisors need to use their executive functions to raise critical questions or visit segments of recordings that challenge defensive or naive therapists' clinical roles.

6 Supervisors should use their creativity and imagination in the review of recordings. They should try not to simply comment on minute-to-minute dynamics. Instead, the recordings should be used to explore the therapist's own issues or to challenge the therapist. For example, a particular impasse may be reviewed, the recording paused, and the therapist given space in which to explore thoughts and feelings. Or, having watched a segment, therapists may be asked to relate what they are seeing to theory or to their original assessment.

7 Supervisors may find it helpful to look at the failure to present recordings for the supervision session as an indicator of learning issues. Todd (1997), reported in Lee and Everett, suggested that supervisors and therapists may collude to avoid discomfort. Therapists may 'forget' to record a session or cue a recording in anticipation of the supervisory session, and supervisors may not remind them. This may be because either or both parties are distracted or their energies are spread too thinly. There may also be other interlocking dynamics between the supervisor and the therapist that would cause this issue to be ignored.

8 Quinn and Nagirreddy (1999), cited in Lee and Everett, have created innovative ways, often employing clients themselves, to use video-recordings in family therapy supervision. Their methods offer ideas when supervisors want therapists to discover and reflect on their internal processes while engaged in therapy.

9 Protinsky (1997), cited in Lee and Everett, reported that discussion of associated ethical issues may be reassuring to all members of the training system although comments from participants in their supervision classes and workshops had indicated that the opposite may also occur because raising awareness may also raise concern. They argued that the supervisor needs to recognise this, but must raise such issues and process them thoroughly before moving on with training. This is based on the first priority of establishing and protecting the working alliance.

The use of recordings in supervision and training has a relatively short history in the helping professions, its use first being reported by Rogers (1942) and Covner (1942), but the advantages identified by Rogers continue to be of relevance today:

- Clinical trainees tended to be more directive in their interviews than they had supposed and this was only identified when they had direct access to the content of their sessions.
- Recordings have a remarkable capacity to reveal resistances, conflicts and blocks that can occur in a session.
- Recordings provide information about areas for supervisee development, in addition to abilities and strengths.

Other technological developments in supervision

The development of distance learning programmes for supervisees who live a long way from an educational establishment and for those who live in rural areas has been facilitated by technological developments. Miller and Crago (1989) found audio-recordings to be a useful source of information regarding the practice of isolated therapists who lived in remote areas of Australia. Video-conferencing has been used (Marrow *et al.*, 2002; Troster *et al.*, 1995) with further and rapid developments taking place based on the Internet and electronic communication.

Distance learning was initially supported through telephone and telegraph communications in the context of correspondence courses and some students continue to prefer regular telephone calls to electronic communications. Stephen Goss (2000) reviewed new technologies and the ways in which they might be developed in the context of supervision. He asked the question as to whether meaningful relationships can be developed through email, video-conferencing and futuristic systems. In the paper by Marrow *et al.* (2002) one of the authors reported difficulties in maintaining eye contact with her supervisor while using video-conferencing technology. She found that it was easier to look at the computer screen instead of at the camera and this appeared to have a negative effect on her motivation.

Kanz (2001) argued that telephone and online supervision is plagued by a lack of perceptual cues and can be very costly due to long-distance telephone charges. He concluded that although the Internet has potential as an important tool for supervision, there are several ethical and relationship concerns with which to contend. He recommended that supervisors and supervisees first establish a supervisory alliance prior to proceeding with online supervision because relationships established online tend to be qualitatively different from face-to-face relationships. This type of approach has been referred to as 'blended', in which the participants meet live, usually at the outset, with supplementary electronic communication (Janoff and Schoenholtz-Read,

1999; Myrick and Sabella, 1995). Kanz went so far as to suggest that the client should not only be aware of the supervision relationship but should be able to communicate directly with the supervisor as well so that any concerns the client has about the supervisee can be addressed. He argued that this may also help the supervisor to identify supervisee resistance.

Face-to-face meetings enable supervisors to develop their personal commitment to the supervisee, and they are supportive to the supervisor in becoming a stakeholder in the supervisee's learning. For the supervisee, the supervisor has more substance in which they can invest their energies and ideas. Face-to-face interaction is so much richer because it involves body language, the use of inflection, laughter and rubato, and variations in pace and phrasing which often carry momentum. On the other hand, in electronic methods the hidden nature of personal characteristics protects the communication from being overly influenced by visible differences such as gender, ethnicity and disability.

Instant messaging, chat rooms and synchronous online communication make for an immediacy of response which is sometimes enjoyed. However, in my own experience of WebCT, for example, I have found that students are often reluctant to commit their views to cyberspace, since they are unable, with reasonable certainty, to comprehend responses to their online posts without the usual accompanying cues. They are unwilling to risk destabilising relationships in which they have a long-term investment and in which the supervisor, and possibly fellow students, are perceived as occupying an evaluative role.

Asynchronous communication by email has the advantages of slowing down the communication process in ways that can be helpful, although the absence of additional cues can lead to significant misunderstandings. It is because of the asynchronous nature that they enable worldwide supervision across different time zones. Supervisees typically prefer prompt replies before the topic has 'gone off the boil'. Telephone and email communication between meetings allows students to consult when suffering a crisis of confidence and faced with the need to make decisions within a short time-scale. However, in comparison with a diary date, the live context for which is governed by rules of social grace and politeness, an email stands the risk of being just another among a potential deluge which may be ignored.

Electronic and telephone communications potentially allow access to specific expertise not available locally provided that the 'expert' agrees to being consulted. A pilot study to test the feasibility of providing training and supervision in child psychiatry, a neglected specialty, to a centre in Pakistan using the Internet was reported by Rahman *et al.* (2006). The objective of the e-clinic was to train and empower existing staff, rather than provide a satellite service. Informal feedback suggested that participants had begun to improve their diagnostic and management skills. They felt well supported and, in turn, felt they could support other trainees. The activity generated new interest in collaborating with existing child welfare organisations and schools. Feedback from patients indicated that they valued expert opinion from abroad, and that the overall profile of the service had been raised as a result of the activity.

When electronic methods of communication are adopted, clients must give full informed consent since there are many hazards which can threaten confidentiality when using the Internet. Kanz (2001) advised the judicious use of initials or pseudonyms and encryption programmes where these are available in order to provide some safeguards. Remote supervision can be a powerful supplement when supervisors approach the limits of their competence. Technical blocks such as firewalls which enhance security sometimes impede legitimate communication and reliability of electronic communication can be an issue. Effective use requires participants to develop their technical competence to the required level.

Watson (2003) argued that computer-based approaches allow for more effective use of time since supervisors have the capability to 'meet' with their supervisees unbounded by the logistics of travel and tight schedules. Students can benefit from practice placements at more distant locations across the world (Coursol and Lewis, 2000). As with any form of technology, the process is vulnerable to system failure, to human frailties involving lack of familiarity or a phobic relationship with technology, and there are serious threats to the security of data. Resolution of these issues is likely to lead to more widespread use of developing technologies, at least as an adjunct to traditional approaches to supervision.

Chapter 11

Live supervision and observation

To have one's work observed is to subject it to the variously passive or active scrutiny of one or more other workers. In many professions work takes place in the presence of colleagues as a natural consequence of sharing an office, operating theatre, building site, kitchen or other workplace. In mental health and social care settings such accidental scrutiny is less likely and special arrangements usually need to be made.

At one end of the spectrum of such arrangements the supervisor may take the position of a 'fly on the wall', out of the line of sight of client and supervisee and passive during the session. This arrangement might appropriately be designated 'observation'. Powell (1993), cited in Campbell (2000: 77), cautioned that the overall quality of a session may be compromised by the increase in anxiety of therapist and client when the method involves non-participant observation and argues that all parties need to be prepared in advance of such an undertaking. At the other end of the continuum of involvement, the supervisor may be highly active and directly in communication with both supervisee and client; the task being participant observation. This is more likely to be called 'live supervision'. It is argued by Goodyear and Nelson (1997) that while direct observation is necessary in live supervision, it is not sufficient, since live supervision implies concurrent supervisor intervention. In my experience, the more effort directed towards ensuring clarity of task and purpose, specification of mutual roles and responsibilities, and rules of engagement, the more effective and less anxiety provoking the experience of live supervision for all parties. As in other arrangements for supervision, but possibly even more salient due to the level of exposure implied by live observation, a relationship of trust between participants is paramount.

Particularly in training contexts, supervisors and supervisees readily acknowledge the theoretical advantages of seeing each other's work. For neophyte therapists, observation of the supervisor offers the opportunity to emulate behaviours and styles they have witnessed rather than those which they have merely heard or read about. The process may involve observation of a model performance but may also allow the supervisee to observe the continuing challenges encountered by even the experienced practitioner. For example, to observe the supervisor struggling to bring a session to a conclusion may enhance supervisees' views of their own performance. Learners may benefit from observation of differing standards of performance at different stages in their training.

For supervisors to observe or participate live in sessions led by supervisees presents a unique opportunity to obtain the maximum information upon which to base interventions towards the goals of supervision. Even recordings provide limited information about the emotional climate of a session. Live supervision also offers additional safeguards to clients (Champe and Kleist, 2003; Levine and Tilker, 1974; Locke and McCollum, 2001) because the supervisor can take the opportunity to intervene during the session rather than after the moment has passed. Levine and Tilker suggested that this approach to supervision is particularly appropriate early on in training when extensive guidance may be indicated. However, caution needs to be exercised regarding supervisor interventions made during a session in case supervisees experience themselves as undermined in front of the client.

While most practitioners acknowledge the theoretical importance of the supervisor and supervisee working alongside each other, opportunities to work in this way are taken less often than might be expected. Live supervision is encountered most frequently in family work where the rationale is encapsulated within the theory and methodology. Its limited use in other approaches to psychological intervention may be explained by the perpetuation of approaches to supervision which supervisors encountered in their own training, high levels of anxiety about being 'found out' as inadequate exponents of the work, arguments regarding the costs of more than a single worker being present in a session with a client, and concern regarding client discomfort (for example, if outnumbered by the workers). In the latter instance, it is the view of some authors that two or more therapists working together with a client is inappropriate since the arrangement threatens to overwhelm the client (Jones, 1996). However, clients seen by therapists who received live supervision reported stronger working alliances than did clients seen by therapists who received videotaped supervision in a study by Kivlingham et al. (1991).

A factor to be considered in opting for live supervision is the effect on anxiety levels of both supervisor and supervisee. Liddle et al. (1988) suggested that supervisees tend to feel positive about the promise of close attention to and feedback about their clinical work but fearful of the attendant exposure of their clinical skills. Costa (1994) suggested a variety of strategies by which anxiety can be reduced; these included negotiating a clear contract for supervision, matching the method to the supervisee's developmental stage, directly addressing anxiety and fear, developing a collaborative supervisory attitude, creating a positive evaluative focus and encouraging independence. Further ideas are offered later in this chapter.

Live supervision may take place with all parties in the same room or by using a one-way screen which more readily lends itself to one or more supervisors participating.

Advantages of live supervision

1 Clients believe that having a team involved enriches their therapy experience (Locke and McCollum, 2001).
2 It allows for direct and immediate guidance and intervention; after the fact supervision leaves a wide margin for human error (Jordan, 1999; Mauzey and Erdman, 1997; Smith *et al.*, 1998).
3 It avoids overreliance on learners' self-reports as accurately representing clinical encounters (Saba, 1999).
4 It enhances student development through a process of observing supervisors, receiving feedback and on-the-job training (Hendrickson *et al.*, 2002).
5 It promotes good relationships between students and supervisors through the team nature of the task and through shared responsibility for interventions (Bernard and Goodyear, 1998: 140; Hendrickson *et al.*, 2002).
6 It enables preceptors (supervisors) to guide learners through difficult aspects of a session (Saba, 1999).
7 The learning that takes place is experientially and patient based (Saba, 1999).
8 It fosters collaborative enquiry (Saba, 1999).
9 It facilitates the generation of a variety of solutions (Saba, 1999).
10 It fosters an appreciation of parallel processes of interaction between patient and learner and learner and teacher (Saba, 1999).
11 It helps students to understand the complexity of practice at the beginning of a course and provides a context for analysing what they have observed (Fish and Twinn, 1997).
12 It offers a sense of the standards that practitioners set (Fish and Twinn, 1997).
13 It shows students different ways of doing things (Fish and Twinn, 1997).
14 It helps them to acknowledge the uniqueness of each practice situation and the need for responsiveness to individual clients (Fish and Twinn, 1997).
15 It helps students to identify what they did not understand and provides a basis for discussion following completion of the observed session (Fish and Twinn, 1997).
16 It helps the therapist to avoid responding to clients in ways that will reinforce the patterns that brought them to therapy (Bernard and Goodyear, 1998: 140; Kingston and Smith, 1983).

Disadvantages of live supervision

1   Time demands and the problem of scheduling cases to accommodate all who are to be involved means that live supervision can be experienced as burdensome (Bernard and Goodyear, 1998: 141; Hendrickson *et al.*, 2002).

2   It may underplay the therapist's own observations and intuitions in favour of those of the supervisor (Bernard and Goodyear, 1998: 140; Carpenter and Treacher 1989, cited in Wong, 1997).

3   The supervisor may be tempted to 'show off' in front of trainees and suggest dramatic but inappropriate interventions (Goodman, 1985: 48).

4   Live supervision generates anticipatory anxiety which typically continues in the early stages of its use (Wong, 1997).

5   Supervisor interventions may be experienced as distracting and intrusive (Hendrickson *et al.*, 2002; Mauzey and Erdman, 1997).

6   It can change the dynamic between the client and therapist in unhelpful ways (Hendrickson *et al.*, 2002).

7   It can lead clients to relate more to the supervisor than to the therapist (Hendrickson *et al.*, 2002).

8   It may encourage imitation of supervisors and inhibit the growth and development of students in the long run (Nichols 1975, cited in Wong, 1997).

9   It may result in boundary blurring between the supervisee's and supervisor's responsibilities (Smith *et al.*, 1998).

Issues in live supervision and observation

Purpose

'Unfocussed observation, without a clear purpose is generally demoralising and counter-productive' (Haggar *et al.*, 1993). From this perspective, clarification of purpose is an essential prerequisite to observation of practice.

A major purpose of observation is to help practitioners and students learn about and refine their practice. This purpose can be achieved when the supervisor is observed by the student, when the student is observed by the supervisor, when both observe a third party, or when experienced practitioners observe each other. When the practitioner's learning and development is the major purpose, prior agreement as to the focus of the observation and the specific skills to be learned can serve to contain attendant anxiety and help the observed party to maintain at least a reasonable measure of control over the process. Giving feedback which facilitates learning is a major challenge to the supervisor and this is addressed in more detail in Chapter 14 on constructive challenge.

Another purpose is to enhance the service to clients and ensure quality of client care. Live supervision can be containing for both client and clinician since changes of direction, or interruption of unhelpful interactional patterns between client and worker can be accomplished in-session rather than through post-session discussion. The client can benefit from the presence of an experienced practitioner and/or a different perspective during the session. Openness of practice is a safeguard in itself. Jordan (1999) cited comments made by three clients about their experience of live supervision at the end of their counselling experiences. As an example, one client is reported to have said:

> You are very young and are still learning. At first we thought you would not be able to help us; however, we saw quickly that you and your supervisor worked together as a team. We felt safe knowing that your supervisor has a lot of experience. We felt that we got great feedback from both of you. We felt that both of you had our best interest in mind.
>
> (Jordan, 1999)

A third major purpose is that of assessment. While it is necessary to base the assessment of fitness to practise on best evidence, and observation is likely to offer good evidence, the momentousness of this purpose for future careers can interfere unhelpfully with the observation process. Overly high levels of anxiety are likely adversely to affect performance. Fish and Twinn (1997: 114) identified other problematic aspects of observation for this purpose when they stated that, 'All seeing is selective, and all reporting of what is seen is interpretive. Thus in all observations the "facts" are coloured by at least two filters.'

Responsibility

An important decision to be reached, when the supervisor is present while the supervisee works, is agreement about the location of responsibility for the management and outcomes of the session. It is important that the supervisee does not feel disenfranchised by the presence of the supervisor and that the client–therapist relationship is sustained. This is probably easier to achieve when the supervisor is in a different room but can be accomplished by the use of appropriate social cues when all parties are in the same room. Under these conditions, if a process of co-therapy develops, it is almost impossible for the client and supervisee not to defer to the more experienced supervisor (Smith et al., 1998).

If the task of the supervisor is one of observation without participation, then the responsibility for the session lies more clearly with the supervisee. When supervisors take a more active role it is desirable to agree whether their interventions must be followed or whether the preferences of the supervisee may prevail. Are interventions suggestions or directives? Similarly, agreement needs to be reached as to who will initiate communication between supervisor and supervisee; the range of possibilities that may comprise these interventions, and the complexity that might be encompassed within them. It is important to guard against imitation of the supervisor by the supervisee which might inhibit the development of appropriate autonomy in the long run.

Potential for distraction

In the complex processes of interaction between client and therapist, it is often difficult both to concentrate fully on the client's issues and concerns and simultaneously to think about relevant theory, ideas and useful interventions. How much more complex when the ideas of the supervisor are added to the brew. They can serve as a distraction to the therapist's sense of direction, and be experienced as confusing and disorienting rather than helpful suggestions and signposts.

In a study of phone-ins (a particular supervisory intervention) Mauzey and Erdman (1997) found that supervisor contributions were most effective when they were clear, precise and brief, infrequent except in crisis situations, were suggestive rather than directive, took into account the level of anxiety and developmental stage of the supervisee, were supportive rather than challenging, and helped the supervisee with administrative control of the session and tracking of the client. Although there may seem to be more arguments for higher levels of supervisor intervention with a novice than with an experienced practitioner, paradoxically, it is also likely to be the novice who struggles with too much simultaneous information. However, on the basis of their research findings Moorhouse and Carr (1999) recommended that supervisors make infrequent phone calls during a session but that it was helpful to offer more than four suggestions within a single call. Agreement may be reached through discussion as to the optimum method for and quantity of supervisory input.

Actions, thoughts and feelings

While observation can provide the supervisor with information not otherwise available, observation alone is of limited value since it omits the thoughts and feelings of the practitioner which can only be inferred from what is observed. Workers who engage in live supervision or observation typically take this into account by recourse to a structured multi-stage process which involves an initial planning phase, a clinical encounter, and a post-session reflective stage (Saba, 1999). Fish and Twinn (1997) drew attention to the importance of the theories-in-use of the practitioner and the need for supervisors to try to understand how workers are thinking and what informs their professional judgements in order to take account of these and to keep a balanced judgement about their observations.

Recording methods

Particularly where the identified primary purpose of observation or live supervision is that of assessment of practice, supervisors may find it helpful to make a record of their observations, thoughts and reflections. More structured methods such as the use of checklists can serve the purpose of recording judgements that a particular skill has been accomplished but can be problematic if it is assumed that this is once and for all, or where a subsequent assessor makes a different judgement. Rich data is lost when the only record is boxes ticked or crossed. In contrast, an unstructured approach can leave supervisors wondering what might be salient about the session they are observing and unsure as to what to capture. Fish and Twinn proposed a method which generates a series of questions with which to explore the session in later discussion with the supervisee. This method may also be usefully adopted where it is the novice observing an experienced practitioner.

Levels of anxiety

This is a subject addressed by most authors on the topic of observation. Typically, the anxiety of the person observed is discussed but Saba also points out that in the context of medical education, some faculty members have initial trepidation about working with live supervision since they feel more on the spot to give immediately helpful and relevant input. The qualitative studies by Hendrickson *et al.* (2002), Mauzey and Erdman (1997), Wark (1995) and Wong (1997) all identified actual and potential anxiety experienced by supervisees particularly in anticipation of and early on in their use of the method. As they became more experienced their levels of anxiety declined and retrospectively they generally perceived their experience as enjoyable and valuable. Factors described as beneficial to the construction of a useful and enjoyable experience were clarification of expectations, a clear structure, a strong supervisory alliance, emphasis on the process as a collaborative endeavour, an emphasis on support as against challenge, and the supervisor taking a lead from the needs of the supervisee. It could be argued that these are qualities that characterise good supervision whatever the specific procedural arrangements.

Practicalities

The simple requirement to gather client, supervisee and supervisor together at the same time and in the same place introduces administrative complexity to the supervision task. This does not appear to have been afforded undue attention in the literature. Some authors (e.g. Saba, 1999) are clear that live supervision is expensive and time-consuming but worthwhile for its effectiveness as a training tool. It may also be argued that several tasks are being accomplished simultaneously: clinical governance, training and therapy.

Formats for live supervision

There are a variety of possible formats for live supervision which may take place with all parties in the same room or using a one-way screen which lends itself to one or more supervisors and/or supervisees participating. In some settings, as part of the process of introducing live supervision to clients, it is useful to ask them which format they would prefer.

What can go wrong with two or more people working together?

In my own experience, several pitfalls can present themselves when working live with a colleague in the room. Probably the most commonly adopted arrangement is some kind of co-work. When the pair shares a common method and approach to the work it may be possible spontaneously to interview together. There is a risk, however, of 'de-consulting' to the other party, leading to feelings of frustration in the workers and a meandering of direction in the therapy. The following is an extract from supervision in which the supervisee takes her difficulties in joint work with a colleague to her supervisor (*S* = supervisee, *Th* = therapist):

> Work is being carried out with a couple, Chris and Mary. Mary was sexually abused in childhood and Chris has been imprisoned in the past for sexual offences against children. He is considered by Social Services to pose a potential risk to Mary's children. The work with the couple is aimed at establishing whether the adults can keep the children safe were they to live together.

S: When you say you, when you say you do this jointly with the probation officer, are you both sitting in the room together?

Th: Yes.

S: And who does the work, or how do you allocate that?

Th: Well this is an issue I think, because we have discussions about that and I've made it clear that my way of working is to do this, is to go through the layers that are necessary, but I don't think that that's his way of working. I think he normally operates more on a how things are now level rather than what used to happen in one's childhood or something.

S: So layers for you are historical layers rather than emotional, or layers of belief or . . .

Th: They're emotional as well, that's right, all those things. But I feel that we. . . . Although I talk with the probation officer about what I'm intending to do and we agree it, when it actually comes to the session I don't feel that we're working in the same direction because he'll ask questions about other things that are current and I'll be asking questions about . . .

S: So there's a struggle for control of the sessions? And how do you think
       Chris responds to that?

Th: [Laughs] Well, I'm sure he'd much rather stay with the probation
       officer's agenda than with mine. Mary would go along with my agenda.

In this example the work might have been enhanced by the prior development
of a greater consensus about the aims of the work, how to achieve them, and
a discussion of the roles of the two workers.

Another potential problem in working live in the room, particularly when
one member of the pair is in training and the other is more experienced, is
the tendency either for the learner to bow to the superior knowledge of the
supervisor or for the supervisor to intervene excessively, leading to the supervisee feeling undermined. One of the most difficult tasks for the supervisor in
such circumstances is to help supervisees carry out the work in their own way,
rather than trying to wrestle the learner into carrying out the work in the way
that would be adopted by the supervisor. This often involves supervisors in
the experience of 'sitting on their hands' and requires the development of a
mindset which differs from that of being the principal therapist. The dilemma
is particularly acute for the supervisor who has responsibility for the clinical
work and observes what he or she construes as missed opportunities, blind
alleys or even explicit errors. On the other hand, there is plenty of pedagogic
potential in these for the supervisee, providing the welfare of the client is not
compromised.

Before embarking on work with a colleague in the room, it is advisable
to engage in a discussion in which the approach to working together is
thoroughly explored, negotiated and agreed. It may not be necessary for the
supervisor and supervisee to work in the same therapeutic model if the role
of the supervisor is agreed as that of helping the other to carry out the work
in the way he or she wishes. What needs to be agreed is who will introduce the
session, who will speak to the client, how the two workers will communicate
with each other, how the process will be respectful to all parties, where the
responsibility for the session lies and so on. A number of options are possible.

Supervisor/s and supervisee in the room together

Co-working

In instances where there is an agreed and tested commonality of approach to
the work, and each party has the confidence and role relationship which
confer equivalence of status, it is likely to be possible successfully to carry
out joint work without risk of 'de-consulting' to each other as outlined
in the example above. Co-working might also turn out to be satisfactory
under less stringent conditions. In this approach, both parties ask questions,
make reflections and so on, probably meeting to plan the session and to

reflect on what transpired during it both before and after the meeting with the client.

Observing role of one party

For beginners, the role of observer can be very freeing and may be preferable to co-work. In this condition, it is agreed that the observer does not actively contribute during the session. The observation may take place without constraint or the observer may be delegated a particular task – for example, to make contemporaneous process notes of the session, to focus on the non-verbal responses of the client, to notice therapeutic process and patterns, or to note her or his own feelings and thoughts as the session progresses. When the observer is the supervisee, the particular task negotiated can relate to current learning needs. The observer might focus on the client, on the clinician or on the therapeutic process, and might note down questions about the progress of the session to be addressed later in supervision. The agreement to undertake a specific task lessens the risks of boredom and of superficial unfocused gazing that can accompany an apparently passive role.

Where it is the supervisor who observes and makes notes, it may be particularly helpful to agree a focus for the supervision in advance. Notes can be descriptive (for example, about the physical layout of the room and the content of the session); evaluative of the work or of the client's presentation; and/or enquiring, inviting the supervisee to reflect further on an episode in the session. Particularly in the supervision of trainees the expectation that the supervisor will adopt an evaluative position can dominate in the mind of the supervisee. The following example of notes made by a supervisor of a family therapy session illustrates how this expectation can be challenged by an orientation to note making that is aimed at stimulating the thinking of the supervisee (the numbers in the left column refer to the time):

15.33   Family opens with tales of improvement and the episode which generated the difference.

15.35   The question, 'Who does she most take after?' follows the mother's story in a particular way. What is the overarching purpose to the telling of the story as well as the content of the story itself?

15.39   You change to the mother's partner at this point. What was your thinking at this point? And on reflection?

15.45   You make a summary here that I would describe as a second-order statement which clarified a significant change.

The final note above offers a judgement, but as a personal view.

Where an observational role is agreed, it is enormously helpful if the learner can first experience the role of observer rather than observed. This establishes the explicit and implicit rules regarding the role of the observer and is likely to be experienced as less threatening than being observed by the supervisor. Following an observation, the supervisor might model non-defensive responses to the supervisee's questions, might illustrate how to invite feedback and so on.

For neophyte supervisors who may never themselves have been observed during their own training, the presence of an observing supervisee might be experienced as nerve-racking, and likely to affect the approach to the work undertaken by the supervisor. Some defensive tactics for dealing with this include only allowing observation of initial sessions or particularly structured assessments. Even those experienced at being observed can find themselves inexplicably nervous in the presence of an unfamiliar observer, especially where fantasies about perceived competence or incompetence of self and other abound. In this case, other methods of working together which involve both parties might be more suitable, or, alternatively, a pre-session discussion in which the supervisor reveals her or his fantasies might evoke a more comfortable scenario. A clearly prescribed role for the observer which focuses specifically on the client rather than on the supervisor might also help.

Once the supervisee has experienced the role of observer and knows what to expect, a reversal of roles is likely to be less anxiety provoking. It is probably helpful if the supervisee feels in control both of the session and of any ensuing discussion and feedback. Careful planning of the session and discussion of contingency plans may also help. Occasionally the supervisee encounters a position of 'stuckness' in a session which can be particularly distressing in the presence of an observer. One way around this is to agree in advance that in such an event the supervisee may introduce a break in the session in which the supervisory dyad leaves the room for a mid-session consultation. During this period it is explained to clients that they are free to take a break themselves, either remaining in the room or returning to a reception area. In this case, it is important that the client is led to expect that such a break may be scheduled by an explanation given in the introduction to the session. It is likely to be seen as logical and helpful by the client that the supervisee may wish to take advice from the supervisor during, rather than between, sessions. As in any such explanation, it is helpful for the worker to include an explanation of the usefulness of the process for the client.

Joint participation, different roles

Under conditions in which supervisee and supervisor are relatively unfamiliar with each other and without a clearly shared and agreed approach to the work, the most successful way of working jointly may be for each party to contribute to the session, but with clearly delineated roles.

The specificity of roles would be agreed through discussion in advance. An adjunct to this option is to role play the agreed relationship process with a third colleague in order to ensure that both parties feel relatively comfortable working together in the way proposed. It is usually helpful that one person be designated as the leader of the session. It is this person who is responsible for participative management of the session, who makes the introductions and describes the approach to joint working to the client. This person also asks any questions and speaks directly to the client. It might be agreed that the other party may also speak to the client, but in my experience this can be confusing and my own preference is that the non-leader speaks only to the leader but in the presence of the client who sees and hears the communication between the two workers. Clients in such an arrangement frequently attempt to involve the non-leader through eye contact and social reference, as would usually be the case in a social interaction. The non-leader can respond to this by eye reference to the leader and avoiding gaze. This helps all parties to be clear about the roles and responsibilities within this arrangement.

When the session is planned in this way, the leader invites the other therapist to contribute at intervals during the session. It is best if the first invitation takes place early in the session in order to establish the pattern. The non-leader may be invited to share her or his ideas evoked during the session so far or to suggest questions the leader may wish to ask. In such cases it is often helpful to the leader if the rationale behind the question is included in the communication. It is agreed that while the client hears and may respond spontaneously to the contribution of the non-leader, it is at the discretion of the leader whether to follow up the contribution or to continue along a different path of her or his own determination. In this approach the control of the session lies clearly with the leading practitioner. The advantages of this approach are clarity regarding who is managing the session; little risk of one party feeling undermined by the other; the ideas of both parties being transparent to the workers and clients; conveying of mutual respect and open participation; and active involvement of both supervisor and supervisee.

The contributions of the non-leader benefit from being tentative, respectful to the client and the leader, and focused on the material brought by the client rather than on feedback to the leader. Feedback of the latter kind may be offered later by arrangement but not undertaken in front of the client. Such contributions often helpfully begin with 'I noticed that . . .', 'I was wondering if . . .', 'When that happened I felt like . . .'.

Responsibility for closing the session also lies with the leader. It is important that the non-leader is invited to make contributions at intervals with sufficient frequency that the comments are timely, but not so often as to effectively represent a handing over of control of the session. Offerings from the non-leader should be brief and contain only that number of ideas that could reasonably be taken on board by the leader and/or the client at one go. It should be agreeable that the non-leader may not have a comment to offer at times, in which case the leader progresses the session as he or she sees fit. This is particularly important when the non-leader is in training. The pair may also agree that the non-leader may interrupt the session with an idea if to withhold it would constitute a significant opportunity missed.

Additional advantages of this approach lie in its flexibility, the safeguarding of the welfare of the client since the supervisor is able to intervene respectfully during the work, and the availability of ideas to supervisees should they experience 'stuckness' in the session. (On respectful approaches to the work also see Anderson, 1997; Hoffman, 1991.)

As in other forms of live working, offering supervisees an initial opportunity to adopt the role of non-leader provides a relatively safe context in which to become familiar with the approach. It also provides an active role in which they can make a valuable contribution to the work without taking undue responsibility. Role reversal can be agreed once learners indicate that they have sufficient confidence to proceed. Further details of this approach to live supervision may be found in Smith and Kingston (1980) and Kingston and Smith (1983).

Shared leadership

Sometimes a structured form of shared leadership can be very helpful. An example might be where two workers of equivalent status are both reluctant to be the first to adopt the leadership role. While the 'rules' of interaction described above might be applied, it could be agreed that the leadership role switches from one party to the other halfway through the session. This might help the pair to overcome the initial hurdle with regard to feelings of vulnerability and exposure. Such an approach also allows both parties to use their ideas and to follow different directions where this seems helpful.

Effects on the client

While it is acknowledged that the presence of two or more workers is likely to influence the dynamics of the relationship, I have used the above methods successfully in work with individual clients. It has been possible to approximate the level of intimacy that is achievable with one client and one clinician, particularly when the method has been introduced at the first session and continued. Once familiar with the approach, additional possibilities reveal themselves. The worker is less likely to be drawn into a pattern of relating that is counter-productive as there is always someone else present who can take more of an observer perspective. The work tends to feel safe as it is conducted in the presence of another, and an experience of shared responsibility can develop which is less frightening and distressing than lone exposure to the 'narcissistic insults' that can arise in the work (Mollon, 1989).

On the other hand, the client may feel outnumbered and less able to exert influence in the therapeutic relationship than in a one-to-one setting. This may be a hindrance, though in certain work it may be helpful; it is important to address the effects on the client of two workers together both through discussion in the supervisory pairing and explicitly with the client. Clients may experience the approach as particularly respectful and attentive to their needs, or as socially obtuse and uncomfortable. Live supervision is most often used in the context of family or couples therapy. In these settings research evidence suggests that clients generally subscribe to the notion that 'two heads are better than one' (Locke and McCollum, 2001). As in all therapeutic work, the needs of the client and the usefulness of the approach adopted should be kept under review.

Live supervision outside the room

One-to-one supervision

Live supervision with the supervisor outside the room can be implemented when a one-way screen or video-link is available. Typically, when such technology is available, supervision is undertaken by a team, but the arrangement is also suitable for one-to-one supervision. Berger and Dammann (1982) suggested that two effects result from the supervisor being outside the room in which the consultation is taking place. First, the supervisor may more readily notice interaction patterns from the observer perspective. When these observations are conveyed to supervisees, they may experience a sense of feeling unintelligent insofar as they have not noticed these patterns themselves. Berger and Dammann suggested that supervisors prepare supervisees for this experience. Second, the supervisor may not experience the full intensity of the client's affect and the supervisee may feel that the supervisor does not adequately understand the client and the process in the room. In order to take account of this issue it is proposed that contributions from the supervisor should be regarded as advisory rather than mandatory.

Research on supervision employing a one-way screen suggests that supervisees can experience high levels of vulnerability and embarrassment in anticipation of, and when first using, the approach (Gershenson and Cohen, 1978; Wong, 1997). However, they reported that this initial stage is usually short-lived and is rapidly replaced by a stage in which the supervisor is perceived as a supporter rather than a critic. Feelings of vulnerability in the initial stages can be addressed by introducing the method in the manner outlined earlier in this chapter.

In a qualitative study of the views of supervisors and supervisees regarding helpful aspects of live supervision Wark (1995) identified three categories of supervisor behaviour: 'teaching/directing', 'supporting' and 'collaboration'. The 'teaching/directing' dimension was identified only by supervisors, whereas 'supporting' and 'collaboration' were identified as helpful by both groups. Collaboration was the most heavily supported dimension and was reflected in the supervisor attempting to proceed from the supervisee's position and attending to the needs of the supervisee. Wark proposed that the experience of collaboration can be fostered when, as Schwartz *et al.* (1988) suggested, the supervisor exercises conscious restraint so that supervisees learn to monitor, trust and use their own skills.

Live team supervision

Live supervision by a team of workers was developed in the context of family therapy. The rationale for the approach included the notion that multiple perspectives and hypotheses were preferable when working with a family group, the individuals within it being likely to hold different perspectives on and explanations for their difficulties. This way of working is intended to generate a range of options for change from which family members can select a route best suited to their personal circumstances.

Early approaches to such team supervision tended to follow a pattern of pre-session consultation and discussion, an interview with the family by one team member, a mid-session discussion break in which the therapist consulted with the team, a second half-session with the family, and a final break for consultation with the team followed by an intervention given to the family, who then departed. Over time, variations in this approach have been developed with the intention of showing greater respect to clients, an increased sense of partnership with clients, and a reduction in the mystery of the team behind the screen (Andersen, 1987; Hoffman, 1991).

Team supervision may be used concurrently with other models of therapy and may be viewed as a subset of group supervision. This is discussed in Chapter 6, and there are many important issues to consider in establishing group supervision that are of relevance and will not be repeated here. While the team approach may be perceived as a costly use of resources, it may also be argued that therapy, supervision, teaching and training are being carried out simultaneously, thus representing an economy over time spent individually on each of these tasks.

Many of the issues that apply to live supervision involving two workers are also relevant to live team work, but in addition sheer numbers can complicate matters further. Team involvement usually benefits from the use of technology in order not to overwhelm the client. The team may observe from behind a one-way screen or through a video-link, each of which needs to be introduced to the client. Clients are usually introduced to team members and invited to see the viewing arrangements. In my own work, clients sometimes prefer the team to sit in the room in which the interview is being conducted, and these preferences are always accommodated. Some authors have described the family, clinician, supervisor, learning team and video technician all sitting in the same room as a matter of course (Pegg and Manocchio, 1982). It is important in live team supervision to agree how communication from the team will take place. This could be through one or several team members, and may involve a single idea or several ideas. The communication may be in the form of an instruction or an offer to the lead clinician. The worker may offer the ideas to the client alongside and indistinguishably from her or his own, or specifically as those of the team. The effects of such interventions are various but often have the result of enhancing engagement between the clients and clinician who occupy the same space and who are both subject to the interventions of the team.

Where the clinician and team occupy different rooms, communication between them may be effected through the use of an internal telephone, a 'bug in the ear' through which the team can speak to the worker, or by knocking on the door to set up a mid-session consultation.

A development of the ear-bug used by the supervisor to communicate with the supervisee during sessions, which has been contingent on the increasing use and availability of computers, is the 'bug in the eye' (Klitzke and Lombardo, 1991) which involves the provision of regularly updated feedback to the supervisee on a monitor usually placed out of view of the client. The supervisor, while observing the supervisee from an observation room, types feedback to inform supervisees about aspects of their performance. It is suggested that this method maintains the benefits of the use of the earphone without its drawbacks because it reduces trainee distraction while permitting longer messages (Watson, 2003).

In one version of this arrangement, the clinician was presented with a graph line on a computer monitor located behind the clients (Follette and Callaghan, 1995). As therapist performance improved the graph line rose, with less satisfactory performance resulting in a decline in the graph. In my view the limited information provided by this method would suggest that it best be restricted to use where there has been clear prior agreement as to the goals for therapist behaviour during the session. Without this, the therapist would be left to guess which aspects of performance had led it to be adjudged as improving or declining.

Smith et al. (1998) described a system of live supervision that provided direct and immediate feedback regarding the supervisor's perceptions of the client's 'clinically relevant behaviours', the therapist's therapeutic intervention behaviours, the expected class of therapeutic behaviours in response to the client's behaviour and an indication of whether the therapist was 'on target' with these expected therapeutic behaviours. The computer screen was refreshed at ten-second intervals. This method was at an early stage of development. Early indications were that beginning therapists found it useful, as they were able to access information from the screen at times when they felt stuck and uncertain as to how to proceed. A further advantage is the preservation of information on a database, making it available for subsequent review.

The use of communication devices such as the 'bug in the ear' and telephone present their own challenge in the context of live supervision. These devices have typically been used in training contexts as a means whereby the supervisor can intervene while the therapy is in progress. Not only might this be regarded as of benefit to a client who is being seen by a practitioner-in-training, but there are potential advantages for the supervisee's learning. Byng-Hall (1982) regarded the use of the earphone as offering a much quicker way of learning than by observing or reading about a technique and tentatively trying it out at a later date. Because the earphone can be experienced as highly intrusive, Byng-Hall recommended that it only be used once a trusting relationship between supervisor and supervisee had been established. He also suggested that the style of the supervisor's interventions should be adapted to suit the needs of individual supervisees, and that the device should initially be used in role play until the supervisee is comfortable.

The earphone has been regarded as the most intrusive of the communication devices (Lowenstein *et al.*, 1982) and the supervisee's sense of autonomy may be disrupted by the one-way communication inherent in its use. A number of difficulties can arise from this challenge to the supervisee's autonomy. For example, if the supervisor proposes a course of action that the supervisee was about to take, he or she is robbed of the opportunity to demonstrate this. On the other hand, if the supervisor proposes a plan of action contrary to the one in the supervisee's mind, the supervisee may be prevented from taking the initiative. Potential reactions to these situations include feelings of rage and/or relinquishing responsibility and authority to the supervisor. Lowenstein *et al.* suggested that a means of overcoming these difficulties is for the supervisee to be responsible for initiating consultation with colleagues behind the screen.

Mauzey and Erdman (1997) studied trainees' perceptions of phone-ins, focusing on how phone-ins are used, the effects on trainees, the trainees' views of the effects on clients, and the effects on the supervisor–supervisee relationship. They carried out a qualitative study based on interviews with eight participants. They found that while the process served as a constant reminder that participants were in training, the overall use of phone-ins was perceived as being more helpful than it was distracting. The most useful phone-ins occurred when the supervisee was feeling stuck. At times, trainees reported that they had secretly hoped that the phone would ring during difficult sessions, and especially during crisis moments with the client, as they felt supported by the sharing of responsibility. As supervisees became more familiar with the process their levels of anxiety diminished and they became more prepared to take risks and learn new skills. Mauzey and Erdman argued that supervisors and supervisees benefit from preparatory training in the use of the earphone and that a good phone-in was characterised by the following features:

- Brief, clear, precise
- Less frequent, except in crisis situations
- Focused on welfare of client more than training

- Suggestive rather than directive
- Had clear instructions when a directive was necessary
- Was on track, rather than in a new direction
- Was supportive more often than challenging in initial training
- Considered current perspective of trainee
- Came from supervisor more often than from other team member
- Avoided strident tones
- Was timely
- Flowed from a trusting relationship with supervisor/team
- Helped supervisee with administrative control and tracking client
- Often came when the supervisee was confused
- Considered anxiety level of supervisee
- Considered developmental level of supervisee

An empirical study of the bug-in-the-ear (BITE) was carried out by Jumper (1999). Ten participants received immediate feedback via the BITE in conjunction with live supervision and ten participants served as a control group, receiving live supervision without the BITE. Results indicated that the group that received immediate feedback during the sessions demonstrated significantly greater increases in counselling self-efficacy than did the control group. Changes in participant anxiety levels were not significantly different between the two groups.

More lengthy consultations with the team may take place behind the screen and be summarised to the client, or be presented by a 'reflecting team' in which the team comes into the room occupied by the client and therapist. In this arrangement team members discuss their ideas together while the clinician and client listen. At the end of the reflection the team retires to the other side of the screen and the client is free to respond to the team's ideas. In one service in which I have worked, clients were offered a choice of whether the team talked behind the screen or in front of the client. My experience over several years was that clients invariably requested that the discussion took place in front of them. Team members to whom the reflecting team has been a new concept have reported it as causing them to focus positively on the client rather than critically on the therapist, and as helping them to create views and opinions in positive frames to be offered to the client. When ideas are shared behind the screen a worker might clumsily refer to a parent as 'overprotective', for example. When instead this is reflected to the parent it might be presented as 'I was struck by what an affectionate and loving mum Charlotte has – she's very precious and so she's always kept very safe. I wondered if Charlotte sometimes feels that she wants to learn more about how to keep herself safe.' This is the same idea offered more respectfully and with the 'blame-frame' removed.

In Andersen's (1987) description of the reflecting team, the family-interviewer system is not interrupted and the reflecting team members listen quietly behind the screen, each generating their own ideas. When the team members are invited to reflect on what they have heard, they take a speculative view. It is hypothesised that family members will select those ideas that fit and reject or ignore others. Following the reflection, the therapist invites the family members to comment on the team's reflections. In this approach the team does not offer feedback to the therapist and the therapist does not invite a discussion connected with her or his own learning needs. However, this is not precluded by the method, although it is likely to take place after the session with the family has ended.

Research by Young *et al.* (1989) and Smith *et al.* (1993) explored supervisee and client reactions to the reflecting team. The majority of both groups found the reflecting team to be either extremely or moderately helpful. Clients in particular reported valuing the reflecting team's ability to offer them multiple perspectives (i.e. two or more credible explanations of the same event). There is also more recent evidence to support the value to families of multiple perspectives (Champe and Kleist, 2003; Locke and McCollum, 2001). Participants in Locke and McCollum's study reported, 'Different perspectives on the same problem. If the therapist can't identify, maybe someone behind the mirror will,' and, 'The team is helpful in guiding sessions. I like the idea of several heads working on the problem rather than just one. There is a greater chance of achieving a successful approach to problems,' and, 'When I would be a little confused about a question . . . the team could call and reword the question . . . to communicate to me in a way that I understood.' Although the majority of responses were positive some clients felt that it was difficult to be themselves, felt uneasy, or were concerned with who was observing the sessions. Others were bothered by the disruptions caused by telephone calls, for example.

Live team supervision offers options for intervention that are more difficult to reproduce under other conditions. For example, team members may offer different perspectives to the client in the form, 'My colleague Jan is of the view that . . . but John thinks . . .'. This can help to separate the position from the person, thus facilitating a more reasoned debate. In addition, there are options to introduce ideas based on differences such as age, gender and ethnicity. Team members may also be able to offer particularly challenging ideas to the client with less risk to the therapeutic alliance than if they were to be offered by the therapist.

Feedback in live supervision

Lee and Everett (2004: 107) argued that seeking feedback to inform supervision should not come as a surprise either to therapists or their clients. They suggested that talking about therapy with the clients 'underscores the humanity of all participants and validates the risk that everyone takes in therapy' (Dwyer, 1999: 143, cited in Lee and Everett, 2004). They outlined a number of approaches to the involvement of clients in the evaluation of the therapy and the supervision as an ongoing process. For example, supervisors can enter therapy sessions at mid-point and ask questions of the therapist and the client/s about how the session is progressing: 'How is this session going?', 'What things are you experiencing as helpful?', 'How could therapy be changed better to meet your needs?' A supervisor could also interview the worker in front of the family. Supervisors could interview supervisees about what had been most and least useful to their learning and development. In the latter case the supervisees are described as effecting a consulting role for their supervisor. Lee and Everett counselled that this approach is dependent on all relationships within the system being open and supportive so that the parties can share ideas, solve problems and negotiate change together. All participants in the training system need to view the others as ethical, relate to each other respectfully, and be open to differing theoretical philosophies, values and beliefs.

Establishing a supervisory team

The process of establishing a supervisory team and the range of options for models of leadership is explored in greater depth in Chapter 6. It is important that differences in hierarchy, status and professional discipline, including differential clinical and administrative responsibilities, are addressed. Methods for resolving differences of opinion are required, including who has the final say during a session when differences cannot be reconciled. Such discussions will need to be revisited from time to time and particularly at points of transition when members join or leave the group.

The focus of the supervising team can be on developing shared understandings of the client, but can also be on the developmental needs of its members. The giving and receiving of feedback or making constructive challenges usually needs careful handling and is discussed in Chapter 14. The structured group supervision model (Wilbur *et al.*, 1994) offers a process in which feedback is followed by a period of reflection and a response statement. In this process constructive challenge is a circular process in which all group members hear views of their contributions from team members.

Live team supervision offers the same advantages as other methods of live supervision, with the further complexities of the need to establish a functional staff group and the need for familiarity with the chosen technologies for communicating with the lead clinician. It is likely to continue being primarily of application in work with families or groups of clients, but can be adapted successfully in a training context in which more than one supervisee is working with a single supervisor.

Chapter 12

Creative approaches

This chapter is an acknowledgement of and tribute to the ideas of colleagues who over the years have developed strategies and techniques for approaching supervision that help to keep the process alive and fresh. My own profession of clinical psychology is dominated by talking as the medium of communication, and this can be a very effective way for people to connect, both in clinical work and in supervision. This chapter describes techniques for talking in different ways, and for using other materials and methods to widen the scope of the collaborative enquiry in supervision. Lahad (2000) suggested that creative methods are particularly helpful in situations where the supervisee is 'stuck', where there is resistance or rationalisation. In such situations creative methods are intended to strengthen introspection and the visualisation of problems.

By the use of alternatives to talking, knowledge and understanding that a supervisee has about a client that is at the edge of awareness may be accessed. We perceive others with all of our senses, and creative methods aim to make the most of our perceptions, generating insight through creative thinking, methods and frameworks. Creative methods work in tandem with more conventional supervision. They may involve creating a representation of a client, problem or the problem system external to the supervisee which can be the focus of study by each of the participants in supervision. Shared contemplation helps to create and sustain an atmosphere of collegiality.

Some of these methods may also be used when time is short since they can quickly reach the heart of the matter. For example, a supervisee may be asked to identify her or his dilemma with a client in a single sentence, to represent this pictorially or diagrammatically as quickly as possible, and discuss the ideas that emerge. Consideration may then be given to any implications for the work and the whole episode may have taken no longer than 15 minutes. Such a brief review of a piece of work may be appropriate when the majority of a supervision session has been given over to one client but the supervisee wishes to take away some tentative ideas about another. The use of brief periods of time also helps to create a boundary that maintains a clear focus on the needs of supervisees in respect of their work. Such brief reviews can sometimes enable a wider perspective and clearer overview of the case.

Creative methods can also serve to lighten what is being experienced as an emotionally taxing and particularly heavy piece of work. Playfulness, so long as it is respectful to clients and their difficulties, can not only be enlightening in supervision but also serves as a model for creative exercises that might be carried out by the supervisee with the client. The work can continue to be serious but the enjoyment of it may be enhanced.

The use of these different methods has greater or lesser appeal for supervisees, just as it will have for clients. While encouragement to try something different is appropriate, particularly when the supervision or the work with the client hits a snag, alternative approaches to generating the material for supervision require the commitment of the supervisee to the process. Inskipp and Proctor (1995) regard the results of adopting creative methods as unpredictable because they can cut through surface presentation to something 'raw'. They therefore caution against pressing supervisees to take part against their better judgement, and charge the supervisor with careful and respectful management of the process. They also propose that debriefing, a method for disengaging from the material explored, be undertaken as a way of closing down the exercise. This can be as simple as chatting or moving positions and relaxing but may involve more formal de-roling. It is also wise to ensure that there is time to reflect on what has been learned and its implications for the work with the client.

The creative methods described in this chapter include visual and active methods of varying degrees of sophistication. Some require familiarity with and experience of a particular therapeutic approach. An example of this would be VanderMay and Peake's (1980) adaptation of psychodrama as a psychotherapy supervision technique. Other methods are less tied to a specific therapeutic model. Creative methods have in common the aim of providing new information based on images, actions and talking. As a result of this Williams (1995: 161) noted that, 'The tale trainees tell about therapy is the tale they spin; when they access the world of visual images, however, the tale spins them.'

Some methods for encouraging creativity are entirely verbal and involve interrupting normal patterns and routines to see if new ideas emerge. Deacon (2000) reported that creativity theorists identify four aspects of divergent thinking; fluency to generate many ideas, flexibility to think of varied ideas, originality to produce new ideas, and originality to produce unique ideas. She described a number of exercises which are primarily cognitive in nature. These included SCAMPER, creative pause and pattern interruption. SCAMPER is an acronym for a checklist: substitute, combine, adapt/adopt, minify/magnify, put to other uses, eliminate, reverse. These words are inserted into a sentence such as, 'What might we ... for/about/in our problem in order to improve it?' There are many such exercises based on the work of

Eberle (1997) and De Bono (2007), for example, that can be adapted for supervision.

Metaphor and imagery

It has been argued that an advantage of using metaphor is that it allows for the assembly of a complex array of information into a relatively simple conceptualisation or image (Rule, 1983). The image provides a springboard for developing further insights (Hampden-Turner, 1981). If the medium of the metaphor is visual, it offers possibilities of elaboration from the linearity of speech to a two- or three-dimensional representation (Arnheim, 1969: 232).

Metaphors often naturally occur to people and may be introduced by clients themselves. Using metaphors in supervision can lead to an exploration of the work through discussion and extension. In an example from my own practice, a child described his family as a battery with a negative and positive pole. This represented the relationship between his parents in which one was viewed as an optimist and the other as a pessimist. During the session I had asked what it was like to be in the middle of a live circuit. Later, in supervision, the metaphor was extended to create an explanation about the marital relationship in that the polarity neither allowed the parents to separate nor to be intimate. This idea fitted with other information about the family and it was possible for the metaphor to be explored further in the next family session. It can be more creative to discuss the problem in the form of a metaphor as the issue becomes one removed from the actual problem and widens the thinking. This distancing effect can offer some safety (be less threatening) to explore difficult areas.

Metaphors may also be created in supervision and introduced to the client by the supervisee, or simply used in further understanding of the case (Ronen and Rosenbaum, 1998). It is suggested that metaphors should be simple and new in order to engage interest or can usefully be developed when introduced by the client (Goncalves and Craine, 1991; Kopp, 1995), thereby creating a context for opening up new ideas and directions.

A review of the literature on the use of metaphors in clinical supervision concluded that the process may enhance case conceptualisation (Guiffrida et al., 2007). Amundson (1988) described a method for using visual metaphors as an aid to case conceptualisation in supervision. The method is flexible and responsive, both to the needs of the service context and of individual supervisees. He cautioned that participation should be voluntary since some supervisees respond negatively to the use of metaphors by reason of not being 'visualisers', by lack of drawing ability, or by other feelings of insecurity.

The procedure involves four basic stages and takes place in a supervision group context. Initially, the case is summarised by the supervisee with the aid of a drawing he or she has made in advance. The picture should illustrate, metaphorically, how the supervisee sees the client and her or his problems. Supervisees are asked to include how they see the case proceeding.

In the second stage the representation is discussed by the group. In the third stage the focus of the discussion shifts to the relationship between the supervisee and the client. In the final stage the focus is on how the drawing might be altered to reflect a different therapeutic orientation or approach. Amundson argues that the impact of the case drawing method can come from the development and drawing of the metaphor, or from the case discussion, or by sharing the drawing with the client.

Ronen and Rosenbaum described a technique for overcoming obstacles in treatment through exploring and modifying a video image of a therapy session. In reviewing a session in which the supervisee had felt helpless and bored, the supervisor suggested, 'Close your eyes and think of your session with that client. Try to concentrate on the room, the smell, the colors, the noises around you. Imagine you are sitting in front of a video, looking at a video cassette of your session with that client. Look at the two of you. How are you sitting? How far from each other? Pay attention to your nonverbal movements – what do you see? Listen to your voices – what do you hear? . . . Now use the remote control and lower the voices – what do you see?' and so on. The second phase of the process was used to create change, the supervisee being encouraged to visualise changes to position, posture and the tempo of the conversation. In the case example given, the supervisee learned that she might try to change her experience with the client by moving closer, leaning in and increasing the tempo of the conversation.

Writing and drawing

Amundson's method involves drawing, and, as he noted, people have a range of reactions to the proposal to use visual methods to further their understanding of the work they are conducting. However, visual methods can range from diagrammatic representation of the formulation of a problem to more sophisticated use of artists' materials. Diagrams can provide an easy transition from talk to vision and may be a good starting point for those who feel less confident about the use of alternatives to talking.

The act of writing words on paper or a drawing-board serves to externalise some ideas so that they are no longer just in one person's head but are 'out there' for the purpose of shared contemplation. The act of, say, drawing a family tree or genogram on a white-board can reveal a pattern not previously noted. The use of white-boards to note keywords and make links as supervisees talk about their work can proceed as a natural extension of the discussion. In my experience, supervisees report finding this process a particularly helpful aid to case conceptualisation and formulation.

Ronen and Rosenbaum (1998) described some applications of techniques from cognitive behaviour therapy to supervision which included the use of book proposals to decide on supervision goals and increase collaboration. Using this method, the supervisee creates a table of contents for a book on the ideal therapist, and a second list relating to self as therapist. The supervisor prepares a table of contents for a book about the supervisee at work. The supervisee's chapter headings help the supervisor to understand the worker's beliefs and frame of reference while the supervisor's headings allow the supervisor to describe the strengths of the worker and provide positive feedback.

For those supervisees who feel at ease with a transition from diagrams to drawings, a variety of frameworks have been proposed for providing structure, two of which are described in more detail below.

Drawing the client as a fish

A useful exercise in a group context introduced to me by Inskipp and Proctor (1997) was to draw the client as a fish. The choice of the fish reflects their view that everyone is capable of drawing a fish irrespective of artistic skill. The exercise may thus be experienced as less threatening for those who are uncertain with the medium. Further containment was provided by boundaries to the task. The drawing was to be accomplished within five minutes and without talking. We were then asked to put ourselves as the therapist into the drawing. In small groups we contemplated each other's offerings with a view to noticing whatever struck us about the picture. The other participants were to follow the request of the 'artist' regarding what was desired from the group members. This exercise would adapt to individual supervision. Whether or not connections are subsequently made to the work with the client could be optional. In my case I produced the drawing shown in Figure 12.1.

My colleagues noticed the height afforded by the dais from which I

Figure 12.1 A drawing of the client as a fish.

apparently conducted the work and suggested that this level of protection seemed responsive to the illustrated threat of the large teeth! I talked of my preference for an enquiring rather than conducting approach to the work and wondered how I might have got myself into the position that seemed to be represented in the drawing. None of this had been in my awareness prior to making the drawing, but helpfully informed my subsequent thinking.

The technique of asking the supervisee to represent some aspect of the work in a drawing was extended during a workshop led by Val Wosket (1998). She offered Ishiyama's (1988) framework for undertaking the drawing in a series of steps.

Ishiyama's framework

Ishiyama (1988) argued that Amundson's instructions for case drawing should be more specific and the procedure operationalised for practical and research purposes. Ishiyama provided a set of instructions that could help the introduction of the use of drawings into supervision for supervisors who are unfamiliar with this approach. A four-stage process was proposed, beginning with a more conventional approach to case conceptualisation. The supervisee is asked to respond to six-sentence stems on a 'Cognitive Case Processing Form' with a view to clarification of present perceptions of the client, the therapeutic process and the client–therapist relationship. Sentence stems are: 'What I see as the client's main concern is . . .', 'The way the client interacted with me is . . .', 'What I was trying to do in the session is . . .', 'What I felt or thought about myself as a counsellor during this session is . . .', 'The way this session went is . . .', 'What I think the client gained from this session is . . .'.

In order to encourage metaphoric thinking the supervisee then responds to a further four-sentence stems, the responses to which may or may not be written down according to preference. These stems are as follows: 'The way I perceive the client with her or his concern may be characterised by a metaphor or image like . . .', 'The way the client responded to me or felt towards me during this session may be characterised by a metaphor or image like . . .', 'The way I conducted myself during this session may be characterised by a metaphor or image like . . .', 'The way this session went may be characterised by a metaphor or image like . . .'.

Using large sheets of paper and coloured pens, supervisees are then given instructions for case drawing that emphasise the irrelevance of artistic qualities and aesthetic factors. Symbols, words, phrases or sentences may be included in the drawing, which should incorporate:

- Yourself as a counsellor and a person.
- The client and her or his concerns.
- Your relationship with the client (i.e. how you and the client related to each other).

- How the sessions went.
- Where the case is going.

In the final step, supervisees present their drawings and explain their thinking and the images to the supervisor and fellow supervisees. Further exploration can be encouraged by questioning, by sharing personal reactions to and impressions of the drawings, and by extending and developing the metaphors used. The supervisor's task is seen as one of facilitation.

Ishiyama illustrated the method with the example shown in Figure 12.2. The supervisee described the client as a man drowning in a glass of beer, calling for help and having available some life preservers/lifebuoys that are within his grasp. The supervisee's experience as a counsellor in the session was as in the role of life preserver, a role enacted by throwing a lifeline and struggling to pull it in. Reflecting on how the session proceeded, the

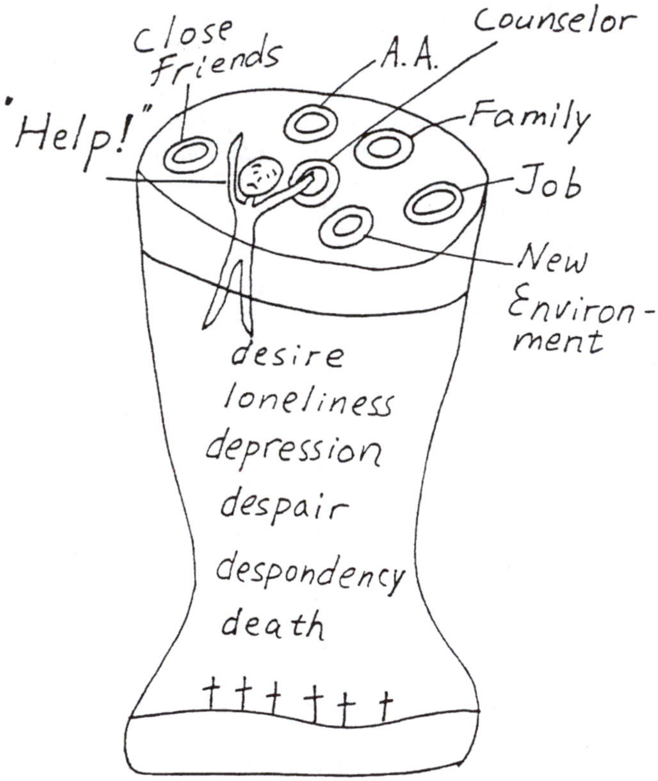

Figure 12.2 A man drowning in a glass of beer.

Source: Ishiyama (1988: 157). Reprinted with permission of the American Counseling Association.

swimmer–drowner was described as half-way home but in need of a larger life preserver in order to complete the work.

Ishiyama described positive reactions of supervisees to the procedure while cautioning that the method does not suit everyone, and that additional preparation time for supervision is needed. In addition, there was a tendency of case presenters to become more self than client focused when using visual methods. This can be appropriate and educational in that it enables supervisees' feelings, anxiety and self-doubt to surface and be explored. Whether or not this is helpful will depend upon multiple factors, including the objectives of the supervision and the dynamics of the relationship within the supervision group. The case conceptualisations produced were viewed as developing ideas that can inform the work and not as static and unchanging formulations.

Using objects in visual supervision

A number of authors have proposed that visualisation of a case can be aided by the symbolic use and arrangement of objects. Their use in supervision could be seen as a development and adaptation of the use of objects in therapy. Objects are probably more widely used in therapeutic work with children than with other client groups. Toys and play are not infrequently used as a means to enhance communication and to facilitate the expression of ideas that may not be amenable to more direct verbal expression given the developmental status of the child.

The use of objects and of play as therapy have a long tradition in the helping professions. One such method employs miniature models of people and objects which children use to construct their 'worlds' (Lowenfeld World Technique) in sand-filled trays (Lowenfeld, 1979). The method was extended to use with adults by Nourry et al. (1978) and by Kalff (1980). Further applications in the supervision of couples therapy have been described and proposed (Dean, 2001). This might involve the exploration of intergenerational patterns as supervisees create a world in the sand-tray about their family-of-origin. Case material could be presented in the sand-tray, illustrating the relationship dynamics of families with which supervisees are working.

Williams (1995) helpfully identified differences between the use of objects for therapeutic purposes and for the purposes of supervision as follows:

- The subjects which the objects are used to represent in supervision are the therapy systems and the supervising system. The supervisee is not a client and thus not a subject of therapy or healing.
- Supervisees do not construct their personal world but rather a representation of some therapy in which they may or may not be included.
- The use of objects in supervision is not associated with a particular model of therapy.

- The supervisor takes a directive role in managing the supervisory process and gives instructions. A non-directive approach would typify therapy.
- The supervisor encourages the supervisee to make associations and interpretations as part of the supervisory process, focusing on the conceptualisation of the work.
- However the materials are used in supervision, they are dismantled by the supervisee during the session rather than being seen as completed creations representing processes in the client and between the client and therapist. When used in therapy the creation would be preserved at the end of the session.
- The nature of the objects and the manner in which they are used in supervision is not specified and there is room for flexibility according to circumstance and need. No standard procedure is followed as in their use in therapy.

Williams (1995) has gathered together a set of evocative objects which are attached to magnets so that they can be moved around on a marker board. In supervision these are used to represent people, roles, 'states' or relationships. He argued that the sophistication of the objects is not important provided that they can be moved around. Visual presentation enables viewing of the objects and their relationship with each other in terms of similarity, distance and continuity. In Williams' method, the objects are used by the supervisee to show or define the therapeutic system as currently perceived. The supervisor as facilitator questions the supervisee about the arrangement with a view to creating a second arrangement that is different from the original and which gives pointers for the future directions of the work. The interpretation of the arrangement is the responsibility of the supervisee. The role of the supervisor is to enquire into the positioning of the objects so that supervisees can use their imaginations to create their own interpretations.

Williams suggested a number of routines for supervisors who wish to experiment with the use of symbolic objects. The recommendations for supervisors new to this approach are as follows:

- Clients are represented by one figure each when more than one person is included in the client system.
- Up to four figures may be used to represent a single client, each representing different aspects or features of the client as perceived by the supervisee.
- Typically three figures are used to represent the roles of the supervisee with the client.
- The supervisor asks supervisees to select objects to represent their roles in the work, and to represent the client.
- When several objects have been placed, the supervisor's usual first instruction is to 'move one of the figures to a place where you think it would be better employed'. The next instruction is to ask the supervisee

to show on the board what happens next. These instructions are repeated until no more moves are desired by the supervisee.

- It is often preferable that the first figure to be moved is one representing the supervisee's roles, but exceptions can be made when this seems more helpful.
- The supervisor does not question the supervisee about why particular figures have been selected or where they have been placed until the above moves have been completed.
- When the moves have been completed a rerun of the process may be carried out with the supervisor asking questions such as, 'What do you make of having chosen a lion to represent yourself?', 'Why do you think you have positioned yourself between the husband and wife?'

Williams has a preference for simple and naive questions. The decisions about the figures are about form rather than language. The supervisor's questions aim to help the supervisee to translate from the visual medium to articulation in speech so as to inform the direction of the work and to connect with theoretical underpinnings.

Williams described some specific procedures for the use of objects to aid visualisation and case conceptualisation. In addition, insights may be obtained by the use of simple materials such as buttons or stones with which to create representations of the therapeutic system through a process of sculpting (discussed later in this chapter).

Lahad (2000: 85) referred to the use of objects in a representational sense to create a 'spectrogram'. He uses his collection of small objects not only to enable supervisees to understand what is happening with their clients but also with their colleagues. Yosuf, head of a Social Services department in an Arab town, chose seven pieces to represent his team. He described the characters thus: 'Miss Piggy is this new lazy woman that is in charge of the rehabilitation program. She never does anything but she will always have advice and (generally negative) things to say. She is young and I feel she is stupid. The shepherd is my assistant. He comes in only three days a week the rest of the time he is at court. He is an older man, a former teacher and is very efficient.' He went on to describe each of the characters in detail and was then asked to position the team from each staff member's point of view. As the exercise progressed, he reported that he had learned that 'the shepherd wished to see Yosuf leave so that he could take the lead, that the snail saw herself left out once the new team had formed, that Miss Piggy wanted his lead but would block anyone from approaching him, and that the duke was challenging his authority at the same time as joining forces with Miss Piggy against the strong lad.' After further rearrangements of the figures Yosuf shared his astonishment at what he had learned, in that moving one figure would change the whole situation. He decided that he would use the learning to inform individual conversations with each member of his team.

Sociograms

As in the example above, the issues that people are experiencing in their work sometimes stem from the wider context in which it is taking place. It can be helpful to identify all the elements that comprise the work system and to explore their relationship with each other and how they might be having an impact on the work. For example, an 11-year-old girl with terminal cancer for which all treatments had failed was brought as a case to supervision by a Macmillan nurse who was concerned that the child was depressed. The nurse believed that the child should take antidepressant medication and had convinced the consultant paediatrician of the same. The family context was that the child had been raised largely by paternal grandparents after the early separation of the parents, and the child's mother had pursued a successful career. Following the mother's establishment of a new relationship and the birth of a half-sibling, the girl had moved to live with her mother and her new partner, continuing to spend weekends and holidays with her grandparents. The view of the mother was that since the child had only a short life remaining, all efforts should be made to make it as enjoyable and comfortable as possible. The view of the grandparents was that the child should be treated like any other. The child's behaviour tended to conform to each of the different family circumstances. She did not complain of pain or show sadness when with the grandparents but did both when with her mother.

The child was taken to the appointment with the consultant paediatrician by her grandparents, and he was persuaded that the child was well and did not require antidepressant medication. The Macmillan nurse referred to child psychiatry as an alternative source for a diagnosis of depression. She expressed grave concern that the effects of the two strongly held views in the family were very unhelpful for the well-being of the child.

In supervision a sociogram or relationship map of the different involved parties was created and positions arranged in relation to each person's connection with the different views of the mother and the grandparents. This revealed that there was the potential for an increasing number of professionals to become 'stuck' to each side of the argument. It was agreed that this was unhelpful and that neither the mother nor the grandparents would be prepared to change their position if they perceived the source of influence to be the other side of the family. It was felt, however, that both the mother and the grandparents would listen to the child's opinion if this could be given freely to a 'neutral' party. The focus of the discussion then moved to a decision about who might be perceived as neutral and who would also have the skills to interview the child. It was agreed that the interview be video-recorded and shown to both sides of the family. This might allow for a decision regarding the use of antidepressant medication to be freed from the influence of the wider context.

Through the sociogram described above, the nurse discovered that in order for her views to be influential she needed to think carefully about how to introduce them to the different family members.

The use of sociograms can be particularly helpful in exploring the wider influences on the work. Blocks to progress can be distant from the client–therapist relationship and a broader analysis can help prevent the frustrations of trying to accomplish outcomes that are impossible in the wider scheme of things.

Sculpting

Sculpting is a method in which people or objects are placed in relation to each other to represent a person's view of a system (Lawson, 1989; Lesage-Higgins, 1999). Where people are the objects placed they can be asked to describe the experience of physically being in the system – who else they could see, whether they were physically comfortable, and so on. In individual supervision, the objects used to make a sculpt cannot be interrogated in such a fashion, but a useful alternative perspective can be created in the process of representation using objects.

In a group, the materials used for sculpting can be the group members. A supervisee is invited to think about a client in their family or social context. The supervisee then chooses two members of the family, possibly the client and a significant other, and is asked to select two group members to represent these people. The supervisee then places these two in relationship to each other. This positioning includes the features of distance, orientation, position in space and relationship to each other. The positions may be static or moving. It is not necessary or desirable to give background to the case.

A third group member is then selected to represent another member of the client's system and he or she is placed in relation to the other two. Group members are selected until all of the people in the client's system have been represented. The supervisee may then stand back and look at the system with a view to identifying what can be seen only in the sculpt, rather than attempting to make interpretations in relation to the case itself. All the participants are then asked in turn to describe their experience of their position in the sculpt, again without making any interpretation or link to the client's family or system.

The sculpt can be repeated for a past or future time, perhaps choosing a time of transition in the system or family, such as a child leaving home or at the time of a bereavement, birth or schism. The supervisor facilitates the sculpt by a process of enquiry regarding how the people have been placed and whether this satisfies the mental picture that the supervisee has of the family.

In the absence of a group, objects such as buttons or small stones can be arranged by the supervisee to represent her or his view of the client's relationship with the family-of-origin, current social circle or therapeutic system. The objects provide for the representation of texture, colour and relative size and distance. Sculpts can be made of the past, present and future to incorporate the dimension of time. Supervisees can use an object to represent themselves in the client's system. Alternatively, the objects may be used to represent features, qualities, or roles played by the individual client.

The medium of clay may also be used to make models or representations of individuals. Because clay is malleable, it has the advantage that shapes and sizes of images can be altered as the process of moving them into different positions and relationships develops. For example, you can ask the question, 'What would it look like if this moved closer to that?'

When using such methods in individual supervision, there is a choice regarding the degree to which observations are made only of the representation, or how far each participant has permission to go further and make interpretations linked directly to what is known about the client.

The supervisor may choose to facilitate the sculpting process by prompting the supervisee with enquiries regarding whether all relevant people have been included. The sculpt could be completed by the supervisee trying to take the position of each of the members of the system with a view to further developing an understanding of conflicts and alliances. Many options are available. The method offers an alternative to a verbal medium and may reveal understandings not yet verbally formulated by the supervisee. Where people are the materials sculpted, they may need to de-role at the conclusion of the exercise.

Use of therapeutic cards

Historically, cards and illustrations have been used to encourage children and adults to tell stories for therapeutic purposes (for example, Rorschach inkblots, the Thematic Apperception Test and the Children's Apperception Test were used by Oaklander (1970) for this purpose). Lahad (2000) has explored the use of therapeutic storytelling cards which depict characters, scenes and objects that serve as a springboard for a story. He described a series of steps which involved dividing the cards into five piles face down and then thinking about a 'problem case'. Five cards are dealt into a star pattern, one card is turned over and the clinician thinks about how the card represents the client's problem. The second and third cards are to be connected to the origins of the problem, the fourth addresses the hopes and fears of the supervisee and the fifth is connected to the issues with which the therapy is dealing. After some shared discussion the supervisee chooses the card that most suggests 'Stop it all, there is no hope' and the card that suggests 'Yes, this is difficult but you can do it'. The supervisee is encouraged to 'let the cards "talk" to each other' and to engage in dialogue and interview in relation to the selected characters, further exploring hope and hopelessness. It is suggested that the supervisor help in this process perhaps by holding a card facing the supervisee or joining in an interview. After a number of repetitions, the process is evaluated with a view to extracting elements that are helpful to a broader understanding or new perspective on the work. Lahad uses SAGA and PERSONA therapeutic faces cards which are available from www.oh-cards.com. In my experience the use of these cards can lead to energetic and uplifting exchanges which shed different light on and thereby illuminate a client's difficulties or a practitioner's difficulty with a client.

Action methods

Action methods in supervision are probably more typically employed in group than in individual contexts. But since they include role play and role training, they can also be fruitful in individual supervision. Experimenting with taking the role of the client can be an effective way of obtaining different perspectives on the work. Working on a new technique as modelled by the supervisor, or rehearsing a strategy in supervision prior to using it with a client, can foster the development of new skills and give supervisees the confidence to proceed with new approaches to their work. Such practice also serves to help safeguard the welfare of the client.

Williams (1995: 215) advocates the introduction of an 'action culture' as early as possible if this is to be a feature of the supervision, and it would be an appropriate topic to be addressed in the contracting process.

Physical scaling

The use of rating scales is widespread in the helping professions. In addition to their use as assessment tools they can be used to evaluate progress and can be a focus of the therapeutic dialogue with the client. Williams (1995) advocated their adaptation as an action method in supervision as a gentle introduction to such methods.

An example of the use of physical scaling concerns the process of contracting about the learning needs of the supervisee. The supervisee might identify 'using Socratic questioning' as a learning need. The supervisor asks at what level of skill on a scale of 1–10 the supervisee evaluates her or his current performance. The supervisee then stands on an imaginary line on the office floor and chooses, say, scale point 3. The supervisor interviews the supervisee about the meaning of a score of 3 on 'using Socratic questioning'. He or she is then asked to move to the point that will be reached after a period of time. The supervisee then moves along the line to occupy the new position and is interviewed about what he or she will be doing differently at this point.

This procedure may be used in either individual or group supervision and does not have to include physical movement along an imaginary line. However, the inclusion of the physical action provides the additional experience of walking through the difference between, say, 3 and 7.

Empty chairs

Williams (1995) described the use of empty chairs in the context of group supervision. Any method of supervision adopted in the context of a group requires careful consideration of group processes and the reader is referred to Chapter 6 for consideration of supervision in groups. While the use of the empty chair in a group setting may provide a richer source of data, it is a technique that will also translate to individual supervision. Opportunities for using an empty chair arise particularly when supervisees make two statements that encapsulate two different courses of action: 'Part of me would like to . . . And another to . . .'. Two empty chairs can serve to represent the two positions. The supervisee can be invited to talk to each with a view to identifying costs and benefits and potential outcomes of following one or the other view. The effect of separating the two positions is to enable a clearer and more passionate exposition of each view. Williams (1995: 256) elaborates on a range of options for the use of the empty chair in supervision.

Role play

Bradley (1989: 165) described role playing in learning contexts as 'the exercise of behaving in a contrived experience according to a prescribed role, and by altering roles a number of learning situations can be presented'. Role play has often been advocated as a useful method in supervision (Errek and Randolph, 1982; Meredith and Bradley, 1989; Strosahl and Jacobson, 1986) by practitioners from a range of theoretical persuasions from behaviour therapy to psychodrama.

Adopting different roles enables supervisees to move from their current perspective to explore from a different angle the knowledge they have about the piece of work in focus. There are many roles the supervisee might adopt, including that of the central client, of another person connected to the client, of a piece of furniture, of a part of the client, of a previous 'helper' and so on. There is also an option for the supervisee to interview the supervisor in the role of a client in order to illustrate what happened in a session or to experiment with how a particular approach might be received. The example below describes an experiment involving the kind of letter to write to a non-attending client.

The supervisor's habit was to write to clients beginning, 'I am sorry that you could not attend for your appointment today . . .'. The supervisee was concerned that to write this to clients who wished to communicate something deliberate through their non-attendance might be unhelpful. She invited the supervisor to take the role of clients who did not attend for a range of reasons and experimented with how they might respond to a letter commencing in alternative ways, 'I am sorry that you did not attend for your appointment . . .', 'As you did not attend for your appointment . . .', etc.

Role play also enables a supervisor to demonstrate a method or technique to a supervisee, and/or a supervisee to practise a technique in the relative safety of the supervision. This can range from something relatively straight-forward such as how to introduce oneself to clients, to something more complex such as the use of guided imagery in relaxation training.

Occasionally, supervisees experience some difficulty in taking on the role of the other. Various techniques can help. The methods of psychodrama pre-scribe that protagonists are helped by being 'warmed-up' to working on their issues, and this is accomplished through the use of specifically designed exer-cises (Karp *et al.*, 1998) which could be adapted for individual use. Energy can be generated by having supervisees rearrange furniture in the room to represent the physical layout of the space in which they meet with the client. At the least it is often helpful for the supervisee to change chairs when taking another role. In order to help the supervisee to adopt the designated role, the supervisor can ask a number of 'grounding' questions prior to focusing on the identified issues for supervision. These include referring to the supervisee by the name of the person whose role they are taking and asking questions about their age, family circumstances, how they came to seek help, how long they have known the clinician and so on. When the supervisee is responding consistently in the first person rather than the third person it is probably germane to move on to more central issues.

The use of role play can have a powerful impact through the creation of different perspectives on the work. It can also be fun and provide a diversion through lighter moments that can lift supervisees who are feeling worn down with their efforts to help. In one example of couple therapy, a supervisee role played the clients' bed! This required the supervisor to also get down on the floor to talk with 'bed'. Once the supervisee was grounded in the role through conversation about the layout of the room and the bedcovers, the supervisor said, 'So, I bet you've seen a lot of action.' The supervisee's response, 'Well, that's the problem really.'

Another important issue in the use of role play is the need for the super-visor to ensure that the supervisee has de-roled before proceeding further to discuss the meaning of the role play for future work with the client, although this in itself can aid the de-roling process. Simple de-roling manoeuvres include asking supervisees to say how they are the same and how they are different from the role, or to say their name and their intentions for the rest of the supervision and for the remainder of the day. As a transition to de-roling supervisees may wish to describe their experiences in the role in general. Role plays should be set up with a particular intention in mind. After de-roling the discussion might focus on any insights gained and should connect back to the original purpose in having set it up.

Williams (1988) described a training group for supervisors. Real dilemmas were acted out employing some of the methodology of psychodrama without engaging in the full process. The procedure involved a group member in giving a brief narrative description of the case, concretising the multiple roles that were hidden in the description, setting out the roles spatially, an enactment, and the identification of a role for the supervisor that could lead to movement in the others. The aim of the process was to explore possibilities for the supervisor in the task of assisting the supervisee with her or his client.

Internalised-other interviewing

'Internalised-other' interviewing (Burnham, 2000; Epston, 1993) offers a method for exploring the relationships people have with the various facets of their own being. Casement (1990) referred to the voices in oneself of personally influential people as one's internalised significant others. Interviews may not only be restricted to the voices of significant others. For example, an interview with a client might explore the relationship the person has with 'having fun' or with 'excellence' or with a number of different elements that might have been mapped as relating to the presenting difficulties – 'feeling guilty', 'feeling responsible', 'feeling a failure'. In this technique the clinician speaks with the client as the selected element. The initial questions are designed to help interviewees 'ground' themselves in the identity of the other, and subsequent ones to explore the relationship of the other with the client. For example, 'Hello, "feeling-good" ', 'How old are you?', 'How big are you?', 'Do you have a particular colour or do you change colour?', 'When were you last in touch with Jane?', 'Does she contact you or do you call on her?', 'Who else comes along when you meet up?', and so on.

The stages of the internalised-other interview were identified as follows by Burnham (2000):

- Choose the person, idea, ability, problem or emotion that will be the 'other'. This choice takes place through negotiation and is best when connected with the flow of the conversation or a purpose of the interview.
- Propose the way of working as a way of fulfilling a goal of the interview.
- Explain the process as much as necessary to begin with, or politely accept if the person declines the offer.
- Begin by 'grounding' the person being interviewed in the identity of the 'other'. This is accomplished by talking to the person as if meeting them for the first time and asking questions about everyday aspects of the 'other's' life.
- Continue by exploring more deeply the experience of the other in relation to the goals of the interview. These questions may be related to emotions, actions and meanings. Burnham argued that the interviewer need not be discouraged by 'don't know' responses since these are potential triggers to the curiosity of the interviewee.
- Explore the relationship between the 'other' and the person being interviewed.

- Prompt the person that this stage of the interview is ending by saying 'goodbye' to the 'other' and 'hello' to the person sitting in front of you.
- Reflect on the process and its effects in relation to the purpose of the interview.

Internalised-other interviewing can be adapted for use in supervision. The supervisee might take the role of the client, or the method could be used, for example, to explore the supervisee's relationship with an element of the work such as 'stuckness' or 'despair'. The possibilities are limited only by the imaginations of the participants. The method serves to encourage the taking of a different perspective on the subject and from this an action plan can be devised.

Williams (1995: 233) described this approach as 'interviewing for a role', a role being defined as 'a person's functioning with one or more persons at particular times in specific situations', suggesting that people are many 'selves' in many contexts. For the use of the method in group supervision the reader is directed to Williams (1995). My own experience suggests that for effective and safe use of the method in a group setting the supervisor should be experienced in the techniques and methods of drama-based therapy that includes the use of auxiliaries, identification of the protagonist, doubling, de-roling and so forth. These methods are described in Howells *et al.* (1994) and Yablonsky (1992).

The use of creative methods in supervision is more typically found in those helping professions in which such methods are adopted with clients. This does not prevent their translation to those professions more typically engaged in verbal approaches and they are recommended as a way of obtaining alternative perspectives and keeping supervision fresh.

This chapter has offered a range of methods for presenting work in supervision that go beyond the traditional medium of talking. It is recommended that these methods are adapted to suit the experience and confidence levels of the participants and that they should be used as tools to enhance the work of supervision in specific ways rather than as techniques to turn to when one does not know what to do next. All creative methods can tap into unconscious material and may produce unexpected results. This needs to be acknowledged by supervisors using these approaches. For readers who are interested in and wish to develop the use of metaphor and the physical representation of relationships in supervision further, original sources include Robbins and Erismann (1992) on the development of a stone sculpting workshop, Barnat (1977) on the use of metaphor in allaying supervisee anxiety, McNamee and McWay (2004) on the use of bilateral art in supervision, Noucho (1983) on the use of visual imagery in training, and Friedman and Rogers Mitchell (2007) on supervision of sandplay therapy.

Chapter 13

The influence of different models of therapeutic intervention on the supervisory process

Across different models of therapy and counselling there are common themes and ideas that inform both the practice and the supervision of the practice. Whatever the model of therapy, there will be differences between practitioners in style and understanding of the parameters of the model and hence much diversity of supervision within and between models. As long as half a century ago Fiedler's (1950, 1951) studies established that those who adhere to a particular therapeutic theory cannot be regarded as interchangeable units. He found that there could be more difference between two therapists who espoused the same theory than between two therapists with apparently dissimilar theories. A psychologist's espoused theory may correspond only imperfectly with what he or she does in actual practice (Goodyear *et al.*, 1983). It has also been proposed that the manner in which most clinicians work in the field is convoluted and that the approach is self-correcting – if one thing fails to work the clinician tries another (Seligman, 1995). In their practice placements, students are thus likely to encounter a mix of therapeutic approaches rather than work carried out within a 'pure' model.

This chapter focuses on the differences between models of therapy insofar as these influence the way in which supervision is likely to be conducted. This is against the background of differences in style and understanding between therapists of the same theoretical persuasion. The influence of the supervisor's preferred theoretical model/s can be a focus of discussion in the contracting process.

Differences between supervisors from different theoretical orientations were studied by Putney *et al.* (1992). Cognitive behavioural supervisors were perceived to be more likely to act in a consultant role and to focus on skills and strategies than did humanistic, psychodynamic and existential supervisors, who were regarded as more often operating within a relationship model and in a therapist role. Supervisors were not perceived to differ with regard to their focus on growth and skill development and their focus on the supervisee.

Goodyear *et al.* (1984) used videotapes of supervision of the same piece of therapeutic work to compare approaches to supervision undertaken within Gestalt (Erving Polster), Client-centred (Carl Rogers), Psychoanalytic (Rudolph Ekstein) and Rational–Emotive Therapy (Albert Ellis) models. Videotapes were rated along a number of dimensions by 58 experienced supervisors. Of the four supervisors, Rogers was perceived as the person most likely to favour a modelling role and Ellis as the least likely. Ekstein and Ellis were perceived to function more in the role of critic than were Polster and Rogers. Ellis took the role of teacher more often than Rogers, and focused on skills and strategies to a greater extent than the other three supervisors. Ekstein and Ellis were seen as focusing more on case conceptualisation. The authors concluded that their results confirmed the findings of Miars et al. (1983) that there is a relationship between theoretical orientation towards therapy and a supervisor's manifest behaviour, roles and attitudes. Friedlander and Ward (1983) found similar results in a different study using the same stimulus materials. It might be argued that these particular therapists would have adhered more closely to pure models than would typical practitioners in the field. The following sections of this chapter describe the influence on supervision of four theoretical approaches to therapy.

Psychodynamic models

Traditionally, there have been three principal elements that have comprised training in a psychodynamic approach to counselling and therapy. These are a personal analysis or personal therapy, a taught theoretical component and supervised practice. This tripartite model was developed when formal psychoanalytic institutes and societies were established in the 1920s (Moldawsky, 1980).

Two schools of thought developed in relation to the roles of teacher and analyst. The Hungarian position advocated combining the roles of supervisor and analyst, whereas the Viennese position promoted the idea that the pursuit of resolution of personal conflicts through personal therapy should be undertaken with a different person than should supervised practice (Caligor, 1984; Thorbeck, 1992). Binder and Strupp (1997) argued that these two positions became increasingly integrated over time. The supervision is centred on the therapy with the client, while the supervisee is simultaneously seen as unwittingly enacting with the supervisor important dynamics occurring in her or his relationship with the client. Historically, psychodynamic training emphasised this enactment through the notion of 'parallel process' in which the interpersonal processes taking place in the dyads supervisor–supervisee and supervisee–client are seen as influencing and informing each other.

Doehrman's (1976) view of parallel process was that conflicts arising in supervision tended to be replayed in the therapy with the supervisee's client. Thus, supervisees might identify with their supervisor and act towards the client as they had experienced the supervisor acting towards them or, by counter-identification, act towards the client in the opposite fashion. Most subsequent writings emphasise the source of parallel process as being in the therapy with replay in the supervision (Binder and Strupp, 1997). For example, the supervisee is receptive to messages from the client and becomes the transmitter of these messages in supervision, evoking responses in the supervisor that were evoked in herself or himself in the therapy. More recently, it has been suggested (Berman, 2000; Frawley O'Dea and Sarnat, 2001; Lesser, 1984) that the notion of parallel process carries a risk of creating a dogmatic expectation of finding exact parallels while avoiding more direct sources of conflict within the supervisory dyad itself, and that supervisory stalemates require attention despite being 'unparalled'.

The psychodynamic supervisor integrates didactic and therapeutic roles to varying degrees to achieve the educational goals of supervision. The purpose is always educational. Historically, the supervisor's role was to provide theoretical and technical input and to interpret the parallel process. Recently, the role has been more broadly defined (Wharton, 2003). In psychoanalytic training independent personal analysis continues to be a requirement (Dewald, 1997) and this is also predominantly the case generally in psychodynamic therapy training.

The theory of learning in psychoanalytic supervision traditionally was that of a developmental progression taking place through the establishment of a learning alliance. In the beginning the supervisee was seen as being heavily and explicitly reliant on the supervisor and the focus was on learning technical strategies. Gradually the supervisee begins to emulate the supervisor through having internalised or introjected images and qualities of the supervisor. At this stage the supervisee is seen as developing a capacity to reflect on her or his functioning within the supervisory relationship which then generalises to the therapeutic relationship. Gradually supervisees are seen as developing the capacity to engage in the reflection process through the mechanism of their own internal supervisor (Casement, 1985). Casement argued that towards the end of training the process of supervision should develop into a dialogue between the external supervisor and the supervisee's internal supervisor.

Within a psychodynamic framework the source of data for discussion is usually the supervisee's notes made contemporaneously or immediately following a therapy session, or the supervisee's free associations. Recordings have been regarded as useful (Perr, 1986), while other supervisors maintain that recordings make an unjustified intrusion into the therapeutic relationship (Tennen, 1988).

One of the implications of these ideas is the importance of establishing a sound supervisory relationship as a platform from which to discuss the processes that are taking place in the supervision, the processes that are taking place in the therapy, and how these relate to each other. This is also central to contemporary accounts of supervision in a psychodynamic frame (Frawley O'Dea and Sarnat, 2001).

Supervisees can also expect to bring the issue of how the work makes them feel to the supervision, using this to understand the client's transference and the therapist's counter-transference. One of the roles of the supervisor is to help the supervisee to see how he or she is being drawn into unconscious enactments with the client. These may be necessary to the work but is detrimental if they are not identified. For example, therapists may find themselves extending the boundaries of the sessions with a particular client – where, when and for how long the sessions take place – as they are drawn into a pattern of relating with its origins in the client's history. The supervisor can help the supervisee to notice such patterns. Their meaning can be explored in supervision through the notions of transference and counter-transference, and the new awareness and understanding used to facilitate the therapy with the client.

This use of feelings to inform the work is brought out in the following extract from a supervision session (where S = supervisor, and T = trainee) reported in Scaife (1995). The commentary was added to the transcript by the supervisor in order to highlight some features of a psychodynamic model.

S: You've mentioned she's quite good at mothering.

T: Watching her in the room she is good at mothering.

S: But it's harder for her to mother herself?

T: Yes, because she sees herself as ugly inside. That she's so ugly inside that if she goes out in the street, people will see it, and that she can't bear to go out or come and see me because people will see her absolute ugliness. That's one day, but another day . . .

S: I'm wondering what those ugly feelings are.

T: It's the anger and the hatred I think.

S: That seems likely, the anger and the hate. Maybe in the sessions with you she could express them.

T: That's been one of my themes, to get her to express that, not just in the present, but to events in the past and I've tried to do that using drama because it seems to need a fairly powerful expression, but she's very frightened of the power of those feelings.

S: Power of them, and I wonder if she's frightened at showing *you* what they are because you might again reject her. If she shows you those ugly awful feelings, are you going to do the same as the rest and reject, abandon. She's got herself some mothering, and if she expresses those, maybe the fear would be that she's got a lot to lose.

[Commentary: Fear of these primitive emotions of anger, rejection, hatred, envy and abandonment are a typical focus of a psychodynamic model.]

T: Would it be appropriate to raise that as an idea?

S: Yes. Certainly would, and even maybe, does she feel angry with you, or even envious. She's got a woman therapist, and I'm wondering if she also has feelings towards women. Does she know you're a mother?

T: Yes, I would think so. It's fairly obvious.

S: It could be that there's some envy around. That she can see you are together with a good job.

T: I think there is anger towards women as well. She almost got close to a woman who she met at a course she went on, and clearly prevented the relationship developing further.

S: That could be another reason why the sessions haven't developed. It's quite dangerous for her to show those feelings, not just because they're dangerous feelings as such but also they may be towards you. This thing of her ugly feelings, can you remember what you said that you feel when she picks up the phone? What do you feel towards her?

T: I said I didn't feel as sympathetic.

S: What does that mean?

T: Well it's actually a slight feeling of detachment. Is it rejection? I don't know.

S: You do feel detached?

T: Well, I think I see it, when she phones and it's a crisis time, I see it as part of a repeating pattern. I don't get overtaken by the current crisis like I think I would do, or I'm capable of being with some other people. I think, 'Well, here's another crisis, and I know I'm not going to be able to do anything to put this right, so I don't actually need to dive in here.' I suppose with some people I would dive in and rescue them or something. It's hard to put a label on it.

S: Do you feel that in the sessions? Does she give you any other strong feeling?

T: Yes, some of the things she's described about her life have been very sad. I've felt very sad about them and I've felt very much like wanting to help her put those right as far as it's possible to do that.

S: I think what I was wondering about, I seemed to pick up something from what you said earlier which was different from, what you say, experience with your other clients, and I was trying to put that together with the case. Given the fact that in your experience of her, you've been seeing her a long time, and there hasn't been much apparent change. Putting that together with, you said you feel detached in some ways as though here's another crisis and you can't do anything. I'm wondering if that's how she feels.

[Commentary: Part of the transference experience is one of the client projecting her feelings on to the therapist.]

T: Helpless would be the right thing, I think, which prompted me to start writing this letter which I've decided not to send because I think it was prompted by speaking to her on the phone, which was a helpless letter to the GP basically, saying I can't do anything.

(Scaife, 1995: 121–123)

This extract shows briefly how the model and theory in which the therapy is conducted are used reflexively to inform the process of supervision. Identifying the implications of the therapeutic model for the process of supervision may constitute part of the discussion undertaken in the contracting process. This will help the supervisee to know where to look for the data to bring to supervision.

Wharton (2003) took the view that supervision in analytic training is a 'space for play', a rewarding opportunity to reflect on material together without feeling that a conclusion must be reached. Learning is primarily experiential and emotional rather than cognitive although she argues that a thorough discussion of the wording of interpretations and the various meanings for the patient is an essential aspect of supervision. The supervisor models an enquiring non-judgemental reflectiveness and an ability to tolerate a state of not knowing in which hypotheses are tested rather than correct conclusions reached. She suggested that supervisors should try to avoid giving any impression that the trainee's intervention was wrong and that if the assessment role is continually in focus this is like digging up a plant to see if the roots are growing. Supervisors need to be alert to: supervisees' fears about hearing unconscious communications from clients which can lead to a 'flight into action'; anticipate sensitivity to losses which can be particularly acute because the loss of the supervisee's own childhood is acutely emphasised; and recognise that a vague style of reporting is a common symptom of trainee anxiety. Wharton's approach contrasts with more traditional approaches to supervision in analytic training.

Issues of transference and counter-transference

Transference and counter-transference are regarded as a cyclical process where studying one part would be like studying only one set of the figures on a chessboard (Berman, 2000). Like Wharton, Berman argued that purely didactic supervision which relegates the supervisee's counter-transference to her or his own analysis is untenable. His approach is therefore to follow the analytic interaction carefully, with close attention to minute details, pausing to consider the intersubjective implications of each verbal and non-verbal exchange. Since what is required is introspective and empathic sensitivity to the sources and impacts of the parties' actions and non-actions, personal exposure is essential, the capacity for which is strongly influenced by the supervisory climate.

The management of counter-transference was discussed by Wakefield (1995). He argued that when the supervisee's counter-transference arises from unresolved personal issues it is advisable that the supervisor does not explore the reactions but when it is a reaction to the client's material (referred to as projective or syntonic counter-transference) then it is an appropriate focus of supervision. The emphasis is on education rather than on therapy. Transference projections from both the supervisor and supervisee are built into the supervisory situation and by definition at first are not conscious and may not be recognised by either party. Wakefield argued that supervision contains many of the same factors that generate transference in analysis, such as personal contact over an extended period of time and the revealing of important personal matters. The supervisor is a powerful figure whom the candidate not unreasonably may wish to please, especially given the supervisor's role as evaluator. He used three overarching theories to explore potential transference reactions.

Drive theory (Freud)

Within this theory the primary instincts are sex and power (see Freud and Gay, 1995). Either supervisee or supervisor may experience the other as a source of gratification of instinctive desire. This gives potential for the development of dual-role relationships, for example where the supervisor engages socially or sexually with the supervisee in addition to occupying a formal position, and this threatens the integrity of the supervision process.

Object relations theory (Harry Stack Sullivan, Melanie Klein, Michael Balint and others)

Object relations is a set of theories (see Gomez, 1997) which propose that the relationship within the primary carer–infant dyad lays the foundation for the development of individual identity. The individual's interpretation and understanding of primary relationships, both conscious and unconscious, becomes the basis for later relations with others, in friendships, partnerships, and in parenting. Early life patterns may become transference projections between supervisor and supervisee; for example, the supervisor may represent the caring, guiding parent the supervisee never had. For supervisors the supervisee may represent the child they never had or the child in themselves to be nourished as they would have wished. Some of these projections are disapproved but others are socially reinforced; for example, the supervisor taking a special interest in a particular supervisee.

Kohut's self-psychology

In this model three types of narcissistic transferences are identified (see Mollon, 2001). In the idealising transference the person projects ideals on to the other and expects them to live up to them. This clearly has the potential for difficulties in a supervisory relationship. In the mirror transference the projector expects the recipient of the projection to mirror back what the projector wants to see of herself or himself. Failure to do so can generate rage and complaints that the other 'just will not listen'. In the twinship transference the projector wishes the other to be a double, failing to take account of the power differential and the evaluative role of the supervisor. Wakefield argued that while such transference projections remain unconscious between supervisor and supervisee, closeness is problematic and that therefore the mutual exploration of these interpersonal dynamics is an essential part of the work of supervision.

The essence of supervision within a psycho-analytic frame as being essentially a space for thinking which is characterised by a quality of attention that is not dissimilar to that of analysis was asserted by Rustin (1996) cited in Astor (2003). However, supervision is unlike analysis in that the supervisee's transference to the supervisor is not systematically analysed or interpreted. Astor (2003) sees the supervisory relationship as mutual, acknowledging that as a supervisor he is also learning from the relationship. He encourages supervisors to pay attention to what is being reported, how it is being reported and what the supervisor experiences while listening, taking into account what is known about the supervisee, the tendencies of the supervisee to report material in particular ways, and the residual psychopathology of the supervisee as revealed in relation to the supervisor. He argued that if there is too much focus on the supervisee and insufficient focus on the client, the knowledge gained can take on a persecutory quality through the knowledge of hindsight. It can seem like 'wisdom after the event' with the implication that the supervisee should have done something about what they now know earlier.

In contrast, too much focus on the patient, particularly where the supervisor's view is emphasised over that of the supervisee, while it can be inspirational, can also trample on the individuality of the patient and supervisee and lead to 'analysis by ventriloquism'. This is more of a risk when the supervisor concentrates on what he or she has understood and hardly at all on what the supervisee has reported. In this circumstance the supervisee is likely to have to repeat the supervisor's formulations without being able to follow them up if they have not been integrated into the supervisee's own learning.

Astor (2003) gives a number of examples of how supervisees may be helped to recognise their difficulties in projection without it becoming an analytic process and how the counter-transference can be an appropriate focus of supervision. The following is one example (author's italics).

Projective identification and counter-transference

A colleague with a specific problem asked me for a few sessions of supervision. On the telephone he stated that he had difficulty getting his patients to come more than once a week. In the event, when he arrived he told me first of all something of his own biography and then gave an account of a patient who he felt treated him disdainfully. At the same time, this patient was also having consultations with another therapist, thinking they might be a more suitable choice. He described her as rich and rather grand by marriage, but ill at ease internally with her family of origin.

My internal transference commentary at this point was that this therapist was wondering whether, if he were to have a different analyst for himself, it would improve his work. He was having difficulty thinking about the feelings stirred in him by this patient and was looking elsewhere for the solution to the problem. My hypothesis at this stage, based on the material he brought about his patient, was that he had become identified with the projective identification content of her material and that this was probably due to some personal difficulty that he had with envy.

My colleague talked and talked, filling the whole session with material. He was determined to get through everything he had brought, leaving no time for discussion or examination of the material. I indicated that time was up and that we would have to return to this in a fortnight. He said in a some-what peevish tone of voice, 'Is that all?' meaning, 'Was that the best that I could do?' I was put in the position at that point of the analyst/supervisor who was not able to produce enough, which was exactly his dilemma with his patient and within his practice. I was the recipient of the feelings the super-visee had when he was with his patient, but which he was unable to interpret to her satisfactorily. I said that his comment, 'Is that all?' sounded like the sort of thing his patient said to him. This struck a chord with him and he agreed that it did seem to be the nature of the transference.

(Astor, 2003: 56)

Astor suggested that this final exchange encapsulated the issue. In the ensuing period the colleague internally elaborated the idea and felt greater freedom from his patient's projections of inferiority and anger. He was able to process these feelings inside himself and to work more productively with the client, interpreting his patient's consultation with the other analyst as potentially the better one.

Whether or not supervisors work within a psychoanalytic or psychodynamic frame, these theories offer useful ideas with which to consider and address issues that arise in supervision. For example, Berman (2000) argued that teachers are always a major focus of transference feelings and supervisors would do well to consider that supervisee responses to them will have resonances from earlier student–teacher relationships. Supervisees often experience rescue fantasies towards their clients (Berman, 2000), projecting their own vulnerability. The involvement of a supervisor unavoidably reminds the supervisee of her or his own vulnerability and in the wider picture the supervisor may be viewed as a potentially superior rescuer which vision it would be instructive for the supervisor to dismantle. Berman reminds us that in supervision mutual evaluation is going on, even if the evaluation of the supervisor by the supervisee is muted and only articulated informally outside of supervision. The supervisor's need to be valued can lead to anxiety about what the supervisee reports to others. The supervisor's awareness of these issues is crucial to the outcomes of supervision. For Berman, no personal topic is out of place in supervision. The difference between supervision and therapy is that in the former, only aspects of the personal theme that can be directly related to the work are a legitimate focus of supervision.

Finally, in this section, a psychodynamic frame reminds us that the supervisory relationship is often influenced by the context of the institution in which it takes place, since supervisees also develop transferential feelings towards their institute (identification, reservations, idealisation, rebellion and so on). The supervisor is therefore well advised to develop a multi-eyed perspective when attempting to understand the transactions taking place in supervision and the responses that might best bring about the aims and objectives of the process.

Person-centred model

In a person-centred model the focus is upon the needs of the client, not on what the therapist might want to happen or believe to be in the best interests of the client. Translated to supervision, the supervisor focuses exclusively on the needs and understandings of the supervisee rather than on the supervisor's own ideas about the work or about the supervisee's needs. The process gives primacy to active listening in an attempt to obtain a deep understanding – the core condition of accurate empathy. The main goal of therapy is to become connected with the client rather than to specify the goals and outcomes of the work. Similarly, in supervision the assumption is that change will emerge from the state of being connected. As in psychodynamic models, the relationship between the participants is seen as key.

Philosophy of a person-centred approach to therapy and supervision

Supervisees and clients are regarded as tending innately towards actualising their potential as fully as possible in their circumstances. Rogers (1959) described this as the 'inherent tendency of the organism to develop all its capacities in ways which serve to maintain or enhance the organism'. In consequence, supervisors can place a high level of trust in the work being carried out by supervisees and do not need to police it. Full attention can be focused on helping supervisees explore their own thoughts and feelings about the work (Tudor and Worrall, 2004). Evaluation conducted by the supervisor is inimical to the approach and this has left person-centred supervision open to criticism on these grounds. For example, Davenport (1992) argued that such a position fails to meet the ethical and legal guidelines for the practice of counselling and counsellor training.

Tudor and Worrall (2004) outlined the tenets of person-centred theory and then examined whether the necessary and sufficient conditions for therapy defined by Rogers also fitted for supervision. They argued that he did not specifically develop a theory of supervision but that such a theory may be constructed from his theory of therapy. They proposed that the process of personality development outlined by Rogers in which the individual moves from unselfconscious organismic integrity through conditions of worth to a limiting self-concept is a process that repeats, within a narrower frame, as people become therapists. Thus, training imposes a new set of conditions of worth, and the professional self-concept which emerges as a result of training limits what practitioners think they are able and unable to do. In supervision, practitioners may review and dissolve that part of their self-concept concerned with being a professional, with the potential effects of expanding horizons and actualising their potential in the role.

Rogers (1959) argued that there are six conditions which are both necessary and sufficient for change to be effected in therapy. Tudor and Worrall examined each of these in turn with a view to establishing whether they are both necessary and sufficient for change to be effected through the process of supervision.

The six conditions

PSYCHOLOGICAL CONTACT

This was defined by Rogers (1959: 207) as the 'minimum essential of a relationship, when each makes a perceived or subceived difference in the experiential field of the other'. Both parties need to be sufficiently aware of the presence of the other through reciprocal and simultaneous contact. Tudor and Worrall take the view that the condition of psychological contact, while necessary for therapeutic change, is not necessary for supervision. They cite the example of email through which they argue supervision is a possibility. In my experience, emails are not infrequently open to misinterpretation and appear to suit certain kinds of communications, particularly instrumental ones, rather than others. It is apparent that electronic media can lend themselves to emotion-laden interchanges for some, in that it is possible for relationships to develop at a distance through initial contacts made online.

CLIENT INCONGRUENCE

A further condition for therapeutic change is that the client must experience some discrepancy 'between the self as perceived and the actual experience of the organism'. The perception of such incongruence may well be the motivating factor in the seeking of therapy. Supervision is sought for different reasons, one of which is the mandatory requirement in counselling and therapy training. Tudor and Worrall stated that while incongruence is endemic, its presence may not be necessary in the process of supervision. Supervisees may wish to use supervision for a range of purposes; for example, to share their successes and confusions, without the motivating experience of incongruence.

CONGRUENCE

Congruence is described as occurring when 'the feelings the therapist is experiencing are available to him, available to his awareness, and he is able to live these feelings, be them, and able to communicate them if appropriate' (Rogers, 1967: 61). Tudor and Worrall take the view that this condition is necessary for supervision. Supervisees need to be in a relationship in which it is possible to explore their work honestly with a supervisor whom they trust and who is congruent.

UNCONDITIONAL POSITIVE REGARD

Tudor and Worrall believe that this is the most crucial condition which must be present for supervision to be effective. Supervisees' willingness to explore the most difficult aspects of the work relies on the supervisor's unconditional acceptance of them. They follow Rogers in taking the view that total unconditional regard is not possible but something to which a relationship can aspire. Unconditional acceptance implies the absence of external evaluation and this is an increasingly difficult position to hold in an evidence-based world. The historical widespread trust invested in institutions, professions and political figures has been increasingly eroded throughout the twentieth century with extensive ramifications for formal ongoing practitioner assessment, recording, accreditation and registration. It is difficult to see in these circumstances how this tenet of the model can be maintained, although formal methods of self-evaluation may go some way towards meeting the requirements of the method and of the institutions within which the training is accredited.

EMPATHIC UNDERSTANDING

Empathic understanding is defined as 'to sense the client's world as if it were your own but without losing the "as if" quality' (Rogers, 1967: 284). Tudor and Worrall see this condition as one of the central requirements for good supervision. Since the tasks of therapy and counselling are conducted in isolation, supervision may be the only place where supervisees are able legitimately to talk about the intimacies of their work with an empathic supervisor.

PERCEPTION

Positive regard and empathic understanding are of no value to the client, and in parallel, to the supervisee, if they are not perceived by the intended recipient. A supervisor's empathic stance is to no effect without openness on the part of supervisees. This will be determined in part by their prior experiences in educational settings which will have generated a set of expectations influenced by the prevailing culture. The tenets of person-centred philosophy are not the first that come to mind in conjunction with contexts of education and training in the UK.

While taking the view that these conditions are necessary and sufficient for supervision, Tudor and Worrall suggest that other conditions can also be of help. These are that supervisors have some knowledge of and confidence in the approach, enough experience that they can listen without over- or under-reacting, are currently practising in the field using up-to-date knowledge, and are willing to share what they know and have experienced.

Tudor and Worrall go on to map some of the processes regarded as taking place in therapy on to those taking place in supervision.

Mapping therapeutic process on to supervision

A loosening of feelings

Encouragement is given to supervisees to reduce their attention to the cognitive in favour of the affective aspects of the clients, their problems and the therapeutic relationship. This supervisory focus is regarded as making more effective inroads to the work when the supervisee experiences stuckness.

A change in the manner of experiencing and the capacity for greater congruence

This is a development where supervisees are increasingly able to take a position of curiosity towards their experiences and the meaning of them which allows for the greater flexibility and spontaneity that characterises skilled performance.

Communication

The features of the empathic relationship encourage the development of greater willingness to describe experiences honestly and to be transparent in relationships with clients and the supervisor.

Constructs

This is the development of an attitude that allows reduced adherence to pre-existing cognitive maps and habits. Instead of an orientation towards fitting new experiences into existing frameworks for understanding, there develops a capacity to allow new experiences to change what is believed about the world.

The individual's relationship to the problem/s

This is a change in attitude whereby greater responsibility for difficulties and problems in work with clients is taken by the supervisee. Tendencies to attribute blame externally become reduced. This is adaptive in that the only change mechanisms available to supervisees are their own acts and, through this, change in others can be evoked.

The individual's manner of relating

As supervisees develop, their manner of relating changes in a direction of greater openness and freedom, since relationships have less potential to evoke fearful responses. Tudor and Worrall note that in the context of person-centred supervision, practitioners 'come to relish close relationships more actively and to embrace more warmly the joys and challenges of such relationships'.

A number of practices that characterise supervision within other models are regarded as antithetical to person-centred supervision. One of these is modelling; there is no sense in the person-centred approach of supervisors showing the supervisee the ways in which they themselves conduct therapy. It could be argued, though, that the stance taken by supervisors in their approach to supervision is an implicit model of appropriate attitude towards clients. Live supervision is regarded as raising too many issues of contracting, confidentiality, ethics and transferential attitudes although recording is considered useful. Developmental models are regarded as inherently infantilising (Tudor and Worrall, 2004). Strategies for intervention and a technique-driven approach are all problematic within a person-centred approach since they imply 'doing' something to the client often without their cognisance or consent.

Example of supervision within a person-centred approach

The following (where R = Rogers and H = Hackney[1]) is a passage from a supervision session led by Carl Rogers, described in Bernard and Goodyear (1992).

R: . . . it interests me that she said, 'When I make up my mind to do it, I'll go ahead and do it.'

H: Yeah.

R: And when you responded accurately to that . . . that threatened her . . .

H: Uh-uh.

R: Which I think means that that was a very important statement for her.

H: Uh-huh.

R: I've often noticed that if a person takes quite a positive step-uh-expresses a feeling quite positively, and you understand it accurately, God, that's almost too much for them.

H: Huh.

R: They tend to draw away from what they just said.

H: Right. Right. That was the reaction I got from her when I said that.

R: [Pause] The-uh . . . when you say she has a sort of differing type of motivation, different . . . reason for motivation each time she comes in-uhm . . . that wouldn't bother me. I-I would-I would-uh . . . go with whatever . . . shred of feeling she would let me have at the time.

H: Uh-huh. [Pause] I'd like to be able to do that. [Laughs]

R: [Laughs] Well, I'm saying what I would do; that doesn't mean that's necessarily what you should do.

H: Well, I don't think what I'm doing is working for me. Uh . . . and I don't think it really is working for her either, so-uhm . . . and I think it would be – I think I'd be better-uh . . . in this case if I-uh . . . could feel a little bit less responsible when she comes in with less motivation.

R: She came in of her own accord. She asked to see you.

H: That's right. That's right. And she's been very faithful-uh . . . so far in the case.

R: Wonderful. So then anything that you do that takes any responsibility away from her is really quite unnecessary.

H: Uh-huh.

R: She did decide to come; and she comes.

H: Right.

R: [Pause] An interesting, mixed-up, modern young woman, it seems like.

H: Yes, it is. Uh . . . and a delightful young woman, too. She really is. Uh . . . she's the person I think I like most among the people I'm working with.

R: OK. OK, that's important. That's one reason why you want it to go well.

H: That's right. Right.

R: [Pause] My feeling of her is very . . . good . . . feeling, and I like that. It means you will get somewhere, but-uh . . . [Pause]. But if you like her enough to want her to go your way, that's-that's a different matter.

H: Yeah. Well . . . you – that's especially true because I'm not really sure . . . what way it would be if it was going my way. And I-I'm not clear there either, so . . .

R: Well, you were – you were somewhat clear toward the end of the interview as to a step that you clearly thought was advisable for this coming week.

H: Right. I had an agenda at that point; I was wanting to set up . . . an opportunity for her and-and her husband to-uh-to have a conversation. Whether that came off or not was another matter. But part of the sense that I was picking up at that point was that because of the pace of their lives they never even really had the opportunity. And then she got-uh ignored or missed-uh.

R: Well, that's where you did feel a responsibility for helping set up something that would make that come off.

H: Oh, I was – I was taking care of it all. Yes. [Pause] Where do you think it might go if I were to-uh . . . that – that's maybe an impossible question to ask.

R: Uh-huh.

H: If I were to-uh . . . to try to follow what her inclinations were-uh-as far as . . . her trying to find a moment with her husband, where do you think that might go? Do you think – do you think she would bring the initiative out of that?

R: I haven't any idea where it would go, but to me that's the fascination of – of therapy, is not knowing; and yet-uh-connecting just as deeply as I can with the, in this case, the confusion, the-uh . . . 'Maybe I will; maybe I won't. Maybe I like Don; maybe I like John.' Uh . . . just connecting as deeply as possible with that feeling and following it wherever she leads me . . .

(Bernard and Goodyear, 1992: 322–323)

In this extract Rogers highlighted the requirement of the method for the therapist to follow the client rather than the therapist's own inclinations, and to resist any invitation to provide answers. Haynes *et al.* (2003: 119) suggested some examples of the kinds of statements or questions typically used by person-centred supervisors:

- I'd like to hear you talk more about how it was for you to be with the client for that session.
- I encourage you to begin to trust more your own internal direction.
- Even though you are saying you really don't know how to proceed, if you did know, what actions might you take?
- Tell me what you found to be important about the experience you shared with your client today.
- I'd like to hear you talk more about the climate you are creating with your client.
- To what degree do you feel you understand the world of your client?
- What are your expectations for what we might do in today's session?

Patterson (1997) stated that the supervisor offers a supervisee-centred relationship in which the qualities of genuineness, respect and empathy are key.

These are viewed as the core conditions for therapeutic progress. The supervisee is identified as responsible for setting the agenda for supervision, and for choosing the material to be examined and the issues on which to focus. The requirement of the training is that supervisees work within the assumption that the core conditions are sufficient for therapeutic progress to be made, and thereby put the assumption to the test. Supervisees are not expected to depart from the agenda of creating the core conditions and are explicitly required not to try other techniques. The criterion for evaluation is effectiveness in providing the core therapeutic conditions. Supervisees evaluate themselves against this criterion and make recordings of their sessions from which extracts are used as the material for supervision. Self-evaluation is regarded as making a significant contribution to the establishment of a constructive supervisory relationship.

Within this approach, supervisees are expected to take major responsibility for their own learning. However, supervisors effect their responsibility to clients by recommending personal therapy for the supervisee should they perceive the supervisee's personal adjustment to be problematic. This could result where some parallel process is not being resolved or where the supervisee's personal material is persistently intruding and making it difficult for her or him to stay in the client's frame of reference. If necessary the supervisor will discontinue the practicum should it be considered that clients could be damaged. Thus, in this model as in others, ethical considerations will override all others.

Patterson highlighted the following features of person-centred supervision:

- In preregistration training the supervisor bears responsibility for the supervisee's clients, and in order to keep track the supervisee begins each supervision by reviewing each client. The level of detail varies according to perceived need and it is recommended that one client is the subject of continuing detailed focus.
- The approach is little concerned with diagnosis and personality dynamics since the focus of the work is on the acceptance and understanding of the client as a person. Rather than diagnostic assessment, the therapist is more concerned with the 'stage in process' of the client, as in Rogers' seven stages of process, and the supervisor may need to know that the supervisee has some understanding of this with each client. Supervision nevertheless helps supervisees to identify evidence of severe disturbance or organic presentations that may warrant referral elsewhere.
- Didactic instruction by the supervisor is minimal.
- The intention of supervision is to facilitate the supervisee's development in work and the supervisor responds to the difficulties the supervisee has in her or his relationships with clients. Because of the commonality in core conditions for the relationships supervisor–supervisee and client–therapist, and between the skills of supervision and therapy, there can be

an overlap in which the line between supervision and therapy may be difficult to determine (Bonney, 1994). However, the roles and responsibilities of the supervisor and supervisee are agreed in a process described as 'structuring the relationship', and this agreement may be reviewed as the supervision proceeds.

Patterson views these features as appropriate to more generic ways of working in addition to their specificity to a client-centred approach. While other elements may be added from a preferred theory, he regards these additions as inconsistent with a client-centred approach.

Cognitive behavioural models

Cognitive behavioural psychotherapy developed from the separate traditions of behavioural and cognitive approaches which shared some common underpinning philosophies. Behavioural approaches derived from experimental psychology and the paradigms of classical and operant conditioning which generated interventions such as systematic desensitisation, functional analysis and token economy. Cognitive theories proposed that emotional disturbance was mediated by the way in which individuals constructed their worlds. The therapies that were devised from this position encouraged clients to identify these cognitions and to test them through practical assignments. The resulting cognitive behavioural therapies place a primary emphasis on cognitive processes as they influence behaviour and emotions. The approaches involve the identification of underlying schemas (Padesky, 1994) or philosophies (Woods and Ellis, 1997) that play a causal role in the client's emotions and behaviour. A task of the therapist is to help the client to develop more helpful cognitions through a process of challenge and reconstruction which leads to symptom reduction and problem resolution.

Ricketts and Donohoe (2000) identified the common philosophical underpinnings of the behavioural and cognitive traditions as follows:

- That the therapy should be problem focused, and applied to a specified and agreed area of current dysfunction, rather than attempting to enhance general well-being.
- The importance of aiming to operationalise and make explicit procedures being used.
- The link between theory and practice, psychological research being given equal weight with the need for empirical evaluation of the developing techniques.
- The focus on detailed assessment of the individual, leading to a case formulation as the basis for individualised treatment.
- The active, educational and collaborative nature of the therapies.

There is a spectrum of approaches within this group of therapies including, for example, the cognitive therapy (CT) of Aaron Beck (1988) and Judith Beck (1995) and the Rational Emotive Behaviour Therapy (REBT) of Ellis (Ellis and Dryden, 1987). While these approaches are classified here under the same umbrella, exponents of each specific method would highlight differences as well as similarities. My own understanding suggests that in REBT, for example, the therapist tends to be more overtly directive whereas in CT a process of collaborative guided discovery is the aim. In REBT unhelpful thought sequences are referred to as 'irrational' whereas in CT they are described by the term 'negative automatic thoughts'. An example of such a thought in both models would be 'I am an unlovable person'.

Descriptions of supervision in both models (Liese and Beck, 1997; Woods and Ellis, 1997) have emphasised the educational role of the supervisor. Training methods include reading and discussion, direct observation of therapy and the provision of opportunities for practice. In cognitive therapy supervision the use of recordings is recommended, with a view to identifying the strengths and weaknesses of the supervisee. It is suggested that reluctance to make recordings be addressed by identifying the automatic thoughts (for example, 'recording will cramp my style') of the supervisee in a process similar to the one adopted with clients. The supervision is structured with an emphasis on skill development towards specified goals.

Goals of CBT supervision

The literature on clinical supervision of cognitive behaviour therapy emphasises the need for congruence between the approach to therapy and the approach to supervision since both are intended to effect development and change and to reflect the theory of change. This means that parallels may be drawn between aspects of the approach; the structure of a therapy session and a supervision session, for example, both featuring processes such as agenda setting and bridging from the previous session.

The major goal of supervision has been described as that of bringing about a philosophical change in the supervisee. Rosenbaum and Ronen (1998) argued that CBT is 'not only a profession but also a philosophy of life; a way of living. You cannot ask your clients (or your supervisees) to practice this approach while you do not live according to its principles'. One of the supervisor's tasks is to encourage supervisees to become aware of the different belief and value systems of their clients and themselves, thereby enhancing the therapist's sensitivity to differences in individual meaning-making systems which can otherwise lead to unhelpful misunderstandings.

A second goal of CBT supervision is to teach supervisees specific techniques. Ultimately the goal is for supervisees to develop a commitment to and skills in the approach which will enable them to practise independently, employing their creativity further to develop the methods and techniques in the service of their clients. Supervision and therapy in CBT are congruent and follow the same principles, distinguished by the primary aims. For the purposes of therapy the aim is to help clients cope with specific personal problems, and for the purposes of supervision to help supervisees become effective therapists who can facilitate the desired change in clients.

Liese and Beck (1997) described the key features of cognitive therapy supervision as follows:

- First, the supervisor identifies any misconceptions the supervisee may hold about cognitive therapy. Such misconceptions are frequently associated with beliefs that the model takes no account of clients' emotions, childhood experiences, the therapeutic relationship or interpersonal factors.
- Where misconceptions are identified, the supervisor educates supervisees through direct instruction, discussion, role play, assigned readings and direct observation of cognitive therapy in action.
- Supervisees usually undertake individual supervision with a weekly frequency for an hour per session. In addition, biweekly group supervision is prescribed.
- Supervision sessions follow a format akin to that of cognitive therapy, proceeding through the stages of check-in, agenda setting, bridging to the previous supervision session, enquiry, review of homework, prioritisation and discussion of agenda items, new homework, brief summarising of key points, ending with the supervisee's feedback about the supervision session.
- Since the quality of the supervisory relationship is considered a central feature in the success of the enterprise, the above format is not rigidly followed.
- The main style of supervisory intervention is direct instruction, although guided discovery is also employed.
- Role play in which the supervisor demonstrates techniques and the supervisee plays the role of the client is considered to be helpful to learning.
- Recordings of therapy sessions are viewed as a useful medium for presenting the work with the client. Where supervisees are reluctant to use recordings in supervision the supervisor helps them to examine their negative automatic thoughts about them. Supervisees are seen as learning from their own review of session recordings, thus enabling identification of strengths and weaknesses. In addition, supervisors may use standardised scales such as the Cognitive Therapy Adherence and Competence Scale (Liese et al., 1995) to evaluate the work of the supervisee.

The parallels in the structure of supervision and therapy sessions are outlined by Liese and Beck in Table 13.1. The table brings home the similarity of

Table 13.1 Comparative structures of cognitive therapy sessions and supervision sessions

Step	Cognitive therapy session	Supervision session
1	Agenda setting	Check-in
2	Mood check	Agenda setting
3	Bridge from previous therapy session	Bridge from previous supervision session
4	Enquiry about primary problems	Enquiry about previously supervised therapy case/s
5	Review of homework since previous therapy session	Review of homework since previous supervision session
6	Prioritisation and discussion of agenda items	Prioritisation and discussion of agenda items
7	Assignment of new homework	Assignment of new homework
8	Therapist's capsule summaries (throughout session and at end)	Supervisor's capsule summaries (throughout session and at end)
9	Elicit feedback from the patient (throughout session and at end)	Elicit feedback from the therapist (throughout session and at end)

Source: Watkins (1997: 121).

structure between CBT therapy and supervision sessions. Rosenbaum and Ronen (1998) stated that there is currently a lack of a well-defined methodology for CBT supervision. This could be accounted for by the broad church of therapies which are subsumed by this overarching title. Armstrong and Freeston (2006) also argued that there is a sparse literature and very small evidence base concerning CBT supervision, identifying only one key study examining efficacy (Sholomskas *et al.*, 2005). They have begun to address this by describing a structure within which to conceptualise supervision in order to support a more systematic approach. Rosenbaum and Ronen (1998) provided a detailed account of the ways in which they conceptualise seven common themes across these therapies applied to the process of supervision as follows.

Supervision as a meaning-making process

A basic tenet of CBT is that psychological problems are in large part determined by the way people construe their experiences, assigning positive and negative meanings to their experiences according to their basic schemata and belief system. Emotions are conceived as the 'barometers of meaning', or the affective experiences associated with states of mind that are out of awareness. The goal of the therapy, and reflexively of supervision, is the development of new and possibly more complex meanings which lead to reconstruction. Socratic questioning is a major technique used to accomplish this and is defined as 'asking questions which clients have the knowledge to answer, and which draw their attention to relevant information which may be outside their current focus' (Hackmann, 1997: 130). Rosenbaum and Ronen particularly argue against viewing the client through specific diagnostic categories which cannot take account of the individual nature of each client's experience.

In supervision, three meaning-making systems are at issue: those of the client, the supervisee and the supervisor. Each party cannot have direct access to that of the others, but the aim is to remain open to the different options for construing problems, identifying goals and the manner in which they might be achieved. This exploration takes place in supervision, as in therapy, through the process of Socratic questioning, through the creation of an accepting relationship that provides emotional support, and through guidance of the supervisee's actions.

Systematic and goal-directed action

The systematic approach is expressed both in how the treatment is planned and implemented and in how the session is structured. Therapists and clients mutually decide on the goals of therapy, criteria for achieving these, and the identification of the steps needed in order to attain them. Rosenbaum and Ronen argued that there is a systematic ongoing process of assessment and evaluation whereby the treatment and assessment aspects of CBT are interwoven rather than undertaken in sequence. This systematic process is also applied to supervision where the goals might be as broad as helping the supervisee introduce CBT methods to an agency where they are not currently practised, and helping the therapist to cope with personal problems that interfere with the implementation of a treatment plan. One method by which the supervisor accomplishes this is by demonstration of a systematic way of thinking and problem solving.

Practising and experiencing

Rosenbaum and Ronen draw a parallel with other practical skills such as swimming where learning only through cognitive means seems an unlikely proposition. Practising can take place either in therapy sessions or through set homework tasks. Practical methods include role play, behavioural rehearsal, guided imagery and relaxation exercises. Specific behavioural tasks might include confronting fear-arousing situations, practising assertiveness, positive self-talk and experiencing novel situations. These exercises are also applicable in the supervisory setting. Role play can aid the supervisee in obtaining insight into the client's behaviour and the supervisor in evaluating supervisee skill development. Supervisees are also encouraged to try out techniques on themselves before trying them with clients. This encourages the development of greater awareness of how such tasks might be perceived by clients. For example, supervisees might first play back a relaxation tape made for a client to themselves.

Therapy and supervision as a collaborative effort

A collaborative relationship characterised by trust and openness is regarded as a fundamental requirement for change both in the context of supervision and therapy. It is suggested that the creation of such an atmosphere may be more taxing in the supervisory context since the supervisor is responsible for the formal assessment of the supervisee's work and/or has the power to affect the professional status of the supervisee. The parties to supervision may not share the same theoretical orientation and this difference may be manifest in apprehension or scepticism.

The issue of resistance may be more to the fore in therapy but can be manifest also in supervision. In this case, Rosenbaum and Ronen argued that the supervisor should avoid challenging the supervisee's basic belief system, and instead raise with the supervisee hypotheses to be tested empirically. Pushing against the therapist's resistance is predicted to be ineffectual.

Person focus

Rosenbaum and Ronen argued that CBT is person focused and that in every-day practice it is the person rather than their 'problem' that is the focus of intervention. This is despite the extensive literature that relates outcomes to specific diagnostic categories. Rosenbaum (1990) asserted that assessing clients' resourcefulness and positive forces may be as important as assessing pathology. Perhaps this links CBT to other therapies such as solution-focused approaches (Thomas, 1996) and the narrative therapy of Michael White (White and Epston, 1990).

Supervisors are advised to match their approach to the therapist's unique characteristics, enabling them to unlearn previously habitual ways of acting and thinking through being treated respectfully and through acceptance of the supervisee's current views. Rosenbaum and Ronen stated:

> The two persons in the focus of CBT supervision are the therapist and the therapist's client. Attention shifts continuously from the therapeutic self of the therapist to the client's personality. These shifts are dictated by the emerging needs in the supervisory process. . . . The focus shifts to the therapists' therapeutic selves when they face personal difficulties in applying CBT or problems in developing a therapeutic relationship with clients.
>
> (Rosenbaum and Ronen, 1998: 226)

The CBT supervisor as the facilitator of change

In CBT treatment, failures are not attributed to the client's resistance or lack of motivation but rather to the therapist's inability to overcome these obstacles. Similarly, since the role of the supervisor is to facilitate change in the supervisee, the responsibility for creating the facilitative conditions for change lies with the supervisor. Rosenbaum and Ronen borrowed from Marsha Linehan (1993) the notion of balancing change with acceptance. The first step in the process of change is for clients to accept their actions and experiences without judgement. The notion of acceptance does not imply approval. Examples of strategies through which acceptance may be achieved are mindfulness and learning to focus on momentary experiences. These are regarded as relevant to supervision in cases, for example, where supervisees constantly evaluate their own performance at the expense of being open fully to experience what is being transacted between themselves and their clients. Supervisors are advised to balance change and acceptance in supervisory sessions in order better to enhance the professional development of their supervisees.

The ultimate goal of empowerment and resourcefulness

Although CBT therapists take full responsibility for the therapeutic process, they guide their clients towards becoming their own agents of change by taking a collaborative stance, sharing information about the therapeutic strategy, by teaching self-control and self-acceptance and by increasing clients' self-belief in their own efficacy. Therapy is time limited, clients taking over further responsibility for their own development once they have developed the skills for change.

Similarly, CBT supervision is regarded as time limited, its primary role being to develop creative and open-minded therapists who are capable of enhancing their clients' resourcefulness and openness to new and challenging experiences. Throughout their paper, Rosenbaum and Ronen emphasised that what's sauce for the goose is sauce for the gander: the process of supervision should replicate the process of therapy. There is one point at which they diverge from this position when commenting on the dearth of evidence and outcome research regarding supervision within this model. This may in part be accounted for by the absence of a well-defined protocol for CBT supervision; the process has not been manualised. They argued that despite this being the approach to CBT therapy, the process of CBT supervision cannot be manualised but should be individually tailored according to their seven basic principles. Ronen and Rosenbaum (1998) further developed their ideas about the role of CBT in generating enhanced therapist sensitivity to possible discrepancies in the meaning-making systems of self and other. They proposed a number of creative methods which go beyond direct verbal instruction through the use of writing techniques, metaphors and imagery which could be adapted in supervision.

Some of the ideas developed in CBT therapy and supervision have found their way into training and supervisory practices outside the specific CBT field. For example, Fitch and Marshall (2002) made the point that students who are training as counsellors experience many self-defeating thoughts and anxieties. These can interfere adversely with performance. Fitch and Marshall used Ellis and Grieger's (1986) model of Activating event, Belief about the event, Consequence of the event, Disputing belief and New effect (ABCDE) with a group of students who were given examples of self-defeating thoughts and then encouraged to dispute them. This served the dual purpose of improving coping skills and modelling cognitive therapy interventions.

Problems arising in supervision

Finally, in this section on CBT supervision, Liese and Beck (1997) identified a number of problems that can arise in supervision and described some of the beliefs that they hypothesised may underlie the difficulties.

Problems related to the supervisor

*   *The Mister Rogers Supervisor*. Many therapists have had supervisors like Mister Rogers: warm, pleasant, kind and good-natured, but failing to provide substantial critical feedback or education. Therapists supervised by 'Mister Rogers' may develop exaggerated positive views of their competencies and not progress as they should. Some likely thoughts and beliefs associated with Mister Rogers supervisors are:

    'It is bad when someone's feelings get hurt.'
    'If I am nice and kind, no one will ever dislike me.'
    'Therapists are fragile and will be destroyed by any criticism.'

*   *Attila the Supervisor*. These supervisors believe that there is only one correct way to do things: *their* way. They may become upset or angry when therapists do not follow their commands. Some specific beliefs of these supervisors are:

    'I need to be right all the time.'
    'It's awful if someone in my command doesn't do what I say.'
    'Not listening to me is a sign of disrespect.'
    'Disrespect is intolerable.'

*   *The 'How do you feel?' Supervisor*. This supervisor believes that everything learned in supervision results from therapists' reflections on personal feelings about the patient (i.e. counter-transference). The patient comes in, for example, wishing to quit smoking and the supervisor asks

the therapist: 'How do you feel when your patient wants to quit smoking?' rather than asking, 'What is your conceptualisation of this patient?' or 'What interventions are most appropriate for smoking cessation?' or 'What will you do next?'

Problems related to the therapist

- *Unfocused therapists.* Some psychotherapists have difficulties focusing in therapy sessions and in supervision. Such difficulties may be due to stylistic preferences, prior training or conscious choice. Beliefs associated with therapists' lack of focus may include:

  'I need to know everything, and I should jump around to get it all.'
  'If we talk enough, the important stuff will eventually emerge.'
  'Focusing is too difficult or uncomfortable.'
  'If we do focus too much, we might focus on the wrong issue.'

- *Passive or avoidant therapists.* Some therapists do not actively participate in the supervision process. These therapists seem aloof, distant or uninterested. Beliefs associated with such passivity or avoidance in supervision may be:

  'If I reveal my thoughts, I'll reveal my weaknesses.'
  'If my supervisor sees me as imperfect, I'm a failure.'
  'I shouldn't have to make a strong effort; my supervisor should always tell me what to do.'
  'I need to show my supervisor my best side.'

- *Defensive or aggressive therapists.* Some therapists respond to supervision with defensive explanations for their behaviours or with aggressiveness when supervisors question them. Beliefs associated with defensiveness and aggressiveness might include:

  'I need to be perfect' or 'my supervisor needs to believe I'm perfect'.
  'I know better than my supervisor.'
  'If I don't defend my position, I'm weak or inadequate.'
  'It's catastrophic when I'm wrong.'
  'If I'm aggressive, my supervisor won't criticise me.'

(Liese and Beck, 1997)

Systemic model

Summary of systemic ideas

Supervising teams

While a systemic approach, which is a particular philosophy of psychological therapy, can be used effectively in work with individuals, it has been used most frequently with families. The approach emphasises the importance of viewing clients in the context of their family and wider systems. In order to be congruent with this emphasis, systemic therapy typically employs live team supervision. The theory proposes that the client and therapist together comprise a newly created system and that patterns of interaction will develop that are influenced by the client's and therapist's habitual ways of relating. It is easy for the therapist implicitly to be invited to join the client's patterns, the supervising team's presence helping to provide a more detached, different or 'meta' perspective on the therapist–client system. Supervision within this model is characterised by attention to interlocking family and supervisory systems. The term 'isomorphism' is used to describe reciprocal relationships between different parts of systems, for example, reciprocity between client–therapist and therapist–supervisor interactions. It is also used to refer to the parallels between the principles that organise therapy and those that organise supervision (Liddle *et al.*, 1997). For example, if a 'learning by doing' philosophy is used in therapy, it can also be used in supervision. Systemic theory also emphasises the desirability of staying open to many and different ideas about clients and their situation. The presence of several people in the supervising team with a range of backgrounds and personal characteristics helps to ensure that the therapy does not become unduly constrained by a particular way of viewing things.

Hypothesising, circularity and neutrality

The original tenets of the approach, described by the Milan team, continue to have relevance. In therapy and in supervision a position is adopted that includes a preference for openness to multiple hypotheses rather than the creation of a static explanation or diagnosis, rejection of a causal-linear way of thinking in favour of circularity and a focus on *patterns* of interaction, and the taking of a stance of 'neutrality', subsequently developed into the notion of a position of 'curiosity' (Cecchin, 1987; Palazzoli *et al.*, 1980).

The history of the client's developing system and transitions within it such as new partnerships, the birth of children, moves of house and so on may be important in the generation and naming of what is presented as a problem. Problems may represent the struggles of the system and the individuals within it to adapt to a transition. Habitual patterns of interaction may no longer fit the new circumstances. A major intervention strategy of the therapy is the use of questions – known as 'circular' (Burnham, 1986), 'reflexive' (Tomm, 1987) or 'leading' (Swann *et al.*, 1982) – with the aim of enabling clients to develop new meanings or stories about themselves and their situation as a result of which the problem is seen differently. These different visions, beliefs or new meanings generate the potential for the client to experiment with novel and more useful actions and approaches.

Formal interventions

More formal interventions associated with the Milan model included reframing, in which the therapist suggested a new meaning for the same data, or the prescription of rituals in which the element of time was introduced with the intention of punctuating habitual sequences of interaction to create difference. For example, if two parents have conflicting ideas about how to manage their child's behaviour, the therapist might prescribe that both parents follow the ideas of one parent on Mondays, Wednesdays and Fridays, and of the other on Tuesdays, Thursdays and Saturdays.

The constructive therapies

The systemic approach has developed away from the idea of the therapist as expert towards a greater sense of collaboration between client, therapist and supervising team as it has incorporated ideas from constructivism (Glasersfeld, 1991), social constructionism (Gergen, 1985), postmodern narrative approaches to therapy (Anderson and Goolishian, 1988), ideas about relationships based on feminism (Gilligan (1982), and solution-focused approaches. Together, a range of approaches has been entitled 'constructive therapies', an umbrella term used by Hoyt (1994) for a number of time-limited therapies which include solution oriented, solution focused, possibility, narrative, postmodern, cooperative, competency based and constructivist.

Implications for supervision

Translated reflexively from the model of work to the model of supervision the following are key issues based on the ideas underpinning systemic and constructive therapies.

Postmodern and constructivist perspectives on supervision

Model of change processes in individuals and systems

In a constructivist paradigm no being has direct access to the mental life of another. On the basis of their experiences individuals construct, in interaction with their environment, ideas which underpin their actions. Therefore, multiple perspectives are valued; a 'both/and' rather than an 'either/or' position is adopted. Instead of highlighting family roles, structures and interactional patterns, constructivism shifts the focus to an understanding of the assumptions and beliefs that maintain problem situations and narrow options for change (Anderson *et al.*, 1995). The emphasis is on encouraging individuals, be they clients, supervisees or supervisors, to co-construct alternative assumptions or narratives that are less focused on problems or deficits and more on strengths and capabilities. The process intends to be empowering in opening up options for change. For clients this means a greater sense of self-efficacy in solving the problems they bring to therapy, and for supervisees, enhanced confidence about their capabilities to develop professionally and become effective therapists.

Nature of the supervisory relationship

Rather than viewing the educational task as one of disseminating a fixed body of knowledge, constructivist educators introduce new perspectives and create an atmosphere of dialogue aimed at developing, guiding and sharing meaning systems (Anderson *et al.*, 1995). Supervisees are regarded as active participants in understanding events, co-creating meaning and constructing their own reality (Wetchler, 1990). The supervisory process aims to facilitate dialogues that generate multiple perspectives and practices rather than 'correct' assessments and plans of action. The intention of the supervisor is to create conditions that can make a difference without prescribing the direction of the difference.

Emphasis on strengths rather than deficits

In the context of pre-qualification training, Presbury *et al.* stated:

> Of course, counsellors in supervision have deficits that monitoring can identify and that training can address. With their shortage of experience, rudimentary knowledge and fundamental skills, supervisees certainly benefit from the wisdom and guidance of their supervisors. However, it is vital to recognise that supervisees also possess latent resources within themselves that can be developed and actualized. If the supervisor focuses on the deficits, he or she trains the supervisee by correcting mistakes and alleviating ignorance. If, in addition to training, a supervisor accepts the challenge of facilitating a supervisee's development, the supervisor is more like a sculptor who is attempting to bring to the surface the supervisee's inchoate potential. Demoralisation, which is far too common among beginning counsellors, can sabotage development (Watkins, 1996). Focusing on what the counsellor is doing that is effective

not only improves morale, it also encourages the counsellor to attribute these behaviours to his or her agency rather than as an accident.

(Presbury *et al.*, 1999: 149)

As one of the authors (McKee) says to his supervisees: 'What you are doing seems to be working well: now you just need to do it on purpose.'

Principal methods for bringing about learning are questioning and adaptations of interventions from therapy

Systemic and constructive therapies offer a number of approaches to questioning with a view to encouraging learning. Essentially, the supervisor takes a genuine position of curiosity although questions may also be asked with the intention of leading the supervisee to new insights. Solution-focused approaches to therapy specifically emphasise the use of presuppositional as opposed to subjunctive language. Subjunctive language supposes a possibility whereas presuppositional language assumes an actuality. For example, a question in subjunctive mode might be, 'Can you think of a time that you were more in tune with the client?' A presuppositional version would be, 'Tell me about a time that you were more in tune with the client.' Presuppositional questions asked by the supervisor such as, 'How did you know to do that at just that moment?' help to create a positive mindset in both the supervisor and supervisee (Swann *et al.*, 1982). Presbury *et al.* (1999) suggest that from day one the supervisor is best advised to phrase questions and statements to include the assumption of competence. Examples of different typologies of questions may be found in Burnham (1986) and Tomm (1987). Interventions such as 'externalisation' (White, 1988) have been adapted by supervisees with the support of their supervisor as an aid to learning. For example, the process was used to marginalise anxiety and self-doubt by a group describing themselves as anxious women trainees who were experiencing shame and self-doubt associated with former experiences in their families of origin and educational settings (Lee and Littlejohns, 2007). A fictional character 'Agnes' was created to embody these feelings which were regarded as anathema to clear and creative thinking. Supervisees were subsequently on the look-out for 'Agnes' interfering with their confidence and self-belief.

A focus on structures and processes that support the notion of multiple perspectives and the development of self-awareness

It is incumbent in the approach, in which multiple perspectives are valued, that each practitioner, whether occupying the role of supervisor or supervisee, engages in a continuous process of developing self-awareness. This extends to the awareness of one's own culturally prescribed values and beliefs.

Live team supervision provides a context in which the ideas of the supervisor or supervising team are available to the client/s and therapist during the therapy session. When the team members possess diverse characteristics, attitudes and beliefs, greater opportunities for multiple perspectives pertain. When work is reported in individual supervision, the segment of communication on which a therapist most characteristically focuses is thought to say more about the therapist than about the client (Hoffman, 1991). The family therapy supervision course based at the Child and Family Department of the Tavistock Clinic in London aims for multi-layered learning (Burck and Campbell, 2002). The training consists of five components:

1   Theory seminar
2   Live supervision of live supervision
3   Agency-based supervision seminar
4   Personal/professional development seminar
5   Observation of supervision groups

Trainees are learning to be supervisors and are therefore live supervised in the role (live supervision of live supervision) by one of the course staff. Students learn in groups, taking turns as the therapist, supervisor or observer. The structure provides opportunities for all parties to reflect on the session with the client/s together, facilitating the development of self-reflexivity at all levels (Burnham, 1993). The reflexive process includes the staff members. The student observers are in a useful position to be able to offer insights into issues such as isomorphism of the relationships between family and therapist, therapist and supervisor and live supervisor of live supervisor. The personal and professional development (PPD) seminar also focuses on multiple layers which include the trainees' own PPD work, the PPD work they carry out in their role as supervisor, and that of the course staff. Seminars include experiential exercises and role play. Issues of difference and power are regarded as central.

Approaches to the development of self-awareness have taken a number of directions within the systemic and constructivist field. For example, Matthews and Treacher (2004) ask their family therapy trainees to complete their own genograms in small groups. Each genogram begins as a narrative: 'this is my personal story about me and my family'. The trainee can invite questions and be offered supportive comments but reserves the right to say what is 'off-limits'. In order to model maintenance of the boundary between therapy and supervision, supervisors also discuss their own genograms, linking what has emerged to working with clients. For example, the information is used to consider with which clients the worker feels most and least at ease. Explanations for this are sought within the genograms. The final part of the approach involves the supervisor initiating a discussion about how the two genograms set up interesting hypotheses about how the supervisor and supervisee will work together. The genogram work is also regarded as facilitative of the relationship-building process at the outset of a new supervisory relationship.

Evaluative role of the supervisor

Because at its heart the approach aims to adopt positive constructions of the actions of the individuals involved, a dilemma could be posed with regard to the assessment role of the supervisor. Flemons *et al.* (1996) stated, 'if, as postmodernists assert, there is no privileged, expert position, how can supervisors evaluate their trainees?' They concluded that evaluation can be undertaken within their family therapy doctoral training programme, but that this is in the context of collaborative relationships with students. Both supervisor and supervisee are seen as being able to learn from each other and evaluations are made of each party by the other.

In order to effect their gatekeeping role, it may be helpful for supervisors to draw on the ideas of Lang *et al.* (1990) who identified different domains of action. In the domain of explanation the focus is on understanding and the style is non-judgemental. In the domain of production the position is one of evaluation in a world of rights and wrongs. The supervisor may find it helpful to identify the domain from which he or she is operating at any particular time yet to intervene sensitively and aesthetically within Lang *et al.*'s third domain of aesthetics, whether acting within the domain of explanation or the domain of production.

Since systemic approaches have increasingly become influenced by postmodern philosophies, alternative approaches to evaluation have been developed. Lowe (2000) described an approach which aims to develop the supervisee's self-supervision. Case consultation is viewed as an embedded narrative involving the case story, the therapist story and the supervision story. A process of constructive enquiry is used to connect these stories in order to construct the identity of a self-sustaining therapist. Emphasis is placed on teaching by coaching expertise, rather than on direct coaching or formal instruction.

Summary

In this chapter the approach to supervision within four different models of therapy has been described. The selection of these particular models is to a degree serendipitous, although between them they illustrate some of the major differences of emphasis in approaches to therapy translated to the supervision process. Each model shows some congruence between the approach to therapy and the approach to supervision, albeit influenced by differences of style between individual supervisors. Discussion of these may be used in contracting for supervision in order to facilitate supervisors and supervisees in debating and negotiating the arrangements and practices they wish to make for themselves.

Note

1 From Bernard, Janine M. and Rodney K. Goodyear *Fundamentals Of Clinical Supervision*, 1/e Published by Allyn and Bacon, Boston, MA. Copyright © 1991 by Pearson Education. Reprinted by permission of the publisher. First published by the Greenwood Publishing Group in *Client-Centred Therapy* by R.F. Levant and J.M. Shlien. Copyright © 1984 by Praeger Publishers. Reproduced with permission of Greenwood Publishing Group. Inc. Westport, CT.

Chapter 14

Challenge and the assessment role

Evaluation and assessment

Evaluation and assessment involve making judgements of a person's work. Inextricably linked with a person's work are the personal qualities they bring to their work. Self-assessment is relatively non-problematic in terms of its potential to evoke negative reactions, whereas evaluative comments offered by a supervisor can readily engender defensive reactions on the part of the person being assessed, particularly where these are taken personally. There is a great deal of skill in carrying out the assessment process in a manner which fosters openness and an orientation towards personal and professional development in the supervisee. Central to the process of assessment is the crucial issue of purpose. Identification of purpose is the first step in making a judgement about one's own or another person's work.

Purposes and types of assessment

There are three major purposes of assessment: diagnostic, formative and summative. Diagnostic or formulatory assessment is a process in which someone's current knowledge and skills are assessed with a view to aiding the teacher or supervisor to arrange a series of learning opportunities and experiences that will encourage development in the identified domains. This is discussed in Chapter 2 on learning. It first involves the supervisee in showing what they know and can do now. From this is devised a programme of work that offers the opportunity to develop professional knowledge and skills further.

Evaluation aimed at fostering development is known as formative evaluation, and that made as a judgement of professional fitness is known as summative assessment. The nature of assessment is such that it is a complex and potentially problematic process in which these two purposes may suggest conflicting approaches.

Summative assessment

Particularly in training contexts supervisors are required to make summative judgements about a practitioner's competence. They are aided in this task by reference to specifications of the knowledge, skills and values required which are typically provided by the profession, by licensing bodies and by institutions of higher education. Specifications of the knowledge, skills and values required to offer competent supervision are also available (British Psychological Society, 2007b; Falender and Shafranske, 2004: 257; Getz, 1999).

When addressing summative assessment it should be borne in mind that there is little consistent agreement about the qualities that make someone fit to be a professional helper or about the skills that make up the work. Attempts to assess competence have often defined their measures around adherence to a particular model of psychotherapy. However, the transactions between clinician and client take on particular meanings and derive their therapeutic effectiveness from the interpersonal context of the therapy (Butler and Strupp, 1986). Studies of competence have often found difficulties resulting from poor inter-rater reliability (Shaw and Dobson, 1989), poor association between measures and client outcome (Svartberg and Stiles, 1992) and difficulties in reaching agreement about what features are central to the task (Fordham et al., 1990). There are also difficulties about the level at which a skill must be demonstrated. Should a predetermined criterion be reached or is the judgement norm-referenced or referred to an average performance? What if the skill is demonstrable within one context but not in another; on one occasion but not on another?

Increasingly, professional psychology has emphasised competency-based approaches to education and training. However, the difficulties described above show no significant signs of resolution (Falender and Shafranske, 2007; Rubin et al., 2007). Some authors have argued that a competency-based approach does not necessarily reflect competence and 'fails to take account of the real character of professionalism on the one hand and the artistry of practice [in medicine] on the other' (Fish and de Cossart, 2006: 404). In light of a vastly expanding knowledge base in psychology, it has been argued that 'half of the facts' in psychology are replaced within the span of a typical graduate school stint (Flannery-Schroeder, 2005: 389). Competence thus requires 'a deep vein of creativity that is constantly renewing itself' (National Center on Education and the Economy, 2006: 6). This report asserted that the American education system 'rewards students who will be good at routine work, while not providing opportunities for students to display creative and innovative thinking and analysis' and argued that the standards movement has reached a point where it is no longer leading to educational gains that will fit students to be members of the twenty-first-century workforce. Falender and Shafranske drew attention to the notion of metacompetence: the use of available skills and knowledge to solve problems or tasks and to determine which skills or knowledge are missing, how to acquire these, and whether they are essential to success. Metacompetence is dependent on self-reflection and self-awareness (Weinert, 2001) and is achieved through self-assessment. Falender and Shafranske (2007) argued that self-assessment is at the heart of developing and maintaining competence, although even this is a novel and uncharted course.

With these factors in mind, it is as well to obtain clarity about what constitutes competence, to identify any overriding concerns that might lead to consideration of unsuitability as a professional helper and to share these concerns with the supervisee early on in the process of establishing the supervisory alliance. For example, the majority of supervisors tolerate or even welcome mistakes, including their own, providing there is willingness to learn from them. Supervisors cannot abdicate the task of summative assessment, and must be satisfied that the supervisee is fit as a professional even where the arrangement for supervision is between peers. The role is particularly salient, however, in the case of preregistration training.

The role of assessor is typically found difficult by supervisors (Hahn and Molnar, 1991; Holloway and Roehlke, 1987). The assertive skills of assessing and challenging others constructively about their work can be difficult to learn, not only in the context of the helping professions but in life more generally. Attempts to challenge others can turn into confrontation or be received as negative and unsolicited criticism, the effects of which can be to damage relationships rather than to facilitate learning and development. This has been recognised by the Probation Service in the UK in relation to the appraisal process:

> There is evidence that employees do not respond well to any substantial degree of criticism, and that it does not lead to improvement in the criticised areas of performance. It is important that this is recognised but equally important that it does not lead to the production of bland appraisal reports that fail to deal with the real developmental issues. It is more helpful and stimulating to make a concrete, time limited statement of what you expect an employee to achieve in the future, than to make critical statements of what he or she has failed to achieve in the past.
>
> (Association of Chief Officers of Probation, 1989: 2)

In clinical work, as opposed to supervision, evaluation may be contraindicated, since the literature suggests that potential impediments to mental health can result. High levels of criticism in families (known as expressed emotion) (Butzlaff and Hooley, 1998; Jacobsen, 1998) have been shown to be associated with mental health difficulties of children in their adult lives. The core conditions for psychotherapy (Rogers, 1980: 486) include unconditional positive regard, an attitude that might be perceived as incompatible with giving feedback and making evaluations. People whose primary training has been as clinicians may therefore find switching to the role of assessor particularly difficult. Unfamiliarity may result in clumsy attempts to provide feedback. The role is therefore worthy of careful consideration, with attention given to the aims of evaluation and the conditions that best support the task.

It is worth keeping in mind that the values and views of assessors inevitably play a part in their judgements of suitability. An extreme example would be to imagine that the cardinals of the Catholic Church, in the firm belief that a flat earth was the centre of the universe, were interviewing for the post of principal astronomer. Would they have offered it to Galileo, a highly competent applicant whose experiments were providing evidence that contradicted this position?

Formative assessment

Summative assessment most helpfully emerges out of formative assessment so that there are no surprises for supervisees at the end of a training placement or supervisory arrangement in terms of how their supervisor views their work. The supervisor has available a range of assessment interventions that might be expected to facilitate learning. These might include:

- Organising learning contexts which of themselves provide information to the supervisee about how they are doing.
- Encouraging the supervisee to self-assess, possibly with the aid of checklists, through observation of the supervisor with a focus on aspects of performance that the supervisee wishes to attain.
- Providing support for arrangements in which peer evaluation is possible.
- Debriefing following observation of a session led by the supervisee.
- Provision of feedback about performance.
- Constructively challenging supervisees to develop their strengths.

Debriefing

Fish and Twinn (1997: 126) used the term 'debriefing' to denote 'the activity of talking with the student or practitioner about practice that has been shared by both the supervisor and that person, and in which either was the main actor and the other the main observer'. They prefer this term over 'feedback' and 'critique' since it is regarded as more neutral and encompasses a sense of the process as one of being helped to uncover and work on what someone already tacitly knows. They argued that the term 'debriefing' is nonjudgemental and that feedback may be a constituent element in the debriefing process. The process does require that both supervisor and supervisee have been party to a piece of work either directly or through review of recorded material.

Fish and Twinn suggested a framework for debriefing with six dimensions:

- *Aims.* These are identified as assisting someone to reflect critically, guiding and supporting, supporting and building, leading by example, leading towards independent practice, building confidence in own skills, facilitating behavioural change, and helping the supervisee to arrive at a complete view of the professional role as well as attending to details within it. These aims are intended to be very learner-centred and supervisors may have to suspend other aspects of their role while focusing on the aims of debriefing.
- *Orientation.* Fish and Twinn suggested that there are three aspects to the general orientation of the debrief. These are an orientation towards improvement of practice, towards deliberation about issues, or on the health needs of the client, some of which may have been identified by the supervisee and others which have been omitted but which are apparent to the supervisor.
- *Mode.* The term 'mode' subsumes both feedback and critique, these being conducted within the 'critique mode'. The lead observer picks out salient points of positive and negative aspects of the observed practice and offers professional judgements about them and about how the person observed might improve on subsequent occasions. In this mode, the parties may refer to a checklist of competencies. In 'reflective mode' both parties reflect on what happened during the practice, including the thinking that underlay the actions with a view to providing an opportunity to refine future professional judgements and actions. The 'formal assessment mode' provides an opportunity to review the specific performance against a set standard. This process is regarded as formative if it occurs during the practice, and summative if it occurs at the end.
- *Pedagogic style.* This mode refers to the debriefer's supervisory role behaviour, which may involve telling or asking.
- *Format.* The format can be oral or written or both. It is suggested that written notes can be taken to subsequent supervision sessions, providing continuity in regard to the learning process. The written basis can be discursive, descriptive and/or completed checklists or forms and this will be in large part determined by the purpose of the debrief.
- *Nature and use of evidence.* It is suggested that the data collected during observation may be regarded as evidence for critiques or as a basis for discussion, in the former case being treated as unproblematic hard data and in the latter as subjective material used as a means of exploring ideas and practice.

Fish and Twinn appropriately pointed out that debriefing must take into account the emotional aspects of the supervisee's experience. They identified some rules of thumb for debriefing that encourage a collaborative process and a focus on clear and specific aspects of practice rather than on personal qualities. Ultimately, as with all methods and approaches to the evaluation of practice, the quality of the relationship between the participants is crucial.

Feedback

Feedback is defined here as a response or reaction providing useful information or guidelines for further action and development. This suggests a very constructive role for feedback in skill development. Feedback from the materials operated upon (in this case from the clients) is likely to be very useful to a practitioner. It may not be explicit but may be inferred from the responses and reactions of the client in the work. If the client responds positively to the work this is likely to produce feelings of efficacy and pleasure for the therapist. If the response of the client is perceived as ambivalent or negative, this is likely to spur workers into seeking changes to their approach. There is sound research evidence to support this proposition.

In a series of studies (Harmon *et al.*, 2007; Lambert *et al.*, 2005) therapists were provided with questionnaire data from outcome measures completed by clients between sessions which informed them about the response of the client to intervention. Feedback to therapists reduced deterioration rates and improved outcomes, particularly in those predicted from the scores to be treatment failures. In these studies, the work was conducted by practitioners schooled in different therapeutic methods who were able to adjust their interventions both in terms of approach and duration. Clients whose progress was not on track were on average provided with a greater number of sessions if their therapist received feedback than similar clients of therapists who were given no feedback. Effect size was greater when the feedback included information about the client's social support, readiness to change and the quality of the therapeutic alliance. Anecdotal data suggested that therapists used the information in different ways. One informant said, 'The information showed that there was not a good therapeutic alliance. It provided a good opportunity to use that information to process how she was experiencing therapy and what she thought of the relationship. We were able to talk through expectations, goals and process issues.' The task of the supervisor with regard to client feedback might be seen as helping the supervisee to interpret and explore the options for learning from this data.

While client feedback can be used to very good effect, there can be problems with feedback given by a third party such as a supervisor:

*   *The recipient needs to be open to engaging with the feedback or else it will have little useful effect on learning.* This is the case irrespective of the feedback being positive or negative. If the supervisor comments, for example, that the supervisee introduced herself or himself and the way of working clearly, but the supervisee does not agree, the supervisee will

give precedence to her or his own self-assessment unless open to the possibility of a change of mind on this subject. The wider effect may be for the supervisee to devalue other feedback given by the supervisor – 'What does he or she know?' – evaluating the supervisor as unfit to judge.

- *The feedback should connect with the issues of the learner.* Something of particular importance to the supervisor may not yet be within the scope of the supervisee at this stage of learning. A supervisee preoccupied with surviving a session is unlikely to be able to respond to fine detail even if this is acknowledged as a future learning goal.

- *Feedback will have no positive effect unless offered in the context of a sustaining supervisory relationship.* It may be necessary to allow time for the relationship to develop prior to attempting to critique the work in order for the recipient to understand the intent of the provider. The context of the supervisory relationship is crucial. It may not be essential for the supervisee to like the supervisor, but other features such as respect and trust are necessary in order for the feedback to be accepted.

- *Feedback in respect of issues about which the recipient feels vulnerable may produce a defensive response rather than learning and development.* If perceived as hurtful to a sensitive spot supervisees may feel it necessary to disguise their vulnerabilities in general and to effect a façade of competence or withdraw from the relationship.

- *If the giver of feedback believes it to be the 'truth' rather than an opinion, it may be given in such a way as to be irrefutable.* While this may be effective in some instances – 'Saying that to the client was wrong in this model of work' – feedback is more generally found acceptable when offered as an opinion – 'At that point in the session I would probably have said . . .'.

- *Feedback statements beginning with 'You . . .' are more likely to be perceived as focused on personal qualities rather than on practices.*

- *Feedback implies unidirectionality rather than mutuality.* It suggests a transmission mode of teaching which is unlikely to engage the adult learner. Feedback could be mutual and it would be important for the recipient to be able to give feedback about the feedback in order to make the view open to debate.

- *In order to be effective, the feedback must be perceived as genuine.* Where it is seen as masking the supervisor's actual opinion or given in a convoluted and clumsy fashion, the effect will be to generate uncertainty and insecurity.

- *Feedback needs to be specific.* Where a bland general comment is made – 'The session was fine' – supervisees find it difficult to identify pointers for learning.

With these issues in mind I have come to the view that feedback from a third party is of limited value except under certain conditions. In particular, it is probably helpful if the feedback is invited rather than unsolicited. This allows recipients to have a degree of control, enables them to protect their vulner-abilities, and enhances the possibility that the feedback will connect with their learning needs. It also gives some protection to supervisors, preventing them from inadvertently undermining rather than enhancing the confidence of the supervisee.

Challenge

The meaning of challenge here is taken as an invitation or undertaking to test one's capabilities to the full. Supervisors might thus challenge supervisees to use their identified strengths and capabilities, suggesting how these may be further developed. Supervisees might also be challenged to identify new skills they wish to learn, building on current capabilities. Particularly early on in their training, supervisees tend to have difficulty in identifying their own strengths, as they are unclear about the features of the skills they are trying to learn. The supervisor can help by noticing these and inviting the supervisee to use them more widely and in different contexts. For example, the supervisor may have noticed the supervisee feeling so overwhelmed with sadness as a client described the loss of her father that he or she was unable to speak. The supervisor might challenge the supervisee through identifying the strength of the capacity to experience deep empathy and, with the supervisee's agree-ment, use the supervision to consider how to manage this strength, which could include allowing a period of quietness during the session with the client. The purpose of challenge is to generate new perspectives at a cognitive level and to create options for action. The challenge is to the current way of seeing or doing things.

The benefit of challenging strengths rather than weaknesses is the context of a positive frame which better supports learning and development. The risk of challenging weaknesses is that of prompting defensiveness, possibly leading to confrontation and argument and a hindrance to learning.

Aims of challenge

In this section 'challenge' is the preferred term for the action supervisors might take to foster a supervisee's development. In the event of serious con-cerns regarding the supervisor's capability to reach a satisfactory level of competence, or in the event of impaired performance or unethical conduct, more stringent measures may be required and these are discussed in the final section of this chapter.

Ownership

The supervisor is only one element of the supervisory environment that offers opportunities for challenge. In addition to the feedback from the client, a most important element is supervisees' own assessment of their strengths and points for development. The supervisor has a role in helping supervisees to challenge themselves and this role is less likely to produce defensiveness or confrontation. In this role, the supervisor may help the supervisee to identify core skills that comprise the helping task and against which supervisees might evaluate their current functioning for evidence not of attainment, but of progress to date, prioritising some issues for learning on which they might invite the supervisor to comment. Professional bodies are a useful source of statements of core knowledge, skills and values.

Principles underlying challenge

Egan (1994, 2002) helpfully outlined the principles underlying effective challenge of clients by professional helpers. In respect of supervision the following are offered as principles which can guide decisions about how and when to challenge supervisees:

- *Keep in mind the goals of challenge.* The purpose of challenge was identified earlier as formative and addressed the supervisees' learning and development. Supervisors who keep this in mind will be trying to understand the stage of the supervisee's learning and connect their challenges to this. It is also helpful for supervisors to check that their challenges fit with the supervisee's needs and this can be achieved explicitly by the supervisor asking the supervisee whether challenges proposed or already made have been useful to learning and development.
- *Encourage self-challenge.* This can be done explicitly by asking supervisees on which topics they would wish to challenge themselves, or by choosing a specific topic and inviting supervisees to consider whether this is a good time for them to challenge themselves to develop further on this issue. The supervisor will also notice when the supervisee has seemed to be attempting to take a new stance or approach and enquire into this.
- *Work to establish a relationship in which challenge is constructive.* A fundamental requirement for a functional supervisory alliance is mutual respect. If this is absent, and where there is a choice, it is better not to begin the relationship in the first place. Where there is no choice, open discussion of the preconceptions about the other in the beginning may be difficult but may enable a reassessment which allows for the development of mutual respect. The supervisor also needs to keep in mind the inequity of the positions of supervisor and supervisee, particularly in the context of training relationships. It may be helpful to hold a discussion early on about each person's typical defensive reactions and the most constructive responses to them. Supervisors should state clearly what issues they would perceive as seriously problematic as well as issues that would not trouble them. This prevents the supervisee from having to fantasise about

this. Supervisors can usefully model positive responses to being challenged themselves. They can refer to their own difficulties with the work, their own progress and development, and thereby normalise mistakes or lack of knowledge. Such references should always be driven by the learning needs of the supervisee and not stray into meeting the affirmation needs of the supervisor.

- *Show openness to learning and being challenged oneself.* This may be apparent through observations the supervisee might suggest of the challenges made to the supervisor by clients, colleagues or the supervisee. On the other hand there may be limited opportunities, but this could be accomplished by supervisors challenging themselves about the supervision they are offering or inviting the opinions of the supervisee. The supervisor may identify a learning need on which they are working in the role of supervisor, and invite comments from the supervisee.
- *Be authentic.* For example, if there are serious concerns that a supervisee has been unable to remedy in a training placement, it is ingenuous to feign continued interest in challenging strengths.
- *Balance tentativeness with assertiveness.* Messages delivered in an overly assertive manner may not leave room for disagreement, may be experienced as accusations, and produce confrontation and defensiveness. On the other hand, too many qualifications can sound apologetic, devalue the point being made and can leave someone uncertain as to what the supervisor thinks. For example:

  'You asked me to notice how the client responded to you interrupting him because you are experimenting with challenging your idea that interruptions may be disrespectful to the client. Maybe you were more ready to interrupt than previously and perhaps this helped the session along so that you may have stayed with your plan for the session more than before.'

  'You asked me to notice how the client responded to you interrupting him because you are experimenting with challenging your idea that interruptions may be disrespectful to the client. You certainly interrupted more than previously and I think you could easily go further without showing disrespect. Do you want to experiment more in the next session or try it with me now?'

- *Build on success.* This links with the idea of challenging strengths that are underused or could be more widely applied. It is important not to expect great leaps in learning and to encourage even small changes, helping supervisees to notice these changes and making plans to build on them.
- *Be specific.* Vague and overly broad observations tend to be experienced as challenges to the whole being of the person rather than to specific aspects of knowledge or performance that might be developed.

In addition to evoking strong feelings in the supervisee, it is much more difficult to change something that is experienced as central to one's self. For example, challenging a supervisee's whole approach to clients by saying, 'When you are with clients I observe that you are overly friendly and that limits what you can do as a therapist' is likely to be perceived as a criticism and may produce a defensive response. An alternative is to say, 'Talking to clients in the waiting room like a friend might not orient them to your professional role as a therapist. I would like us to think about how to start when clients have to be brought from the waiting area, and how you might use your strengths of warmth and friendliness in other ways in the work.'

The process of challenging

The following steps are suggested as a format for challenging a supervisee. This is not to suggest that challenge is necessarily a major undertaking, rather it can be a small part of the work of the supervisor, undertaken naturally as part of the regular supervisory process. The skills of challenging do require supervisors to acknowledge their own authority which is afforded by the role, even in peer arrangements. The format is designed to help people new to taking a position of authority to think about and practise the skills.

*   *Identify the purpose of the challenge.* In planning to challenge a supervisee it is helpful to be clear that the desired outcome is some particular learning. The purpose may be described to the supervisee as a preface to introducing the subject matter, and the desired outcome should be specific and clear. The benefit to the supervisee can be included – 'I think that you could be even more effective in your work with Jane if you were to develop your skills in helping her to work harder and participate more in the sessions, perhaps by staying more quiet yourself.'
*   *Decide whether you have the authority to make this challenge.* The degree of authority vested in the supervisor depends on the specific arrangement made. If in doubt, for example, in a peer arrangement, ask the supervisee for their opinion on this – 'Would you prefer me to challenge your approach to this client or would you like me to help you with the approach you're now taking?' The responsibility for some kinds of learning may lie elsewhere in the work system – for example, with a line manager or member of a training institution. In order to challenge confidently it is important to believe that one is operating within the agreed brief of the relationship.
*   *Get your facts clear.* If you are unsure about what you believe it would be helpful for the supervisee to change in their work – for example, because something has been reported to you by another person – make sure that you are clear about the facts and that you subscribe to the idea that

change is needed. If not, work out how to gain greater clarity before treating it as a matter on which to challenge the supervisee.

- *Practise making clear and direct statements.* If this is a new skill for you, rehearsal will help you to feel comfortable. You might also ask for feedback from the supervisee. This could be part of your learning agenda as a supervisor and could be introduced to the supervisee as such – 'I am trying to develop my skills in challenging and I would like to make a suggestion to you about your learning. I would welcome your opinion about how my suggestion affects you.'

- *Consider starting sentences with 'I'.* This indicates that you are offering an opinion which could in turn be challenged by the supervisee. 'I have noticed that I seem to be talking a lot in supervision. I wonder if you think that my opinions are more important than yours. I would like to talk about what I can do that would make your ideas more important.' This is clear and purposeful and less likely to be perceived as a criticism than saying, 'You need to share more of your own ideas in supervision.'

- *Use immediacy if things seem to be getting out of hand.* Immediacy in the context of supervision is using perceptions of what is currently taking place between the participants in the supervisory dialogue as information for the purposes of learning and development. The concept was introduced by Carkhuff and his colleagues (Carkhuff, 1969; Carkhuff and Anthony, 1979). If the supervisee responds defensively or aggressively to a challenge, do not be afraid to comment on what seems to be happening between you in the present. If it is appropriate, be prepared to take responsibility for the direction the conversation has taken. 'My intention in raising this is to help you to develop your confidence in your own ideas about the work but that doesn't seem to be happening. What can I do that would better achieve that?' Don't second-guess the mood of the supervisee with a 'you' statement, such as, 'You seem to be getting very angry.'

- *Offer to come back to the matter after further thought.* Sometimes you may anticipate that the issue you are planning to raise will be difficult for the supervisee to address no matter how sensitively it is raised; for example, continuing to work despite significantly poor health. 'In your position I would want to be considering whether to take a period of sick leave. One of the problems in our profession is that people are often reluctant to do that because they feel that they are letting their clients down or believe that their colleagues will be critical. Don't let me know what you think now but I would like you to think about it between now and our next supervision and put it on the agenda for then.' This can also be suggested if the conversation has proved difficult, deferring any decisions until the supervisee has been able to go beyond her or his initial response.

- *If you meet with blank refusal to consider the issue, ask the supervisee what he or she would do in your shoes.* This would more typically occur in the context of the managerial function of supervision. You may have had to raise an issue such as the supervisee coming to work with the smell of alcohol on her or his breath. The supervisee will not necessarily be thinking of your dilemma but you can introduce this by asking her or him to consider what action he or she would take in your place. You are showing authority with respect to the issue of drink and the workplace, and showing openness to learning about the process of dealing with it.

- *Be prepared to show humility.* While the skills of challenging involve taking authority, this does not have to be across the board, only in relation to the specific issue raised. It is important that supervisors model a non-defensive approach with regard to their own skills in challenging.

Challenging is about the learning of the supervisee. Ultimately if the supervisee does not seem amenable to learning, then supervisors will need to consider whether to exert their formal evaluative role as gatekeeper to the profession. This is explored in the final section of this chapter.

Challenge of a different kind

Sometimes supervisors find that they are in a difficult relationship with a supervisee. It is not the learning and development of the supervisee that is at stake, but rather a change in the nature of the relationship. Supervisors may feel that the relationship is too distant, that they cannot trust the word of the supervisee, or that the supervisee is acting strategically or inauthentically in supervision. However, the work carried out may meet the requirements of the profession and the issue is not therefore one of normative standards. Here, the difficulty is or may be specific to the supervisory relationship. The aim is to create a more effective and satisfying supervisory alliance. The challenge here is to both parties, with no predetermined intention to facilitate change in the supervisee. The aim is to facilitate change in the supervisory relationship which will probably involve change in the supervisor.

Since the difficulty is being identified by the supervisor, it is the supervisor who is experiencing the problem and inviting the assistance of the supervisee in its solution. This may require a different approach since it is in the nature of a request which may be met or refused. There may be a consequence for the supervisee of refusing the request. Where the arrangement is voluntary the supervisor may conclude that he or she no longer wishes to participate, and where it is mandatory supervisees who refuse to engage may find that their learning needs are given reduced priority.

The challenge in this context may need to be introduced in a different way, and the value to the supervisee of agreeing to engage in solving the supervisor's problem may be part of the introduction. For example, 'I'm finding some difficulties in how my relationship with you is working and I would like to ask if you are prepared to talk to me about it because I think that we could both have a lot more enjoyment than we are having at the moment if I felt differently. Would it be OK with you if I tell you a little more about it?' Another method of introducing the topic may be first to comment on what is working well in the relationship in order to provide a context in which the supervisee is encouraged to work to preserve it. This may mean noting the professionalism of the person, her or his commitment to learning, and so on. It is helpful to avoid noting strengths and then following them up with a 'but'.

Attribution of the difficulty to the pattern rather than the person is probably helpful. It may also help to be specific in identifying particular examples of the difficulty, the events that have contributed to establishment of the pattern and the effects on self. For example, where the supervisor does not find the supervisee's contributions to have an authentic quality the supervisor could refer to examples. 'When you were talking to Mrs Brown I just had the feeling that you didn't mean what you said and I felt the same when you were asking to have a shorter supervision session last week. I may be misreading your tone of voice or eye contact – I'm not sure what it is – can you help at all? Am I doing something that makes you uncomfortable or that you would rather I did differently?'

Another strategy is to work together on the pattern by enlisting the support of the supervisee in committing what is known to paper in the form of data or a diagram. In this way the parties are on the same side in studying the problem that is outside them as individuals. From time to time the best efforts of the supervisor appear to have no impact and a state of impasse is reached. In voluntary arrangements, the supervision contract can be terminated. In pre-registration arrangements supervisors may conclude that their repertoire of approaches to the difficulties has been exhausted and the help of a third party may be invoked. Another conclusion may be that the supervisee is unfit to join the profession. It is important for this to be acknowledged and the supervisor will need to communicate with the training agency in order to effect the gatekeeping function.

Unsatisfactory performance

Definitions of unsatisfactory performance

From a thorough review of the literature pertaining to the training of clinical psychologists in the USA, Forrest et al. (1999) concluded that there is a lack of clear, shared and consistent language to represent different types of problematic behaviour. They recommended distinguishing between impairment, incompetence and unethical practice. Impairment refers to diminished functioning after reaching an adequate level of professional competence. It has been suggested (Falender and Shafranske, 2007) that this term is unsuitable since it has a specific legal definition under the Americans with Disabilities Act. It has been proposed that the terms 'problematic professional competence', 'professional competence problems' or 'problems with professional competence' be used in its place (Elman and Forrest, 2007). Such problems are likely to arise from situations of extreme personal stress, or alcohol or substance misuse. Incompetence refers to an absence of qualities or skills necessary to attain adequate levels of professional performance (Kutz, 1986). Unethical practice refers, for example, to entering into a sexual relationship with a client where there is no temporarily diminished functioning.

Forrest *et al.* noted that current definitions of impairment mix descriptions of problematic behaviour (e.g. defensiveness in supervision) with descriptions of explanations (e.g. depression, personality disorder) and that this creates confusion for both supervisors and supervisees. They made a number of recommendations through which training courses may develop helpful policies and procedures in order to fulfil their gatekeeping role.

Palmer Barnes (1998) offered another model for classifying unacceptable practice into the categories of 'mistakes', 'poor practice', 'negligence' and 'malpractice'. Mistakes feature in the work of all practitioners, although the degree of severity will differ. They are defined by Palmer Barnes as 'an unintended slip in good practice'. At the other end of the continuum, malpractice usually involves a practitioner following a course of action designed to meet her or his own needs. For a wider discussion of these categories the reader is referred to Daniels (2000).

Supervisors, faced with managing unsatisfactory performance, need to find a path that takes into account the needs of clients and of the supervisee that is as pain-free as possible for all. Balancing educational responsibilities with gatekeeping obligations continues to be a struggle for supervisors (Hahn and Molnar, 1991; Holloway and Roehlke, 1987).

Dealing with unsatisfactory performance of a supervisee in training

In the contracting process, the supervisor's requirements of the supervisee should have been made clear. For example, the supervisor may have agreed that supervision will take place at a regular time and venue and that this should also be the case for the work carried out by the supervisee with the client. If the supervisee shows unreliable timekeeping, this will need to be addressed in supervision. The supervisor needs some skills in challenging in order to accomplish this. In preregistration training, students have a right of due process, violation of which allows them recourse to legal redress. This is explored more fully in Chapter 7. Since a future career can weigh in the balance, supervisors need to take a well-considered and ethical approach to the management of unsatisfactory performance.

There is sometimes a temptation for the supervisor to hope that supervisees' evaluations of their own performances equate with those of the supervisor. There may be a temptation to ask a question rather than to make a statement. The question, 'How satisfied were you with the way the session ended?' may be asked either from a position of genuine curiosity or when the supervisor has already decided that the supervisee needs to develop skills in closing down sessions. In the latter case, the supervisor is faced with a continuing dilemma regarding how to pursue this unless the supervisee responds to the question with the same opinion as the supervisor regarding endings. Whatever the supervisee's response, be it neutral, with openness or defensively, supervisors can make diagnostic use of this in order to judge their next action.

It may be helpful for supervisors to practise making preference and purpose statements and evaluative statements in which they make their opinions and requirements clear. Here are some examples:

'In the contact we agreed that I would need to hear you working and next week I would like you to bring a recording of a session of your choice. This week I would like us to spend the first 15 minutes or so working out how to use the recording in ways that you are comfortable with.'

'When you asked Janet to keep a diary record of her automatic thoughts, I felt that she would find the task too difficult without more structure. I tend to make a record during the session of an example, and then ask the client to do this for a second example so that any uncertainties can be dealt with at the outset. What do you think about trying that?'

'When we discussed how to keep case-files in this service I explained that they needed to be completed each time you saw a client. I was very surprised to find that the files are a month behind and completing them must be a priority for this week. Can you tell me how they came to be so far behind?'

'When you come to supervision I would prefer it if you have thought about a focus for the session in advance as at this stage I think it is no longer necessary to take a look at each of your cases every week.'

'We have talked a lot about how anxious the work makes you feel and how when you feel anxious one way of coping is to avoid seeing clients. Now we are half-way through the placement and I'm worried that when we reach the end you will not have achieved the aims and activities that we agreed at the beginning because you will not have had enough contact with the clients. If this happened you would not pass the placement so I think that we need to work out how to deal with the anxiety in a different way. There has to be a change but we can work out together what would be needed to help you to make the change.'

The last example leads on to failure and the gatekeeping role of the supervisor in the context of preregistration training.

When to fail a supervisee

It is important that the supervisor and supervisee are both aware at the outset of the criteria upon which the assessment of the supervisee's work will be made. These may be set by the training institution, but with room for modification according to the individual judgement of the supervisor. The kinds of behaviours that might lead to failure are usually within the domain of unprofessional behaviour, unethical behaviour, and unwillingness or inability to learn. Occasionally the supervisor may judge the candidate to be unsuitable for the profession because of an unwillingness to examine blind spots that are considered central to conducting the work soundly. The following are some examples of issues that might prompt consideration of failure:

- The supervisee makes appointments with clients but is unreliable in turning up for them, or is repeatedly late and unresponsive to suggestions for change.
- The supervisee shows hostility in interactions with staff, losing her or his temper and attributing the difficulty to others. A pattern of such behaviour emerges particularly in relation to authority figures. Attempts to discuss the difficulties lead to further expressions of hostility, with the supervisee walking out of meetings arranged to explore the difficulties.
- The supervisee violates ethical codes or the rules of the organisation in which the work is conducted, engaging in gross professional misconduct (for example, turning up to work when under the influence of drugs or alcohol, or engaging in a sexual relationship with a client).
- The supervisee achieves only a superficial level of engagement with clients, talking about them rather as objects than people. Clients regularly fail appointments after the first one or two sessions. When these issues are raised the supervisee acts avoidantly.
- The supervisee's work is adversely influenced by earlier life experiences which constitute major blocks to her or his work with certain issues and clients. It is inappropriate to continue in training until these have been addressed in personal development work.
- The supervisee engages in inappropriately immature or defensive behaviour such as attempting to lie her or his way out of a difficulty rather than engaging actively with the issue and taking responsibility for the difficulties.
- The supervisee presents with very unbalanced professional capabilities. For example, there is a mismatch of skills in an academic high-flyer who has very limited interpersonal skills for work in a people-centred profession.

When a supervisee's performance is unsatisfactory supervisors often try to find alternatives to failing the practice placement. Some of these alternatives do not help with the problem. Wilson (1981) described the following:

- Ignore the problematic performance and award a 'satisfactory' grade.
- Lower performance expectations.
- Wait and see if the supervisee's performance improves in the next practice placement.
- Make the supervisee's experience so miserable that he or she withdraws from the training programme.

Since these solutions are unsatisfactory, constitute a danger to future clients, and are misdirected in the best interests of the supervisee, it would be better for supervisors to 'bite the bullet' and raise their concerns with the training institution, having first discussed with the supervisee the manner in which this will be conducted.

How to fail a supervisee

When serious difficulties arise it is essential to keep records of the reasons for concern, the attempts that have been made to raise them with the supervisee and what would be required in order for the supervisee's performance to be assessed as adequate. Where possible it is also desirable to involve the training institution at an early stage. When such decisions are to be made it is usually wise to involve a group of people or a committee in order to ensure fairness and to establish that the difficulty does not arise from a single problematic supervisory relationship. It is essential that the supervisee has had the opportunity to make improvements – discussed in Chapter 7 under the issue of due process.

To fail a placement is a very difficult decision for one individual to make. It is important not to avoid the issue, however. A test of the level of one's concern is to imagine the supervisee being consulted by one's best friend, partner or child. If it is concluded that there is an unacceptable risk of the loved one being damaged by the contact, then it would surely be irresponsible not to take action.

Following from the decision to fail is either the construction of a plan for remediation or a decision to dismiss, the latter being a process which is likely to be informed, but not taken, by the supervisor. While a decision to fail a training placement is usually a source of anxiety and heart-searching for supervisors, it can be the crisis that enables a supervisee to face up to her or his difficulties in a constructive way since they can no longer be avoided.

Dealing with impairment and unethical behaviour

When the supervisor has serious concerns regarding the practice of a supervisee who is a qualified practitioner, the path for dealing with this may be even more complex and challenging than in the case of preregistration training. A range of explanations for the impairment or unethical conduct may suggest different approaches in the longer term. Schoener and Gonsiorek (1988) reported their work in the rehabilitation of more than a thousand cases of therapists who had committed sexual transgressions with clients. They concluded that their sample varied from individuals whose conduct had arisen from naivety to those who showed psychotic symptoms. They identified the need for careful assessment of practitioners whose performance is believed to be impaired or unethical. This entails the use of clinical judgement.

Supervisors experience contradictory pulls between their nurturing and evaluative roles and are likely to have to deal with impairment in supervisees only on rare occasions. They may also fear the reaction of the supervisee to their attempts to take the matter forward. When the level of supervisors' concerns leaves them with no alternative but to act, this needs to be done with care for the individual and concern for the practitioner's clients. Supervisors in such circumstances would be wise to take advice and guidance from their professional network, out of which consultation process should emerge a suitable plan for action. This will almost certainly involve the supervisee, although her or his consent to the action may be unobtainable. Professional regulatory bodies provide advice for members, often laying out a procedure which helps practitioners to structure their intervention (see e.g. General Medical Council, 2006). Many psychologists have self-reported continuing to work, even when they are too distressed to function effectively (Pope et al., 1987; Wood et al., 1985). Supervisors are in a pivotal position to help such practitioners to make the difficult decision to stop work, or in extreme circumstances to take the decision for them.

At times, experienced supervisors may be asked to aid a colleague whose practice has been deemed impaired. In the USA one such intervention is known as 'sanctioned supervision'. Sanctioned supervision usually involves the clinician whose practice is problematic being monitored and supervised by specified colleagues (Thomas, 2005). Sanctioned supervision has been described as a mechanism for helping the disciplined professional develop in areas that have been defined as lacking or impaired (Cobia and Pipes, 2002). Rapisarda and Britton (2007) suggested that while it makes some intuitive sense that professionals whose performance has been deemed impaired need to be 'watched', at least for a while, to ensure that remediation and rehabilitation efforts are successful, the manner in which sanctioned supervision should be carried out is still undefined. Through a focus group study they identified a number of very difficult issues associated with this circumstance:

- Sanctioned counsellors typically seek a known colleague to occupy this role which would make an honest appraisal of performance very difficult.
- If the sanctioned counsellor has taken a negative attitude to the disciplinary process, this may not be conducive to a positive orientation towards learning and development.
- The legal and professional liability of the sanctioned supervisor was questioned. What if the sanctioned counsellor were to reoffend either during or following the period of intervention?
- Typically it is sanctioned counsellors who pay for their supervision. One participant in the study offered the comment: 'You know you give me [supervisor] a check and it's hard to tell you [sanctioned counselor] "you're terrible, thank you. I don't think you should do this anymore, so you want to come next Thursday?" '
- The supervisors in this study recognised that they lacked training for the role.
- The need for firsthand information about the counsellor's practice, rather than reliance on reported work, was regarded as essential.
- The group identified a lack of clarity about what would need to be assessed and recorded in order for the counsellor to be regarded as fit to practise.
- The group engaged in a discussion of the appropriateness of the term 'sanctioned supervision'. Several participants liked the idea of using the term 'clinical monitoring' in place of sanctioned supervision. One participant expressed this very clearly: 'Supervision refers to a growth and development, and a positive thing, and yet here they [licensure board] are saying, "You're in trouble, now you have to go to supervision," which kind of destroys the whole thing.'

Before taking on such a role it would be advisable for supervisors to give full consideration to these issues, and to obtain written clarification from the professional body about the difficult but important task they are being asked to undertake.

Although this chapter has dealt with some of the challenges to supervisors generated when supervisees are struggling with their practice, the majority of supervisory relationships are rewarding and satisfactory to the participants most of the time. When there are difficulties, it is wise to bear in mind that with rare exceptions, people are doing their very best at work, and the supervisor's capability to instil confidence can make all the difference, as Otter, in Charles Kingsley's *The Water Babies*, did to Tom:

And now, by the flashes of the lightning, Tom saw a new sight – all the bottom of the stream alive with great eels, turning and twisting along, all down stream and away. They had been hiding for weeks past in the cracks of the rocks, and in burrows in the mud; and Tom had hardly ever seen them, except now and then at night; but now they were all out, and went hurrying past him so fiercely and wildly that he was quite frightened. And as they hurried past he could hear them say to each other, 'We must run, we must run. What a jolly thunderstorm! Down to the sea, down to the sea!'

And then the otter came by with all her brood, twining and sweeping along as fast as the eels themselves; and she spied Tom as she came by, and said:

> 'Now is your time, eft, if you want to see the world. Come, children, never mind those nasty eels: we shall breakfast on salmon tomorrow. Down to the sea, down to the sea!'

. . . 'Down to the sea?' said Tom; 'everything is going to the sea and I will go too. Goodbye, trout.' But the trout were so busy gobbling worms that they never turned to answer him; so that Tom was spared the pain of bidding them farewell.

(Kingsley, 1994: 78)

Chapter 15

Outcome studies of supervision

There has been a developing expectation across professions in health, education and social services in the UK that ongoing supervision throughout a professional career be mandated. Explanations for the proliferation of supervision in these settings have looked to factors such as the introduction of clinical governance. This is a mechanism 'by which organisations ensure the provision of quality clinical care by making individuals accountable for setting, maintaining and monitoring performance standards' (Department of Public Health, 1998). Davy (2002) argued that the drivers for the proliferation of supervision have been the prevailing political and social conditions, and that it merits much more critical attention through research. Some authors are sceptical about the evidence base supporting the value of the enterprise:

> In my view there is curiously little evidence, but much emotional rhetoric, supporting the value or clarifying the purposes of supervision. Even Roth and Fonagy (1996) resort to purely rhetorical support for supervision in their otherwise evidence-obsessed study. Supervision, I submit, is highly problematic terrain. And any consideration of the problems of supervision implicitly reminds us of the problems simmering throughout the entire counselling and psychotherapy enterprise.
>
> (Feltham, 2000: 21)

Methodological issues

Those attempting to seek evidence about the outcomes of supervision have adopted a wide range of methods including randomised controlled trials, satisfaction surveys, systematic reviews involving meta-analysis of a body of work and small-scale qualitative studies.

The literature is difficult to assess because some studies have failed adequately to define their terms, some have studied the process within one discipline and others across disciplines, some have attempted to link supervisor interventions with client outcomes, some have confined themselves to the study of supervisor behaviours, supervisee satisfaction and so on. Ultimately, it can be argued that effective supervision demands a causal link between supervisor interventions and client outcomes. This is a tall order.

Bernard and Goodyear (1998: 254) described a tension between rigour and relevance in supervision outcome studies, which might be exemplified by the difference between efficacy studies and effectiveness studies. According to Seligman (1995), efficacy studies of *psychotherapy* are characterised by:

- Random assignment to treatment and control conditions
- Controls are rigorous
- Treatments are manualised
- Patients are seen for a fixed number of sessions
- Target outcomes are well operationalised
- Raters and diagnosticians are blind to which group the patient belongs
- Patients meet the criteria for a single diagnosed disorder
- Patients are followed for a fixed period after termination and an assessment battery administered.

In this type of study the research protocol sets the criteria for practice in order to make it more amenable to measurement. Efficacy studies leave out the way that clinicians work in the field:

- The manner in which most clinicians work in the field is too cumbersome and convoluted to be evaluated using an efficacy study
- Therapy is not of fixed duration
- The approach is self-correcting – if one thing doesn't work the clinician tries another
- Patients who come for psychological therapy get there by active shopping around, not passive random allocation
- Patients usually have multiple problems or issues
- Concern is with improvement in general functioning, not only specific symptom alleviation.

Effectiveness studies sample treatment provided in the field. It may be argued that there are many methodological flaws. Advantages suggested are:

- Studies can be very large scale
- They sample treatment as offered in the field
- They sample those who seek out treatment
- They measure multiple outcomes
- They capture how and to whom treatment is provided and to what end.

The classical efficacy study, the randomised controlled trial, which examines a highly selected population is high in terms of internal validity but may not be representative of the general population. Observational data which is routinely collected in clinical practice may be more highly reflective of outcomes in practice. The work of Michael Lambert (Harmon *et al.*, 2007; Lambert *et al.*, 2005) and his colleagues has constructed something of a bridge between these two types of study by randomly assigning clients to control and experimental conditions while allowing clinicians to work as usual in the field.

Towards the end of the twentieth century a number of thorough and extensive reviews of supervision outcome studies were published which often raised doubts about methodology and the conceptualisation of the studies. The difficulties inherent in the studies were attributed to a number of factors:

- Supervision research has been limited by the extent to which effective therapist behaviours have been identified (Lambert and Arnold, 1987). It has been argued that progress in psychotherapy research and the advent of therapy manuals provide potential standards of therapist behaviour (Neufeldt *et al.*, 1997) which will facilitate the progression of supervision research.
- It is difficult to compare therapist behaviours across clients and even more difficult to compare therapy outcomes across clients with differing presenting problems and diagnoses (Neufeldt *et al.*, 1997).
- One oft-stated intention of supervisors is to facilitate development of their supervisees (the formative role of supervision). This implies changes in the ways practitioners conceptualise their work and interact with their clients. To obtain samples of behaviour and thinking at different points in a professional training or subsequent career is a massive undertaking. Even where change can be demonstrated, to link it specifically to supervisor interventions presents a further challenge.
- There are no adequate measures that link therapist thoughts and behaviours to therapist development, and no empirically defined models on which these could be based (Neufeldt *et al.*, 1997).
- Studies have not set about testing existing supervisory theory. This may have been hindered by a lack of common agreement about what constitutes supervisory theory.
- There is a scarcity of replication studies (Ellis and Ladany, 1997), which means that findings from one study cannot be generalised to supervision in other contexts.
- 'Supervision' and 'training' have been considered as interchangeable whereas it may be argued that training refers to the teaching of more specific skills in laboratory courses without direct client contact (Bernard and Goodyear, 1998).
- There has been a widespread reliance on satisfaction measures to assess supervision outcomes (Bernard and Goodyear, 1998). Bernard and Goodyear argued that this approach is unsatisfactory; they likened it

to asking a number of people leaving a doughnut shop whether they were satisfied with their doughnuts. Most would probably give an answer in the affirmative but their answers would be of no value in establishing the nutritional value of doughnuts. Enquiry into the shopper's view of the nutritional value, however, might yield appropriately relevant and useful information.

In order to address the balance between rigour and relevance, Milne *et al.* (2007) argued the case for an approach to reviewing the literature entitled Best Evidence Synthesis (Petticrew and Roberts, 2006). The reviewer works with whatever evidence is available, however flawed, rather than lamenting the lack of methodologically rigorous material. In this approach, studies are not excluded for lack of rigour, but those with findings based on sound methodology are given greater weight. The approach combines the meta-analytic approach of extracting quantitative information from a series of studies while taking into account study quality and relevance. It takes the perspective of reaching a richer picture of what is regarded as a high standard or good practice through critical judgement and selection.

The effects of supervision on client outcomes

Some studies have attempted directly to link client outcome with supervisory input.

Ellis and Ladany's (1997) extensive review of the supervision literature found only nine studies carried out between 1981 and 1997 that included client outcome data. Milne *et al.* (2007) reported 17 studies conducted between 1991 and 2005 that included client variables. One field study by Harkness and Hensley (1991) investigated the effects of adding client-focused supervision to what they called 'traditional' supervision which focused more on adminis-trative matters. A tentative conclusion from the data was that the addition of client-focused supervision was related to an increase in client satisfaction with the therapeutic relationship, to goal attainment and to therapist helpfulness across the therapist's case load.

A randomised controlled trial carried out by Heaven *et al.* (2006) examined the difference between two groups of clinical nurse specialists who had attended a three-day workshop on communication skills. Twenty-nine of the 61 participants were then randomised to four weeks of clinical supervision, aimed at facilitating the transfer of newly acquired skills into practice. Assessments using real and simulated patients were carried out before the course, immediately after the supervision period and three months later. Assessments with simulated patients showed that the training programme was extremely effective in changing competence in key skills, responding to patient cues and identifying patient concerns. However, only those who experienced supervision showed any evidence of transfer to the workplace in real client encounters. The nurses who participated in supervision were found significantly to increase their use of open questions, explore their patients' cues and identify more patient-related psychological concerns.

In another study (Bambling *et al.*, 2006) 127 clients with a diagnosis of major depression were assigned randomly to supervised or unsupervised therapists who provided eight sessions of problem-solving treatment. Supervised therapists were randomly assigned to either alliance skill- or alliance process-focused supervision and participated in eight supervision sessions. Both approaches to supervision were intended to enhance the therapists' working alliance with their clients. Standard measures of therapeutic alliance and symptom change were completed. The results showed a significant effect on working alliance from the first session of therapy, on symptom reduction, and on treatment retention and evaluation for both supervision conditions but there were no effect differences between the two supervision conditions.

A quasi-experimental controlled design was used to assess whether clinical supervision provided by workplace-based supervisors enhanced outcomes for mental health nurses attending a psychosocial intervention education programme and for the service users with whom they worked (Bradshaw *et al.*, 2007). Service users seen by the students in the supervised group showed significantly greater reductions in positive psychotic symptoms and total symptoms compared with those seen by students without work-based supervision. Improvements in social functioning were observed in service users treated by the students in both groups, but there was no significant difference in this outcome between the two groups. Methodological limitations included the adoption of a retrospective comparison group (the supervised group participated in education and supervision one year after those students in the control group had completed the course) and data on client outcome was collected by the nurses themselves.

Outcome research addressing the educational pyramid

The challenge of linking supervisory interventions to client outcomes derives from the multiple variables influencing clients' progress. Over one hundred published studies support the idea of the therapeutic relationship as an important predictor of final outcome, along with client variables such as readiness to change, and the availability of social supports as important mediators and moderators of recovery (Harmon *et al.*, 2007). Supervisory interventions bring about their effect through the supervisee, only one factor among the many that impact upon the client. Many studies have therefore attempted to examine individual links in a chain which runs from consultant to supervisor, supervisor to supervisee and supervisee to client. Milne (2007a) described this as an educational pyramid and reviewed 24 studies reported between 1991 and 2005 which focused on different parts of the pyramid. The studies included an overall total of 13 consultants, 72 supervisors, 499 supervisees and 711 clients. The review concluded that supervisors learn from consultancy (sample size 10, 87 per cent impact), supervisees learn from supervision (sample size 24, 79 per cent impact), and clients benefit clinically (sample size 17, 76 per cent impact).

Ellis and Ladany's (1997) extensive review of the supervision literature identified what they referred to as six cardinal inferences about supervision. These are the core premises or assumptions believed to be central to clinical supervision and supervisees. Supervisory theories were incorporated as more focused sub-inferences within these categories. The six categories identified in order of prevalence within the literature were:

1   A broad premise of supervision leading to supervisee development including theories about this.
2   Inferences about the supervisory relationship.
3   Matching of supervisees and supervisors in terms of individual differences and/or specific needs.
4   Evaluation of supervisees.
5   Relationship of supervision to client outcomes.
6   The use of measures of supervision.

They adopted a rigorous process for the inclusion or exclusion of studies in their review such as whether the study addressed supervision of individual counselling or therapy as an integral part of the research, was empirically based and published since 1981, and was focused on inferences about supervisee and/or client variables. Tentative conclusions from this comprehensive review were as follows.

Supervisee development

Much of the research around the premise of supervisee development has been conducted within the frame of developmental theories of supervision. The reviewed research was regarded as having failed to demonstrate that something called 'development' takes place over the course of supervision and that a different construct of cognitive development or cognitive complexity may be more potent.

The supervisory relationship

The consensus in the field of clinical supervision appears to be that the supervisory relationship is theorised as an important aspect of supervision process and outcome. The studies reviewed presented some evidence that the supervision relationship may be related to a number of delimited and specific processes and outcomes but it was not clear what it was about the relationship that was effective.

Matching in supervision

Studies based on Bernard's (1979) discrimination model investigated supervisory behaviours according to focus and role. There was no satisfactory evidence to the effect that supervision outcomes are related to the responsiveness of supervisors along these dimensions to supervisor needs. Studies were criticised for failing to present arguments to explain the importance of matching according to supervisees' needs and for a general lack of conceptual and methodological rigour.

Matching supervisory dyads by gender was generally not found to produce significant effects. A study by Nelson and Holloway (1990) of Masters' level counsellors suggested that female counsellors may be less encouraged and supported to assume power in supervision by both male and female supervisors. The study also suggested that female supervisees may more often defer power to female and male supervisors than do male supervisees. It was suggested that the way in which gender differences manifest themselves in supervision is subtle and highly complex.

The reviewed studies provided some evidence that 'race' may play an important part in the supervision process and outcome but the extent and nature of this were not adequately tested.

Evaluation of supervisees

The reviewers asked the question as to whether supervisees could be evaluated effectively by their supervisors. They concluded that supervisees may be evaluated primarily through a qualitative process, that perceptions of the supervisee by the supervisor may influence the evaluation, and that the most frequently used measure to aid evaluation (the Counselor Evaluation Rating Scale (Myrick and Kelly, 1971)) was seriously flawed.

Relationship of supervision to client outcomes

Ellis and Ladany reviewed a number of studies of parallel process which suggested a link between therapist–client interactions and supervisor–therapist interactions but they concluded that a link with parallel process theorising has yet to be established.

The use of measures of supervision

Ellis and Ladany were a little less critical of the measures devised to evaluate aspects of the supervision process than of other research reviewed.

Nevertheless, they recommended only two scales as meeting rigorous statistical standards and reflecting the theoretical basis from which they were compiled. These are the Relationship Inventory (Schact *et al.*, 1988) and the Role Conflict and Role Ambiguity Inventory (RCRAI) developed by Olk and Friedlander (1992). The former measure was constructed to assess 'empathy', 'congruence', 'unconditionality' and 'willingness to be known', yielding a total score termed 'quality of relationship'. It was used by supervisees to rate former supervisors according to their greatest or least contribution to therapeutic effectiveness. Ellis and Ladany suggested that this instrument may be a viable measure of most or least effective supervision.

In summary, Ellis and Ladany's wide-ranging review of the literature on supervision research reached some fairly depressing conclusions regarding the state of *reliable* knowledge about the endeavour. Other reviews have reached similar conclusions (e.g. Bogo and McKnight, 2005; Holloway and Neufeldt, 1995; Lambert and Ogles, 1997; Wheeler and Richards, 2007b). In the latter study only two of the 18 studies reviewed met the criteria to be classified as 'very good'.

In any system which has an inherent complexity (a multi-variable system) and/or where there is a significant time lag between the action of the 'input' variables or design factors and the outcomes; where various paths of causality or causal loops may pertain, then it is not suited to an analysis which is conducted on the expectation of a measurable or a clear and direct simple connection between input and outcome (Scaife, 2004, personal communication). Complex processes do not lend themselves to simple statements of linear causality. It is also important to remember that measurement typically plays a very restricted part in the achievement of outcomes – a pig is not fattened by weighing it.

The approach suggested by Milne *et al.* (2007) takes a much more optimistic position and there is evidence of increasing efforts to explore supervision outcomes in creative and original ways.

Selected large-scale studies

Beinart (2004: 48) reported a study which she carried out to test aspects of two models of the supervisory relationship propounded by Bordin (1983) and Holloway (1995). Data were collected on just under a hundred supervisory relationships involving trainee and newly qualified clinical psychologists. Supervisees were asked to rate and describe the characteristics and qualities of the supervisory relationships that had contributed most and least to their effectiveness as a clinical psychologist. The main qualities of the relationship which were reported to have contributed to effectiveness were rapport between supervisee and supervisor and the supervisee feeling supported by the supervisor. Beinart (2004) stated:

Clinical psychology supervisees described a strong preference for collaborative supervisory relationships where both parties were involved in setting the agenda and goals of supervision. A certain amount of flexibility of both approach and therapeutic model seemed to aid the collaboration. The two tasks of education and evaluation were helped if the supervisor was sensitive to the supervisee's needs, both in terms of their previous experience and stage of training and the personal impact of the work. Unlike in findings from previous studies, the wisdom and experience of the supervisor seemed less important than opportunities to observe the supervisor's work and have curious and stimulating discussions. The most important aspect of the educative code seemed to be collaborative work on formulation, which included theory–practice links. Again, flexibility was important to supervisees who found didactic supervision or inflexible adherence to models less helpful. Interestingly, the evaluative aspect of supervision was only an issue in poorer-quality supervisory relationships. Supervisees valued and appreciated feedback and challenge in good collaborative relationships, and the formal elements of evaluation did not seem to impact on this.

Beinart concluded that helpful supervisory relationships are similar to other good relationships and are based on mutual trust and respect. The setting of clear boundaries at the outset, both in terms of structure and what can be brought to supervision, was also regarded as facilitative of effective supervisory relationships.

Another large-scale study was reported by Anderson *et al.* (2000). This was a study of family therapy trainees' evaluations of their best and worst supervision experiences. The sample size was 160, representing a 51 per cent response rate. The results were consistent with those reported in Beinart's study. Factors contributing to best experiences were 'openness of the supervisory environment (open to feedback, respecting value differences)', 'communicating respect, support and encouragement', emphasis on the personal growth aspect of supervision', and 'conceptual and technical guidance and direction'. Worst experiences were characterised by 'students' weaknesses and shortcomings were emphasised', 'heavy emphasis on evaluation', 'encouraging unthinking conformity' and 'intolerance for divergent viewpoints'.

In a study of 201 nurses in the UK, Bowles and Young (1999) attempted to examine whether clinical supervision outcomes could be related to each of the three functions of supervision described in a framework of supervision by Inskipp and Proctor (1988) as Normative, Formative and Restorative. An instrument was developed to examine reported benefits and attitudes towards clinical supervision. The findings indicated that clinical supervision relationships reflected each of the three functions with no single function dominating the other two. Respondents reported obtaining greater benefits the longer they had participated in supervision. The normative function appeared to increase in salience with the greater experience of the participants.

A survey of 280 BABCP accredited cognitive behavioural psychotherapists (Townend *et al.*, 2002) indicated that satisfaction levels were high and that the ratio of time spent in supervision to therapeutic contact was, on average, higher than the recommended minimum.

Selected small-scale studies since 2000

A small-scale qualitative study carried out in 2000 by Wulf and Nelson reached similar conclusions to the larger scale studies about the importance of the supervisory relationship. This was a retrospective study of six psychologists who had been accredited for at least five years. They were asked to reflect on their pre-doctoral training experiences through the use of a semi-structured interview. A grounded theory approach was used to identify superordinate categories, the first of which was 'supervision dynamics'. Positive experiences were evidenced in the following quotes:

'He had a pretty profound impact on my clinical style, helping me to become more practical, maybe more results-oriented, less theoretical in my thinking, and less kind of ethereal and pedantic in my thinking – being more of a human being.'

'It was just a wonderful experience that really kick-started me in a lot of ways in family work. And so that's had a long-term impact. And in the context of feeling kind of beat up by a couple of these other supervisors, it was a really good experience in constructive feedback. They had good things to say about my work, and bad things to say about my work . . . I was able to really take in the constructive criticism and use it.'

Examples of negative experiences were cited thus:

'It was a bit her style to be aghast at anything that wasn't quite in its little place. . . . I still think that way of going about is really not helpful, at all, and added in a really ridiculous stress that really didn't need to be there.'

'He would tell me things that nobody would ever tell anybody, like which hand to hold out to shake hands with, stuff like that, just bizarre stuff, just very nitpicky. My sense in looking back on it was that he really could not take criticism or disagreement, and all he was dishing out was criticism and disagreement. Whenever I criticised his criticism, he would just get furious. He screamed at me a couple of times; just weird stuff.'

The authors argued that their study provided evidence in support of the findings of Worthen and McNeill (1996: 29):

> The most pivotal and crucial component of good supervision experiences that was clearly evident in every case studied was the quality of the supervisory relationship. All trainees described the supervisor as conveying an attitude that manifested empathy, a non-judgemental stance toward them, a sense of validation of affirmation, and encouragement to explore and experiment.

This is convergent with the finding that *non-confirming* supervision experiences are so potent that the memory of them remains affectively charged, even years later (Skovholt and Ronnestad, 1992).

Another small-scale study by Milne *et al.* (2003) examined a single supervisor–supervisee–client triad using a grounded theory approach to explore the extent to which themes evident in the supervisory relationship were transferred to the therapeutic relationship. The supervisee was a trainee on a diploma course in cognitive therapy. Videotaped data from 20 observed supervision and therapy sessions were examined. The data provided very strong evidence for the transfer of supervision themes to therapy.

The development of training for supervision

Historically there has been little requirement for formal training in supervision and no formal process for the recognition and development of supervisory skills, although more than 25 years ago clinical psychologists in the Trent region of the NHS in the UK were privileged to attend a three-day training laboratory devised and led by Janine Bernard. More recently, she has argued (Bernard and Goodyear, 1998: 231) that all effective supervisor training should have both didactic and experiential components. Statements listing the skills of supervision have been available for some time (e.g. Borders and Leddick, 1987). Some disciplines are starting to accredit their supervisors and to specify requirements that candidates must meet in order to be accredited. For example, the American Association for Marriage and Family Therapy (AAMFT, 1997) requires that candidates complete the following in order to be designated an 'approved supervisor':

1   Accumulate at least 3,000 post-Masters'-degree hours of clinical experience in marital and family therapy over a minimum period of three years.
2   Provide 180 hours of marital and family therapy supervision over a minimum period of 18 months.
3   Supervise at least two supervisees on a regular schedule.
4   Complete a graduate course in supervision that has didactic and interactive components.

5   Participate in 36 hours of supervision with an 'approved supervisor' over an 18-month period of time.
6   Submit a philosophy statement and a case study.

Currently various professional bodies in Europe, the USA and Australia offer or are developing opportunities for their membership to be accredited as supervisors (e.g. British Association of Counselling and Psychotherapy; British Psychological Society, Division of Clinical Psychology). Training manuals for supervisory skills are beginning to appear (Milne, 2007b). The formalisation of the training process is likely to make supervision more amenable to empirical study while qualitative studies will continue to put flesh on the bones.

Conclusions

The study of supervision outcomes in the research literature is well and thriving despite some of the criticisms voiced in systematic reviews concerning methodological limitations. These are inevitable given the complexities of the supervisor/supervisee/client relationship system. Qualitative methodologies and Best Evidence syntheses are offering constructive and creative ways forward in examining the impacts of supervision. Research efforts may be focused on any of the links in the chain between supervisors and clients. Continuing efforts have been directed towards researching the impact of supervision on supervisee self-awareness and self-reflection (Burkard *et al.*, 2006; Connor, 1999; Fowler and Chevannes, 1998; Kilkullen, 2007; Raichelson *et al.*, 1997), supervisee satisfaction (Bruijn *et al.*, 2006; Busari *et al.*, 2005; Edwards *et al.*, 2005; Ho and McConville, 2004), the impact on therapeutic skills (Alleyne and Jumaa, 2007; James *et al.*, 2008; Ogren and Jonsson, 2003; Patton and Kivlighan, 1997), confidence and self-efficacy (Cashwell and Dooley, 2001; Lehrman-Waterman and Ladany, 2001) and client outcomes.

In my experience, clinicians are increasingly welcoming supervision as a process that enables them to cope with an emotionally demanding workplace, although this is highly dependent upon the perceptions they have of the matter. Is it an entitlement or an imposition? From the point of view of the employer, participating in supervision in an active way is a clear demonstration of individuals exercising their responsibility under clinical governance. It has a place in the wider framework of activities that are designed to manage, enhance and monitor the provision of high-quality clinical services (Butterworth and Woods, 1999). But also, 'properly conducted it will ensure that standards are maintained, that interventions are appropriate, and that despite a frenetic pace of work, individuals can function therapeutically, rather than become mini bureaucrats or broken professionals distanced from the humanity of care' (Bishop, 2008).

Supervisors serve as the keepers of the faith and the mentors of the young. Theirs is a quiet profession that combines the discipline of science with the aesthetic creativity of art. They teach, inspire, cajole, and shape their students towards their own standards of professional excellence. It is a curious paradox that at their best they are the least visible.

(Alonso, 1985: 3)

Self-assessment schedule for supervisees

(adapted from Pomerantz, 1992; Wilson, 1981)

Introduction

The following Self-Assessment Schedule is designed to shape your thinking before engaging in an initial meeting with a placement supervisor. Previous experience has shown that supervisees and supervisors do not necessarily share common ideas about supervision. There is no universal supervision manual dictating formal structures or procedures other than some general guidelines and some formal course requirements. Within these constraints there is a great deal of flexibility to tailor supervision to meet the individual needs of the participants.

It is recommended that this schedule be completed as a private exercise. You may then wish to identify matters for discussion that might enable your supervisor better to understand your needs.

- Most people will already have had some experience of being supervised in a job or when undertaking research and so on. What specific activities during supervision do you recall as being particularly helpful?
- There are many different ways to offer supervision. What are the conditions that would be most helpful to you?
- What would you personally expect to gain from being supervised?
- What would you want to get from supervision but anticipate that will not be on offer? What could you do about this?
- There are a number of difficult issues that can arise in supervision. Below is a list on which to indicate issues where you expect that there may be some problems for you. Feel free to add other issues to the end of the list:

  - Having too much to do.
  - Having too little to do.
  - Having insufficient guidance as to what is required.
  - Having too little autonomy to plan and carry out your work.
  - Feeling constrained during supervision by the fact that your supervisor is also your assessor.
  - Receiving too much negative criticism during supervision.

- Receiving too little critical appraisal from your supervisor.
- Not getting enough time from your supervisor for adequate supervision.
- Being given too few opportunities to see your supervisor working.
- Being given too few opportunities to be observed working by your supervisor.
- Disagreeing with your supervisor on how to proceed with some aspects of the work.
- Disagreeing with your supervisor on how some aspects of supervision should proceed.
- Holding values concerning the role of a professional helper that seem incompatible with those of your supervisor.
- Having to cope with different styles of work and supervision from your supervisor compared to previous supervisors.
- Having to cope with different styles of work and supervision from your supervisor compared to your course tutors.
- Feeling that your supervisor is too formal with you.
- Feeling that your supervisor is too informal with you.
- Experiencing problems from having more than one supervisor during your placement.
- Add in any other issues that concern you.

- Now return to the above list and identify the two issues which seem to be the most important ones for you. What steps can be taken now to minimise the chances that these two issues will seriously interfere with your placement?
- Going into this supervisory relationship what would you consider to be your greatest strengths that you would expect your supervisor to notice? List three.
- Likewise, list three points for your development that may or may not be obvious to your supervisor. Try to be specific.
- Practitioners frequently find themselves in face-to-face contact with people labelled by society as belonging to a particular subgroup. Which subgroups make you feel uncomfortable for any reason? Do you want to do anything about this during supervision?
- What background information do you think your supervisor needs to know about you at the outset? This might include a curriculum vitae listing your relevant previous experience. What would be the best way to convey this information?
- Is there any difference between what you want out of this placement and what you feel you need from it? Be specific.
- What background information about this placement and this supervisor do you have? How does this make you feel? Is there any more information you need?

- What do you hope and expect your supervisor to focus on in supervision?
- What roles would you like your supervisor to take in relation to you and your work?
- What media of supervision would you like to experience (e.g. taped, 'live', reported)? How do you feel about these? What do you want to do about your feelings?
- Consider your feelings now about your work being evaluated at the end of placement by your supervisor. Do you have a reasonable idea of how that evaluation will be conducted? If the answer is 'no', what do you need to clarify with your supervisor?

Examples of rating scales of supervision

Manchester Clinical Supervision Scale

(Winstanley, 2000)

A 36-item measure with six factors exploring the normative, formative and restorative functions of supervision. The six scales assess 'Trust/rapport', 'Supervisor advice/support', 'Improved care/skills', 'Importance of the value of clinical supervision', 'Finding time' and 'Personal issues/reflection'.

Supervisory Styles Inventory

(Friedlander and Ward, 1984; unpublished instrument printed in Bernard and Goodyear, 1998)

A 33-item measure with seven-point rating scales. The same version may be completed by supervisors or supervisees. Each item lists a single-word descriptor of supervisor style (e.g. sensitive, affirming, creative, didactic). Subsets of scores are summed to give scores on three dimensions of 'Attractive', 'Interpersonally sensitive' and 'Task oriented'.

Supervisory Working Alliance Inventory

(Efstation et al., 1990 reprinted in Bernard and Goodyear, 1998)

There are two versions for supervisors and supervisees. A 23-item supervisor form with seven-point rating scales and a 19-item supervisee form with seven-point rating scales. The supervisor form has three scales of 'Rapport', 'Client focus' and 'Identification' scored by summing and taking the mean of subsets of items. The supervisee form has two scales of 'Rapport' and 'Client focus' scored by taking the mean of a subset of items. Includes items such as 'I encourage my trainee to talk about the work in ways that are comfortable for him/her.' 'My supervisor stays in tune with me in supervision.'

Supervisee Perceptions of Supervision

(Olk and Friedlander, 1992 reprinted in Bernard and Goodyear, 1998)

A 29-item measure with five-point scales for supervisees. Lists issues with which supervisees may have found difficulty in their current or most recent supervision. There are two scales of 'Role ambiguity' and 'Role conflict' derived by summing scores on two subsets of items. Includes items such as 'My supervisor's criteria for evaluating my work were not specific.' 'My supervisor gave me no feedback and I felt lost.'

Self-Assessment Questionnaire for Supervisors

(Hawkins and Shohet, 2006)

A 37-item questionnaire with five-point rating scales for supervisors designed to help self-identification of learning needs. Includes subscales of 'Knowledge', 'Supervision management skills', 'Supervision intervention skills', 'Capacities or qualities', 'Commitment to own ongoing development' and optional scales for group supervisors and senior organisational supervisors. There is no summing of scores.

Psychotherapy Supervisory Inventory

(Shanfield *et al.*, 1989)

Rating scales include the dimensions of 'Intellectual and experiential orientation', 'Number of clarifying and interpretive comments', 'Intensity of confrontation', 'Depth of exploration', 'Comfort and tension levels', 'Degree of focus on the therapist and on the patient', 'Verbal activity level', 'Dominance', 'Comfort and tension levels' and 'Empathy'. The measure is designed for completion by an observer.

The Supervisory Focus and Style Questionnaire

(Yager *et al.*, 1989)

A 60-item scale for supervisors that has nine scores in the areas of 'Personality' (Affection, inclusion and control), 'Supervisory focus' (Process, conceptualisation and personalisation) and 'Supervisory style' (Teaching, counselling and consultation).

Other Scales

Other scales include the Supervisor role analysis (Johnston and Gysbers, 1966), Supervisor questionnaire (Worthington and Roehlke, 1979), Trainee personal reaction scale (Holloway and Wampold, 1983), Psychotherapy supervisor development scale (Watkins *et al.*, 1995) and the Training reaction questionnaire (Berg and Stone, 1980).

Learning objectives to be addressed by introductory supervisor training programmes

British Psychological Society, Membership and Professional Training Board, Criteria for the Accreditation of Post-graduate Training Programmes in Clinical Psychology (2007)

The following are the key learning objectives for introductory supervisor training for clinical psychologists and related professions. It is recommended that clinical psychologists should attend this training one to two years post-qualification. It is also recommended that the training should be for a minimum of three days (ideally spread over time to allow for the practical application of the training). The learning objectives include knowledge, understanding and the development of key skills, attitudes and the capability to generalise and synthesise these components.

It is envisaged that training providers will use the learning objectives to develop their individual training packages. These will include specified learning outcomes tailored to each programme.

Understanding and application

1   Have knowledge of the context (including professional, ethical and legal) within which supervision is provided and an understanding of the inherent responsibility.
2   Have an understanding of the importance of modelling the professional role (e.g. managing boundaries, confidentiality, accountability).
3   Have knowledge of developmental models of learning which may have an impact on supervision.
4   Have knowledge of a number of supervision frameworks that could be used for understanding and managing the supervisory process.
5   Have an understanding of the importance of a safe environment in facilitating learning and of the factors that affect the development of a supervisory relationship.
6   Have skills and experience in developing and maintaining a supervisory alliance.
7   Have knowledge of the structure of placements including assessment

procedures at different levels of qualification up to doctorate level, and the expectations regarding the role of a supervisor.

8 Have skills and experience in contracting and negotiating with supervisees.

9 Have an understanding of the transferability of professional skills into supervision and the similarities and differences.

10 Have an understanding of the process of assessment and failure, and skills and experience in evaluating trainees.

11 Have skills and experience in the art of constructive criticism, ongoing positive feedback and negative feedback where necessary.

12 Have knowledge of the various methods to gain information and give feedback (e.g. self-report, audiotapes and videotapes, colleague and client reports).

13 Have skills and experience of using a range of supervisory approaches and methods.

14 Have knowledge of ethical issues in supervision and an understanding of how this may affect the supervisory process, including power differentials.

15 Have an understanding of the issues around difference and diversity in supervision.

16 Have an awareness of the ongoing development of supervisory skills and the need for further reflection/supervision training.

17 Have knowledge of techniques and processes to evaluate supervision, including eliciting feedback.

Attitudes (value base)

1 Respects trainees
2 Sensitive to diversity
3 Committed to empowerment of supervisees
4 Values the ethical base guiding practice
5 Believes in balancing support and challenge
6 Committed to a psychological knowledge-based approach to supervision
7 Recognises need to know own limitations
8 Supports principle of lifelong learning.

Capabilities

1 The capability to generalise and synthesise supervisory knowledge, skills and values in order to apply them in different settings and novel situations.

References

Adair, J.E. (1983). *Effective Leadership: A Self-development Model*. Aldershot: Gower Publishing.

Akamatsu, M.N. (1998). The talking oppression blues: including the experience of power/powerlessness in the teaching of 'cultural sensitivity'. In M. McGoldrick (ed.) *Re-visioning Family Therapy. Race, Culture and Gender in Clinical Practice*. London: Guilford Press.

Alderfer, C. and Lynch, B. (1987). Supervision in two dimensions. *Journal of Strategic and Systemic Therapies*, 5, 70–73.

Alleyne, J. and Jumaa, M.O. (2007). Building the capacity for evidence-based clinical nursing leadership: the role of executive co-coaching and group clinical supervision for quality patient services. *Journal of Nursing Management*, 15(2), 230–243.

Alonso, A. (1985). *The Quiet Profession: Supervisors of Psychotherapy*. New York: Macmillan.

Altfeld, D.A. (1999). An experiential group model for psychotherapy supervision. *International Journal of Group Psychotherapy*, 49, 237–254.

American Association for Counseling and Development (1988). Ethical standards (3rd revision, AACD Governing Council). *Journal of Counseling and Development*, 67, 4–8.

American Association of Directors of Psychiatric Residency Training (2005). *Psychotherapy Competency Assessment Tools*. Retrieved 2 January 2008 from: http://www.aadprt.org/training/assesment_tools/default.aspx.

American Association for Marriage and Family Therapy (1997). *AAMFT-approved Supervisors: Mentors and Teachers for the Next Generation of MFTs*. Washington, DC: American Association for Marriage and Family Therapy.

American Association for Marriage and Family Therapy (2004). *Sample Supervision Contract*. Retrieved 12 October 2007 from: 2004http://www.aamft.org/membership/approved%20supervisor/sample%20supervision%20contract.pdf.

Amundson, N.W. (1988). The use of metaphor and drawings in case conceptualisation. *Journal of Counseling and Development*, 66, 391–393.

Andersen, T. (1987). The reflecting team: dialogue and meta-dialogue in clinical work. *Family Process*, 26, 415–428.

Anderson, H. (1997). *Conversation, Language and Possibilities. A Post-modern Approach to Therapy*. New York: Basic Books.

Anderson, H. and Goolishian, H. (1988). Human systems as linguistic systems. *Family Process, 27*, 371–395.

Anderson, J.R. (1980). *Cognitive Psychology and its Implications*. San Francisco, CA: W. H. Freeman.

Anderson, L., Scrimshaw, S., Fullilove, M., Fielding, J., Normand, J., and the Task Force on Community Preventive Services (2003). Culturally competent healthcare systems: a systematic review. *American Journal of Preventative Medicine, 24*, 68–79.

Anderson, S.A., Rigazio-DiGilio, S.A. and Kunkler, K.P. (1995). Training and supervision in family therapy: current issues and future directions. *Family Relations, 44*, 489–500.

Anderson, S.A., Schlossberg, M. and Rigazio-DiGilio, S. (2000). Family therapy trainees' evaluations of their best and worst supervision experiences. *Journal of Marital and Family Therapy, 26*, 79–92.

Applebaum, R.A. and Austin, C.D. (1990). *Long-term Care Case Management: Design and Evaluation*. New York: Springer Publishing.

Armstrong, P.V. and Freeston, M.H. (2006). Conceptualising and formulating cognitive therapy supervision. In N. Tarrier (ed.) *Case Formulation in Cognitive Behaviour Therapy: The Treatment of Challenging and Complex Clinical Cases*. Hove, Sussex: Routledge.

Arnheim, R. (1969). *Visual Thinking*. London: Faber and Faber.

Arvidsson, B., Löfgren, H. and Fridlund, B. (2000). Psychiatric nurses' conceptions of how group supervision in nursing care influences their professional competence. *Journal of Nursing Management, 8*, 175–185.

Ashforth, B.E. and Humphrey, R.H. (1995). Emotion in the workplace: a reappraisal. *Human Relations, 48*(2), 97–125.

Association of American Medical Colleges (AAMC) (1999). *Communication in Medicine: Spirituality, Cultural Issues and End of Life Care*. Washington, DC: Association of American Medical Colleges.

Association of Chief Officers of Probation (ACOP) (1989). *Staff Appraisal in the Probation Service*. Wakefield: ACOP.

Astor, J. (2003). Empathy in the use of counter-transference. In J. Wiener, R. Mizen and J. Duckham (eds) *Supervising and Being Supervised: A Practice in Search of a Theory*. Basingstoke: Palgrave Macmillan.

Aten, J.D. and Hernandez, B.C. (2004). Addressing religion in clinical supervision: a model. *Psychotherapy: Theory, Research, Practice, Training, 41*(2), 152–160.

Atkinson, D., Morten, G. and Sue, D.W. (1989). *Counselling American Minorities: A Cross-cultural Perspective*. Dubuque, IA: William C. Brown.

Aveline, M. (1997). The use of audiotapes in supervision of psychotherapy. In G. Shipton (ed.) *Supervision of Psychotherapy and Counselling*. Buckingham: Open University Press.

Ayvazian, A. (1995). Interrupting the cycle of oppression: the role of allies as agents of change. *Smith College School of Social Work Journal, 13*, 17–20.

Baldwin, S. and Barker, P.J. (1991). Putting the service to rights. In P.J. Barker and S. Baldwin (eds) *Ethical Issues in Mental Health*. London: Chapman & Hall.

Bambling, M., King, R., Raue, P., Schweitzer, R. and Lambert, W. (2006). Clinical supervision: its influence on client-rated working alliance and client symptom reduction in the brief treatment of major depression. *Psychotherapy Research, 16*(3), 317–331.

Banks, S. (1998). Professional ethics in social work: what future?, *British Journal of Social Work*, *28*, 213–231.

Barnat, M.R. (1977). Spontaneous supervisory metaphor in the resolution of trainee anxiety. *Professional Psychology*, *8*, 307–315.

Barnes, L.H. and Pilowsky, I. (1969). Psychiatric patients and closed-circuit television teaching: a study of their reactions. *British Journal of Medical Education*, *3*, 58–61.

Barrett, M.S. and Barber, J.P. (2005). A developmental approach to the supervision of therapists in training. *Journal of Contemporary Psychotherapy*, *35*, 169–183.

Bauman, W.F. (1972). Games counselor trainees play: dealing with trainee resistance. *Counselor Education and Supervision*, *11*, 251–256.

Baumann, Z. (1993). *Post-modern ethics*. Oxford: Blackwell.

Beach, M.C., Cooper, L.A., Robinson, K.A., Price, E.G., Gary, T.L., Jenckes, M.W., Gozu, A., Smarth, C., Palacio, A., Feversein, C.J., Bass, E.B. and Powe, N.R. (2004). *Strategies for Improving Minority Healthcare Quality. Evidence Report/Technology Assessment No. 90*. (Prepared by Johns Hopkins University Evidence-based Practice Center, Baltimore, MD.) AHRQ Publication No. 04-E008–02. Rockville, MD: Agency for Healthcare Research and Quality.

Beauchamp, T.L. and Childress, J.F. (2001). *Principles of Biomedical Ethics* (5th edn). Oxford: Oxford University Press.

Beck, A.T. (1988). *Love is Never Enough*. New York: Harper & Row.

Beck, J.S. (1995). *Cognitive Therapy: Basics and Beyond*. New York: Guilford Press.

Bégat, I.B.E., Severinsson, E.I. and Berggren, I.B. (1997). Implementation of clinical supervision in a medical department: nurses' views of the effects. *Journal of Clinical Nursing*, *6*, 389–394.

Behnke, S.H. and Kinscherff, R. (2002). Confidentiality in the treatment of adolescents. *Monitor on Psychology*, *33*, 44–45.

Beinart, H. (2004). Models of supervision and the supervisory relationship and their evidence base. In I. Fleming and L. Steen (eds) *Supervision and Clinical Psychology*. Hove: Brunner-Routledge.

Bell, M. (2001). A case study of an online role play for academic staff. *Australian Society for Computers in Learning in Tertiary Education*. Retrieved 30 July 2007 from: http://www.ascilite.org.au/conferences/melbourne01/pdf/papers/bellm.pdf.

Bell, M. and Sinclair, I. (1993). *Parental Involvement in Initial Child Protection Conferences in Leeds: An External Evaluation*. York: University of York, Department of Social Policy and Social Work.

Bennett, J. (2007). The struggle for 'cultural competence'. *Guardian*, 12 April 2006. Accessed 8 August 2007 from: http://society.guardian.co.uk/publicfinances/story/0,,1751529,00.html.

Bennett S., Plint, A. and Clifford, T.J. (2005). Burnout, psychological morbidity, job satisfaction, and stress: a survey of Canadian hospital based child protection professionals. *Archives of Diseases in Childhood*, *90*, 1112–1116.

Berg, A. and Hallberg, I.R. (1999). Effects of systematic clinical supervision on psychiatric nurses' sense of coherence, creativity, work-related strain, job satisfaction and view of the effects from clinical supervision: a pre-post test design. *Journal of Psychiatric and Mental Health Nursing*, *6*, 371–381.

Berg, K.S. and Stone, G.L. (1980). Effects of conceptual level and supervision structure on counselor skill development. *Journal of Counseling Psychology*, *27*, 500–509.

Berger, M.M. (ed.) (1978). *Videotape Techniques in Psychiatric Training and Treatment*. New York: Brunner/Mazel.

Berger, M. and Dammann, C. (1982). Live supervision as context, treatment and training. *Family Process*, *21*, 337–344.

Berman, E. (2000). Psychoanalytic supervision: the intersubjective development. *International Journal of Psychoanalysis*, *81*, 273–290.

Bernard, J.M. (1979). Supervisor training: a discrimination model. *Counselor Education and Supervision*, *19*, 60–68.

Bernard, J.M. (1981). In-service training for clinical supervisors. *Professional Psychology*, *126*, 740–748.

Bernard, J.M. (1989). Training supervisors to examine relationship variables using IPR. *The Clinical Supervisor*, *7*, 103–112.

Bernard, J.M. and Goodyear, R.K. (1992). *Fundamentals of Clinical Supervision*. Boston, MA: Allyn & Bacon.

Bernard, J.M. and Goodyear, R.K. (1998). *Fundamentals of Clinical Supervision* (2nd edn). Boston, MA: Allyn & Bacon.

Bernard, J.M. and O'Laughlin, D.L. (1990). Confidentiality: do training clinics take it seriously? *Law and Psychology Review*, *14*, 59–69.

Bhugra, D. and De Silva, P. (2007). The silver screen, printed page and cultural competence. *The Psychologist*, *20*(9), 528–540.

Bickhard, M. (1995). World mirroring versus world making: there's gotta be a better way. In L.P. Steffe and J. Gale (eds) *Constructivism in Education*. Hove: Lawrence Erlbaum Associates.

Binder, J.L. (2004). *Key Competencies in Brief Dynamic Psychotherapy: Clinical Practice Beyond the Manual*. New York: Guilford Press.

Binder, J.L. and Strupp, H.H. (1997). Supervision of psychodynamic psychotherapies. In C.E. Watkins, Jr. (ed.) *Handbook of Psychotherapy Supervision*. New York: John Wiley & Sons.

Bion, W.R. ([1961] 1974). *Experiences in Groups and Other Papers*. New York: Ballantine.

Bishop, V. (2008). Clinical governance and clinical supervision: protecting standards of care. *Journal of Research in Nursing*, *13*(3), 3–5.

Blackburn, I.M., James, I.A., Milne, D.L., Baker, C., Standart, S., Garland, A. and Reichelt, F. (2001). The revised Cognitive Therapy Scale (CTS-R): psychometric properties. *Behavioural and Cognitive Psychotherapy*, *29*, 431–446.

Blake, R.R., Mouton, J.S. and Bidwell, A.C. (1962). The managerial grid. *Advanced Management Office Executive*, *1*(9), 12–15.

Blotzner, M.A. and Ruth, R. (1995). *Sometimes You Just Want to Feel Like a Human Being*. Baltimore, MD: Paul H. Brookes Publishing.

Bogo, M. and McKnight, K. (2005). Clinical supervision in social work: a review of the research literature. *Clinical Supervisor*, *24*(1–2), 49–67.

Bolton, G. (2001). *Reflective Practice*. London: Paul Chapman.

Bolton, G. (2005). *Reflective Practice* (2nd edn). London: Sage.

Boltuch, B.S. (1975). The effects of a pre-practicum skill training program: influencing human interaction: on development of counselor effectiveness in a Master's level practicum. Unpublished doctoral dissertation, New York University. Reported in N. Kagan (1984). 'Interpersonal process recall: basic methods and recent research.' In D. Larson (ed.) *Teaching Psychological Skills*. Monterey, CA: Brooks/Cole.

Bond, T. (2000). *Standards and Ethics for Counselling in Action* (2nd edn). London: Sage.

Bonney, W. (1994). Teaching supervision: some practical issues for beginning supervisors. *The Psychotherapy Bulletin, 29*, 331–336.

Borders, L.D. and Leddick, G.R. (1987). *Handbook of Counseling Supervision.* Alexandria, VA: American Association for Counseling and Development.

Bordin, E.S. (1979). The generalizability of the psychodynamic concept of the working alliance. *Psychotherapy: Theory, Research and Practice, 16*, 252–260.

Bordin, E.S. (1983). A working alliance model of supervision. *Counseling Psychologist, 11*, 35–42.

Boud, D., Keogh, R. and Walker, D. (eds) (1985). *Reflection: Turning Experience into Learning.* London: Kogan Page.

Boudreaux, C.T. (2001). Psychologist disclosures of client information to significant others. *Dissertation Abstracts International, 62*, 1566.

Bowers, B. (1995). *Best Practice in Wisconsin's Long-term Support Network.* Wisconsin: Policy paper for Wisconsin's Bureau of Long-term Support, Division of Community Services, Department of Health and Social Services. Retrieved 11 October 2007 from: http://dhfs.wisconsin.gov/WIpartnership/pdf-wpp/appc.pdf.

Bowers, B., Esmond, S. and Canales, M. (1999). Approaches to case management supervision. *Administration in Social Work, 23*, 29–49.

Bowles, N. and Young, C. (1999). An evaluative study of clinical supervision based on Proctor's three function interactive model. *Journal of Advanced Nursing, 30*, 958–964.

Bradby, H. (2003). Describing ethnicity in health research. *Ethnicity and Health, 8*, 5–13.

Bradley, I. (ed.) (1989). *Counselor Supervision: Principles, Process and Practice.* Muncie, IN: Accelerated Development Inc.

Bradshaw, T., Butterworth, A. and Mairs, H. (2007). Does structured clinical supervision during psychosocial intervention education enhance outcome for mental health nurses and the service users they work with? *Journal of Psychiatric and Mental Health Nursing, 14*, 4–12.

Bridge, P. and Bascue, L.O. (1990). Documentation of psychotherapy supervision. *Psychotherapy in Private Practice, 8*, 79–86.

British Association for Behavioural and Cognitive Psychotherapies (BABCP) (2005). *Mapping Psychotherapy – What is CBT? What are Cognitive and/or Behavioural Psychotherapies?* Retrieved 20 January 2008 from: http://www.babcp.org.uk/babcp/WhatisCBT-Aug2005.pdf.

British Association for Counselling and Psychotherapy (1996). *What is Supervision? Information Sheet 6.* Rugby: BACP.

British Association for Counselling and Psychotherapy (n.d.). *Ethical Framework for Good Practice in Counselling and Psychotherapy.* Retrieved 19 January 2007 from http://www.bacp.co.uk/ethical_framework/.

British Psychological Society (BPS) (1995). *Professional Practice Guidelines, Division of Clinical Psychology.* Leicester: BPS, 27–28.

British Psychological Society (BPS) (1998a). *Guidelines for Clinical Psychology Services, Division of Clinical Psychology.* Leicester: BPS, 18–23.

British Psychological Society (BPS) (1998b). *Responsibility and Accountability in*

Clinical Psychology: Professional Practice and Multidisciplinary Teamwork. Leicester: BPS.

British Psychological Society (2002). *Criteria for the Accreditation of Postgraduate Training Programmes in Clinical Psychology.* Retrieved 23 January 2007 from: http://www.bps.org.uk/careers/committee-on-training-in-clinical-psychology-guidance-documents/committee-on-training-in-clinical-psychology-guidance-documents_home.cfm.

British Psychological Society (BPS) (2007a). *Generic Professional Practice Guidelines.* Leicester: BPS.

British Psychological Society (2007b). Membership and Professional Training Board. *Criteria for the Accreditation of Postgraduate Training Programmes in Clinical Psychology.* Retrieved 20 January 2008 from: http://www.bps.org.uk/download file.cfm?file_uuid=48516386-1143-DFD0-7E99-DBB0AE131B71&ext=pdf.

Brookfield, S.D. (1986). *Understanding and Facilitating Adult Learning.* Buckingham: Open University Press.

Brookfield, S.D. (1995). *Becoming a Critically Reflective Teacher.* San Francisco, CA: Jossey-Bass.

Brown, T.L., Acevedo-Polakovich, I.D. and Smith, A.M. (2006). Cross-cultural issues affecting the supervisory relationship in counseling children and families. In T. Kerby-Neill (ed.) *Helping Others Help Children.* Washington, DC: American Psychological Association.

Bruijn, M., Busari, J.O. and Wolf, B.H.M. (2006). Quality supervision as perceived by specialist registrars in a university and district teaching hospital. *Medical Education, 40,* 1002–1008.

Burck, C. and Campbell, D. (2002). Training systemic supervisors: multi-layered learning. In D. Campbell and B. Mason (eds) *Perspectives on Supervision.* London: Karnac.

Burkard, A.W., Johnson, A.J., Madson, M.B., Pruitt, N.T., Contreras-Tadych, D.A., Kozlowski, J.M., Hess, S.A. and Knox, S. (2006). Supervisor cultural responsiveness and unresponsiveness in cross-cultural supervision. *Journal of Counseling Psychology, 53,* 288–301.

Burnham, J. (1986). *Family Therapy. First Steps Towards a Systemic Approach.* London: Tavistock.

Burnham, J. (1993). Systemic supervision: the evolution of reflexivity in the context of the supervisor relationship. *Human Systems, 4,* 349–381.

Burnham, J. (2000). Internalised other interviewing: evaluating and enhancing empathy. *Clinical Psychology Forum, 140,* 16–20.

Busari, J.O., Weggelaar, N.M., Knottnerus, A.C., Greidanus, P-M. and Scherpbier, A.J.J.A. (2005). How medical residents perceive the quality of supervision provided by attending doctors in the clinical setting. *Medical Education, 39,* 696–703.

Butler, C. (2004). An awareness-raising tool addressing lesbian and gay lives. *Clinical Psychology Forum, 36,* 15–17.

Butler, S.F. and Strupp, H.H. (1986). Specific and nonspecific factors in psychotherapy: a problematic paradigm for psychotherapy research. *Psychotherapy, 23,* 30–40.

Butterworth, C.A. and Woods, D. (1999). *Clinical Governance and Clinical Supervision: Working Together to Ensure Safe and Accountable Practice.* Manchester: University of Manchester.

Butterworth, T. (1992). Clinical supervision as an emerging idea in nursing. In T. Butterworth and J. Faugien (eds) *Clinical Supervision and Mentorship in Nursing*. London: Chapman & Hall.

Butzlaff, R.L. and Hooley, J.M. (1998). Expressed emotion and psychiatric relapse. *Archives of General Psychiatry*, *55*(6), 547–552.

Byng-Hall, J. (1982). The use of the earphone in supervision. In R. Whiffen and J. Byng-Hall (eds) *Family Therapy Supervision: Recent Developments in Practice*. London: Academic Press.

Byng-Hall, J. (1995). *Rewriting Family Scripts*. New York: Guilford Press.

Caligor, L. (1984). Parallel and reciprocal processes in psychoanalytic supervision. In L. Caligor, P.M. Bromberg and J.D. Meltzer (eds) *Clinical Perspectives on the Supervision of Psychoanalysis and Psychotherapy*. New York: Plenum.

Campbell, J.M. (2000). *Becoming an Effective Supervisor: A Workbook for Counselors and Psychotherapists*. Philadelphia, PA: Accelerated Development (Taylor & Francis).

Capodanno, K.H. (1998). *The effects of countertransference on the therapist treating borderline personality disorder: a review of the literature*. Doctoral dissertation, Biola University. Retrieved 2 January 2008 from: http://www.eric.ed.gov/ERICDocs/data/ericdocs2sql/content_storage_01/0000019b/80/15/b9/62.pdf.

Carey, J.C., Williams, K.S. and Wells, M. (1988). Relationships between dimensions of supervisors' influence and counselor trainees' performance. *Counselor Education and Supervision*, *28*, 130–139.

Carkhuff, R.R. (1969). *Helping and Human Relations* (Vols 1 and 2). New York: Rinehart & Winston.

Carkhuff, R.R. and Anthony, W.A. (1979). *The Skills of Helping: An Introduction to Counseling*. Amherst, MA: Human Resource Development Press.

Carroll, L. (1872). *Through the Looking Glass and What Alice Found There*. John Tenniell. Retrieved 9 September 2007 from: www.jabberwocky.com/carroll/jabber/jabberwocky.html.

Carroll, M. (1996). *Counselling Supervision: Theory, Skills and Practice*. London: Cassell.

Carroll, M. and Gilbert, M.C. (2005). *On Being a Supervisee: Creating Learning Partnerships*. London: Vukani.

Casement, P. (1985). *On Learning From the Patient*. London: Routledge.

Casement, P. (1990). *Further Learning From the Patient*. London: Routledge.

Cashwell, T.H. and Dooley, K. (2001). The impact of supervision on counselor self-efficacy. *Clinical Supervisor Special Issue*, *20*(1), 39–47.

Catcliffe, J.R. and Lowe, L. (2005). A comparison of North American and European conceptualisations of clinical supervision. *Issues in Mental Health Nursing*, *26*, 475–488.

Cecchin, G. (1987). Hypothesising, circularity, and neutrality revisited: an invitation to curiosity. *Family Process*, *26*, 405–413.

Chambers, M. and Cutcliffe, J.J.R. (2001). The dynamics and processes of 'ending' in clinical supervision. *British Journal of Nursing*, 10(21), 1403–1411.

Champe, J. and Kleist, D.M. (2003). Live supervision: a review of the research. *The Family Journal*, *11*, 268–275.

Christensen, T.M. and Kline, W.B. (2001). Anxiety as a condition for learning in group supervision. *Journal for Specialists in Group Work*, *26*, 385–396.

Clark, J.J. and Croney, E.L. (2006). Ethics and accountability in supervision of child psychotherapy. In T. Kerby Neill (ed.) *Helping Others Help Children: Clinical Supervision of Child Psychotherapy*. Washington, DC: American Psychological Association.

Clarke, P. (1997). Interpersonal process recall in supervision. In G. Shipton (ed.) *Supervision of Psychotherapy and Counselling*. Buckingham: Open University Press.

Cloke, C. and Davies, M. (eds) (1995). *Participation and Empowerment in Child Protection*. London: Pitman.

Clouder, L. and Sellars, J. (2004). Reflective practice and clinical supervision: an inter-professional perspective. *Journal of Advanced Nursing, 46*, 262–269.

Coaching and Mentoring Network (n.d.). *Coach and Mentor Definitions*. Retrieved 19 December 2006 from http://www.coachingnetwork.org.uk/ResourceCentre/WhatAre CoachingAndMentoring.htm.

Cobia, D.C. and Pipes, R.B. (2002). Mandated supervision: an intervention for disciplined professionals. *Journal of Counseling and Development, 80*, 140–144.

Cogan, M.L. (1973) *Clinical Supervision*. Boston, MA: Houghton Mifflin Co.

Connor, M. (1999). Training and supervision make a difference. In C. Feltham (ed.) *Controversies in Psychotherapy and Counselling*. London: Sage.

Constantine, M. (1997). Facilitating multicultural competency in counseling supervision: operationalizing a practical framework. In D.B. Pope-Davis and H.L.K. Coleman (eds) *Multicultural Counseling Competencies: Assessment, Education and Training, and Supervision*. Thousand Oaks, CA: Sage.

Constantine, M.G. and Ladany, N. (2001). New visions for assessing multicultural counseling competence. In J.G. Ponterotto, J.M. Casas, L.A. Suzuki and C.M. Alexander (eds) *Handbook of Multicultural Counseling* (2nd edn). Thousand Oaks, CA: Sage.

Cook, D.A. (1994). Racial identity in supervision. *Counselor Education and Supervision, 34*, 132–141.

Corey, G., Corey, M.S. and Callanan, P. (1993). *Issues and Ethics in the Helping Professions* (4th edn). Pacific Grove, CA: Brooks/Cole.

Costa, L. (1994). Reducing anxiety in live supervision. *Counselor Education and Supervision, 34*, 30–40.

Cott, C. (1998). Structure and meaning in multidisciplinary teamwork. *Sociology of Health and Illness, 20*, 848–873.

Cottrell, D., Kilminster, S., Jolly, B. and Grant, J. (2002). What is effective supervision and how does it happen? A critical incident study. *Medical Education, 36*, 1042–1049.

Coulshed, V. (1990). Soapbox. *Social Work Today*, 11 October, 42.

Coursol, D.H. and Lewis, J. (2000). Cybersupervision: close encounters in the new millennium. *Cybercounseling, 1–12*. Retrieved 8 August 2007 from: http://cybercounseling.uncg.edu/manuscripts/cybersupervision.htm.

Covner, B.J. (1942). Studies in phonographic recordings of verbal material. I: The use of phonographic recordings in counseling practice and research. *Journal of Consulting Psychology, 6*, 105–113.

Cross, M.C. and Papadopoulos, L. (2001). *Becoming a Therapist: A Manual for Personal and Professional Development*. Hove, East Sussex: Brunner-Routledge.

Cutcliffe, J.R. (2000). To record or not to record: documentation in clinical super-vision. *British Journal of Nursing, 19*(6), 350–355.

Cutcliffe, J.R. (2005). From the guest editor – clinical supervision: a search for homo-geneity or heterogeneity? *Issues in Mental Health Nursing, 26,* 471–473.

Cutcliffe, J.R. and Lowe, L. (2005). A comparison of North American and European conceptualisations of clinical supervision. *Issues in Mental Health Nursing, 26,* 475–488.

Cutcliffe, J.R., Butterworth, T. and Proctor, B. (2001). Introduction: Fundamental themes in clinical supervision – national and international perspectives of educa-tion, policy, research and practice. In J.R. Cutcliffe, T. Butterworth and B. Proctor (eds) *Fundamental Themes in Clinical Supervision.* London: Routledge.

Czander, W.M. (1993). *The Psychodynamics of Work and Organizations: Theory and Application.* New York: Guilford Press.

Daniels, J. (2000). Whispers in the corridors and kangaroo courts: the supervisory role in mistakes and complaints. In B. Lawton and C. Feltham (eds) *Taking Super-vision Forward: Enquiries and Trends in Counselling and Psychotherapy.* London: Sage.

Daniels, J. and Feltham, C. (2004). Reflective and therapeutic writing in counsellor training. In G. Bolton, S. Howlett, C. Lago and J.K. Wright (eds) *Writing Cures: An introductory handbook of writing in counselling and therapy.* Hove: Brunner-Routledge.

Davenport, D.S. (1992). Ethical and legal problems with client-centred supervision. *Counselor Education and Supervision, 31,* 227–231.

Davies, F. (2007). Personal communication.

Davies, J. and Coleman, B.A. (1999). Peer consultation – more than just a trip to the pub? *Clinical Psychology Forum, 131,* 13–16.

Davy, J. (2002). Discursive reflections on a research agenda for clinical supervision. *Psychology and Psychotherapy, 75,* 221–238.

Deacon, S. (2000). Using divergent thinking exercises within supervision to enhance therapist creativity. *Journal of Family Psychotherapy, 11,* 67–73.

Dean, J.E. (2001). Sandtray consultation: a method of supervision applied to couple's therapy. *The Arts in Psychotherapy, 28*(3), 175–180.

De Bono, E. (2007). *How to Have Creative Ideas: 62 Exercises to Develop the Mind.* London: Vermilion.

Dennett, D.C. (1993). *Consciousness Explained.* London: Penguin Science.

Department of Health (1993). *A Vision for the Future: Report of the Chief Nursing Officer.* London: DOH.

Department of Health (2000). *Making a Difference: Clinical Supervision in Primary Care.* London: DOH.

Department of Health (2007). Improving access to psychological therapies (IAPT) programme: computerised cognitive behavioural therapy (cCBT) implementation guidance. Retrieved 15 October 2007 from http://www.dh.gov.uk/en/Publications andstatistics/Publications/PublicationsPolicyAndGuidance/DH_073470.

Department of Psychology, University of Calgary (2005). *Art, Vision and the Dis-ordered Eye.* Retrieved 3 February 2007 from: http://www.psych.ucalgary.ca/ PACE/VA-Lab/AVDE-Website/monet.html.

Department of Public Health (1998). *Clinical Governance in North Thames: A Paper for Discussion and Consultation.* London: NHSE North Thames Regional Office.

Despenser, S. (2004). Case notes in private practice. *Counselling and Psychotherapy Journal*. Retrieved 5 January 2008 from: http://www.bacp.co.uk/cpj/jul2004/cover_feature2.htm.

Dewald, P.A. (1997). The process of supervision in psychoanalysis. In C.E. Watkins Jr. (ed.) *Handbook of Psychotherapy Supervision*. New York: John Wiley & Sons.

Disney, M.J. and Stephens, A.M. (1994). *Legal Issues in Clinical Supervision*. Alexandria, VA: American Counseling Association.

Divac, A. and Heaphy, G. (2005). Space for GRRAACCES: training for cultural competence in supervision. *Journal of Family Therapy*, *27*, 280–284.

Dodenhoff, J.T. (1981). Interpersonal attraction and direct-indirect supervisor influence as predictors of counselor trainee effectiveness. *Journal of Counseling Psychology*, *28*, 47–62.

Dodge, J. (1982). Reducing supervisee anxiety: a cognitive-behavioural approach. *Counselor Education and Supervision*, *22*, 55–60.

Doehrman, M.J.G. (1976). Parallel processes in supervision and psychotherapy. *Bulletin of the Menninger Clinic*, *40*, 9–104.

Dogra, N. and Karim, K. (2005). Training in diversity for psychiatrists. *Advances in Psychiatric Treatment*, *11*, 159–167.

Dogra, N., Vostanis, P., Abuateya, H. and Jewson, N. (2007). Children's mental health services and ethnic diversity: Gujurati families' perspectives of service provision for mental health problems. *Transcultural Psychiatry*, *44*, 275–291.

Donaldson, M. (1978). *Children's Minds*. London: Fontana.

Duan, C. and Roehlke, H. (2001). A descriptive 'snapshot' of cross-racial supervision in university counseling center internships. *Journal of Multicultural Counseling and Development*, *29*, 131–146.

Dudley, E. (1988). Ethical complaints against family therapists submitted to the AAMFT Ethics Committee. Paper presented at the National Meeting of the American Association of Marriage and Family Therapists, New Orleans, LA. Reported in L.C. Baker and J.E. Patterson (1990). The first to know: a systemic analysis of confidentiality and the therapist's family. *The American Journal of Family Therapy*, *18*, 295–300.

Dwyer, T.F. (1999). Barging in. In R.E. Lee and S. Emerson (eds) *The Eclectic Trainer*. Galena, IL: Geist & Russell.

Eberle, B. (1997). *Scamper On: More Creative Games and Activities for Imagination Development*. Austin, TX: Prufrock Press.

Eckler-Hart, A. (1987). True self and false self in the development of the psychotherapist. *Psychotherapy*, *24*, 683–692.

Edelman, G.M. and Tononi, G. (2000). *Consciousness: How Matter Becomes Imagination*. London: Penguin.

Eder, R.W. and Ferris, G.R. (eds) (1989). *The Employment Interview: Theory, Research and Practice*. Thousand Oaks, CA: Sage.

Edwards, D., Cooper, L., Burnard, P., Hanningan, B., Adams, J., Fothergill, A. and Coyle, D. (2005). Factors influencing the effectiveness of clinical supervision. *Journal of Psychiatric and Mental Health Nursing*, *12*, 405–414.

Efstation, J.F., Patton, M.J. and Kardash, C.M. (1990). Measuring the working alliance in counselor supervision. *Journal of Counseling Psychology*, *37*, 322–329.

Egan, G. (1976). *Interpersonal Living: A Skills–Contract Approach to Human Relations Training in Groups*. Pacific Grove, CA: Brooks/Cole.

Egan, G. (1994). *The Skilled Helper* (5th edn). Monterey, CA: Brooks/Cole.

Egan, G. (2002). *The Skilled Helper* (7th edn). Monterey, CA: Brooks/Cole.

Ehrencrona, A. (2002). *The History of Sexuality by Michael Foucault.* Retrieved 18 February 2002 from: andreas.ehrencrona@home.se. (Also available as: Author unknown (n.d.) The history of sexuality – About Foucault. Retrieved 13 June 2008 from: http://www.ipce.info/ipceweb/Library/history_of_sexuality.htm).

Ekstein, R. and Wallerstein, R.S. (1972). *The Teaching and Learning of Psychotherapy* (2nd edn). New York: International Universities Press Inc.

Eleftheriadou, Z. (1997). Cultural differences in the therapeutic process. In I. Horton, E. van Deurzen and V. Varma (eds) *The Needs of Counsellors and Psychotherapists: Emotional, Social, Physical, Professional.* London: Sage.

Elliott, R. (1986). Interpersonal Process Recall (IPR) as a psychotherapeutic process research method. In L.S. Greenberg and W.M. Pinsof (eds) *The Psychotherapeutic Process: A Research Handbook.* New York: Guilford Press.

Ellis, A. and Dryden, W. (1987). *The Practice of Rational–Emotive Therapy (RET).* New York: Springer.

Ellis, A. and Grieger, R. (1986). *Handbook of Rational Emotive Therapy.* New York: Springer.

Ellis, M.V. and Ladany, N. (1997). Inferences concerning supervisees and clients in clinical supervision: an integrative review. In C.E. Watkins, Jr. (ed.) *Handbook of Psychotherapy Supervision.* New York: Wiley.

Elman, N.S. and Forrest, L. (2007). From trainee impairment to professional competence problems: seeking new terminology that facilitates effective action. *Professional Psychology: Research & Practice*, *38*(5), 501–509.

Engel, A., House, R., Pearson, C. and Sluman, S. (1998). Report of a supervisors' workshop. *Training Link*, *28*, 1–2. Sheffield: University of Sheffield.

Engleberg, S. and Storm, C.L. (1990). Supervising defensively: advice from legal counsel. *Supervision Bulletin*, *3*, 24.

Entwistle, N.J. (1981). *Styles of Teaching and Learning.* Chichester: Wiley.

Epston, D. (1993). Internalised other questioning with couples: the New Zealand version. In S. Gilligan and R. Price (eds) *Therapeutic Conversations.* New York: W.W. Norton.

Errek, H. and Randolph, D. (1982). Effects of discussion and role-playing activities in the acquisition of consultant interview skills. *Journal of Counseling Psychology*, *29*, 304–308.

Falender, C.A. and Shafranske, E.P. (2004). *Clinical Supervision: A Competency-based Approach.* Washington, DC: American Psychological Association.

Falender, C.A. and Shafranske, E.P. (2007). Competence in competency-based supervision practice: construct and application. *Professional Psychology, Research and Practice*, *38*(3), 232–240.

Falvey, J.E. (2002). *Managing Clinical Supervision: Ethical Practice and Legal Risk Management.* Pacific Grove, CA: Brooks/Cole.

Falvey, J.E. (2004). The buck stops here: documenting clinical supervision. *The Clinical Supervisor*, *22*, 63–80.

Falvey, J.E., Caldwell, C.F. and Cohen, C.R. (1996). *Focused Risk Management Supervisory System (FoRMSS).* Unpublished document.

Faulks, S. (2005). *Human Traces.* London: Hutchinson.

Feasey, D. (2002). *Good Practice in Supervision with Psychotherapists and Counsellors.* London: Whurr.

Feltham, C. (2000). Counselling supervision: baselines, problems and possibilities. In B. Lawton and C. Feltham (eds) *Taking Supervision Forward.* London: Sage.

Fiedler, F.A. (1950). A comparison of therapeutic relationships in psychoanalytic, non-directive and Adlerian therapy. *Journal of Consulting Psychology, 14,* 436–445.

Fiedler, F.A. (1951). Factor analyses of psychoanalytic, non-directive and Adlerian therapeutic relationships. *Journal of Consulting Psychology, 15,* 32–38.

Figley, C.R. (1995). *Compassion Fatigue: Coping with Secondary Traumatic Stress Disorder in Those Who Treat the Traumatized.* New York: Brunner-Mazel.

Figley, C.R. (ed.) (2002). *Treating Compassion Fatigue.* New York: Brunner-Routledge.

Fine, M., Ibrahim, S. and Thomas, S. (2005). The role of race and genetics in health disparities research. *American Journal of Public Health, 95,* 2125–2127.

Fish, D. and de Cossart, L. (2006). Thinking outside the (tick) box: rescuing professionalism and professional judgement. *Medical Education, 40,* 404–406.

Fish, D. and Twinn, S. (1997). *Quality Clinical Supervision in the Health Care Professions.* Edinburgh: Butterworth Heinemann.

Fitch, T.J. and Marshall, J.L. (2002). Using cognitive interventions with counseling practicum students during group supervision. *Counselor Education and Supervision, 41,* 335–342.

Flannery-Schroeder, E. (2005). Treatment integrity: implications for training. *Clinical Psychology: Science and Practice, 12,* 388–390.

Fleming, I., Gone, R., Diver, A. and Fowler, B. (2007). Risk supervision in Rochdale. *Clinical Psychology Forum, 176,* 22–25.

Flemons, D.G., Green, S.K. and Rambo, A. (1996). Evaluating therapists' practices in a postmodern world: a discussion and a scheme. *Family Process, 35,* 43–56.

Follette, W.C. and Callaghan, G.M. (1995). Do as I do, not as I say: a behavior-analytic approach to supervision. *Professional Psychology: Research & Practice, 26*(4), 413–421.

Ford, N. (1985). Learning styles and strategies of postgraduate students. *British Journal of Educational Technology, 2*(16), 65–77.

Fordham, A.S., May, B., Boyle, M., Bentall, R.P. and Slade, P. (1990). Good and bad clinicians: supervisors' judgements of trainees' competence. *British Journal of Clinical Psychology, 29,* 113–114.

Forrest, L., Elman, N., Gizara, S. and Vacha-Haase, T. (1999). Trainee impairment: a review of identification, remediation, dismissal and legal issues. *The Counseling Psychologist, 27,* 627–686.

Fotaki, M. (2006). Choice is yours: a psychodynamic exploration of health policy-making and its consequences for the English National Health Service. *Human Relations, 59*(12), 1711–1744.

Fournier, V. (2000). Boundary work and the (un-)making of the professions. In N. Malin (ed.) *Professionalism, Boundaries and the Workplace.* London: Routledge.

Fowler, J. and Chevannes, M. (1998). Evaluating the efficacy of reflective practice within the context of clinical supervision. *Journal of Advanced Nursing, 27*(2), 379–382.

Frame, M.W. (2001). The spiritual genogram in training and supervision. *Family Journal, 9,* 109–115.

Frawley O'Dea, M.G. and Sarnat, J. (2001). *The Supervisory Relationship: A Contemporary Psychodynamic Approach*. New York: Guilford Press.

Freud, S. and Gay, P. (1995). *The Freud Reader*. London: Vintage.

Friedlander, M.L. and Snyder, J. (1983). Trainees' expectations for the supervisory process: testing a developmental model. *Counselor Education and Supervision, 23*, 342–348.

Friedlander, M.L. and Ward, L.G. (1983). Dimensions of supervisory style. Cited in R.K. Goodyear, P.D. Abadie and F. Efros (1984). Supervisory theory into practice: differential perceptions of supervision by Ekstein, Ellis, Polster and Rogers. *Journal of Counseling Psychology, 31*, 228–237.

Friedlander, M.L. and Ward, L.G. (1984). Development and validation of the Supervisory Styles Inventory. *Journal of Counseling Psychology, 31*, 542–558.

Friedman, H. and Rogers Mitchell, R. (2007). *Supervision of Sandplay Therapy*. London: Routledge.

Friedmann, C.T., Yamamoto, J., Wolkon, G.H. and Davis, L. (1978). Videotape recording of dynamic psychotherapy: supervisory tool or hindrance? *American Journal of Psychiatry, 135*, 1388–1391.

Gabbard, G.O. and Lester, E.P. (2003). *Boundaries and Boundary Violations in Psychoanalysis*. Arlington, VA: American Psychiatric Press.

Gagné, R.M. (1967). Instruction and the conditions of learning. In L. Siegel (ed.) *Instruction: Some Contemporary Viewpoints*. San Francisco, CA: Chandler.

Gammon, D., Sorlie, T., Bergvik, S. and Sorensen-Hoifodt, T. (1998). Psychotherapy supervision conducted via videoconferencing: a qualitative study of users' experiences. *Nordic Journal of Psychiatry, 52*, 411–442.

Gatmon, D., Jackson, D., Koshkarian, L. and Martos-Perry, N. (2001). Exploring ethnic, gender, and sexual orientation variables in supervision: do they really matter? *Journal of Multicultural Counseling and Development, 29*, 102–114.

General Medical Council (2006). *Fitness to practise procedures*. Retrieved 21 January 2008 from: http://www.gmc-uk.org/concerns/printable_documents/index.asp.

Gergen, K. (1985). The social constructionist movement in modern psychology. *American Psychologist, 40*, 266–275.

Gergen, K.J. and Gergen, M.M. (1991). Towards reflexive methodologies. In F. Steier (ed.) *Research and Reflexivity*. London: Sage.

Gershenson, J. and Cohen, M. (1978). Through the looking glass: the experiences of two family therapy trainees with live supervision. *Family Process, 17*, 225–230.

Gert, B. (2004). *Common Morality: Deciding What to Do*. New York: Oxford University Press.

Getz, H.G. (1999). Assessment of clinical supervisor competencies. *Journal of Counseling and Development, 77*, 491–497.

Getzel, G.S. and Salmon, R. (1995). Group supervision: an organizational approach. *Clinical Supervisor, 3*, 27–43.

Gibbs, G. (1988). *Learning by Doing: A Guide to Teaching and Learning Methods*. Oxford: Further Education Unit, Oxford Brookes University.

Gilbert, M.C. and Evans, K. (2000, 2007). *Psychotherapy Supervision: An Integrative Relational Approach to Psychotherapy Supervision*. Buckingham: Open University Press.

Gilbert, M. and Sills, C. (1999). Training for supervision evaluation. In E. Holloway and M. Carroll (eds) *Training Counselling Supervisors*. London: Sage.

Gilligan, C. (1982). *In a Different Voice: Psychological Theory and Women's Development*. Cambridge, MA: Harvard University Press.

Gilmore, S.K., Fraleigh, P.W. and Philbrick, R. (1980). *Communication at Work*. Eugene, OR: Friendly Press.

Gitterman, A. (1988). Teaching students to connect theory and practice. *Social Work with Groups*, *11*, 33–41.

Glaser, R.D. and Thorpe, J.S. (1986). Unethical intimacy. *American Psychologist*, *41*, 43–51.

Glasersfeld, E. von (1991). Knowing without metaphysics: aspects of the radical constructivist position. In F. Steier (ed.) *Research and Reflexivity*. London: Sage.

Glasersfeld, E. von (1995). *Radical Constructivism*. London: Falmer.

Goffman, E. (1968). *Asylums*. Harmondsworth: Penguin.

Goldhammer, R., Anderson, R.H. and Krajewski, R.J. (1980). *Clinical Supervision: Special Methods for the Supervision of Teachers*. New York: Holt, Rinehart & Winston.

Goldstein, W.N. (2006). *Using the Transference in Psychotherapy*. Northvale, NJ: Jason Aronson.

Gomez, E.A., Ruiz, P. and Langrod, J. (1980). Multidisciplinary team malfunctioning on a state hospital unit: a case study. *Hospital and Community Psychiatry*, *31*, 38–40.

Gomez, L. (1997). *An Introduction to Object Relations*. London: Free Association Books.

Goncalves, O.F. and Craine, M.H. (1991). The use of metaphors in cognitive therapy. *Journal of Cognitive Psychotherapy*, *4*(2), 135–149.

Gonsoriek, J.C. (ed.) (1995). *Breach of Trust: Sexual Exploitation by Health Care Professionals and Clergy*. London: Sage.

Goodman, R.W. (1985). The live supervision model in clinical training. *Clinical Supervisor*, *3*, 43–49.

Goodyear, R.K. (2007). Toward an effective signature pedagogy for psychology: comments supporting the case for competent supervisors. *Professional Psychology: Research and Practice*, *38*(3), 268–275.

Goodyear, R.K. and Nelson, M.L. (1997). The major formats of psychotherapy supervision. In C.E. Watkins, Jr. (ed.) *Handbook of Psychotherapy Supervision*. New York: Wiley.

Goodyear, R.K. Abadie, P.D. and Efros, F. (1984). Supervisory theory into practice: differential perceptions of supervision by Ekstein, Ellis, Polster and Rogers. *Journal of Counseling Psychology*, *31*, 228–237.

Goodyear, R.K., Bradley, F.O. and Bartlett, W.E. (1983). An introduction to theories of counselor supervision. *The Counseling Psychologist*, *11*, 19–20.

Goss, S. (2000). A supervisory revolution? The impact of new technology. In B. Lawton and C. Feltham (eds) *Taking Supervision Forward*. London: Sage.

Gottlieb, M.C., Robinson, K. and Younggren, J.N. (2007). Multiple relations in supervision: guidance for administrators, supervisors, and students. *Professional Psychology: Research and Practice*, *38*(3), 241–247.

Gould, S.J. (1980). *The Panda's Thumb*. New York: W.W. Norton.

Gowdy, E., Rapp, C. and Poertner, J. (1993). Management is performance: strategies for practice in social service organizations. *Administration in Social Work*, *17*(1), 3–22.

Grahame, K. (2005). *The Wind in the Willows*. Lawrence, KS: Digireads.com.

Granello, D.H., Beamish, P.M. and Davis, T.E. (1997). Supervisee empowerment: Does gender make a difference? *Counselor Education and Supervision*, *36*, 305–317.

Gray, L.A., Ladany, N., Walker, J.A. and Ancis, J.R. (2001). Psychotherapy trainees' experience of counterproductive events in supervision. *Journal of Counseling Psychology*, *48*, 371–383.

Greenberg, Jay (1996). Psychoanalytic words and psychoanalytic acts: a brief history. *Contemporary Psychoanalysis*, *32*, 195–213.

Greenberg, Joanne (1992) *I Never Promised You a Rose Garden*. New York: Signet.

Grimmer, A. and Tribe, R. (2001). Counseling psychologists' perceptions of the impact of mandatory personal therapy on professional development: an exploratory study. *Counselling Psychology Quarterly*, *14*(4), 287–301.

Guest, D.E. and Conway, N. (2002). *Pressure at Work and the Psychological Contract*. London: CIPD. Accessed 24 January 2007 from: http://www.cipd.co.uk/subjects/empreltns/psycntrct/psycontr.htm.

Guiffrida, D.A., Jordan, R., Saiz, S. and Barnes, K.L. (2007). The use of metaphor in clinical supervision. *Journal of Counseling and Development*, *85*(4), 393–400.

Gutheil, T.G. and Gabbard, G.O. (1993). The concept of boundaries in clinical practice: theoretical and risk-management dimensions. *American Journal of Psychiatry*, *150*, 188–196.

Hackmann, A. (1997). The transformation of meaning in cognitive therapy. In M. Power and C.R. Brewin (eds) *The Transformation of Meaning in Psychological Therapies: Integrating Theory and Practice*. Chichester: John Wiley.

Haggar, H., Burn, K. and McIntyre, D. (1993). *The School Mentor Handbook*. London: Kogan Page.

Haggard, E.A., Hiken, J.R. and Isaacs, K.S. (1965). Some effects of recording and filming on the psychotherapeutic process. *Psychiatry*, *28*, 169–191.

Hahn, W.K. (2001). The experience of shame in supervision. *Psychotherapy*, *38*, 272–282.

Hahn, W.K. and Molnar, S. (1991). Intern evaluation in university counseling centers: process, problems and recommendations. *Counseling Psychologist*, *19*, 414–430.

Halpert, S.C., Reinhardt, B. and Toohey, M.J. (2007). Affirmative clinical supervision. In K.J. Bieschke, R.M. Perez and K.A. DeBord (eds) *Handbook of Counseling and Psychotherapy with Lesbian, Gay and Transgender Clients* (2nd edn). Washington, DC: American Psychological Association.

Hamilton, J.C. and Spruill, J. (1999). Identifying and reducing risk factors related to trainee–client sexual misconduct. *Professional Psychology: Research and Practice*, *30*, 318–327.

Hampden-Turner, C. (1981). *Maps of the Mind*. New York: Collier Books.

Handelsman, M.M., Gottleib, M.C. and Knapp, S. (2005). Training ethical psychologists: an acculturation model. *Professional Psychology: Research and Practice*, *36*, 59–65.

Haringey Council: Barnet Enfield and Haringey Mental Health NHS Trust (2005). *Integrated Supervision Policy for Mental Health Community Teams*. Retrieved 15 April 2006 from: www.haringey.gov.uk/integrated_supervision_policy.pdf.

Harkness, D. and Hensley, H. (1991). Changing the focus of social work supervision. *Social Work*, *36*, 506–512.

Harmon, S.C., Lambert, M.J., Smart, D.M., Hawkins, E., Nielson, S.L., Slade, K. and Lutz, W. (2007). Enhancing outcome for potential treatment failures:

therapist–client feedback and clinical support tools. *Psychotherapy Research*, *17*(4), 379–392.

Harrar, W.R., Vandercreek, L. and Knapp, S. (1990). Ethical and legal aspects of clinical supervision. *Professional Psychology: Research and Practice*, *21*, 37–41.

Hawkins, P. and Miller, E. (n.d.). *Psychotherapy In and With Organisations*. Bath: Bath Consultancy Group.

Hawkins, P. and Shohet, R. (1989). *Supervision in the Helping Professions*. Milton Keynes: Open University Press.

Hawkins, P. and Shohet, R. (2006). *Supervision in the Helping Professions* (3rd edn). Milton Keynes: Open University Press.

Haynes, R., Corey, G. and Moulton, P. (2003). Models of supervision. In R. Haynes, G. Corey and P. Moulton (eds) *Clinical Supervision in the Helping Professions: A Practical Guide*. Pacific Grove, CA: Brooks/Cole-Thomson Learning.

Heaven, C., Clegg, J. and Maguire, P. (2006). Transfer of communication skills training from workshop to workplace: the impact of clinical supervision. *Patient Education and Counseling*, *60*, 313–325.

Heginbotham, C. (1999). The psychodynamics of mental health care. *Journal of Mental Health*, *8*(3), 253–260.

Helms, J.E. (ed.) (1990). *Black and White Racial Identity: Theory, Research and Practice*. Westport, CT: Greenwood Press.

Hendrickson, S.M., Veach, P.M. and LeRoy, B.S. (2002). A qualitative investigation of student and supervisor perceptions of live supervision in genetic counseling. *Journal of Genetic Counseling*, *11*, 25–49.

Heppner, P.P. and Handley, P.G. (1982). The relationship between supervisory expertness, attractiveness, or trustworthiness. *Counselor Education and Supervision*, *22*, 23–31.

Hewson, J. (1999). Training supervisors to contract in supervision. In E.L. Holloway and M. Carroll (eds) *Training Counselling Supervisors*. London: Sage.

Hildebrand, J. (1998a). Personal communication.

Hildebrand, J. (1998b). *Bridging the Gap: A Training Module in Personal and Professional Development*. London: Karnac Books.

Hinshelwood, R.D. (1994). *A Dictionary of Kleinian Thought*. London: Free Association Books.

Hitchings, P. (1999). Supervision and sexual orientation. In M. Carroll and E. Holloway (eds) *Counselling Supervision in Context*. London: Sage.

Ho, H. and McConville, P. (2004). Who's happy with supervision? *Psychiatric Bulletin*, *28*, 87–90.

Hoffman, L. (1991). A reflexive stance for family therapy. *Journal of Strategic and Systemic Therapies*, *10*, 4–17.

Hoggett, P. (2006). Conflict, ambivalence, and the contested purpose of public organizations. *Human Relations*, *59*, 175–194.

Holloway, E.L. (1992). Supervision: A way of teaching and learning. In S. Brown and R. Lent (eds) *The Handbook of Counseling Psychology* (2nd edn). New York: Wiley.

Holloway, E.L. (1995). *Clinical Supervision: A Systems Approach*. Thousand Oaks, CA: Sage.

Holloway, E.L. and Neufeldt, S.A. (1995). Supervision: its contributions to treatment efficacy. *Journal of Consulting and Clinical Psychology*, *63*, 207–213.

Holloway, E.L. and Roehlke, H.J. (1987). Internship: the applied training of a counseling psychologist. *Counseling Psychologist, 15*, 205–260.

Holloway, E.L. and Wampold, B.E. (1983). Patterns of verbal behaviour and judgements of satisfaction in the supervision interview. *Journal of Counseling Psychology, 30*, 227–234.

Holt, J. (1969). *How Children Fail*. Middlesex: Penguin.

Holt, J.L. (2001). Impact of gender, organisational role and multicultural status on conflict resolution style preference. *Dissertation Abstracts International: Section B: The Sciences and Engineering, 61*, 4457.

Honey, P. and Mumford, A. (1992). *The Manual of Learning Styles*. Maidenhead: Honey (available from 10 Lindon Avenue, SL6 6HB).

Horton, I. (1993). Supervision. In R. Boyne and P. Nicholson (eds) *Counselling and Psychotherapy for Health Professionals*. London: Chapman & Hall.

Horvath, A.O. (2001). The alliance. *Psychotherapy, 38*, 365–372.

Houston, G. (1997). *The Red Book of Counselling and Supervision*. London: Rochester Press (9 Rochester Terrace, London N1).

Howell, W.C. (1982). *Information Processing and Decision Making*. Mahwah, NJ: Lawrence Erlbaum Associates.

Howells, W.D., Karp, M., Watson, M., Sprague, K. and Moreno, Z.T. (1994). *Psychodrama Since Moreno: Innovations in Theory and Practice*. London: Routledge.

Hoyt, M.F. (ed.) (1994). *Constructive Therapies Volume 2*. New York: Guilford Press.

Hoyt, M. (2000). *Some Stories are Better than Others: Doing What Works in Brief Therapy and Managed Care*. Lillington, NC: Taylor & Francis.

Hughes, J. and Massey, C. (2000). Personal communication.

Hughes, J. and Youngson, S. C. (in press). *Personal Development and Clinical Psychology*. Oxford: Blackwell.

Hurley, G. and Hadden, K. (2005). Online video supervision: a case study. *National Register of Health Service Providers in Psychology*. Retrieved 5 January 2008 from http://www.e-psychologist.org/index.iml?mdl=exam/show_article.mdl&Material_ID=2.

Husband, C. (1995). The morally active practitioner and the ethics of anti-racist social work. In R. Hugman and D. Smith (eds) *Ethical Issues in Social Work*. London: Routledge.

Hyrkäs, K. (2005). Clinical supervision, burnout and job satisfaction among mental health and psychiatric nurses in Finland. *Issues in Mental Health Nursing, 26*, 531–556.

Inskipp, F. and Proctor, B. (1988). *Skills for Supervising and Being Supervised*. Twickenham, Middlesex: Cascade Publications.

Inskipp, F. and Proctor, B. (1993). *The Art, Craft and Tasks of Counselling Supervision. Part 1. Making the Most of Supervision*. Twickenham, Middlesex: Cascade Publications.

Inskipp, F. and Proctor, B. (1995). *The Art, Craft and Tasks of Counselling Supervision. Part 2. Becoming a Supervisor*. Twickenham, Middlesex: Cascade Publications.

Inskipp, F. and Proctor, B. (1997). Personal communication. Trent Region supervisors' workshop.

Inskipp, F. and Proctor, B. (2001a). *The Art, Craft and Tasks of Counselling Super-*

vision. Part 1. Making the Most of Supervision (2nd edn). Twickenham, Middlesex: Cascade Publications.

Inskipp, F. and Proctor, B. (2001b). *The Art, Craft and Tasks of Counselling Supervision. Part 2. Becoming a Supervisor* (2nd edn). Twickenham, Middlesex: Cascade Publications.

Inskipp, F. and Proctor, B. (2007). *Creative Supervision with Francesca Inskipp and Brigid Proctor* (DVD). Newport: University of Wales School of Health and Social Sciences.

Ishiyama, F.I. (1988). A model of visual case processing using metaphors and drawings. *Counselor Education and Supervision, 28*, 153–161.

Ivey, A.E. (1974). Micro-counselling: teacher training as facilitation of pupil growth. *British Journal of Educational Technology, 5*, 16–21.

Jacobs, D., David, P. and Meyer, D.J. (1995). *The Supervisory Encounter. A Guide for Teachers of Psychodynamic Psychotherapy and Psychoanalysis.* New Haven/London: Yale University Press.

Jacobsen, T. (1998). Delay behaviour at age six: links to maternal expressed emotion. *Journal of Genetic Psychology, 159*(1), 117–120.

James et al. (2008). Microskills of clinical supervision. *Journal of Cognitive Psychotherapy,* 22, 29–36.

James, S. and Foster, G. (2006). Reconciling rules with context: an ethical framework for cultural psychotherapy. *Theory and Psychology, 16*, 803–823.

Janoff, D.S. and Schoenholtz-Read, J. (1999). Group supervision meets technology: a model for computer-mediated group training at a distance. *International Journal of Group Psychotherapy, 49*, 255–272.

Johns, C. and Graham, J. (1996). Using a reflective model of nursing and guided reflection. *Nursing Standard, 11*(2), 34–38.

Johnson, B. (1996). Feeling the fear. In D. Boud and N. Miller (eds) *Working with Experience.* London: Routledge.

Johnston, J.A. and Gysbers, N.C. (1966). Practicum supervisory relationships: a majority report. *Counselor Education and Supervision, 6*, 3–10.

Jones, C., Shillito-Clarke, C., Syme, G., Hill, D., Casemore, R. and Murdin, L. (2000). *Questions of Ethics in Counselling and Psychotherapy.* Buckingham: Open University Press.

Jones, S. (1996). *Training Link. Newsletter of the Universities of Leicester and Sheffield Clinical Psychology Training Courses, 13*, 1–2. Sheffield: University of Sheffield.

Jordan, K. (1999). Live supervision for beginning therapists in practicum: crucial for quality counselling and avoiding litigation. *Family Therapy, 26*, 81–86.

Jumper, S.A. (1999). *Immediate feedback using the bug-in-the-ear in counselor training: implications for counseling self-efficacy, trainee anxiety and skill development.* Dissertation, University of North Dakota. Grand Forks, North Dakota.

Kadushin, A. (1985). *Supervision in Social Work* (2nd edn). New York: Columbia University Press.

Kadushin, A. (1992). What's wrong; what's right with social work supervision. *Clinical Supervisor, 10*(1), 3–19.

Kagan, N. (1984). Interpersonal Process Recall: basic methods and recent research. In D. Larson (ed.) *Teaching Psychological Skills.* Monterey, CA: Brooks/Cole.

Kagan, N. and Kagan, H. (1991). Teaching counselling skills. In K.R. Cox and C.E. Ewan (eds) *The Medical Teacher.* Edinburgh: Churchill Livingstone.

Kagan, N. and Krathwohl, D.R. (1967). *Studies in Human Interaction: Interpersonal Process Recall Stimulated by Videotape*. East Lansing: Michigan State University.

Kagan, N., Krathwohl, D.R. and Miller, R. (1963). Stimulated recall in therapy using videotape: a case study. *Journal of Counselling Psychology, 10*, 237–243.

Kagan-Klein, H. and Kagan, N. (1997). Interpersonal Process Recall: influencing human interaction. In C.E. Watkins, Jr. (ed.) *Handbook of Psychotherapy Supervision*. New York: John Wiley & Sons.

Kalff, D. (1980). *Sandplay: A Psychotherapeutic Approach to the Psyche*. Santa Monica, CA: Sigo Press.

Kanz, J.E. (2001). Clinical-supervision.com: issues in the provision of online supervision. *Professional Psychology: Research and Practice, 32*, 415–420.

Karp, M., Holmes, P. and Tauvon, K.B. (1998). *The Handbook of Psychodrama*. New York: Routledge.

Katz, J.H. (1985). The sociopolitical nature of counseling. *The Counseling Psychologist, 13*, 615–624.

Kees, N.L. and Leech, N.L. (2002). Using group counselling techniques to clarify and deepen the focus of supervision groups. *Journal for Specialists in Group Work, 27*, 7–15.

Kent, G. and McAuley, D. (1995). Ethical difficulties faced by trainee clinical psychologists. *Clinical Psychology Forum, 80*, 26–30.

Kerby Neill, T., Holloway, E.L. and Kaak, H.O. (2006). A systems approach to supervision of child psychotherapy. In T. Kerby Neill (ed.) *Helping Others Help Children: Clinical Supervision of Child Psychotherapy*. Washington, DC: American Psychological Association.

Kilkullen, N. (2007). An analysis of the experiences of clinical supervision on Registered Nurses undertaking MSc/graduate diploma in renal and urological nursing and on their clinical supervisors. *Journal of Clinical Nursing, 16*, 1029–1038.

King, D. and Wheeler, S. (1999). The responsibilities of counsellor supervisors: a qualitative study. *British Journal of Guidance and Counselling, 27*, 215–228.

Kingsley, C. (1994). *The Water Babies*. Bath: Robert Frederich.

Kingston, P. and Smith, D. (1983). Preparation for live consultation and live supervision when working without a one-way screen. *Journal of Family Therapy, 5*, 219–233.

Kipling, J.R. (n.d.). *In the Neolithic Age*. Retrieved 22 October 2007 from http://www.kipling.org.uk/poems_neolithic.htm.

Kivlingham, D.M. Jr., Angelone, E.O. and Swafford, K.G. (1991). Live supervision in individual psychotherapy: effects on therapist's intention use and client's evaluation of session effect and working alliance. *Professional Psychology: Research and Practice, 22*(6), 489–495.

Klitzke, M.J. and Lombardo, T.W. (1991). A 'bug-in-the-eye' can be better than a 'bug-in-the-ear'. *Behavior Modification, 15*, 113–117.

Knapp, S. and VandeCreek, L. (2006). *Practical Ethics for Psychologists: A Positive Approach*. Washington, DC: American Psychological Association.

Koenig, T.L. and Spano, R.N. (2004). Sex, supervision and boundary violations: pressing challenges and possible solutions. *The Clinical Supervisor, 22*(1), 3–19.

Kolb, D.A. (1984). *Experiential Learning – Experience as the Source of Learning and Development*. Engelwood Cliffs, NJ: Prentice-Hall.

Kollock, P., Blumstein, P. and Schwartz, P. (1985). Sex and power in interaction: conversational privileges and duties. *American Sociological Review, 50*, 34–46.

Kopp, R.R. (1995). *Metaphor Therapy: Using Client-generated Metaphors in Psychotherapy*. New York: Brunner/Mazel.

Kuhn, T.S. (1962). *The Structure of Scientific Revolutions*. Chicago, IL: University of Chicago Press.

Kumar, S. (2000). Client empowerment in psychiatry and the professional abuse of clients: where do we stand? *The International Journal of Psychiatry in Medicine, 30*, 61–70.

Kurpius, D., Gibson, G., Lewis, J. and Corbet, M. (1991). Ethical issues in supervising counseling practitioners. *Counselor Education and Supervision, 31*, 48–57.

Kutz, S.L. (1986). Defining 'impaired psychologist'. *American Psychologist, 41*, 220.

Ladany, N. and Lehrman-Waterman, D.E. (1999). The content and frequency of supervisor self-disclosure and their relationship to supervisor style and supervisory working alliance. *Counselor Education and Supervision, 38*, 143–160.

Ladany, N., Friedlander, M.L. and Nelson, M.L. (2005). *Critical Events in Psychotherapy Supervision*. Washington, DC: American Psychological Association.

Ladany, N., Walker, J.A. and Melincoff, D.S. (2001). Supervisory style: its relation to the supervisory working alliance and supervisor self-disclosure. *Counselor Education and Supervision, 40*, 263–275.

Ladany, N., Hill, C.E., Corbett, M.M. and Nutt, E.A. (1996). Nature, extent and importance of what psychotherapy trainees do not disclose to their supervisors. *Journal of Counseling Psychology, 43*, 10–24.

Lahad, M. (2000). *Creative Supervision: The Use of Expressive Arts Methods in Supervision and Self-supervision*. London: Jessica Kingsley.

Laireiter, A.R. and Willutzki, U. (2005). Personal therapy in cognitive behavioural therapy: traditions and current practice. In J.D. Geller, J.C. Norcross and D.E. Orlinsky (eds) *The Psychotherapist's Own Psychotherapy: Patient and Clinician Perspectives*. New York: Oxford University Press.

Lambert, M.J. (1980). Research and the supervisory process. In A.K. Hess (ed.) *Psychotherapy Supervision: Theory, Research and Practice*. New York: Wiley.

Lambert, M.J. and Arnold, R.C. (1987). Research and the supervisory process. *Professional Psychology: Research and Practice, 18*, 217–224.

Lambert, M.J. and Ogles, B.M. (1997). The effectiveness of psychotherapy supervision. In C.E. Watkins, Jr. (ed.) *Handbook of Psychotherapy Supervision*. New York: Wiley.

Lambert, M.J., Harmon, C., Slade, K., Whipple, J.L. and Hawkins, E.J. (2005). Providing feedback to therapists on their patients' progress: clinical results and practice suggestions. *Journal of Clinical Psychology/In Session, 81*(2), 165–174.

Lang, W.P., Little, M. and Cronen, V. (1990). The systemic professional: domains of action and the question of neutrality. *Human Systems, 1*, 1.

Laplanche, J. and Pontalis, J.B. (1973). *The Language of Psychoanalysis*. London: Hogarth Press.

Lawson, D.M. (1989). Using family sculpting in groups to enrich current intimate relationships. *Journal of College Student Development, 30*, 171–172.

Lawton, B. (2000). 'A very exposing affair': explorations in counsellors' supervisory relationships. In B. Lawton and C. Feltham (eds) *Taking Supervision Forward: Enquiries and Trends in Counselling and Psychotherapy*. London: Sage.

Lee, L. and Littlejohns, S. (2007). Deconstructing Agnes – externalisation in systemic supervision. *Journal of Family Therapy, 29*, 238–248.

Lee, R.E. and Everett, C.A. (2004). *The Integrative Family Therapy Supervisor: A Primer*. New York: Brunner-Routledge.

Lehrman-Waterman, D. and Ladany, N. (2001). Development and validation of the evaluation process within supervision inventory. *Journal of Counseling Psychology*, *48*, 168–177.

Lendrum, S. and Syme, G. (1992). *Gift of Tears: A Practical Approach to Loss and Bereavement Counselling*. Routledge: London.

Lesage-Higgins, S.A. (1999). Family sculpting in premarital counseling. *Family Therapy*, *26*, 31–38.

Lesser, R. (1984). Supervision: illusions, anxieties and questions. In L. Caligor *et al.* (eds) *Clinical Perspectives on the Supervision of Psychoanalysis and Psychotherapy*. New York: Plenum.

Levine, F.M. and Tilker, H.A. (1974). A behaviour modification approach to the supervision of psychotherapy. *Psychotherapy: Theory, Research and Practice*, *2*, 182–188.

Liddle, B.J. (1986). Resistance in supervision: a response to perceived threat. *Counselor Education and Supervision*, *26*, 117–127.

Liddle, H.A., Becker, D. and Diamond, G.M. (1997). Family therapy supervision. In C.E. Watkins, Jr. (ed.) *Handbook of Psychotherapy Supervision*. New York: Wiley.

Liddle, H.A., Breunlin, D.C. and Schwartz, R.C. (eds) (1988). *Handbook of Family Therapy and Training Supervision*. New York: Guilford Press.

Liese, B.S. and Beck, J. (1997). Cognitive therapy supervision. In C.E. Watkins, Jr. (ed.) *Handbook of Psychotherapy Supervision*. New York: Wiley.

Liese, B.S., Barber, J., and Beck, A.T. (1995). The Cognitive Therapy Adherence and Competence Scale. Unpublished instrument. University of Kansas Medical Centre, Kansas City. Reproduced in B.S. Liese and J. Beck (1997). Cognitive therapy supervision. In C.E. Watkins, Jr. (ed.) *Handbook of Psychotherapy Supervision*. New York: Wiley.

Linehan, M.M. (1993). *Cognitive-behavioural Treatment of Borderline Personality Disorder*. New York: Guilford Press.

Linehan, M.M., Comtois, K.A., Murray, A.M., Brown, M.Z., Gallop, R.J., Heard, H.L., Korslund, K.E., Tutek, D.A., Reynolds, S.K. and Lindenboim, N. (2006). Two-year randomised controlled trial and follow-up of dialectical behavior therapy vs therapy by experts for suicidal behaviors and borderline personality disorder. *Archives of General Psychiatry*, *63*, 757–766. Retrieved 3 January 2008 from: http://www.archgenpsychiatry.com/.

Littrell, J.M., Lee-Borden, N. and Lorenz, J.A. (1979). A developmental framework for counseling supervision. *Counselor Education and Supervision*, *19*, 119–136.

Llewelyn, S., Cushway, D. and Vetere, A. (2007). Why a trainer's lot is not a happy one (a happy one . . .). *Clinical Psychology Forum*, *175*, 24–27.

Locke, L.D. and McCollum, E.E. (2001). Clients' views of live supervision and satisfaction with therapy. *Journal of Marital and Family Therapy*, *27*(1), 129–135.

Loganbill, C., Hardy, E. and Delworth, U. (1982). Supervision: a conceptual model. *Counseling Psychologist*, *10*, 3–42.

Lopez, S.R. (1997). Cultural competence in psychotherapy: a guide for clinicians and supervisors. In C.E. Watkins, Jr. (ed.) *Handbook of Psychotherapy Supervision*. New York: Wiley.

Lowe, R. (2000). Supervising self-supervision: constructive inquiry and embedded narratives in case consultation. *Journal of Marital and Family Therapy*, *26*, 511–522.

Lowenfeld, M. (1979). *The World Technique*. London: Allen & Unwin.

Lowenstein, S.F., Reder, P. and Clark, A. (1982). The consumer's response: trainees' discussion of the experience of live supervision. In R. Whiffen and J. Byng-Hall (eds) *Family Therapy Supervision: Recent Developments in Practice*. London: Academic Press.

McAuliffe, D. and Sudbury, J. (2005). Who do I tell? Support and consultation in cases of ethical conflict. *Journal of Social Work*, *5*, 21–43.

McCann, D., Gorrell-Barnes, G. and Down, G. (2000). Sex and sexuality: the supervisory challenge. In G. Gorrell-Barnes, G. Down and D. McCann *Systemic Supervision: A Portable Guide for Supervision Training*. London: Jessica Kingsley.

McCarthy, P., Kulakowski, D. and Kenfield, J.A. (1994). Clinical supervision practices of licensed psychologists. *Professional Psychology: Research and Practice*, *25*, 177–181.

McElfresh, T.A. and McElfresh, S.J. (1998). How being a psychotherapist can imperil personal relationships. In L. Vandercreek and S. Knapp (eds) *Innovations in Clinical Practice: A Source Book*. Sarasota, FL: Professional Resource Press.

McIntosh, P. (1998). White privilege: unpacking the invisible knapsack. In M. McGoldrick (ed.) *Revisioning Family Therapy: Race, Culture and Gender in Clinical Practice*. New York: Guilford Press.

McNamee, C.M. and McWey, L.M. (2004). Using bilateral art to facilitate clinical supervision. *The Arts in Psychotherapy*, *31*, 229-243.

McNeill, B.W. and Worthen, V. (1989). The parallel process in psychotherapy supervision. *Professional Psychology: Research and Practice*, *20*, 329–333.

Macran, S. and Shapiro, D. (1998). The role of personal therapy for therapists: a review. *British Journal of Medical Psychology*, *71*, 13–25.

Magnuson, S., Wilcoxon, S.A. and Norem, K. (2000). A profile of lousy supervision: experienced counselors' perspectives. *Counselor Education and Supervision*, *39*, 189–202.

Mahoney, M.J. (1986). The tyranny of technique. *Counseling and Values*, *30*, 169–174.

Mahoney, M.J. (2003). *Constructive Psychotherapy: Theory and Practice*. New York: Guilford Press.

Mahrer, A.R. and Boulet, D.B. (1997). The experiential model of on-the-job teaching. In C.E. Watkins, Jr. (ed.) *Handbook of Psychotherapy Supervision*. New York: Wiley.

Manaster, G.L. and Lyons, A. (1994). An exercise in multicultural complexity. *Texas Counseling Association Journal*, *22*, 45–51.

Manosevitz, M. (2006). Supervision by telephone: an innovation in psychoanalytic training – a roundtable discussion. *Psychoanalytic Psychology*, *23*, 579–582.

Marks, D. (1999). *Disability: Controversial Debates and Psychosocial Perspectives*. London: Routledge.

Marrow, C.E., Hollyoake, K., Hamer, D. and Kenrick, C. (2002). Clinical supervision using video-conferencing technology: a reflective account. *Journal of Nursing Management*, *10*(5), 275–282.

Matthews, S. and Treacher, A. (2004). Therapy models and supervision in clinical psychology. In I. Fleming and L. Steen (eds) *Supervision and Clinical Psychology*. Hove: Brunner-Routledge.

Maturana, H. and Varela, F. (1980). *Autopoiesis and Cognition: The Realization of the Living*. Dordrecht, NL: Kluwer Academic.

Mauzey, E., and Erdman, P. (1997). Trainee perceptions of live supervision phone-ins: a phenomenological inquiry. *The Clinical Supervisor*, *15*, 115–128.

Mearns, D. (1997). *Person-centred Counselling Training*. London: Sage.

Megginson, D. and Clutterbuck, D. (2005). *Techniques for Coaching and Mentoring*. Oxford: Elsevier, Butterworth-Heinemann.

Meredith, R. and Bradley, L. (1989). Differential supervision: roles, functions and activities. In L. Bradley (ed.) *Counselor Supervision*. Muncie, IN: Accelerated Development.

Meyer, R.G., Landis, E.R. and Hays, J.R. (1988). *Law for the Psychotherapist*. New York: W.W. Norton.

Mezirow, J. (1985). A critical theory of self-directed learning. In S. Brookfield (ed.) *Self-directed Learning: From Theory to Practice*. San Francisco, CA: Jossey-Bass.

Mezirow, J. (1997). Cognitive processes: contemporary paradigms of learning. In P. Sutherland (ed.) *Adult Learning: A Reader*. London: Kogan Page.

Mezirow, J. (2000). *Learning as Transformation: Critical Perspectives on a Theory in Progress*. San Francisco, CA: Jossey-Bass.

Miars, R.D., Tracey, T.J., Ray, P.B., Cornfeld, J.L., O'Farrell, M. and Gelso, C.J. (1983). Variation in supervision process across trainee experience levels. *Journal of Counseling Psychology*, *30*, 403–412.

Middleman, R.R. and Rhodes, G.B. (1985). *Competent Supervision: Making Imaginative Judgments*. Englewood Cliffs, NJ: Prentice-Hall.

Miller, G.R. (1976). *Explorations in Interpersonal Communication*. Beverly Hills, CA: Sage.

Miller, L. and Twomey, J.E. (1999). A parallel without a process: a relational view of a supervisory experience. *Contemporary Psychoanalysis*, *35*, 557–580.

Miller, N. and Crago, M. (1989). The supervision of two isolated practitioners: it's supervision, Jim, but not as you know it. *Australian and New Zealand Journal of Family Therapy*, *10*, 21–25.

Miller, S. (2004). What's going on? Parallel process and reflective practice in teaching. *Reflective Practice*, *5*, 383–393.

Milne, D. (2007a). An empirical definition of clinical supervision. *British Journal of Clinical Psychology*, *46*(4), 449–459.

Milne, D. (2007b). *Introduction to Clinical Supervision: A Tutor's Guide*. Newcastle: Milne.

Milne, D.L., Pilkington, J., Gracie, J. and James, I. (2003). Transferring skills from supervision to therapy. *Behavioural and Cognitive Psychotherapy*, *31*, 193–202.

Milne, D., Aylott, H., Dunkerley, C., Fitzpatrick, H. and Wharton, S. (2007). What does the empirical literature tell us about 'good' clinical supervision? Paper presented at the DCP annual conference, London.

Minardi, H.A. and Ritter, S. (1999). Recording skills practice on videotape can enhance learning – a comparative study between nurse lecturers and nursing students. *Journal of Advanced Nursing*, *29*, 1318–1325.

MIND Publications (n.d.). *Getting the Best from your Counsellor or Psychotherapist*. London: MIND.

Moldawsky, S. (1980). Psychoanalytic psychotherapy supervision. In A.K. Hess (ed.) *Psychotherapy Supervision: Theory, Research and Practice*. New York: Wiley.

Mollica, K.A. (2003). The influence of diversity context on white men's and racial minorities' reactions to disproportionate group harm. *Journal of Social Psychology*, *143*(4), 415–431.

Mollon, P. (1989). Anxiety, supervision and a space for thinking: some narcissistic perils for clinical psychologists in learning psychotherapy. *British Journal of Medical Psychology*, *62*, 113–122.

Mollon, P. (2001). *Releasing the Self: The Healing Legacy of Heinz Kohut*. London: Whurr Publishers.

Monaghan, L. (2007). *Supervisors' perspectives on difficulties in supervision*. Unpublished thesis submitted to the University of Sheffield for the degree of Doctor of Clinical Psychology.

Moorhouse, A. and Carr, A. (1999). The correlates of phone-in frequency, duration and the number of suggestions made during live supervision. *Journal of Family Therapy*, *21*, 407–418.

Mordock, J. (1990). The new supervisor: awareness of the problems experienced and some of the suggestions for problem resolution through supervisory training. *The Clinical Supervisor*, *8*(1), 81–92.

Morrisey, J. and Tribe, R. (2001). Parallel process in supervision. *Counseling Psychology Quarterly*, *14*, 103–110.

Morrison, T. (1993). *Staff Supervision in Social Care*. Harlow: Longman.

Morrison, T. (2001). *Staff Supervision in Social Care* (2nd edn). Brighton: Pavilion Publishing.

Mothersole, G. (1999). Parallel process: a review. *Clinical Supervisor*, *18*, 107–121.

Mueller, W.J. and Kell, B.L. (1972). *Coping with Conflict: Supervising Counselors and Psychotherapists*. New York: Appleton-Century-Crofts.

Mulholland, J., Dyson, S. and Smaje, C. (2001). Sociological theories of 'race' and ethnicity. In L. Culley and S. Dyson (eds) *Ethnicity and Nursing Practice*. London: Palgrave.

Munson, C.E. (2002). *Handbook of Clinical Social Work Supervision* (3rd edn). New York: Haworth Press.

Murphy, D. (2005). A qualitative study into the experience of mandatory personal therapy during training. *Counselling and Psychotherapy Research*, *5*(1), 27–32.

Myers, D. and Wee, D. (2005). *Disaster Mental Health Services: A Primer for Practitioners*. New York: Routledge.

Myrick, R.D. and Kelly, F.D., Jr. (1971). A scale for evaluating practicum students in counseling and supervision. *Counselor Education and Supervision*, *10*, 330–336.

Myrick, R.D. and Sabella, R.A. (1995). Cyberspace: new place for counselor supervision. *Elementary School Guidance and Counseling*, *30*, 35–44.

National Center on Education and the Economy (2006). *Tough Choices or Tough Times: The Report of The New Commission on the Skills of the American Workforce (Executive Summary)*. Washington, DC: NCEE.

National Health Service National Treatment Agency for Substance Misuse (2004). *Developing Drug Service Policies, No. 6. July 2004 Supervision and Appraisal*. Retrieved 15 April 2006 from: http://www.nta.nhs.uk/frameset.asp?u=http://www.nta.nhs.uk/publications/Drug_service_policies_6.htm.

Nelson, G.L. (1978). Psychotherapy supervision from the trainee's point of view: a survey of preferences. *Professional Psychology*, *9*, 539–550.

Nelson, M.L. and Friedlander, M.L. (2001). A close look at a conflictual supervisory relationship: the trainee's perspective. *Journal of Counseling Psychology*, *48*, 384–395.

Nelson, M.L. and Holloway, E.L. (1990). Relation of gender to power and involvement in supervision. *Journal of Counseling Psychology*, *37*, 473–481.

Neufeldt, S.A. (1999). Training in reflective processes in supervision. In E. Holloway and M. Carroll (eds) *Training Counselling Supervisors*. London: Sage.

Neufeldt, S.A., Beutler, L.E. and Banchero, R. (1997). Research on supervisor variables in psychotherapy supervision. In C.E. Watkins, Jr. (ed.) *Handbook of Psychotherapy Supervision*. New York: Wiley.

Neufeldt, S.A., Karno, M.P. and Nelson, M.L. (1996). A qualitative analysis of experts' conceptualization of supervisee reflectivity. *Journal of Counseling Psychology*, *43*, 3–9.

Newman, A.S. (1981). Ethical issues in the supervision of psychotherapy. *Professional Psychology: Research and Practice*, *12*, 690–695.

Niland, T.M., Duling, J., Allen, V. and Panther, E. (1971). Student counselors' perceptions of videotaping. *Counselor Education and Supervision*, *11*, 97–101.

Noddings, N. (1984). *Caring: A Feminine Approach to Ethics and Moral Education*. Berkeley: University of California Press.

Noucho, A.O. (1983). The use of visual imagery in training professional helpers. In J. E. Shorr, G. Sobel-Whittington, P. Robin and J. Conella (eds) *Imagery. Vol 3: Theoretical and Clinical Applications*. New York: Plenum.

Nourry, C., Samba, D. and Bieder, J. (1978). The mosaic test of Margaret Lowenfeld applied to schizophrenics. *Annales Medical Psychologiques*, *136*, 1217–1224.

Nuttall, D., Goldstein, H., Prosser, R. and Rasbash, H. (1989). Differential school effectiveness. *International Journal of Educational Research*, *13*, 769–776.

Oaklander, V. (1970). *Windows to Our Children*. Utah: Real People Press.

Obholzer, A. (1994). Managing social anxieties in public sector health organisations. In A. Obholzer and V. Zagier-Roberts (eds) *The Unconscious at Work: Individual and Organisational Stress in Human Services*. London: Routledge.

Office of National Statistics (2000). *Psychiatric Morbidity Among Adults Living in Private Households, 2000*. London: The Stationery Office.

Ogren, M.L. and Jonsson, C.O. (2003). Psychotherapeutic skill following group supervision according to supervisees and supervisors. *The Clinical Supervisor*, *22*(1), 35–58.

Ogren, M.L., Apelman, A. and Klawitter, M. (2001). The group in psychotherapy supervision. *The Clinical Supervisor*, *20*, 147–175.

Olk, M. and Friedlander, M.L. (1992). Trainees' experiences of role conflict and role ambiguity in supervisory relationships. *Journal of Counseling Psychology*, *39*, 389–397.

Olkin, R. (1999). *What Psychotherapists Should Know about Disability*. New York: Guilford Press.

Open University (2005). *Observation Skills in Psychology*. Milton Keynes: Open University Press.

Orlinsky, D.E., Norcross, J.C., Rønnestad, M.H. and Wiseman, H. (2005). Outcomes and impacts of psychotherapists' personal therapy: a research review. In J.D.

Geller, J.C. Norcross and D.E. Orlinsky (eds) *The Psychotherapist's Own Psychotherapy: Patient and Clinician Perspectives*. New York: Oxford University Press.

Padesky, C.A. (1994). Schema change processes in cognitive therapy. *Clinical Psychology and Psychotherapy*, *1*, 267–278.

Page, S. and Wosket, V. (1994). *Supervising the Counsellor: A Cyclical Model*. London: Routledge.

Page, S. and Wosket, V. (2001). *Supervising the Counsellor: A Cyclical Model* (2nd edn). London: Routledge.

Palazzoli, M., Boscolo, L., Cecchin, G. and Prata, G. (1980). Hypothesising, circularity, neutrality: three guidelines for the conductor of the session. *Family Process*, *19*, 3–18.

Palmer, R.L. (2002). Dialectical behaviour therapy for borderline personality disorder. *Advances in Psychiatric Treatment*, *8*, 10–16.

Palmer Barnes, F. (1998). *Complaints and Grievances in Psychotherapy: A Handbook of Ethical Practice*. London: Routledge.

Palmer Barnes, F. (ed.) (2001). *Values and Ethics in the Practice of Psychotherapy and Counselling*. Buckingham: Open University Press.

Papadopoulos, I. (2006). The Papadopoulos, Tilki and Taylor model of developing cultural competence. In I. Papadopolous *Transcultural Health and Social Care: Developing Culturally Competent Practitioners*. Oxford: Elsevier.

Parsloe, E. (1999). *The Manager as Coach and Mentor*. London: Chartered Institute of Personnel and Development.

Pask, G. (1976). Styles and strategies of learning. *British Journal of Educational Psychology*, *46*, 128–148.

Patterson, C.H. (1997). Client-centred supervision. In C.E. Watkins, Jr. (ed.) *Handbook of Psychotherapy Supervision*. New York: Wiley.

Patton, M.J. and Kivlighan, D.M. (1997). Relevance of the supervisory alliance to the counseling alliance and to treatment adherence in counselor training. *Journal of Counseling Psychology*, *44*(1), 108–115.

Paul, R.W. and Elder, L. (2002). *Critical Thinking: Tools for Taking Charge of Your Professional and Personal Life*. Englewood Cliffs, NJ: Prentice-Hall.

Pearce, W.B. and Cronen, V.E. (1980). *Communication, Action and Meaning: The Creation of Sound Realities*. New York: Praeger.

Pedder, J. (1986). Reflections on the theory and practice of supervision. *Psychoanalytic Psychotherapy*, *1*, 1–12.

Pegg, P.F. and Manocchio, A.J. (1982). In on the act. In R. Whiffen and J. Byng-Hall (eds) *Family Therapy Supervision: Recent Developments in Practice*. London: Academic Press.

Pelling, N.J. and Renard, D.E. (1999). The use of videotaping in developmentally based supervision. *Journal of Technology in Counseling [On-line serial]*, *1*(1). Retrieved 2 July 2007 from http://jtc.colstate.edu/home.htm.

Pendry, L.F., Driscoll, D.M. and Field, S.C.T. (2007). Diversity training: putting theory into practice. *Journal of Occupational and Organizational Psychology*, *80*, 27–50.

Perr, H.M. (1986). The use of audio-tapes in psychotherapy. *Journal of the American Academy of Psychoanalysis*, *13*, 391–398.

Petticrew, M. and Roberts, H. (2006). *Systematic Reviews in the Social Sciences*. Oxford: Blackwell.

Pettifor, J.L., Estay, I. and Paquet, S. (2002). Preferred strategies for learning ethics in the practice of a discipline. *Canadian Psychology*, *43*, 260–269.

Phillips, D.C. (1995). The good, the bad, and the ugly: the many faces of constructivism. *Educational Researcher*, *24*(7), 5–12.

Phillips, R. and Green, D. (n.d.). *Possible Routes for the Accreditation of Training in Clinical Supervision for Clinical Psychologists*. Retrieved 14 October 2007 from: http://www.leeds.ac.uk/lihs/psychiatry/courses/dclin/cpd/DROSS/ dross_products.htm.

Piaget, J. (1972). *The Principles of Genetic Epistemology*, trans. W. Mays. London: Routledge.

Pilkington, N.W. and Cantor, J.M. (1996). Perceptions of heterosexual bias in professional psychology programs: a survey of graduate students. *Professional Psychology: Research and Practice*, *26*(6), 604–612.

Plotkin, H. (1994). *Darwin Machines and the Nature of Knowledge*. London: Penguin.

Polanyi, M. (1958). *Personal Knowledge*. London: Routledge & Kegan Paul.

Pomerantz, M. (1992) Personal communication.

Pomerantz, M., Leydon, G., Lunt, I., Osborne, E., Powell, M. and Ronaldson, J. (1987). *Report of the Joint DECP/Course Tutors' Working Party on Fieldwork Supervision*. Leicester: British Psychological Society.

Ponterotto, J.G. and Pedersen, P.B. (1993). *Preventing Prejudice: A Guide for Counsellors and Educators*. Newbury Park, CA: Sage.

Poortinga, Y.H. (1995). Cultural bias in assessment – historical and thematic issues. *European Journal of Psychological Assessment*, *11*, 140–146.

Pope, K., Tobachnick, B. and Keith-Spiegel, P. (1987). The beliefs and behaviours of psychologists as psychotherapists. *American Psychologist*, *42*, 993–1006.

Pope, K.S. and Vasquez, M.J.T. (2007). *Ethics in Psychotherapy and Counseling: A Practical Guide for Psychologists* (3rd edn). San Francisco, CA: Jossey-Bass.

Presbury, J., Echterling, L.G. and McKee, J.E. (1999). Supervision for inner vision: solution-focused strategies. *Counselor Education and Supervision*, *39*, 146–156.

Proctor, B. (2000). *Group Supervision: A Guide to Creative Practice*. London: Sage.

Proctor, P. and Ditton, A. (1989). How counselling can add value to organisations. *Journal of Workplace Learning*, *1*(2), 3–6.

Protinksy, H. (1997). Dismounting the tiger: using tape in supervision. In T.C. Todd and C.L. Storm (eds) *The Complete Systemic Supervisor: Context, Philosophy and Pragmatics*. Boston, MA: Allyn & Bacon.

Putney, M.W., Worthington, E.L. and McCullough, M.E. (1992). Effects of supervisor and supervisee theoretical orientations on supervisors' perceptions. *Journal of Counseling Psychology*, *39*, 258–265.

Quality Assurance Agency (2001). *The Framework for Higher Education Qualifications in England, Wales and Northern Ireland – January 2001*. Retrieved 2 January 2008 from: http://www.qaa.ac.uk/academicinfrastructure/FHEQ/EWNI/ default.asp.

Quinn, W.H. and Nagirreddy, C. (1999). Utilizing clients' voices in clinical supervision: the Interpersonal Process Recall model. In R.E. Lee and S. Emerson (eds) *The Eclectic Trainer*. Galena, IL: Geist & Russell.

Rabinowitz, F.E., Heppner, P.P. and Roehlke, J.J. (1986). Descriptive study of process and outcome variables of supervision over time. *Journal of Counseling Psychology*, *33*, 292–300.

Rae, W.A. and Fournier, F.J. (1999). Ethical and legal issues in the treatment of children and families. In T.H. Ollendick and W.W. Russ (eds) *Handbook of Psychotherapies with Children and Families*. Dordrecht, NL: Kluwer Academic.

Rahman, A., Nizami, A., Minhas, A., Niazi, R., Slatch, M. and Minhas, F. (2006). E-mental health in Pakistan: a pilot study of training and supervision in child psychiatry using the Internet. *Psychiatric Bulletin, 30*, 149–152.

Raichelson, S.H., Herron, W.G., Primavera, L.H. and Ramirez, S.M. (1997). Incidence and effects of parallel process in psychotherapy supervision. *Clinical Supervisor, 15*, 37–48.

Randall, R. and Southgate, J. (1980). *Co-operative and Community Group Dynamics*. London: Barefoot Books.

Rapisarda, C.A. and Britton, P.J. (2007). Sanctioned supervision: voices from the experts. *Journal of Mental Health Counseling, 29*, 81–93.

Rapp, H. (2000). Working with difference: culturally competent supervision. In B. Lawton and C. Feltham (eds) *Taking Supervision Forward: Enquiries and Trends in Counselling and Psychotherapy*. London: Sage.

Reavis, C.A. (1976). Clinical supervision: a timely approach. *Educational Leadership, 33*, 360–363.

Rhinds, D. (2003). Secrets of supervision – a trainee's perspective. *Psychiatric Bulletin, 27*, 352–353.

Richards, D.A. and Suckling, R. (2008). Improving access to psychological therapy: the Doncaster demonstration site organisational model. *Clinical Psychology Forum, 181*, 9–16.

Ricketts, T. and Donohoe, G. (2000). Clinical supervision in cognitive behavioural psychotherapy. In B. Lawton and C. Feltham (eds) *Taking Supervision Forwards: Enquiries and Trends in Counselling and Psychotherapy*. London: Sage.

Riding, R. (1992). Cognitive styles: an overview and integration. *Educational Psychology, 11*(3–4), 193–215.

Riding, R. (1994). *Personal Style Awareness and Personal Development*. Birmingham: Learning and Training Technology.

Riding, R. and Rayner, S. (1998). *Cognitive Styles and Learning Strategies: Understanding Style Differences in Learning and Behaviour*. London: David Fulton.

Robbins, A. and Erismann, M. (1992). Developing therapeutic artistry: a joint counter-transference supervisory seminar/stone sculpting workshop. *The Arts in Psychotherapy, 19*, 367–377.

Roberts, C.A. (1985). Viewpoint: the multi-disciplinary team in psychiatry. *Psychiatric Journal of the University of Ottawa, 10*, 147–152.

Roberts-DeGennaro, M. (1987). Developing case management as a practice model. *Social Casework: The Journal of Contemporary Social Work, 68*(8), 466–470.

Robson, D. and Robson, M. (1998). Intimacy and computer communication. *British Journal of Counselling and Guidance, 26*, 33–41.

Rock, M.H. (ed.) (1997). *Psychodynamic Supervision: Perspectives of the Supervisor and Supervisee*. Northvale, NJ: Jason Aronson.

Rogers, C.R. (1942). The use of electronically recorded interviews in improving psychotherapeutic techniques. *American Journal of Orthopsychiatry, 12*, 429–434.

Rogers, C.R. (1959). A theory of therapy, personality and interpersonal relationships, as developed in the client-centred framework. In S. Koch (ed.) *Psychology: A Study of Science, Volume 3: Formulation of the Person and the Social Context.* New York: McGraw-Hill.

Rogers, C.R. (1967). What we know about psychotherapy: Objectively and subjectively. In C.R. Rogers *On Becoming a Person.* London: Constable.

Rogers, C.R. (1974). *On Becoming a Person.* London: Constable.

Rogers, C.R. (1980). Client-centred therapy. In C.H. Patterson (ed.) *Theories of Counseling and Psychotherapy.* New York: Harper & Row.

Ronen, T. and Rosenbaum, M. (1998). Beyond direct verbal instructions in cognitive behavioral supervision. *Cognitive and Behavioral Practice, 5*, 7–23.

Rosenbaum, M. (ed.) (1990). *Learned Resourcefulness: On Coping Skills, Self-control, and Adaptive Behavior.* New York: Springer.

Rosenbaum, M. and Ronen, T. (1998). Clinical supervision from the standpoint of cognitive-behaviour therapy. *Psychotherapy, 35*, 220–230.

Rosenblatt, A. and Mayer, J.E. (1975) Objectionable supervisory styles: students' views. *Social Work*, May, 184–189.

Ross, W.D. (1930). *The Right and the Good.* Oxford: Clarendon Press.

Roth, A. and Fonagy, P. (1996). *What Works for Whom?* London: Guilford Press.

Roth, T. and Pilling, S. (2007). *The Skills Required to Deliver Effective Cognitive and Behavioural Therapy.* Centre for Outcomes, Research & Effectiveness (CORE) UCL Clinical Health Psychology. Retrieved 20 January 2008 from: http://www.ucl.ac.uk/clinical-health-psychology/htmlfiles/LogB_CBT.htm.

Rothschild, B. and Rand, M. (2006). *Help for the Helper: The Psychophysiology of Compassion Fatigue and Vicarious Trauma.* New York: W.W. Norton.

Rowan, J. (1989). *The Reality Game: A Guide to Humanistic Counselling and Therapy.* London: Routledge.

Rowell, J.A. (1989) Piagetian epistemology: equilibration and teaching of science. *Synthese, 80*, 141–162.

Rubin, N.J., Bebeau, M., Leigh, I.W., Lichtenberg, J.W., Nelson, P.D., Portnoy, S., Smith, I.L. and Kaslow, N.J. (2007). The competency movement within psychology: an historical perspective. *Professional Psychology: Research and Practice, 38*(5), 452–462.

Rudduck, J. and Sigsworth, A. (1985). Partnership supervision (or Goldhammer revisited). In D. Hopkins and P. Wiser (eds) *Rethinking Teacher Education.* London: Croom Helm.

Rule, W.R. (1983). Family therapy and the pie metaphor. *Journal of Marital and Family Therapy, 9*, 101–103.

Rustin, M. (1996). *Young minds in the balance.* Unpublished conference paper, Tavistock Conference 50 Years Celebration.

Ryan, F. (1991). Taking care with responsibility. *Clinical Psychology Forum, 35*, 36–37.

Saba, G.W. (1999). Live supervision: lessons learned from behind the mirror. *Academic Medicine, 74*, 856–858.

Sacuzzo, D.T. (2003). Liability for failure to supervise adequately: let the master beware (Part 2). *The Psychologist's Legal Update, 13*, 15–22.

Salzberger-Wittenberg, I. (1983). Part 1: Beginnings. In I. Salzberger-Wittenberg, G. Henry and E. Osborne (eds) *The Emotional Experience of Teaching and Learning.* London: Routledge & Kegan Paul.

Scaife, J.A. (2002). personal communication.

Scaife, J.A. and Scaife, J.M. (1996). A General Supervision Framework: applications in teacher education. In J. Trafford (ed.) *Learning to Teach: Aspects of Initial Teacher Education*. Sheffield: USDE Papers in Education.

Scaife, J.M. (1993a). Setting the scene for supervision: the application of a systems framework to an initial placement consultation. *Human Systems, 4,* 161–173.

Scaife, J.M. (1993b). Application of a General Supervision Framework: creating a context of cooperation. *Educational and Child Psychology, 10*(2), 61–72.

Scaife, J.M. (1993c). *Hierarchy and heterarchy in systemic therapy: reflexivity in therapy and consultation.* Unpublished research dissertation. University of Birmingham.

Scaife, J.M. (1995). *Training to Help: A Survival Guide.* Sheffield: Riding Press.

Scaife, J.M. (2001). *Supervision in the Mental Health Professions: A Practitioner's Guide.* London: Brunner-Routledge.

Scaife, J.M. (n.d.). *Supervising the Reflective Practitioner.*

Scaife, J.M. and Pomerantz, M. (1999). A survey of the record-keeping practices of clinical psychologists. *Clinical Psychology and Psychotherapy, 6,* 210–226.

Schact, A.J., Howe, H.E., Jr. and Berman, J.J. (1988). A short form of the Barrett–Lennard Relationship Inventory for supervisor relationships. *Psychological Reports, 63,* 699–706.

Schaeffer, J.A. (2006). *Transference and Countertransference in Non-analytic Therapy: Double-edged Swords.* Lanham, MD: University Press of America.

Schoener, G.R. and Gonsiorek, J. (1988). Assessment and development of rehabilitation plans for counselors who have sexually exploited their clients. *Journal of Counseling and Development, 67,* 227–232.

Schön, D.A. (1987). *Educating the Reflective Practitioner.* San Francisco, CA: Jossey-Bass.

Schröder, T. and Davis, J. (2004). Therapists' experience of difficulty in practice. *Psychotherapy Research, 14*(3), 328–345.

Schutz, W.C. (1967). *Joy: Expanding Human Awareness.* New York: Grove/Atlantic Incorporated.

Schutz, W.C. (1989). *Joy – Twenty Years Later.* Berkeley, CA: Ten Speed Press.

Schwartz, R.C., Liddle, H.A. and Breunlin, D.C. (1988). Muddles in live supervision. In H.A. Liddle, D.C. Breunlin and D.C. Schwartz (eds) *Handbook of Family Therapy Training and Supervision.* New York: Guilford Press.

Scott, C. and Spellman, D. (1992). Clinical psychology and family therapy training. *Clinical Psychology Forum, 48,* 31–34.

Searles, H.F. (1965). The informational value of the supervisor's experience. In H. Searles (ed.) *Collected Papers on Schizophrenia and Related Subjects.* New York: International Universities Press.

Segal, L. (2001). *The Dream of Reality: Heinz von Foerster's Constructivism* (2nd edn). New York: Springer-Verlag.

Seligman, M.E.P. (1995). The effectiveness of psychotherapy: the Consumer Reports study. *American Psychologist, 50,* 965–974.

Sells, J., Goodyear, R., Lichtenberg, J. and Polkinghorne, D. (1997). Relationship of supervisor and trainee gender to in-session verbal behaviour and rating of trainee skills. *Journal of Counseling Psychology, 44,* 1–7.

Shainberg, D. (1983). Teaching therapists to be with their clients. In J. Welwood (ed.) *Awakening the Heart: East/West Approaches to Psychotherapy and the Healing Relationship.* Boulder, CO: Shambhala.

Shanfield, W.B., Mohl, P.C., Matthews, K. and Hetherly, V. (1989). A reliability assessment of the Psychotherapy Supervisory Inventory. *American Journal of Psychiatry*, *146*, 1447–1450.

Sharpe, M. (1995). *The Third Eye: Supervision of Analytic Groups*. New York: Routledge.

Shaw, B.F. and Dobson, K.S. (1989). Competency judgements in the training and evaluation of psychotherapists. *Journal of Consulting and Clinical Psychology*, *56*, 666–672.

Sheikh, A.I., Milne, D.M. and MacGregor, B.V. (2007). A model of personal professional development in the systematic training of clinical psychologists. *Clinical Psychology and Psychotherapy*, *14*(4), 278–287.

Shohet, R. (2003). Personal communication.

Sholomskas, D.E., Syracuse-Siewert, G., Rounsaville, B.J., Ball, S.A., Nuro, K.F. and Carroll, K.M. (2005). We don't train in vain: a dissemination trial of three strategies of training clinicians in cognitive-behavioural therapy. *Journal of Consulting and Clinical Psychology*, *73*, 106–115.

Sills, C. (ed.) (2006). *Contracts in Counselling and Psychotherapy* (2nd edn). London: Sage.

Silvester, J. (1996). Questioning discrimination in the selection interview: a case for more field research. *Feminism and Psychology*, *6*, 574–578.

Skills for Health (2007). Retrieved 2 January 2008 from: http://www.skillsforhealth.org.uk/.

Skovholt, T.M. and Ronnestad, M.H. (1992). *The Evolving Professional Self: Stages and Themes in Therapist and Counsellor Development*. Chichester: Wiley.

Smith, D. and Kingston, P. (1980). Live supervision without a one-way screen. *Journal of Family Therapy*, *2*, 379–387.

Smith, E.J. (1981). Cultural and historical perspectives in counseling blacks. In D.W. Sue (ed.) *Counseling the Culturally Different*. New York: John Wiley.

Smith, H.D. (1984). Moment-to-moment counseling process feedback using dual-channel audiotape recording. *Counselor Education and Supervision*, *23*, 346–349.

Smith, J.P. (1995). Clinical supervision: a conference by the National Health Service Executive. *Journal of Advanced Nursing*, *21*, 1029–1031.

Smith, L.L., Taylor, B.B., Keys, A.T. and Gornto, S.B. (1997). Nurse–patient boundaries: crossing the line. *The American Journal of Nursing*, *97*, 26–32.

Smith, R.C., Mead, D.E. and Kinsella, J.A. (1998). Direct supervision: adding computer-assisted feedback and data capture to live supervision. *Journal of Marital and Family Therapy*, *24*, 113–125.

Smith, T.E., Yoshioka, M. and Winton, M. (1993). A qualitative understanding of reflecting teams. I. Client perspectives. *Journal of Systemic Therapies*, *12*, 28–43.

Spencer, M. (2000). Working with issues of difference in supervision of counselling. *Psychodynamic Counselling*, *6*(4), 505–519.

Stalker, J. (1996). Sharing the secrets of perspectives: operating honestly in the classroom. In D. Boud and N. Miller (eds) *Working with Experience*. London: Routledge.

Steffe, L.P. and Gale, J. (1995). *Constructivism in Education*. Hove: Lawrence Erlbaum Associates.

Stoltenberg, C.D. and Delworth, U. (1987). *Supervising Counselors and Therapists*. San Francisco, CA: Jossey-Bass.

Stoltenberg, C.D., McNeill, B. and Delworth, U. (1998). *IDM Supervision: An Integrated Developmental Model for Supervising Counselors and Therapists*. San Francisco, CA: Jossey-Bass.

Stone, G.L. (1997). Multiculturalism as a context for supervision: perspectives, limitations and implications. In D. Pope-Davis and H. Coleman (eds) *Multicultural Counseling Competencies: Assessment, Education and Training, and Supervision*. Thousand Oaks, CA: Sage.

Stones, E. (1984). *Supervision in Teacher Education: A Counselling and Pedagogical Approach*. London: Methuen.

Storm, C.L., Todd, T.C., Sprenkle, D.H. and Morgan, M.M. (2001). Gap between MFT supervision assumptions and common practice: suggested best practices. *Journal of Marital and Family Therapy, 27*, 227–240.

Strosahl, K. and Jacobson, N. (1986). Training and supervision of behaviour therapists. *The Clinical Supervisor, 4*, 183–206.

Sullivan, C.G. (1980). *Clinical Supervision: A State of the Art Review*. Virginia, USA: Association for Supervision and Curriculum Development.

Sutter, E., McPherson, R.H. and Geeseman, R. (2002). Contracting for supervision. *Professional Psychology: Research and Practice, 33*(5), 495–498.

Svartberg, M. and Stiles, T.C. (1992). Predicting patient change from therapist competence and patient–therapist complementarity in short-term anxiety-provoking psychotherapy: a pilot study. *Journal of Consulting and Clinical Psychology, 60*, 304–307.

Swann, W.B., Jr., Guiliano, T. and Wegner, D.M. (1982). Where leading questions can lead: the power of conjecture in social interaction. *Journal of Personality and Social Psychology, 42*, 1025–1035.

Tarasoff v. Regents of the University of California (1974). 118 Cal. Rptr. 129, 529 P. 2d 533.

Taylor, F.W. ([1911] 1998). *Principles of Scientific Management*. Norcross: Engineering and Management Press.

Teasdale, K., Brocklehurst, N. and Thom, N. (2001). Clinical supervision and support for nurses: an evaluation study. *Journal of Advanced Nursing, 33*, 216–224.

Tennen, H. (1988). Supervision of integrated psychotherapy: a critique. *Journal of Integrative and Eclectic Psychotherapy, 7*, 167–175.

Thomas, A., Chess, S. and Birch, H.G. (1968). *Temperament and Behaviour Disorders in Children*. New York: University Press.

Thomas, F.N. (1996). Solution-focused supervision: The coaxing of expertise. In S.D. Miller, M.A. Hubble and B.L. Duncan (eds) *Handbook of Solution Focused Therapy*. San Francisco, CA: Jossey-Bass.

Thomas, J.T. (2005). Licensing board complaints: minimizing the impact on the psychologist's defense and clinical practice. *Professional Psychology: Research and Practice, 36*, 426–433.

Thomas, J.T. (2007). Informed consent through contracting for supervision: Minimizing risks, enhancing benefits. *Professional Psychology: Research and Practice, 38*(3), 221–231.

Thorbeck, J. (1992). The development of the psychodynamic psychotherapist in supervision. *Academic Psychiatry, 16*, 72–82.

Thyer, B.A., Sowers-Hoag, K. and Love, J.P. (1988). The influence of field instructor–student gender combinations on student perceptions of field instruction quality. *Clinical Supervisor*, *6*, 169–179.

Todd, T.C. (1997). Purposive systemic supervision models. In T.C. Todd and C.L. Storm (eds) *The Complete Systemic Supervisor: Context, Philosophy and Pragmatics*. Boston, MA: Allyn & Bacon.

Tomm, K. (1987). Interventive interviewing: Part II. Reflexive questioning as a means to enable self-healing. *Family Process*, *26*, 167–183.

Toporek, R.L., Ortega-Villalobos, L. and Pope-Davis, D.B. (2004). Critical incidents in multicultural supervision: exploring supervisees' and supervisors' experiences. *Journal of Multicultural Counseling and Development*, *32*, 66–83.

Torosyan, R. (2001). Motivating students: evoking transformative learning and growth. *ETC*, *58*(3), 311–328.

Tower, K. (1994). Consumer-centred social work practice: restoring client self-determination. *Social Work*, *39*(2), 191–196.

Townend, M., Ianetta, L. and Freeston, M.H. (2002). Clinical supervision in practice: a survey of UK cognitive behavioural psychotherapists accredited by the BABCP. *Behavioural and Cognitive Psychotherapy*, *30*, 485–500.

Tromski-Klingshirn, D.M. (2006). Should the clinical supervisor be the administrative supervisor? The ethics versus the reality. *The Clinical Supervisor*, *25*, 53–67.

Tromski-Klingshirn, D.M. and Davis, T.E. (2007). Supervisees' perceptions of their clinical supervision: a study of the dual role of clinical and administrative supervisor. *Counselor Education and Supervision*, *46*(4), 294–304.

Troster, A.I., Paolo, A.M., Glatt, S.L., Hubble, J.P. and Koller, W.C. (1995). Interactive video conferencing in the provision of neuro-psychological services in rural areas. *Journal of Community Psychology*, *23*, 85–88.

Tschudin, V. (1997). *Counselling for Loss and Bereavement*. London: Baillière Tindall.

Tsui, M.S. (2005). *Social Work Supervision*. Thousand Oaks, CA: Sage.

Tsui, M.S., Ho, W.S. and Lam, C.M. (2005). The use of supervisory authority in Chinese cultural context. *Administration in Social Work*, *29*(4), 51–68.

Tuckman, B.W. (1965). Developmental sequence in small groups. *Psychological Bulletin*, *63*, 384–399.

Tudor, K. and Worrall, M. (2004). Person-centred philosophy and the theory in the practice of supervision. In K. Tudor and M. Worrall (eds) *Freedom to Practise: Person-centred Approaches to Supervision*. Ross-on-Wye, Herefordshire: PCCS Books.

UKCC (1996). *Position Statement on Clinical Supervision for Nursing and Health Visiting*. London: UKCC. The NMC replaced the UKCC and four National Boards in April 2002.

Urdang, E. (1999). The video lab: mirroring reflections of self and the other. *The Clinical Supervisor*, *18*, 143–164.

Urmson, J.O. and Rée, J. (1989). *The Concise Encyclopaedia of Western Philosophy and Philosophers*. London: Routledge.

Ussher, J.M. and Nicolson, P. (1992. *Gender Issues in Clinical Psychology*. New York: Routledge.

VanderMay, J. and Peake, T. (1980). Psychodrama as psychotherapy supervision technique. *Journal of Group Psychotherapy, Psychodrama and Sociometry*, *33*, 25–32.

Vygotsky. L.S. (1962). *Thought and Language*. Cambridge, MA: The MIT Press.

Vygotsky, L.S. (1978). *Mind in Society: The Development of Higher Psychological processes*, ed. Michael Cole. London: Harvard University Press.

Wadsborough Solicitors (1999). Personal communication.

Wakefield, J. (1995). Transference projections in supervision. In P. Kugler (ed.) *Jungian Perspectives on Clinical Supervision*. Einseedeln, Switzerland: Daimon.

Wallace, A.R. (2007). *Borneo, Celebes, Aru*. London: Penguin.

Walsh, S. and Scaife, J.M. (1998). Mechanisms for addressing personal and professional development in clinical training. *Clinical Psychology Forum*, *115*, 21–24.

Warburton, J.R., Newberry, A. and Alexander, J. (1989). Women as therapists, trainees, and supervisors. In M. McGoldrick, C. Anderson and F. Walsh (eds) *Women in Families: A Framework for Family Therapy*. New York: W.W. Norton.

Warburton, N. (1995). *Philosophy: The Basics* (2nd edn). London: Routledge.

Wark, L. (1995). Live supervision in family therapy: qualitative interviews of supervision events as perceived by supervisors and supervisees. *The American Journal of Family Therapy*, *23*, 25–37.

Watkins, C.E., Jr. (1995). Pathological attachment styles in psychotherapy supervision. *Psychotherapy*, *32*, 333–340.

Watkins, C.E., Jr. (1996). On demoralization and awe in psychotherapy supervision. *Clinical Supervisor*, *14*, 139–148.

Watkins, C.E., Jr. (ed.) (1997). *The Handbook of Psychotherapy Supervision*. New York: Wiley & Sons.

Watkins, C.E., Schneider, L.J., Haynes, J. and Nieberding, R. (1995). Measuring psychotherapy supervisor development: an initial effort at scale development and validation. *Clinical Supervisor*, *13*, 77–90.

Watson, J.C. (2003). Computer-based supervision: implementing computer technology into the delivery of counseling supervision. *Journal of Technology in Counseling*, *3*, 1–13. Retrieved 8 August 2007 from: http://jtc.colstate.edu/vol3_1/Watson/Watson.htm.

Webb, A. (2000). What makes it difficult for the supervisee to speak? In B. Lawton and C. Feltham (eds) *Taking Supervision Forward: Enquiries and Trends in Counselling and Psychotherapy*. London: Sage.

Webb, A. and Wheeler, S. (1998). How honest do counsellors dare to be in the supervisory relationship? An exploratory study. *British Journal of Guidance and Counselling*, *26*, 509–524.

Webb, N.B. (1983). Developing competent clinical practitioners: a model with guidelines for supervisors. *The Clinical Supervisor*, *1*(4), 41–52.

Weil, S. (1993). Access: towards education or miseducation? Adults imagine the future. In M. Thorpe, R. Edwards and A. Hanson (eds) *Culture and Processes of Adult Learning*. Milton Keynes: Open University Press.

Weil, S. (1995). Learning by doing – A guide to teaching and learning methods. Personal communication.

Weinert, F.E. (2001). Concept of competence: a conceptual clarification. In D.S. Rychen and L.H. Salganik (eds) *Defining and Selecting Key Competencies*. Seattle, WA: Hogrefe & Huber.

West, J.D. (1984). Utilizing simulated families and live supervision to stimulate skill development of family therapists. *Counselor Education and Supervision*, *24*, 17–27.

Wetchler, J.L. (1990). Solution-focused supervision. *Family Therapy*, *15*, 69–74.

Wetchler, J.L., Piercy, F.P. and Sprenkle, D.H. (1989). Supervisors' and supervisees' perceptions of the effectiveness of family therapy supervisory techniques. *American Journal of Family Therapy*, *21*, 242–247.

Wharton, B. (2003). Supervision in analytic training. In J. Wiener, R. Mizen and J. Duckham (eds) *Supervising and Being Supervised: A Practice in Search of a Theory*. Basingstoke: Palgrave Macmillan.

Wheeler, S. and Richards, K. (2007a). What shall we do with the wounded healer? The supervisor's dilemma. *Counselling and Psychotherapy Research*, *13*(3), 245–256.

Wheeler, S. and Richards, K. (2007b). The impact of clinical supervision on counsellors and therapists, their practice and their clients: a systematic review of the literature. *Counselling and Psychotherapy Research*, *7*(1), 54–65.

White, E., Butterworth, T., Bishop, V., Carson, J., Jeacock, J. and Clements, A. (1998). Clinical supervision: insider reports of a private world. *Journal of Advanced Nursing*, *28*, 185–192.

White, G.E. (2004). Setting and maintaining professional role boundaries: an educational strategy. *Medical Education*, *38*(8), 903–910.

White, M. (1988). The externalizing of the problem and the re-authoring of lives and relationships. *Dulwich Centre Newsletter*, summer.

White, M. and Epston, D. (1990). *Narrative Means to Therapeutic Ends*. New York: Norton.

Wilbur, M.P., Roberts-Wilbur, J., Hart, G.M., Morris, J.R. and Betz, R.L. (1994). Structured group supervision (SGS): a pilot study. *Counselor Education and Supervision*, *33*, 262–279.

Wilkins, P. (1997). *Personal and Professional Development for Counsellors*. London: Sage.

Williams, A. (1995). *Visual and Active Supervision*. New York: Norton.

Williams, A.B. (1997). On parallel process in social work supervision. *Clinical Social Work Journal*, *25*, 425–435.

Williams, A.J. (1988). Action methods in supervision. *The Clinical Supervisor*, *6*, 13–27.

Williams, B. (1982). *Moral Luck: Philosophical Essays, 1973–80*. Cambridge: Cambridge University Press.

Wilson, S.J. (1981). *Field Instruction*. New York: The Free Press.

Winnicott, D.W. (1965). *Maturational Processes and the Facilitating Environment*. Madison, WI: International Universities Press Incorporated.

Winstanley, J. (2000). Manchester clinical supervision scale. *Nursing Standard*, *14*(19), 31–32.

Winter, M. and Holloway, E.L. (1991). Relation of trainee experience, conceptual level, and supervisor approach to selection of audiotaped counseling passages. *Clinical Supervisor*, *9*, 87–103.

WITNESS (n.d.). *Against Sexual Abuse by Health and Care Workers*. Retrieved 5 January 2008 from www.popan.org.uk/index.htm.

Wong, Y-L. S. (1997). Live supervision in family therapy; trainee perspectives. *The Clinical Supervisor*, *15*, 145–157.

Wood, B.J., Klein, S., Cross, H.J., Lammers, C.J. and Elliot, J.K. (1985). Impaired practitioners: psychologists' opinions about prevalence, and proposals for intervention. *Professional Psychology: Research and Practice*, *16*, 843–850.

Wood, J.A.V., Miller, T.W. and Hargrove, D.S. (2005). Clinical supervision in rural settings: a telehealth model. *Professional Psychology: Research and Practice*, *36*, 173–179.

Woods, P.J. and Ellis, A. (1997). Supervision in rational emotive behaviour therapy. In C.E. Watkins, Jr. (ed.) *Handbook of Psychotherapy Supervision*. New York: John Wiley.

Worden, W.J. (1988). *Grief Counselling and Grief Therapy*. London: Tavistock.

Worthen, V. and McNeill, B.W. (1996). A phenomenological investigation of 'good' supervision events. *Journal of Counseling Psychology*, *43*, 25–34.

Worthington, E.L., Jr. (1987). Changes in supervision as counselors and supervisors gain experience: a review. *Professional Psychology: Research and Practice*, *18*, 189–208.

Worthington, E.L., Jr. (2006). Changes in supervision as counselors and supervisors gain experience: a review. *Training and Education in Professional Psychology*, *2*, 133–160.

Worthington, E.L. and Roehlke, H.J. (1979). Effective supervision as perceived by beginning counselors-in-training. *Journal of Counseling Psychology*, *26*, 64–73.

Wosket, V. (1998). Personal communication.

Wosket, V. (1999). *The Therapeutic Use of Self: Counselling Practice, Supervision and Research*. London: Routledge.

Wulf, J. and Nelson, M.L. (2000). Experienced psychologists' recollections of predoctoral internship supervision and its contributions to their development. *Clinical Supervisor*, *19*, 123–145.

Wynne, L.C., McDaniel, S.H. and Weber, T.T. (1986). *Systems Consultation: A New Perspective for Family Therapy*. New York: Guilford Press.

Yablonsky, L. (1992). *Psychodrama: Resolving Emotional Problems Through Roleplaying*. New York: Brunner/Mazel.

Yager, G.G., Wilson, F.R., Brewer, D. and Kinnetz, P. (1989). The development and validation of an instrument to measure counseling supervisor focus and style. Paper presented at the American Educational Research Association, San Francisco. Cited in J.M. Bernard and R.K. Goodyear (eds) (1998). *Fundamentals of Clinical Supervision* (2nd edn). Needham Heights, MA: Allyn & Bacon.

Yalom, I.D. (1989). *Love's Executioner and Other Tales of Psychotherapy*. New York: Basic Books.

Yardley-Matwiejczuk, K.M. (1997). *Role Play: Theory and Practice*. London: Sage.

Yegdich, T. (1999). Clinical supervision and managerial supervision: some historical and conceptual considerations. *Journal of Advanced Nursing*, *30*(5), 1195–1204.

Young, J., Perlesz, A., Paterson, R., O'Hanlon, B., Newbold, A., Chaplin, R. and Bridge, S. (1989). The reflecting team process in training. *Australia and New Zealand Journal of Family Therapy*, *10*, 69–74.

Young, J.E. and Beck, A.T. (1980). *Manual of the Cognitive Therapy Rating Scale*. Philadelphi, PA: University of Pennsylvania, Center for Cognitive Therapy.

Younggren, J. and Gottlieb, M.C. (2004). Managing risk when contemplating multiple relationships. *Professional Psychology: Research and Practice*, *35*, 255–260.

Yourman, D.B. (2003). Trainee disclosure in psychotherapy supervision: the impact of shame. *Journal of Clinical Psychology*, *59*, 601–609.

Yourman, D.B. and Farber, B.A. (1997). Nondisclosure and distortion in psychotherapy supervision. *Psychotherapy*, *33*, 567–575.

Author index

Subject index